Ancient Egypt
and the Old Testament

Ancient Egypt and the Old Testament

John D. Currid

Foreword by Kenneth A. Kitchen

A Division of Baker Book House Co
Grand Rapids, Michigan 49516

© 1997 by John D. Currid

Published by Baker Books
a division of Baker Book House Company
P.O. Box 6287, Grand Rapids, MI 49516-6287

Printed in the United States of America

All rights reserved. No part of this publication may be reproduced, stored in a retrieval system, or transmitted in any form or by any means—for example, electronic, photocopy, recording—without the prior written permission of the publisher. The only exception is brief quotations in printed reviews.

Library of Congress Cataloging-in-Publication Data

Currid, John D., 1951–
   Ancient Egypt and the Old Testament / John D. Currid ; foreword by Kenneth A. Kitchen.
       p.   cm.
   Includes bibliographical references (p.   ) and indexes.
   ISBN 0-8010-2137-5 (pbk.)
   1. Egypt in the Bible. 2. Bible. O.T.—Criticism, interpretation, etc. 3. Excavations (Archaeology)—Egypt. 4. Excavations (Archaeology)—Palestine. 5. Egypt—Antiquities. 6. Palestine—Antiquities. I. Title.
BS1199.E59C87   1997
221.9′5—dc21   97-23829

Unless otherwise indicated, Scripture quotations are from the New American Standard Bible, © the Lockman Foundation 1960, 1962, 1963, 1968, 1971, 1972, 1973, 1975, 1977. Other versions include the Amplified Bible (AMP), the American Standard Version (ASV), the Jerusalem Bible (JB), the King James Version (KJV), the Living Bible (LB), the New English Bible (NEB), the New International Version (NIV), the New Jerusalem Bible (NJB), the New King James Version (NKJV), the New Revised Standard Version (NRSV), and the Revised Standard Version (RSV).

For information about academic books, resources for Christian leaders, and all new releases available from Baker Book House, visit our web site:
       http://www.bakerbooks.com/

To Nancy, Elizabeth, and David

Contents

Illustrations *8*
Foreword *9*
Preface *13*
Abbreviations *15*

Part 1 Introduction
 1. Egypt and the Bible *23*
 2. Cosmologies of the Ancient Near East *33*

Part 2 Egyptian Elements in the Pentateuch
 3. The Egyptian and Genesis Cosmogonies *53*
 4. Potiphar's Standing in Egyptian Society *74*
 5. The Egyptian Setting of the Serpent Confrontation *83*
 6. An Exegetical and Historical Consideration of the Ten Plagues of Egypt *104*
 7. The Travel Itinerary of the Hebrews from Egypt *121*
 8. The Egyptian Complexion of the Bronze Serpent *142*

Part 3 Contacts between Israel and Egypt in the Historical Books
 9. Egyptian Influence on the United Monarchy *159*
 10. Shishak's Invasion of Palestine at the Beginning of the Divided Monarchy *172*

Part 4 Egyptian Wisdom Literature and the Poetical Books
 11. The "Instruction of Amenemope" and the Book of Proverbs *205*

Part 5 Egyptian and Israelite Prophecy
 12. Knowing the Divine Will: The Art of Divination in Ancient Egypt *219*
 13. Hebrew Prophecies against Egypt: The Nile Curse Passages *229*

Bibliography (1973–95) *247*
Scripture Index *253*
Subject Index *259*

Illustrations

Figures
1. Chronology of Egypt and Palestine   *17*
2. The Ancient Egyptian View of the Universe   *34*
3. The Plagues as De-Creation   *115*

Photographs
1. The Narmer Palette: An Egyptian King Hitting an Asiatic   *150*
2. The Narmer Palette: Standard Bearers and Long-necked Lions   *153*
3. The Bubastite Portal at Karnak   *181*
4. Limestone Statue of an Unidentified Scribe (Dynasty 6)   *206*
5. A Relief from the Tomb of King Ra-hotep: Fishing in the Nile   *231*

Maps
1. Ancient Egypt   *22*
2. A Proposed Route of the Hebrew Exodus   *124*
3. Sites on the Invasion List of Shoshenk I   *185*

Foreword

The whole subject of the interrelations of ancient Egypt and the Old Testament is very much larger than most people realize, be they lay or scholars. In this book Currid has thoughtfully selected a series of themes as a sampling from this very wide field; that some of these themes are not among the more obvious and well-worn subjects lends a freshness to his work. Currid early points out that what one may call the more reactionary (nineteenth-century) kind of Old Testament scholarship has preferred to understate the value of Egypt for biblical studies, while not a few others have shown themselves to be more conscious of ancient Egypt's potential as a source of meaningful background to the Old Testament. It is worth recalling that, even merely geographically, Egypt was far closer to the Hebrews and later Israelites in Palestine than was far-distant Mesopotamia, several hundreds of miles to the east.

In dealing with concepts and attitudes common to the biblical world overall, Currid has wisely avoided any temptation to overstress the impact of Egyptian ideas in the way that some past writers overstressed either Egypt or Mesopotamia, or even Ugarit. So in his introduction he evenhandedly presents the various views of origins, and of relations of deity with humanity, as found not only in Egypt and the Bible, but also in Mesopotamia, and in the Levant as represented by Ugarit. Thus he gives a fair-minded and instructive picture of the congruities and contrasts in the beliefs and views of these regions.

After his introduction Currid's work divides into four sections. The lion's share is devoted to Egyptian themes in the Pentateuch. With regard to creation he shows that some features of the Bible have more in common with Egypt than with Mesopotamia. Coming into Joseph's time, he offers a very careful and cautious assessment of Potiphar's official position, and concludes that the evidence is indecisive. At much greater length and with much more positive results, Currid develops the view that Moses and Aaron's confrontation with the magicians at Pharaoh's court in Exodus 7 is a direct polemic against the gods of Egypt and Pharaoh as their representative, a view that is further developed in the discussion of the plagues that befell Egypt on the eve of the exodus. That view (as Currid points out) has some support in the biblical text itself: The Lord said, "Against all the gods of Egypt I will execute judgments" (Exod. 12:12). The effect of the plagues was to turn Egypt from order back into chaos, undoing her much-vaunted concept of *ma'at*. Currid then presents a robust and fascinating defense of the antiquity and integrity of Numbers 33, the itinerary of the Hebrews from Rameses in Egypt via Sinai to the Plains of Moab and verge of the Jordan. Finally, the pentateuchal section turns to the bronze serpent of Numbers 21, where Currid finds usages and concepts that are linked to Egypt and not elsewhere, and that belong in essence to the exodus period and to no other.

For the monarchy period in Israel, Currid takes two themes: the possible role of Egypt's administration as a model for that of David and Solomon, and the invasion of Palestine by Shishak of Egypt. To these he prefaces a hearty and fully justified refutation of the almost neurotic rejection not only of the kingship of David and Solomon, but also of the very clear and firsthand evidence of the Tell Dan stele which, along with its mention of a "king of Israel," has a parallel reference to a "[kin]g of the house of David," indicating beyond rational doubt that by 800 B.C. David was known as a dynastic founder. As for the matter of models in administration, the question of the supposed Egyptian influence is highly controversial (the alleged model from Herakleopolis being a very poor one), especially as we have good antecedents in the Levant itself, from Ebla through Ugarit and down. Our main extrabiblical document for Shishak's invasion of Judah and Israel is (as ever) the list of place-names left by that king as part of his triumphal relief at Karnak. And here Currid offers a full review of the identifications of most of the place-names, testing out previous suggestions along the way.

Returning to more literary matters, Currid enters the lists on the unending debate over the nature and degree of the supposed relationship between the Book of Proverbs and the Egyptian "Instruction of Amenemope." Here he excels in clarity and careful evaluation of the facts about the two books. No close relationship can be proven, as various imagined links are in fact commonplaces of ancient Near Eastern wisdom generally, going well back, it must be said, long before the times of either Amenemope or Solomon. The last two studies in this book concern communications from deity. In the first, Currid deals with oracles and dreams as Egyptian modes of learning from the gods about the future; he very pertinently points out the relevance of Egyptian data as background to the dreams interpreted by Joseph in Egypt. Finally, Currid reviews the famous prophecy of Isaiah 19 in terms of its echoes of Egyptian beliefs as it casts judgment upon Egypt.

In the increasingly erratic world of Old Testament studies, where there is still too often a stubborn refusal to pay proper attention to the firm factual framework of reference that the ancient Near Eastern world offers us in assessing the nature and worth of the biblical writings, Currid's well-documented book is a breath of fresh air and represents a valuable contribution.

K. A. Kitchen
Woolton, September 1996

Preface

In 1872 August Eisenlohr observed, "It has long been the object of Egyptologists to discover in the numerous Egyptian monuments still remaining in stone and papyrus, traces of the Israelites, which might show us the events related in the Old Testament from an Egyptian point of view."[1] Much has changed since Eisenlohr uttered those words. Many scholars today maintain a less judicious approach, arguing that there was little contact between Egypt and the Bible. They say that many biblical references to Egypt are anachronistic. Some are even thought to be figments of the biblical writers' imaginations. In other words, the writers of Scripture possessed a general and vague understanding of Egyptian life and customs, and they used that slim knowledge to formulate many stories dealing with Egypt. To say the least, suspicion rules when it comes to this issue in present-day scholarship.

This volume will argue vigorously against that prevailing minimalistic approach. The reality is that we do not give the biblical writers enough credit for their knowledge of the ancient Near East and of Egypt in particular. A primary aim of this book is to show many firm points of contact between Egypt and the Bible on a variety of levels. The many linguistic connections between the two are well known, and they have been written on extensively. Literary, religious, and cultural points of contact have not been studied and discussed as much. We hope to demonstrate that there was great contact in those areas as well. The use of polemics by the biblical writers will be especially emphasized in this manuscript.

The central ideas of this monograph originally developed in a series of courses I taught on the Pentateuch at Grove City College in Pennsylvania and later at Reformed Theological Seminary in Jackson, Mississippi. Several of the ideas had a special importance of their own, and therefore I published them as articles in scholarly journals or as contributions to larger books. The chapters "The Egyptian and Genesis Cos-

---

1. A. Eisenlohr, "On the Political Condition of Egypt before the Reign of Ramses III," *Transactions of the Society of Biblical Archaeology* 1 (1872): 355.

mogonies" and "The Egyptian Setting of the Serpent Confrontation" have appeared in the German periodical *Biblische Zeitschrift* (204.4 [1991]: 18–40; n.s. 39.2 [1995]: 203–24). The introductory article dealing with the basic formulations of reality held by the Egyptians, Mesopotamians, and Canaanites was first printed in volume 2 of W. A. Hoffecker's *Building a Christian World View* (Phillipsburg, N.J.: Presbyterian and Reformed, 1988). Each of those pieces, however, has been revised for this publication. In the process of writing them, several new studies began to emerge and take shape as I observed the obvious parallels between ancient Egypt and the Bible.

It is a pleasure to take a moment to express my gratitude to those who have aided in the preparation of this manuscript. First, I would like to thank my student assistants, Melissa Cochran and Fred McDowell, for their work on the bibliography included at the end of the book. Two of the Fairbairn scholars at Reformed Theological Seminary, Julie Clinefelter (now instructor of biblical languages) and Albert Bisson, rendered great assistance. For typing much of the manuscript my appreciation goes to Barbara Coppersmith and Amy Gant, the secretaries of the Biblical Studies Department at Reformed Theological Seminary.

I am grateful to Allen Curry, the academic dean, for his continual encouragement during the writing of this book. Thanks to our seminary president, Luder Whitlock, and his wife Mary Lou. Ken Elliott, the head librarian, and his staff were of great help in securing books and articles. My colleagues in the Biblical Studies Department were always a source of reassurance with prayer, words, and laughter: Knox Chamblin, Ralph Davis, and Dennis Ireland.

Both Jim Weaver and Ray Wiersma of Baker Book House were of great encouragement in the preparation of this manuscript. I want to thank them both for their work on this project.

Unless otherwise noted, all translations, both from the Egyptian and the Hebrew, are the author's. And if there are any errors in the book, be they in English or a foreign tongue, they are mine.

Finally, this manuscript would never have seen the light of day without the unfailing support of my family. My wife, Nancy, has proven time and time again that "she is more precious than jewels." And to Elizabeth and David, my prayer is that you would love the Word above all things in this world. I hope this book is an encouragement to both of you in your study of the Bible. May you grow up to love and serve the Lord with all your hearts, minds, and souls.

Abbreviations

AASOR	*Annual of the American Schools of Oriental Research*
ABD	D. N. Freedman, ed., *Anchor Bible Dictionary* (6 vols., 1992)
AEL	M. Lichtheim, *Ancient Egyptian Literature* (3 vols., 1975–80)
AJA	*American Journal of Archaeology*
ANEP	J. B. Pritchard, *The Ancient Near East in Pictures* (1954)
ANET	J. B. Pritchard, ed., *Ancient Near Eastern Texts Relating to the Old Testament,* 3d ed. (1969)
ARE	J. H. Breasted, ed., *Ancient Records of Egypt* (5 vols., 1906)
ASAE	*Annales du service des antiquités de l'Egypte*
BA	*Biblical Archaeologist*
BAR	*Biblical Archaeology Review*
BASOR	*Bulletin of the American Schools of Oriental Research*
BDB	F. Brown, S. R. Driver, and C. A. Briggs, *A Hebrew and English Lexicon of the Old Testament* (1907)
BN	*Biblische Notizen*
BR	*Bible Review*
BZ	*Biblische Zeitschrift*
CBQ	*Catholic Biblical Quarterly*
EI	*Eretz Israel*
GEL	H. Liddell and R. Scott, *A Greek-English Lexicon* (1966)
HTR	*Harvard Theological Review*
IEJ	*Israel Exploration Journal*
ISBE	G. W. Bromiley, ed., *International Standard Bible Encyclopedia* (4 vols., 1979–88)
JANES	*Journal of the Ancient Near Eastern Society of Columbia University*
JAOS	*Journal of the American Oriental Society*
JARCE	*Journal of the American Research Center in Egypt*
JBL	*Journal of Biblical Literature*
JCS	*Journal of Cuneiform Studies*
JEA	*Journal of Egyptian Archaeology*

JNES	*Journal of Near Eastern Studies*
JPOS	*Journal of the Palestine Oriental Society*
JQR	*Jewish Quarterly Review*
JR	*Journal of Religion*
JSOR	*Journal of the Society of Oriental Research*
JSOT	*Journal for the Study of the Old Testament*
JSSEA	*Journal of the Society for the Study of Egyptian Antiquities*
JTS	*Journal of Theological Studies*
NEAEHL	E. Stern, ed., *New Encyclopedia of Archaeological Excavations in the Holy Land* (4 vols., 1992)
PEQ	*Palestine Exploration Quarterly*
RB	*Revue biblique*
SJOT	*Scandinavian Journal of the Old Testament*
SVT	*Supplements to Vetus Testamentum*
TA	*Tel Aviv*
TAPS	*Transactions of the American Philosophical Society*
TDOT	G. J. Botterweck and H. Ringgren, eds., *Theological Dictionary of the Old Testament* (1974–)
TLZ	*Theologische Literaturzeitung*
UF	*Ugarit-Forschungen*
VT	*Vetus Testamentum*
WAS	A. Erman and H. Grapow, *Wörterbuch der ägyptischen Sprache* (6 vols., 1928)
ZA	*Zeitschrift für Assyriologie*
ZAS	*Zeitschrift für ägyptische Sprache und Altertumskunde*
ZAW	*Zeitschrift für die alttestamentliche Wissenschaft*
ZDPV	*Zeitschrift des deutschen Palästina-Vereins*
ZRG	*Zeitschrift für Religionsgeschichte*

Figure 1
Chronology of Egypt and Palestine with a Select List of Kings

Egypt		Palestine	
		Early Bronze Age	**3150–2200**
Early Dynastic Period	**2920–2575**	*Early Bronze I*	3150–2850
Dynasty 1	2920–2770	*Early Bronze II*	2850–2650
Dynasty 2	2770–2649		
Dynasty 3	2649–2575		
Old Kingdom	**2575–2134**	*Early Bronze III*	2650–2350
Dynasty 4	2575–2465		
Snofru			
Cheops			
Dynasty 5	2465–2323		
Userkaf			
Sahoure			
Wenis (Unas)			
Dynasty 6	2323–2150	*Early Bronze IV*	2350–2200
Teti			
Pepy I			
Merenre			
Pepy II			
Dynasty 7/8	2150–2134	*Middle Bronze Age*	**2200–1550**
Ibi			
First Intermediate Period	**2134–2040**	*Middle Bronze I*	2200–2000
Dynasty 9/10	2134–2040		
Merikare			
Dynasty 11	2134–2040		
(Thebes)			

Middle Kingdom	**2040–1640**		
Dynasty 11	2040–1991	*Middle Bronze II*	2000–1550
(All Egypt)			
Mentuhotep I			
Dynasty 12	1991–1783		
Amenemhat I			
Senwosret I			
Amenemhat III			
Dynasty 13	1783–1640		
Sebekhotpe II			
Dynasty 14	no date		
Second Intermediate Period	**1640–1532**		
Dynasty 15	1585–1532	*Late Bronze Age*	**1550–1200**
Apopi		*Late Bronze I*	1550–1400
Dynasty 16	no date		
Dynasty 17	1640–1550		
New Kingdom	**1550–1070**		
Dynasty 18	1550–1307		
Thutmosis I			
Hatshepsut			
Thutmosis III			
Amenophis II		*Late Bronze II*	1400–1200
Thutmosis IV			
Amenophis III			
Akhenaten			
Tutankhamun			
Ay			
Haremhab			
Dynasty 19	1307–1196		
Rameses I			
Sethos I			
Rameses II		Exodus (?)	
Merneptah			
Sethos II			
Dynasty 20	1196–1070	*Iron Age*	**1200–586**
Rameses III			
Rameses IV		*Iron I*	1200–1000
Rameses IX		Period of Judges	
Rameses XI			

Figure 1

Chronology of Egypt and Palestine with a Select List of Kings   19

Third Intermediate Period	**1070–712**	Saul	
Dynasty 21	1070–945	*Iron II*	1000–586
Smendes		David	
Amenemnisu			
Psusennes I			
Amenemope		Solomon	
Siamun			
Psusennes II			
Dynasty 22	945–712		
Shoshenk		Rehoboam (Judah)	
Osorkon I		Jeroboam (Israel)	
Osorkon III			
Takelot II		Uzziah	
Dynasty 23	828–712		
Osorkon IV		Ahaz	
Shoshenk VI			
Dynasty 24	724–712		
Tefnakhte		Hezekiah	
Bakenranef (Bocchoris)			
Dynasty 25	770–712		
(Nubia and Thebes)		Fall of Israel	722–721
Piankhy			
Late Period	**712–343**		
Dynasty 25	712–657		
(All Egypt)			
Shabaka			
Shebitku			
Taharqa			
Tanutamon			
Dynasty 26	664–525		
Amasis		Fall of Judah	586
Dynasty 27	525–404	***Persian Period***	**539–332**
Dynasty 28	404–399		
Dynasty 29	399–380		
Dynasty 30	380–343		

Part 1
Introduction

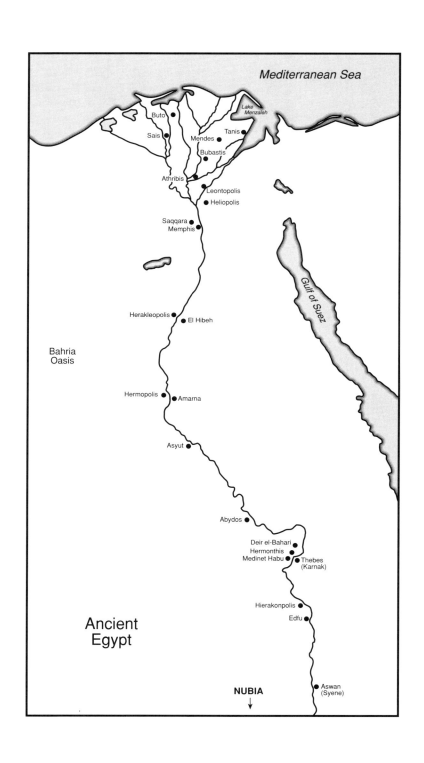

1
Egypt and the Bible

Egypt and the Bible: A Neglected Subject

Over the decades many books have been written regarding the relationship between the Old Testament and Egypt. The contributions of these works have been significant, and they are frequently cited in modern literature. One thinks particularly of titles like Sir Flinders Petrie's *Egypt and Israel* (1911), Archibald Sayce's *Egypt of the Hebrews and Herodotus* (1895), and Abraham Yahuda's *Accuracy of the Bible: The Stories of Joseph, the Exodus, and Genesis Confirmed and Illustrated by Egyptian Monuments and Language* (1934) and *The Language of the Pentateuch in Its Relation to Egyptian* (1933). Although a few such works, notably Pierre Montet's *Egypt and the Bible* (Eng. trans., 1968), Nahum Sarna's *Exploring Exodus* (1986), and Sarah Israelit-Groll's *Pharaonic Egypt: The Bible and Christianity* (1985) are of relatively recent date, most of the works that discuss Egypt and the Old Testament were written no later than the early part of the twentieth century.

A primary reason why Egypt is no longer emphasized in biblical studies is that many scholars today are unconvinced that there are solid historical and cultural connections with the Old Testament. Donald Redford, a leader of this movement, argues that "the Hebrew writer was not so well acquainted with Egypt as has often been imagined. Not a few of the supposed Egyptian parallels, especially titles, vanish under close inspection."[1] On that basis Redford concludes that the story of Joseph actually comes from the Saite–early Persian period (the seventh to fifth centuries B.C.). Elsewhere he claims that "there is little Egyptian

---

1. D. B. Redford, *A Study of the Biblical Story of Joseph (Genesis 37–50)* (Leiden: Brill, 1970), 241–42.

colouring in the Exodus account, almost wholly toponymic in nature; but the Egyptologist would soon sense that it is anachronistic."[2] Redford was not the first to question the reliability of the Egyptian material in the Bible. T. Eric Peet, as early as the 1920s, commented, "The main fact which strikes the Egyptologist is that there is nothing whatsoever in [the biblical accounts with Egyptian colorings] which suggests the Hyksos period, or indeed any particular period at all. It is all the sort of vague general knowledge."[3] That perspective clearly dominates biblical scholarship today.

Many of these same scholars argue as well that any comparison of Egyptian history and the Bible inevitably entails problems because "the purpose of the biblical account is not what we regard as history."[4] Baruch Halpern has described the biblical narrative of the exodus from Egypt as being more like Homer's *Odyssey* than history:

> In both cases, there is evidence of that peculiar process of oral transmission in which the story is renegotiated with each separate audience each time it is told. Each story reflects a healthy admixture of fancy with whatever is being recalled.... The *Odyssey* ... is basically a piece of children's literature. So, in its way, is the story of the Exodus. It is the historical myth of an entire people, a focal point for national identity.... The actual evidence concerning the Exodus resembles the evidence for the unicorn.[5]

Nevertheless, Halpern is convinced that there may be a kernel of historical truth hidden in the exodus account: "Behind the Exodus story events can be discerned that, unlike those of the patriarchal narratives,

---

2. D. B. Redford, "An Egyptological Perspective on the Exodus Narrative," in *Egypt, Israel, Sinai: Archaeological and Historical Relationships in the Biblical Period*, ed. A. F. Rainey (Tel Aviv: Tel Aviv University Press, 1987), 138.

3. T. E. Peet, *Egypt and the Old Testament* (Liverpool: University Press of Liverpool, 1923), 93. Regretfully, academia is cultivating a new generation of minimalists who gleefully separate Egyptology from biblical studies. Consider, for example, a recent piece by a graduate student at the University of Michigan—J. R. Huddlestun, "'Who Is This That Rises like the Nile?': Some Egyptian Texts on the Inundation and a Prophetic Trope," in *Fortunate the Eyes That See*, ed. A. B. Beck et al. (Grand Rapids: Eerdmans, 1995), 338–63. Huddlestun scolds scholars who have recently argued for parallels between the Bible and Egypt. Such claims by well-known authors like N. Sarna and Z. Zevit lack "methodological rigor" and "overestimate the knowledge of the biblical authors." By contrast, Huddlestun makes the bombastic claim that "it is fair to say that we probably know more . . . about the topic [i.e., Egyptian religion] than did the authors or redactors of the biblical texts" (p. 345). Such skepticism permeates his article.

4. H. Shanks, "Defining the Problems," in H. Shanks et al., *The Rise of Ancient Israel* (Washington, D.C.: Biblical Archaeology Society, 1992), 24.

5. B. Halpern, "The Exodus from Egypt: Myth or Reality?" in Shanks et al., *Rise of Ancient Israel*, 88–91.

can be termed historical in scale."⁶ The only real question for scholars like Halpern is which events can be deemed historical in nature—and there is much disagreement over that issue.

To be blunt, there is nothing new here. The present debate is merely the tired old stuff of nineteenth-century liberalism wrapped in a new package. Albert Schweitzer and friends sought the historical Jesus somewhere amid what they termed the myths of the New Testament; now Old Testament scholars search for the historical exodus in the children's literature of the Bible.

Another reason for the lack of study of the relationship between Egypt and the Bible is that a majority of scholars appear to be convinced that the Bible borrowed much of its material, especially for Genesis, from Mesopotamian literature. This view is especially clear in influential commentaries like that of E. A. Speiser on Genesis, which declares that "the background of the patriarchal narratives in Genesis is indeed authentic, so much so in fact that it could have been obtained only in Mesopotamia itself."⁷ Indeed, Speiser's entire discussion of the nature of the contents of Genesis never once mentions an Egyptian setting or background for the primeval and patriarchal histories. By contrast, earlier scholars recognized the importance of Mesopotamian connections and parallels, but they did not ignore or dismiss the obvious correspondences that the Bible has with Egyptian literature. With reference to the Pentateuch C. F. Keil once stated: "How richly stored, again, are all five books with delicate and casual allusions to Egypt, its historical events, its manners, customs, and natural history."⁸ Wilfred Lambert is among those calling for such a balance in scholarship today: "Parallels to Genesis can indeed be sought and found there [i.e., in Mesopotamia], but they can also be sought and found among the Canaanites, the ancient Egyptians, the Hurrians, the Hittites and the early Greeks."⁹

A final reason that scholars have distrusted the biblical accounts that relate to Egypt, particularly the exodus story, is the lack of written evidence from Egypt that would support their historicity. True, the Hebrews are not directly mentioned on Egyptian monuments or in texts from the period of the sojourn.¹⁰ But we need to be careful with this line

---

6. Ibid., 89–90.
7. E. A. Speiser, *Genesis* (Garden City, N.Y.: Doubleday, 1964), lvi.
8. C. F. Keil and F. Delitzsch, *The Pentateuch*, vol. 1 of *Commentary on the Old Testament* (Peabody, Mass.: Hendrickson, 1989 reprint), 23.
9. W. G. Lambert, "A New Look at the Babylonian Background of Genesis," *JTS* 16 (1965): 289.
10. Unless, of course, one identifies the *'apiru* and the Hebrews as one and the same. The Egyptian text Papyrus Leiden 348 mentions the "*'apiru* who drag stone for the great pylon of the structure 'Rameses II–Beloved-of-Truth'" (see R. A. Caminos, *Late-Egyptian*

of reasoning because it is an argument from silence. Such arguments have frequently proved to be fallacious. For example, many of Nelson Glueck's conclusions about the history of Edom and Moab in relation to the biblical record were based upon incomplete surveys of archaeological sites and for the most part upon what he did not find.[11] As more evidence has come to light, many of Glueck's judgments have proven to be faulty.[12] Many similar examples of invalid hermeneutic could be cited.

There is no question that the Egyptians and the Hebrews borrowed many things from one another. One needs only to consider the interrelationship of the Egyptian and Hebrew languages and vocabularies.[13] Numerous cultural and religious practices were similar as well.[14] Therefore, biblical scholars need to be pursuing much work in this field.

Fortunately, biblical scholars today appear to be returning to the study of Egypt and her texts. There seems to be a new appreciation for the connections and parallels between the Bible and Egypt. Some recent studies of the relationship of Egypt and the Bible have provided astounding insights and material for the biblical scholar. The select bibliography of monographs from the years 1973–95 (pp. 247–52) is a clear indication of this heartening trend. In addition, recent symposiums and conferences have heightened the interest in Egypt and the Bible. In particular, the "Exodus Symposium: Who Was the Pharaoh of the Exodus?" sponsored by the Near East Archaeological Society (1987) and

---

Miscellanies [Providence: Brown University Press, 1954], 491). One of the major problems with the identification is that the *'apiru* included many more groups than just the Hebrews, for they were spread over a vast area in antiquity. The first certain reference to Israel from Egyptian monuments is the Israel Stele from ca. 1200 B.C. (see *ANET*, 376–78). The reader should also consider the reliefs at Karnak that may picture Israelites defeated in Merneptah's campaign in Canaan. See F. J. Yurco, "3,200-Year-Old Picture of Israelites Found in Egypt," *BAR* 16.5 (1990): 20–38; and the rejoinder of A. F. Rainey, "Rainey's Challenge," *BAR* 17.6 (1991): 56–60. Another important study is L. E. Stager, "Merneptah, Israel and Sea Peoples: New Light on an Old Relief," *EI* 18 (1985): 56–64.

11. N. Glueck, *Explorations in Eastern Palestine*, vols. 1–4 = AASOR 14 (1934), 15 (1935), 18–19 (1939), and 25–28 (1951).

12. See, e.g., H. J. Franken and W. J. A. Power, "Glueck's *Explorations in Eastern Palestine* in the Light of Recent Evidence," *VT* 21 (1971): 118–23.

13. For many of these linguistic contacts, see T. O. Lambdin, "Egyptian Loan Words in the Old Testament," *JAOS* 73 (1953): 145–55; R. J. Williams, "Egypt and Israel," in *The Legacy of Egypt*, ed. J. R. Harris, 2d ed. (Oxford: Clarendon, 1971), 257–90; and idem, "Some Egyptianisms in the Old Testament," in *Studies in Honor of John A. Wilson*, Studies in Ancient Oriental Civilization 35 (Chicago: University of Chicago Press, 1969), 93–98.

14. It would be worthwhile to consult A. S. Yahuda's *Accuracy of the Bible* (London: William Heinemann, 1934) and *The Language of the Pentateuch in Its Relation to Egyptian* (New York: Oxford University Press, 1933). Frankly, the reader needs to take extreme caution with Yahuda's work because he frequently overstates his case and often misreads both Egyptian texts and the Bible. With that in mind, however, a discerning scholar could glean some rich nuggets from Yahuda's material.

the Egyptology and the History and Culture of Ancient Israel Group of the Society of Biblical Literature ought to be noted. It is hoped that this manuscript will add to the growing interest in and understanding of the Egyptian connections with the Old Testament.

The Bible and Ancient Near Eastern Mythology (Fact Became Myth)

Before we consider the various areas of contact and parallels between Egypt and Israel, we should first briefly tackle one of the most troubling, or let us say nagging, issues for modern biblical scholarship, namely, the relationship between the stories of the Bible and ancient Near Eastern mythology. Before the twentieth century not much of a problem existed because pagan myth from that area was little known. Archaeology has changed all that with the discovery of thousands of clay tablets from Mesopotamia, the decipherment of hieroglyphs, and the unearthing of writings from previously unknown civilizations at Ugarit and Ebla. Among these many writings were found accounts of creation and floods that appear to have some similarities to the biblical stories. Therein lies our dilemma. How should we understand the relationship between the pagan myths of the ancient Near East and the Bible?

An example from ancient Near Eastern literature will help to clarify the issue. One of the more important finds in Mesopotamia is the Epic of Gilgamesh.[15] This is the story of a king and his lonely travels as he seeks to uncover the meaning of life. As the tale unfolds, Gilgamesh's best friend Enkidu dies by decree of the gods. Gilgamesh is crushed, and he becomes obsessed with the awful reality that he too must die. So he searches for a way to escape the fate of all humankind. He eventually hears of one who did escape, a certain Utnapishtim, the only survivor of a great flood. After finding Utnapishtim, Gilgamesh inquires about the secret of eternal life. Utnapishtim tells him about the flood, how he built an ark, loaded it with animals, and survived a torrential rain. Before leaving the ark, he sent forth a dove and a raven, and upon emerging he sacrificed to the gods. The many similarities between the biblical account of the flood and the Gilgamesh Epic suggest a definite relationship between the two. In addition, there are comparable parallels between Genesis and Mesopotamian myths of creation.

Many scholars, perhaps a majority, argue that the Hebrew accounts of the creation and the flood are directly dependent upon earlier Meso-

---

15. A. Heidel, *The Gilgamesh Epic and Old Testament Parallels* (Chicago: University of Chicago Press, 1946); *ANET*, 72–99; *Documents from Old Testament Times*, ed. D. W. Thomas (New York: Harper and Row, 1961), 17–26.

potamian texts. That is the rub: the Mesopotamian accounts were written before the Bible. We have texts of the Gilgamesh Epic that predate the Scriptures by centuries. So from simple chronology scholars have inferred that the biblical stories evolved from the Mesopotamian accounts. Friedrich Delitzsch, for example, "drew sharp attention to the Babylonian ingredient in Genesis, and went on to conclude that the Bible was guilty of crass plagiarism."[16] S. R. Driver argued "that we have in the first chapter of Genesis the Hebrew version of an originally Babylonian legend respecting the beginning of all things."[17]

But how does one account for the many dissimilarities between the Bible and the Mesopotamian legends? How does one explain the absence of polytheism, theogony, cosmic wars, and magic from the biblical episodes of creation and flood? Many argue that the biblical writers stripped the Babylonian stories of such pagan elements—they sanitized and "Yahwehized" the legends! Delitzsch comments, "The priestly scholar who composed Gen. chap. i endeavored, of course, to remove all possible mythological features of this creation story."[18] But despite the cleansing process, "no archaeologist questions that the Biblical cosmogony, however altered and stripped of its original polytheism, is, in its main outlines, derived from Babylonia."[19]

These same scholars also argue that evidences of the original polytheism remain in the biblical text. For example, the plurality of the Godname ʾĕlōhîm suggests an original polytheism that was only later developed into a monotheism. Delitzsch and others also contend that the word tĕhôm ("deep") in Genesis 1:2 is a remnant of Mesopotamian myth. Supposedly it relates to Tiamat, the goddess of the deep sea who was a foe of the creator-god Marduk. In the Babylonian creation account Marduk de-

---

16. Speiser, *Genesis*, lv–lvi. Delitzsch's inflammatory remarks may be seen in his *Babel and Bible* (New York: Putnam, 1903). The influence that this work has had on modern biblical scholarship should not be underestimated. It was a volatile and scathing attack on the reliability of the Bible and divine revelation. For example, he scoffs, "Revelation indeed! A greater mistake on the part of the human mind can hardly be conceived than this" (p. 176). His detesting of the Old Testament is clear: "The more deeply I immerse myself in the spirit of prophetic literature of the Old Testament, the greater becomes my mistrust of Yahweh, who butchers the peoples with the sword of his insatiable anger; who has but one favourite child, while he consigns all other nations to darkness, shame, and ruin" (p. 149). Such distaste for the Old Testament colors the entire book and sets the agenda: "How utterly alike everything is in Babylon and the Bible!" (p. 175). Fortunately, the work suffers from numerous errors that were quickly recognized by scholars of the time. Among these errors is the claim that the first references to Yahweh were Mesopotamian. (It is ironic to note that Friedrich Delitzsch was the son of Franz Delitzsch, the great conservative commentator on the Old Testament.)
17. S. R. Driver, *Genesis* (London: Methuen, 1909), 30.
18. Delitzsch, *Babel and Bible*, 50.
19. Driver, *Genesis*, 30.

feats her, divides her, and forms her into the earth, sea, and heavens. Lying behind the account of God's creation in Genesis 1, therefore, is the Mesopotamian myth that he conquered the chaos deity Tiamat and then created the universe. All the evidence, say many scholars, suggests that the biblical writer was merely demythologizing the pagan world-order. This suggestion has become fact in much recent literature.[20]

We must question, however, whether the position that the Bible demythologizes Mesopotamian legends takes into account all the critical data bearing on the issue. First of all, the common assumption that the Hebrew stories are simplified and purified accounts of Mesopotamian legends is fallacious, for in ancient Near Eastern literature simple accounts give rise to elaborate accounts, and not vice versa. One can view this evolution from simple to complex in the many recensions of the Sumerian/Babylonian flood legends.[21] Ironically, many scholars who accept the model of the complex to the simple would then argue that the Pentateuch is the product of an evolutionary development from the simple to the complex. One cannot have it both ways.

Second, there are no examples from the ancient Near East in which myth later develops into history. Epic simply never transfigures into historical narrative. And, clearly, the creation and flood accounts in Genesis are presented as direct history with no evidence of myth.

Third, the contrasts between the Mesopotamian and biblical accounts are so striking that they cannot be explained by a simple Hebrew cleansing. J. V. K. Wilson agrees: "The many and obvious differences, due in large part to the fact that the essential religious concepts underlying the epic are those of the Sumerians—the non-Semitic predecessors in Mesopotamia of the third millennium Akkadians and later Babylonians and Assyrians—weigh heavily in support of this opinion."[22] Let us consider, for example, four crucial distinctions between Genesis and the *Enuma Elish*, the Mesopotamian creation epic:

1. As its principal theme the Mesopotamian myth promotes polytheism and exalts Marduk to the head of the pantheon. The *Enuma Elish* is an attempt to explain why Marduk was the major

---

20. See, e.g., R. A. Muller, *The Study of Theology* (Grand Rapids: Zondervan, 1991), 76. Frankly, the equation of Hebrew *těhôm* and Babylonian Tiamat is dubious at best—unfortunately, it has worked itself into the scholarly literature as indisputable truth. The case against the alleged parallel is ably presented by A. Heidel, *The Babylonian Genesis* (Chicago: University of Chicago Press, 1951), 99–101.

21. The best-known version is the Gilgamesh Epic as published by George Smith, *The Chaldean Account of Genesis* (New York: Scribner, 1876).

22. J. V. K. Wilson, "The Epic of Creation," in *Documents from Old Testament Times*, ed. Thomas, 14.

god of Mesopotamia. In contrast, the Bible promotes a monotheistic belief in Yahweh as the sovereign God of the universe. In the Bible there is no evidence of theogony, a pantheon, or a cosmic enthronement.

2. *Enuma Elish* pictures a cosmic battle as the catalyst of creation: the forces of order vanquish the forces of chaos. The Bible nowhere claims that Yahweh had to strive against any other force to bring about creation; rather, his activity was effortless. By mere verbal fiat he brought the universe into existence.

3. Ancient Near Eastern myth frequently portrays humans as created to be slaves to the gods. In fact, pagan nations underplayed and de-emphasized human creation. The Bible, on the other hand, portrays humans as created in the image of God *(imago Dei)* to be royal stewards over creation.

4. In pagan myth the gods do not represent the greatest power of the universe—there is something even stronger: magic. Through the use of magic an external and mystical force beyond the ordinary power of both gods and humans can be brought to bear on natural and human events.[23] In both Mesopotamian and Egyptian religion the gods must possess magic to be mighty. They are not supreme, the power of magic is. Consider a brief episode from the *Enuma Elish:*

> Ea, the all-wise, saw through their scheme.
> A master design against it he devised and set up,
> Made artful his spell against it, surpassing and holy.
> He recited it and made it subsist in the deep,
> As he poured sleep upon him. Sound asleep he lay.
> When Apsu he had made prone, drenched with sleep,
> Mummu, the adviser, was powerless to stir.
> He loosened his band, tore off his tiara,
> Removed his halo (and) put it on himself.
> Having fettered Apsu, he slew him.
> Mummu he bound and left behind lock.[24]

In order for Ea to vanquish Apsu and bind Mummu, who were the gods of chaos, he had to use magic. Apart from his spells and craft he would not have succeeded.

---

23. For discussion of Egyptian magical practices see B. Brier, *Ancient Egyptian Magic* (New York: Morrow, 1980); and C. Jacq, *Egyptian Magic* (Chicago: Bolchazy-Carducci, 1985). For a classic study see E. A. W. Budge, *Amulets and Talismans* (New Hyde Park, N.Y.: University Books, 1961). One should especially consider ch. 5 on Egypt and ch. 3 on Babylonia and Assyria.

24. *ANET,* 61.

A later passage describes the choosing of Marduk as king of the gods. He was considered worthy by the other gods because he was a great magician:

> They addressed themselves to Marduk, their first-born:
> "Lord, truly thy decree is first among gods.
> Say but to wreck or create; it shall be.
> Open thy mouth: the cloth will vanish!
> Speak again, and the cloth shall be whole!"
> At the word of his mouth the cloth vanished.
> He spoke again, and the cloth was restored.
> When the gods, his fathers, saw the fruit of his word,
> Joyfully they did homage: "Marduk is king!"[25]

Marduk had to prove his magical prowess in front of the other gods in order to demonstrate his worthiness to be king of the gods—his royal position was dependent upon his magical abilities.

By contrast, in the Bible the primary force and power in the universe is Yahweh himself. He relies and depends upon nothing else for his supremacy.

Even with these major differences, portions of ancient Near Eastern myth are similar to biblical accounts. How should we understand those correspondences? Many of the biblical references to ancient Near Eastern literature can be understood as polemical. For example, Isaiah 19:1 says, "The LORD is riding on a swift cloud." Ugaritic literature uses the same epithet to describe the Canaanite god Baal:

> Seven years Baal will fail *(sb' snt ysrk b'l)*,
> Eight years the rider of the clouds, no dew, no rain
> *(tmn rkb 'rpt bl tl bl rbb)*.[26]

Given the poetical parallelism between the two lines, the attribute "rider of the clouds" is to be ascribed to Baal. We are not to understand from the passage in Isaiah that Yahweh somehow evolved from Baal or to see some type of syncretism here. Rather, the biblical author is making an implicit criticism of Baalism: Baal does not ride the heavens; Yahweh does! That meaning would have been obvious to the Hebrew audience of the time.

Another example of possible polemic is the frequently used motif of the Deity's thundering forth from the clouds and causing the earth to

---

25. Ibid., 66.
26. I Aqht 42–44. Unless specifically noted, all translations are the author's.

quake at his appearance. Yahweh does so at the critical point of his revelation at Sinai:

> So it came about on the third day, when it was morning, that there were thunder and lightning flashes and a thick cloud upon the mountain and a very loud trumpet sound, so that all the people who were in the camp trembled. . . . Mount Sinai was all in smoke because the Lord descended upon it in fire; and its smoke ascended like the smoke of a furnace, and the whole mountain quaked violently. [Exod. 19:16–18]

The authors of the Ugaritic texts employ similar imagery for Baal's theophany:

> Then Baal opened a slit in the clouds,
> Baal sounded his holy voice,
> Baal thundered from his lips. . . .
> The earth's high places shook.[27]

Some scholars argue that such parallels prove syncretism. Michael Coogan, for example, states that "the character of the god of Israel is thus a composite; while Yahweh is primarily an El figure, many of the images and formulae that distinguish him from El are adopted from the theology of Baal."[28] Such parallels, however, hardly prove dependence. They could just as easily be coincidences or, as is more likely, purposeful polemics by the biblical writer against pagan Canaanite belief. It is not Baal but Yahweh who thunders and causes the earth to quake. Later in this volume we will argue that the biblical writers' discussions of Egyptian practices and beliefs were primarily polemics against Egyptian culture.[29]

There is another way of looking at the similarities between biblical accounts and Near Eastern myths. If the biblical stories are true, one would be surprised not to find some references to those truths in extra-biblical literature. And indeed in ancient Near Eastern myth we do see some kernels of historical truth. However, pagan authors vulgarized or bastardized those truths—they distorted fact by dressing it up with polytheism, magic, violence, and paganism. Fact became myth. From this angle the common references would appear to support rather than deny the historicity of the biblical story, a point the reader should keep in mind as we begin our investigation of the relationship between the Old Testament and Egypt.

---

27. M. D. Coogan, *Stories from Ancient Canaan* (Philadelphia: Westminster, 1978), 21.
28. Ibid., 20.
29. See also G. F. Hasel, "The Polemic Nature of the Genesis Cosmology," *Evangelical Quarterly* 46 (1974): 81–102.

2
Cosmologies of the Ancient Near East

Since their creation, humans have pondered the origin, operation, and meaning of the universe, and their particular place within it. As we saw in chapter 1, the Mesopotamian Epic of Gilgamesh, one of the oldest written stories, dating from about 2000 B.C., describes the quest of a king named Gilgamesh to understand the cosmos.[1] He asks some poignant questions regarding the death of a friend and his own end as well:

> I became afraid of death, so that I now roam over the steppe. The matter of my friend rests heavy upon me, hence far and wide I roam over the steppe. The matter of Enkidu, my friend, rests heavy upon me, hence far and wide I roam over the steppe. How can I be silent? How can I be quiet? My friend, whom I loved, has turned to clay; Enkidu, my friend, whom I loved, has turned to clay. And I, shall I not like unto him lie down and not rise forever?[2]

Gilgamesh travels across the earth in an attempt to discover the significance of the universe, the meaning of life and death, and the secret to immortality. In fact, from ancient times until today people individually and collectively have sought answers to these same questions. The

---

1. The earliest fragments of the epic date to the first Babylonian dynasty and are written in Old Babylonian script. Much of the material of the legend was certainly composed earlier, but the precise dates of its origination and compilation are unknown. See the treatment of J. H. Tigay, *The Evolution of the Gilgamesh Epic* (Philadelphia: University of Pennsylvania Press, 1982).
2. A. Heidel, *The Gilgamesh Epic and Old Testament Parallels* (Chicago: University of Chicago Press, 1946), 73.

psalmist put it most eloquently: "When I consider Thy heavens, the work of Thy fingers, the moon and the stars, which Thou hast ordained; What is man, that Thou dost take thought of him? And the son of man, that Thou dost care for him?" (Ps. 8:3–4).

This chapter will summarily examine and explain how the peoples of the ancient Near East understood the origin and workings of the universe. We will focus upon four of the most important and influential societies of antiquity: Egypt, Mesopotamia, Canaan, and Israel. Our study of historical and cultural contexts will point up the striking contrast between the Hebrew cosmology and the cosmologies of the adjoining pagan nations. Only by grasping the major features of the thought and culture of those surrounding nations that had the greatest contact with and impact upon the Hebrews—Egypt, Mesopotamia, and Canaan—can we fully apprehend Israel's cosmological perspective. The obvious differences and antagonism between the cosmological systems are foundational and presuppositional to the remainder of this book.

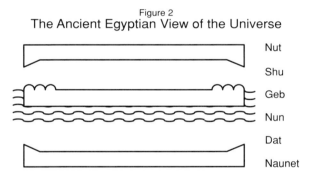

Figure 2
The Ancient Egyptian View of the Universe

Egypt

Egyptian Cosmology

The ancient Egyptians believed that the universe consisted of four principal elements.[3] The first element was the earth, which was

---

3. The written material about Egyptian cosmology is enormous. For a general introduction see A. R. David, *The Ancient Egyptians: Religious Beliefs and Practices* (Boston: Routledge and Kegan Paul, 1982), 46–49; E. Drioton, "Egyptian Religion," in *Religions of the Ancient East*, ed. E. Drioton, G. Contenau, and J. Duchesne-Guillemin (New York: Hawthorn, 1959), 19–59; A. Erman, *A Handbook of Egyptian Religion* (Boston: Longwood, 1977 reprint); idem, *Die Religion der Ägypter* (Berlin: Walter de Gruyter, 1934), 14–24; H. Frankfort, *Kingship and the Gods* (Chicago: University of Chicago Press, 1948); and V. Ions, *Egyptian Mythology* (New York: Bedrick, 1982).

thought to be shaped like a dish with raised or corrugated rims (see figure 2).[4] The central, flat part of the dish represented the Nile Valley (Egypt), and its raised rims symbolized the mountains of countries bordering Egypt. Below the earth lay primeval waters, the universe's second main element, from which life first sprang and upon which the earth floated. Above the earth was the sky, the third element of the universe. The universe's outer limits were bounded both above and below by plates that established the size of the cosmos. These plates were the fourth element.

Each element of the universe was the embodiment of a particular god. For example, between the upper plate and the earth was the air-god Shu, who upheld the plate so that it did not come crashing down upon the earth. The deity Nut, the sky-goddess, personified the upper plate.

Although not included in the figure, the sun (represented by the god Re) was perhaps the most important object in the ancient Egyptian cosmological scheme. The Egyptians believed that the sun journeyed nightly into the underworld (death) and then was reborn each day out of the waters of Nun, the source of life. This emphasis upon the daily rebirth of the sun is evidence of a static view of time and history. The ancient Egyptians believed that cosmic order *(ma'at)* had been firmly established at creation and was maintained throughout subsequent history.[5] Certainly the natural order of things was sometimes disrupted by chaotic events such as the death of a king or a catastrophic storm. But such events were fleeting and did not deeply disturb creational harmony and order.

In addition to the rising and falling of the sun, the entire natural order was thought to reflect a static cosmos. For example, there was the natural rhythm of time in which seasons continually moved from spring (birth) to summer and fall (symbolizing life) to winter (death). Objects within nature followed a similar pattern. The Nile River, upon which Egypt depended for her very existence, inundated yearly.[6] Flora

---

4. The model first appeared in H. Frankfort et al., *Before Philosophy* (Baltimore: Penguin, 1973 reprint), 55.

5. Scholars frequently portray Egyptian cosmology as cyclical. But it is not true that the ancient Egyptians believed that all reality is in a repetitive cycle of birth, life, and death. *Ma'at* is reality, and it is unchanging. In one of my earlier writings (J. Currid, "Cosmologies of Myth," in *Building a Christian World View,* ed. W. A. Hoffecker, 2 vols. [Phillipsburg, N.J.: Presbyterian and Reformed, 1986, 1988], 2:9–20) I am guilty of depicting Egyptian cosmology as cyclical. The Egyptian doctrine of *ma'at* will be discussed in greater detail in ch. 6 (pp. 118–20).

6. The fifth-century B.C. Greek author Herodotus commented, "Egypt to which the Greeks sail is a land that has been given to the Egyptians as an addition and as a gift of the river" (*History* 2.5).

had an identical annual operation. Even humans themselves lived according to a recurring pattern: they were born, lived, and died. In turn, the offspring they produced continued the natural order of things.

Consonant with the static view of reality, ancient Egyptians believed that death was not the end of life; rather, life could be everlasting. Because of that perspective they laid great emphasis on the preservation of the dead in as close to lifelike form as possible. The survival of the body was a necessary requirement for continual existence beyond death. Consequently, in Egypt a rich evolution of burial practices (mummification, elaborate tombs, etc.) has been discovered.

The nation's life, including the religious, economic, and social spheres, was directly related to the static order of things. By arranging their lives so as to be in harmony with the universe, the Egyptians believed that their chances of success in any undertaking would be greatly improved. For example, when a new pharaoh was to be crowned, the ceremony was usually scheduled for the beginning of the natural cycle (which signified birth) in order to provide the new reign with a favorable starting point. So, then, "the coronation could not take place at any time that might seem convenient. It had to wait for some new beginning in the progress of nature."[7] Furthermore, New Year's Day, because it marked the beginning of the natural pattern, was regarded as the most important celebration in Egypt. Elaborate festivities took place, many of which had as their themes the battles between those gods (such as Re) who desired rebirth or the status quo and those other gods (such as Dat) who wanted chaos to reign.

Egyptian Cosmogony

The ancient Egyptians believed that life originated from preexistent primordial waters (Nun). Out of these waters first appeared the "primeval hillocks," islands shaped like mounds or hills. According to Egyptian myth, the creator-god Re entered into the universe through self-creation. As an Egyptian text states, he "became, by himself." The creator-god's principal functions were twofold. First, Re brought order *(ma'at)* out of chaos by seizing control over the eight preexistent gods (including Kuk, who represented darkness, and Amon, who symbolized chaos). Second, Re the sun-god called into being other gods, each of whom, like him, personified a different element of nature.

There are three accounts of how Re created other gods. One account pictures him squatting on a primeval hillock, pondering and inventing names for various parts of his own body. As he named each part, a new god sprang into existence. Another legend portrays Re as

---

7. Frankfort, *Kingship and the Gods,* 102.

violently expelling other gods from his own body, possibly by sneezing or spitting. A third myth describes him creating the gods Shu and Tefnut by an act of masturbation. These gods in turn gave birth to other gods.

The Egyptians had no separate or elaborate account of the creation of humans. References to their origins are found in mere snippets or fragments of literary pieces devoted to other subjects. To the ancient Egyptians a story specifically concerned with the creation of humans would have had no real purpose since humans could not be entirely distinguished from the gods. For creation started with the gods and was thought to continue with humans.

Mesopotamia

Mesopotamian Cosmology

The vast majority of cosmological systems throughout history have divided the universe into the animate and the inanimate, the living and the nonliving. The ancient Mesopotamians, however, believed that each thing in the universe had a will and character all its own.[8] They regarded each object and idea of their experiences as being alive, as having its own personality.

The Mesopotamians thought that all these individual wills and personalities were living together in the community of the universe just as a human state or society would exist. This cosmic state was set up as a "primitive democracy" in which those with the greatest power ran the universe.[9] Powerful natural elements such as water, the sky, and the earth were understood to be political leaders, wielding the most authority in the cosmic society. Other components of the universal state, such as rocks and trees, having less natural power, had no political influence at all. Humans belonged to this latter group; they were considered slaves in the cosmic society.

The Mesopotamians regarded and revered as gods those powerful natural forces that directed the primitive democracy. The highest and most authoritative of the gods was Anu, god of the sky. His duty was to maintain order in the universe and to establish the laws of the cosmic society. Enlil, the second most powerful god, was lord of the storms; he

---

8. The literature on this topic is vast. For a mere taste of it see A. Heidel, *The Babylonian Genesis* (Chicago: University of Chicago Press, 1963); W. G. Lambert, "The Cosmology of Sumer and Babylon," in *Ancient Cosmologies*, ed. C. Blacker and M. Loewe (London: Allen and Unwin, 1975), 42–65; W. G. Lambert and S. B. Parker, *Enuma Elish: The Babylonian Epic of Creation* (Oxford: Clarendon, 1966).

9. T. Jacobsen, "Mesopotamia: The Cosmos as a State," in Frankfort et al., *Before Philosophy*, 137–99.

enforced the decrees of Anu and maintained the assembly of the gods. Considered almost as powerful as Enlil, Ninhursaga was the mother earth who gave birth to all that had the breath of life. Because water was so essential to sustaining life, the water-god, Ea, was as mighty as mother earth. Clearly, the ancient Mesopotamians believed that the gods were totally immanent in nature. These four gods, along with three others, made up the divine assembly of the primitive democracy. This assembly had the power to decide destiny, determining both great and small events of the future.

Mesopotamian Cosmogony

According to Mesopotamian belief, the primitive democracy that controlled the universe was established as a result of the cosmic struggle between order and chaos at the dawn of creation. Order's victory over chaos produced a cosmic hierarchy, which assigned each facet of the universe a proper place. All of this is described in the *Enuma Elish*, the ancient Mesopotamian account of creation, which begins:

> When a sky above had not (yet even) been mentioned,
> (And) the name of firm ground below had not [yet even] been
>   thought of;
> (When) only primeval Apsu, their begetter,
> And Mummu and Tiamat—she who gave birth to them all—
> Were mingling their waters in one;
> When no bog had formed (and) no island could be found;
> When no god whosoever had appeared,
> Had been named by name, had been determined as to (his) lot,
> Then were gods formed within them.[10]

Like the Egyptian cosmogony, these opening lines picture the universe as being originally chaotic, a place where only primeval waters existed. The watery chaos consisted of three gods: Apsu, a male deity representing the sweet waters; Tiamat, the goddess of the sea; and Mummu, who probably was the god of mist. Apsu and Tiamat created other gods through sexual procreation. Each of the gods they generated symbolized an important element of nature (e.g., sky, water, or earth). These created gods came into immediate conflict with Apsu and Tiamat. The former wanted to work actively to preserve order, while Apsu and Tiamat preferred an inactive role, which produced chaos. Apsu complained to Tiamat:

---

10. Ibid., 184. In the quotes from ancient sources, parentheses are used for translations, transliterations, and various interpolations to assist the reader; brackets indicate restorations of missing text.

> Abhorrent have become their (the created gods') ways to me.
> I am allowed no rest by day, by night no sleep.
> I will abolish, yea, I will destroy their ways, that peace may reign (again) and we may sleep.

The conflicting goals resulted in a cosmic battle between the gods of chaos and the gods of order. Ea, god of water, killed Apsu and subdued Mummu by securing a rope through his nose like a leash. Marduk, king of the gods of order, then slew Tiamat, last of the gods of chaos, in a fierce battle:

> They (Marduk and Tiamat) strove in a single combat, locked in battle.
> The lord (Marduk) spread out his net to enfold her;
> The Evil Wind, which followed behind, he let loose in her face.
> When Tiamat opened her mouth to consume him,
> He drove in the Evil Wind [so] that she [could] not close her lips.
> As the fierce winds charged her belly,
> Her body distended and her mouth was wide open.
> He released the arrow, it tore her belly,
> It cut through her insides, splitting the heart;
> Having thus subdued her, he extinguished her life.

After obtaining victory, Marduk used Tiamat's remains to create the cosmos. Ironically, Marduk established the primitive democracy (order) by using the body of Tiamat, who personified chaos. Among his many creations that Marduk set in their proper places in the cosmic state was humanity. Marduk decreed that their life would be uncertain, dependent upon the whims and fancies of the higher gods:

> Blood I will mass and cause bones to be,
> I will establish a savage, "man" shall be his name.
> Verily, savage-man I will create.
> He shall be charged with the service of the gods,
> That they might be at ease!

As we saw in chapter 1, Ea and Marduk were victorious not only because they were inherently more powerful than the gods of chaos, but also because they were better magicians. Ea slew Apsu, for instance, after reciting a magical spell that rendered the god unconscious:

> Surpassing in wisdom, accomplished, resourceful,
> Ea, the all-wise, saw through their scheme.
> A master design against it he devised and set up,
> Made artful his spell against it, surpassing and holy.
> He recited it and made it subsist in the deep,
> As he poured sleep upon (Apsu). Sound asleep he lay.

Similarly, Marduk held a red paste between his lips when he fought Tiamat. The color red in ancient Mesopotamia symbolized the art of magic. Thus, Marduk conquered because of his superior magical skills.

Marduk also used magic to pass a test devised by the gods to see if he should be their king. They laid a piece of cloth in front of Marduk and said:

> "Lord, truly thy decree is first among gods.
> Say but to wreck or create; it shall be.
> Open thy mouth: the cloth will vanish!
> Speak again, and the cloth shall be whole!"
> At the word of his mouth the cloth vanished.
> He spoke again, and the cloth was restored.
> When the gods, his fathers, saw the fruit of his word,
> Joyfully they did homage: "Marduk is king!"

Marduk attained the highest station in the primitive democracy primarily because of his ability as a magician.

Magic was the ultimate power in the universe, even above the gods themselves. All other things in the cosmos—people, animals, plants, rocks—were dependent upon magic to secure their proper places in the primitive democracy. The more magical ability each creature or object had, the greater was its position in the hierarchy of the cosmic state. Ultimately, therefore, the key element in Mesopotamian cosmology was a force external to the universe: magic.

Canaan

Canaanite Cosmology

The Canaanite cosmology is expressed principally in a group of texts called the Ugaritic myths, which explain how the universe operates.[11] Like the Egyptian and Mesopotamian cosmological stories, the Ugaritic myths focus upon the lives of the gods, who as personifications of various aspects of nature ran the universe.

One particular text, the myth of Baal, provides a striking picture of the Canaanite world-and-life view. As Baal (the god of rain, vegetation, and fertility) and his consort Anath (the goddess of love, fertility, and war) are building a palace, Mot (the god of death and summer drought) slays Baal and takes him to the underworld. Anath retaliates by killing Mot, and Baal is resurrected to reclaim his palace:

---

11. See, e.g., M. D. Coogan, *Stories from Ancient Canaan* (Philadelphia: Westminster, 1978); G. R. Driver, *Canaanite Myths and Legends* (Edinburgh: T. and T. Clark, 1956); T. H. Gaster, *Thespis: Ritual, Myth, and Drama in the Ancient Near East* (Staten Island, N.Y.: Gordian, 1975); and H. L. Ginsberg, "Ugaritic Myths, Epics, and Legends," in *ANET,* 129–55.

> She (Anath) seized El's son Mot.
> With a sword she split him;
> With a sieve she winnowed him;
> With fire she burned him;
> With a hand-mill she ground him;
> In the fields she sowed him. . . .
> Baal returned to his royal chair,
> To his dais, the seat of his dominion.

The myth of Baal explains the cycle of seasons. Drought blighted crops in Canaan each summer because the drought-god conquered the fertility-god Baal. But the rainy season appeared each fall because Anath slew Mot, and Baal, the god of rain, was restored to power. The Canaanites believed that this cycle occurred each year (though, of course, with variations, such as the occasional extended drought, which was explained in terms of Mot's holding Baal captive for a longer period of time). This all-pervading cyclical view of life was reflected in Canaanite religious practice and ritual. Through their worship the Canaanites sought to control the yearly cycle by making the gods favorable towards them.

Canaanite Worship

The religion of Canaan revolved around an elaborate system of ritual. Primarily, the Canaanite cults centered upon forms of worship that promoted sex and fertility. Such an emphasis sprang logically from the Canaanites' belief that sustaining the cycle of life and death was absolutely vital for the fertility of their flocks, fields, and wives. The rituals aimed chiefly to invoke the gods' favor upon the worshipers. By manipulating the divine (i.e., through magic), productivity was assured.

One form of Canaanite manipulation was the practice of child sacrifice, especially the offering of firstborn sons to the gods. This ancient society believed that if they gave the first of their offspring to the gods, then the gods would continue to grant fertility to Canaanite women. By sacrificing children, the Canaanites also hoped to compel the gods to intervene in life-threatening situations (see 2 Kings 3:27). Archaeological discoveries at Carthage include the charred remains of hundreds of child sacrifices.[12] Historical records and stone monuments indicate that these victims were sacrificed in order to gain the gods' favors and intervention.

---

12. L. E. Stager, "The Rite of Child Sacrifice at Carthage," in *New Light on Ancient Carthage*, ed. J. G. Pedley (Ann Arbor: University of Michigan Press, 1980), 1–11; L. E. Stager and S. R. Wolff, "Child Sacrifice at Carthage—Religious Rite or Population Control?" *BAR* 10.1 (1984): 30–51. See also 2 Kings 16:3; 17:17; 21:6.

Temple prostitution was another common practice the Canaanites used to gain the gods' good will. Male and female prostitutes attached to the central sanctuaries and shrines were known in the Old Testament and Canaanite literature as the *qĕdēšîm*, the "set apart ones" (1 Kings 14:24; 15:12; 2 Kings 23:7). They were individuals set apart for the special function of ritual prostitution. The Canaanites thought that acts of whoredom at the sacred precincts would guarantee the fertility of their people, land, and animals.

Temple prostitution in Canaan likely centered on the worship of the divinity Baal Peor, a name literally meaning "Lord of the Opening" (a reference to the female vagina). As an example of the Canaanite influence among other peoples, Numbers 25:1–3 reports that by fornicating with the followers of Baal Peor, the Israelites were seduced into worshiping this god. The illicit sexual activity symbolized Israel's unfaithfulness to her God Yahweh. The passage graphically depicts this infidelity and perversion by using the sexual term "coupled or joined together" to describe Israel's union with Baal Peor. As verse 1 relates, Israel "began to play the harlot with the daughters of Moab," even though God had strictly forbidden the Hebrews to do so. (For other instances of such unfaithfulness by Israel, see Deut. 4:3; Ps. 106:28; Hos. 9:10.)

Canaanite religion was also idolatrous. Its various gods were depicted in human form fashioned out of wood or stone. The goddesses of Canaan were generally represented in iconography as naked females with exaggerated and distorted sexual parts. Cult objects such as lilies (representing sexual appeal) and serpents (symbolizing fertility and fecundity) were often associated with the worship of Canaanite goddesses. Thus the Canaanites' obsession with sex and fertility was further demonstrated in their idols.

Most worship occurred at "high places," sacred sites where the Canaanites placed altars for sacrifice, ritual pillars, and idols (see 1 Kings 14:23). One of the more important objects at each high place was the sacred tree or grove, a physical representation of the goddess Asherah. This female deity functioned mainly as the goddess of fertility. When the Canaanites went to the high place to worship Asherah, they were trying to persuade her to make their land, animals, and themselves fertile and productive.

In addition, numerous biblical references (e.g., Deut. 18:9–11) indicate that the Canaanites engaged in soothsaying, divination, sorcery, witchcraft, and necromancy (communication with the dead) as part of their worship. Moreover, they ritually beat and cut themselves during worship (see 1 Kings 18:28; cf. Lev. 19:28). All of these were magical acts intended to discover what decisions the divinities might have made concerning particular situations.

The Hebrews

Hebrew Cosmology

The Old Testament frequently uses a building motif to describe the universe.[13] It figuratively represents the cosmos as a three-storied building composed of the heavens above, the earth beneath, and the sector below the earth (e.g., Exod. 20:4). The heavens consist of windowed vaults held up by columns that reach to the earth (Job 26:11); they are like a veil or tent which God has stretched over the earth (Isa. 40:22; Ps. 104:2). The earth itself is supported by pillars with foundations extending into the subterranean sector (Job 9:6; 38:6; Ps. 18:15; 104:5). The subterranean area, called Sheol by the Hebrews, is the place where humans descend after death (Gen. 37:35; 42:38; 44:29; Num. 16:30–33). Deep beneath the earth in a place where darkness reigns (Ps. 88), Sheol is sometimes pictured as a prison with gates and bars (Job 38:17; Isa. 38:10).

Architectural imagery is also found in the creation account of Genesis 1. The world is divided into compartments or "rooms" for habitation by the various creatures. The sky is a canopy-like covering ("the firmament") serving as a roof for the earth. Lights are installed in the roof in order to provide illumination.

The Hebrew conception of the universe as an architectural structure is clearly figurative. This imagery stresses that the cosmos was designed and constructed with the same care and planning as a building. That the universe was intricately planned emphasizes God's role as designer. The Old Testament repeatedly depicts him as the great architect and builder of the universe. For example, God questions Job: "Where were you when I laid the foundation of the earth! Tell Me, if you have understanding, who set its measurements, since you know? Or who stretched the line on it? On what were its bases sunk? Or who laid its cornerstone?" (Job 38:4–6). Such rhetorical questions indicate that God himself figuratively laid the earth's foundations and determined its measurements with plumb line in hand. Likewise, Proverbs 8:30 pictures God as the master builder who used his wisdom to construct the earth.

The cosmic structure that the Lord created was designed to house more than the earth's creatures. It was built as a holy abode for the living God himself! Psalm 11:4 says, "The Lord is in His holy temple, the Lord's throne is in heaven." The universe is God's kingly residence where he dwells (although he is not limited or contained by it) and his royal court where he presides. Consequently all of creation is to serve

---

13. M. G. Kline has developed this topic in an unpublished manuscript, "Kingdom Prologue" (Gordon-Conwell Theological Seminary, South Hamilton, Mass., 1993), 16–21.

him. "Thus says the LORD, 'Heaven is My throne, and the earth is My footstool'" (Isa. 66:1).

Invisible angelic beings who attend the Lord also reside in the cosmos. Nehemiah 9:6 affirms this point: "Thou alone art the LORD. Thou hast made the heavens, the heaven of heavens with all their host." "All their host" is in part a reference to the invisible angels, who were made by the Lord and dwell in the heaven of heavens (i.e., the cosmos). In addition to the angels who attend the Lord, evil spirits also reside in the cosmos. Satan (a title meaning "adversary") is a rebellious spiritual being who dwells in the cosmic house and roams about the earth, seeking to wreak havoc on humankind.[14] Moreover, he seems to have access to the Lord, sometimes appearing before God's very throne (Job 1:6–12; Zech. 3:1).

Hebrew Cosmogony

The name of the first book of the Hebrew Bible, Genesis, literally means "origin, beginning." It narrates the Hebrew view of the creation of the universe, as well as the beginning of the human race, the nations of the earth, and God's covenant people, Israel. A careful examination of the first chapter of Genesis reveals the basic features of Hebrew cosmogony.

Genesis begins by introducing the power and glory of the Hebrew God: "In the beginning God created . . ." The narrative exalts the great Elohim in his eternal aloneness. In the Hebrew account, Elohim is pictured penetrating the silence and shining into the primordial darkness in order to create a sphere where he might display his sovereignty, incomparability, and power. The Hebrews believed that Elohim revealed himself and his glory through creation: "The heavens are telling of the glory of God; and their expanse is declaring the work of His hands" (Ps. 19:1).

Genesis 1 describes God's creation of "the heavens and the earth." This figure of speech is called a merism, a set of opposite terms with an all-inclusive character.[15] The phrase "the heavens and the earth" is used here and elsewhere in the Hebrew Bible (e.g., Gen. 14:19; Exod. 31:17) to teach that God created everything that exists. How, according to the Hebrews, did God create? The third verse of Genesis 1 indicates that

---

14. That the Hebrews viewed Satan as an individual being and not merely as a representation of the concept of evil is supported by the occasional use of the definite article with the term *Satan* ("the Satan"). See, e.g., Job 1–2 and Zech. 3. The New Testament evidence confirms this understanding (Luke 4; and Rev. 12:9, which, incidentally, connects Satan with the serpent that tempted Eve in the Garden of Eden).

15. Cf. the merism in Ps. 139:8, "If I ascend to heaven, Thou art there; If I make my bed in Sheol, behold, Thou art there!" Where is God? Everywhere.

Elohim declared, "'Let there be light'; and there was light." By simply speaking, God created the universe and all that was in it. Numerous other biblical references indicate that the Hebrews believed that God's speaking was the method of creation. The psalmist declares that "by the word of the LORD the heavens were made" (Ps. 33:6); and Psalm 148:5 exhorts all creation to extol God's name, "for He commanded and they were created."[16]

Furthermore, God's verbal fiat resulted in the creation of the universe *ex nihilo*, "out of nothing." The Hebrew term *bārā'* ("he created") in Genesis 1:1 indicates that all reality (other than God) arose from the nonexistent. A variety of ancient Hebrew verbs express the idea of forming or making, and they may have either God or a human agent as their subject.[17] But the subject of *bārā'* is always and only God, never a human. In addition, as J. Morgenstern has demonstrated, the word *bārā'* "never takes the accusative of the material from which a thing is made, as do other verbs of making, but uses the accusative to designate only the thing made."[18] And the word never refers to creation out of a pre-existent material. It is applied only to creation *ex nihilo*, which no one but God can accomplish.[19]

Each act of Elohim's creation in Genesis 1 follows the same pattern:

1. Pronouncement: "Then God said . . ."
2. Command: "Let there be . . ."
3. Completion: "And it was so."
4. Evaluation: "And God saw that it was good."
5. Temporal framework: "And there was evening and there was morning, a [second] day."

This repetition has four principal theological implications. First, creation was effortless. Elohim spoke and things came into being. The mere verbal fiat that exploded the cosmos into existence displayed Elohim's awesome power. Second, the structure confirms creation *ex nihilo*, that "by the breath of his mouth" the physical came forth from the

---

16. Summarizing the New Testament view, Heb. 11:3 reads, "By faith we understand that the worlds were prepared by the word of God."
17. The words *'āśāh* and *yāṣar* are cases in point. See, e.g., Gen. 3:21 and Exod. 38:1–3.
18. J. Morgenstern, "The Sources of the Creation Story—Genesis 1:1–2:4," *American Journal of Semitic Languages and Literature* 36.3 (1920): 201–2.
19. This last argument that *bārā'* implies *ex nihilo* creation is greatly debated. Morgenstern, "Sources," 202, asserts that it really has "not the slightest foundation." See also B. K. Waltke, *Creation and Chaos* (Portland: Western Conservative Baptist Seminary, 1974), 49–51.

void. Third, creation was an expression of God's will; he was the one who called it forth, and he did so freely without any outside compulsion (Rev. 4:11). Finally, the pattern of creation underscores the doctrine of the sovereignty of God: all things are subject to his rule because he made all things (Ps. 24:1–2).

When God created the cosmos, he installed humans as rulers over the rest of creation. Genesis 1:28 specifies their intended position: "And God blessed them; and God said to them, 'Be fruitful and multiply, and fill the earth, and subdue it; and rule over the fish of the sea and over the birds of the sky, and over every living thing that moves on the earth.'" Psalm 8:5 comments on the human status at creation: "Thou hast made him a little lower than God, and dost crown him with glory and majesty!" God appointed humankind to be the overlords and overseers of the cosmic house and crowned them with glory.

Cosmic Fall

But, according to the Hebrews, humans failed in their task to rule over creation, and a lower creature (i.e., the serpent of Gen. 3) came to dominate them. Instead of responsibly governing creation, they yielded to the enticements of the great tempter. The results of the fall into sin have tremendous cosmological implications.

First, the Hebrews understood that the fall affected the human race in many ways: (1) Man and woman were alienated from God. Genesis 3:7–11 tells us that Adam and Eve hid from God immediately after their sin. (2) The man and woman were alienated from each other. Before sinning they were vulnerable, open, and intimate with each other, a relationship symbolized by their physical nakedness. After sinning they covered themselves, and Adam blamed Eve for his sin. (3) The man and woman were alienated from eternal life.[20] (4) They were alienated from the Garden of Eden. God drove them from the garden and never allowed them to return (Gen. 3:24). (5) Adam and Eve were alienated from themselves. This is evident in their inability, when God confronted them, to accept responsibility for their action.[21]

Second, not only the human race but the entire cosmos was affected by sin. The whole of creation was subjected to vanity, futility, and frustration because of Adam and Eve's fall: "Cursed is the ground because of you; in toil you shall eat of it all the days of your life. Both thorns and thistles it shall grow for you" (Gen. 3:17–18; see also 5:29). Commenting

---

20. That death is a result of sin was later confirmed by the apostle Paul: "The wages of sin is death" (Rom. 6:23).

21. Limitations of space preclude discussion of other effects of the fall, such as the imputation of Adam's sin to the whole human race.

on the fall Ecclesiastes 1:2 declares: "'Vanity of vanities,' says the Preacher, 'Vanity of vanities! All is vanity.'" Subject to deterioration, the universe appeared to be running down. Nature, like humankind, was in a state of decay, pain, and futility.[22]

Cosmological Redemptive Hope

The Old Testament teaches, however, that the present futility to which the whole cosmos was subjected is merely temporary. A time will come when the universe will be delivered from corruption and decay, and restored to its proper order and structure. Hebrew writers prophesy that one day the effects of sin will be removed from the cosmos, and the universe will be regenerated (Isa. 65:17–19).

Two principal elements of the future regenerated cosmos are identified in the Old Testament. First, God will redeem his chosen people, restoring them to a proper relationship with himself (Jer. 24:7; 31:31–34; 32:40; 33:14–16; Ezek. 37:26–27). Second, as the Old Testament prophets announced, God's entire creation will share in the redemption of his people. The cosmos, now subjected to futility, will someday be restored to harmony (Isa. 11:6–9; 35:1–2a, 9–10).

In this chapter we have generally discussed the cosmological views of the ancient Egyptians, Mesopotamians, and Canaanites. Although the three systems had obvious differences, they rested upon the same basic principles:

1. All three societies believed in polytheism, the worship of many gods. These polytheistic religions identified the gods with powers and elements of the universe. They gave names to natural phenomena and endowed them with personalities. Thus the gods were totally immanent—merely part of the universe. And each god was restricted to the capacity of the natural element personified, so that the god's power never exceeded the power associated with the natural phenomenon. Thus the gods were not all-powerful. Rather, the nature deities were severely limited in what they could do. In addition, their characters were often depraved and perverted, reflecting the debased lifestyles of hu-

---

22. Some commentators argue that in the Hebrew perspective the universe was not greatly influenced by the fall into sin. For example, A. H. Lewis, "The Localization of the Garden of Eden," *Bulletin of the Evangelical Theological Society* 11 (1968): 174, observes, "Nothing in the narrative suggests that the realm of nature has been altered in a fundamental way." Kline, "Kingdom Prologue," 81, agrees: "The Bible does not require us, therefore, to think of the character and working of man's natural environment before the Fall as radically different from what is presently the case." However, when Paul comments in Rom. 8:20 that the whole created order "was subjected to futility," he is really saying that nature did not remain the same after the fall. There was indeed a great change, which Paul calls "slavery to corruption" (Rom. 8:21).

mankind. As the powers of the gods reflected the pattern of nature, so the temperament of the gods reflected humans.

2. The gods existed either through self-creation or through creation by other gods. This theogony played a vital and pivotal role in the cosmogonical texts from Egypt and Mesopotamia, almost all of which focused on the origin and genealogy of the gods. Most creation accounts served to establish and justify the particular culture's pantheon and hierarchy of the gods.

3. According to ancient polytheism, the true power of the universe was magic. The god who performed the greatest magical feats was considered the most powerful. Ancient peoples also relied on magic (i.e., omens, sorcery, divinations, and necromancy) to manipulate nature (the gods) for their own benefit. The ultimate power over the cosmos, then, was an element external to the universe.

4. In most ancient Near Eastern societies humans were basically viewed as insignificant. They possessed little dignity and worth and were thought to be merely slaves to the gods. They had no freedom, since the whim and fancy of the gods decided the direction and outcome of their lives.

The Hebrew conception of the universe differs radically from the other ancient Near Eastern cosmologies. Whereas the ancient Egyptians, Mesopotamians, and Canaanites sought to explain the structure and operation of the universe in terms of gods who personified nature, the Old Testament speaks of a deity who is apart from the universe. While ancient pagan societies speculatively searched for elements that ordered the universe internally, the Hebrews presented an external force who created and continually sustained the cosmos. Ancient Israelite cosmology rested upon the Hebrews' unique belief in a single God (monotheism) who began the universe and was completely sovereign over its operation. Old Testament writers taught that the unique, singular God called the people of Israel out of the midst of pagan nations to be his peculiar and distinct agent in the world. He told them: "I am the LORD your God. Consecrate yourselves therefore, and be holy; for I am holy" (Lev. 11:44). The word *holy* in Hebrew *(qādōš)* literally means "to be set apart, separate, distinct, and unique." So it was God's command that Israel repudiate the ways of pagan nations and follow his statutes only.

The Hebrews also understood humans to be essential to the universe. They were creatures of great purpose and dignity. They were not made to be slaves but princes, rulers, the crown of creation.

Given the biblical perspective, all of the thoughts and actions of the Hebrews were to be different from their neighbors—the Egyptians, the Mesopotamians, and the Canaanites. Magical arts, which underlay ancient pagan religions, were forbidden in Israel (Deut. 18:10–11), as were pagan rituals such as temple prostitution and child sacrifice (2 Kings 23:4–10). The sovereign God of Israel could not be manipulated by such rites (see Exod. 7:8–13).

Clearly, the Hebrew conception of reality conflicted with ancient Near Eastern pagan cosmologies. We will see that throughout history these presuppositional differences strikingly affected Israel's relationships with the surrounding cultures and with Egypt in particular.

Part 2
Egyptian Elements in the Pentateuch

3
The Egyptian and Genesis Cosmogonies

In considering the cosmogony of the Hebrews, biblical scholars have laid great stress upon the parallels in Mesopotamian literature. The work of Alexander Heidel is noteworthy in that regard.[1] More recent studies have also affirmed the connection between the two.[2] In fact, many scholars argue that the Hebrew account of creation is directly dependent upon earlier Mesopotamian texts.[3] The material written about the correspondence between the cosmogonic literature of the two cultures has been so vast that few question the veracity of the parallel. It seems to be one of the rare certainties in a field shrouded in disagreement and uncertainty.

While one would not deny that some important parallels do exist between Mesopotamian and Israelite cosmogony,[4] one might wonder if

---

1. See, e.g., A. Heidel, *The Babylonian Genesis* (Chicago: University of Chicago Press, 1951). For the first study of that literature, see George Smith, *The Chaldean Account of Genesis* (New York: Scribner, 1876). The discovery of the Mesopotamian cosmogonic texts is intriguingly reported by W. G. Lambert and A. R. Millard, *Atra-hasis: The Babylonian Story of the Flood* (Oxford: Clarendon, 1969), 1–5.

2. See, e.g., D. Damrosch, *The Narrative Covenant: Transformations of Genre in the Growth of Biblical Literature* (San Francisco: Harper and Row, 1987), 88–143; S. Niditch, *Chaos to Cosmos: Studies in Biblical Patterns of Creation* (Decatur, Ga.: Scholars, 1985); and, especially, W. G. Lambert, "A New Look at the Babylonian Background of Genesis," *JTS* 16 (1965): 287–300.

3. See E. A. Speiser, *Genesis* (Garden City, N.Y.: Doubleday, 1964), liii–lviii. Recall also our quotations of Friedrich Delitzsch and S. R. Driver in ch. 1 (p. 28).

4. For a good parallel see J. Van Seters, "The Creation of Man and the Creation of the King," *ZAW* 101 (1989): 333–42, which discusses a recently published Neo-Babylonian text that speaks of the creation of humans. Van Seters correctly sees features in that text that have much in common with the opening chapters of Genesis. See also W. L. Moran, "The Creation of Man in Atrahasis I, 192–248," *BASOR* 200 (1970): 48–56.

they have not been emphasized to too great a degree, for parallels have scarcely been looked for in other civilizations. Wilfred Lambert comments: "Parallels to Genesis can indeed be sought and found there [i.e., Mesopotamia], but they can also be sought and found among the Canaanites, the ancient Egyptians, the Hurrians, the Hittites and the early Greeks. When the parallels have been found, the question of dependence, if any, has to be approached with an open mind."[5]

A couple of recent studies have attempted to show that the creation account of Genesis may have some striking parallels with the cosmogonic writings of Egypt.[6] James Hoffmeier's work should be especially noted. Old Testament scholars, however, have paid little attention. Indeed, earlier attempts to make such a connection also seemed to fall on deaf ears.[7] Scholars have instead been investigating other areas for possible parallels.[8]

The present study will further analyze the relationship between the Hebrew creation story and Egyptian cosmogony. We will see that there is a significant resemblance between the two creation accounts. This is not surprising since there were frequent connections between the two peoples on many different cultural levels.[9] Our study will focus on the thematic relationship as well as the lexical and philological connec-

---

5. Lambert, "New Look," 289.

6. C. Gordon, "Khnum and El," *Scripta Hierosolymitana* 28 (1982): 203–14; and J. K. Hoffmeier, "Some Thoughts on Genesis 1 and 2 and Egyptian Cosmology," *JANES* 15 (1983): 39–49. This chapter relies heavily on the latter work.

7. A. H. Sayce, "The Egyptian Background of Genesis 1," in *Studies Presented to F. Ll. Griffith* (London: Egypt Exploration Society, 1932), 419–23; and A. S. Yahuda, *The Language of the Pentateuch in Its Relation to Egyptian* (London: Oxford University Press, 1933), 101–294. Though Yahuda overstates his case repeatedly, much profitable material can be gleaned from his work.

8. Some researchers are convinced that there are similarities between the Ugaritic myths and the Bible: L. Fisher, "Creation at Ugarit and in the Old Testament," *VT* 15 (1965): 313–24; R. J. Clifford, "Cosmogonies in the Ugaritic Texts and in the Bible," *Orientalia* 53 (1984): 183–201; J. C. L. Gibson, "The Theology of the Ugaritic Baal Cycle," *Orientalia* 53 (1984): 202–19; and J. H. Grønbaek, "Baal's Battle with Yam: A Canaanite Creation Fight," *JSOT* 33 (1985): 27–44. Certainly some Ugaritic texts were cosmological in nature; that is, they attempted in a mythic manner to describe the operation of the universe. It is debatable, on the other hand, whether any of those texts were cosmogonic, that is, explained the beginning of the cosmos. See the discussions of B. Margalit, "The Ugaritic Creation Myth: Fact or Fiction?" *UF* 13 (1981): 137–45; and M. H. Pope, *El in the Ugaritic Texts* (Leiden: Brill, 1955).

9. Archaeological contacts are discussed by R. Giveon, *The Impact of Egypt on Canaan* (Göttingen: Vandenhoeck and Ruprecht, 1978); literary links can be found in T. O. Lambdin, "Egyptian Loan Words in the Old Testament," *JAOS* 73 (1953): 145–55; R. J. Williams, "Egypt and Israel," in *The Legacy of Egypt*, ed. J. R. Harris, 2d ed. (Oxford: Clarendon, 1971), 257–90; and idem, "Some Egyptianisms in the Old Testament," in *Studies in Honor of John A. Wilson*, Studies in Ancient Oriental Civilization 35 (Chicago: University of Chicago Press, 1969), 93–98.

tions, something other studies have been less willing to do. We will compare three aspects of the Hebrew and Egyptian cosmogonies: (1) the nature and character of the creator-god; (2) the manner in which the creator-god fashioned the universe; and (3) the sequence and constitution of creation.

Before we look at that material, however, a warning must be given to the reader regarding the sources of Egyptian cosmogony, a warning that John A. Wilson expressed as early as 1946: "It is significant that a plural should be necessary, that we cannot settle down to a single codified account of beginnings. The Egyptians accepted various myths and discarded none of them."[10] Similarly, Siegfried Morenz speaks of "an abundance of more or less scanty references in the most varied texts which give us some very disjointed information about Egyptian notions concerning God the creator and the evolution of the world (and life on it)."[11] The fullest Egyptian creation account is the Memphite theology found on the Shabaka Stone, a passage that reflects merely one of many creation myths. Other cosmogonic references appear sporadically in the Coffin Texts, the Pyramid Texts, and sundry other places. The point is that there was no one view of creation held by the Egyptians.[12] Their civilization was long-lasting and, therefore, diverse. Many ideas of creation circulated throughout their history. Consequently, making comparisons between Egyptian cosmogonies and the Bible can be difficult and, indeed, dangerous. But, be that as it may, we are yet convinced of a parallel relationship between the creation accounts in Egypt and the Bible.

The Creator

A fundamental doctrine of the Bible, of course, is the concept of one Creator God. Many texts express this belief (e.g., Job 38; Ps. 24:1–2; 104). But it was an almost unheard of tenet in the remainder of the ancient Near East. The Mesopotamians, for instance, clearly embraced a multiplicity of gods who had creative powers and engaged in creative activity.[13] The ancient Egyptians, however, "believed in a single creator and

---

10. H. Frankfort et al., *Before Philosophy* (Baltimore: Penguin, 1973 reprint), 59.
11. Siegfried Morenz, *Egyptian Religion* (Ithaca, N.Y.: Cornell University Press, 1973), 160.
12. A diversity of beliefs about creation was evident also in Mesopotamia; see Lambert, "New Look," 289.
13. According to the *Enuma Elish*, Ea created the subterranean sea, Marduk then made heaven and earth, and after that Ea fashioned humankind. Apsu and Tiamat, however, were the original creators, for they formed the divine beings who shared in the creation of the universe. For a good discussion see Heidel, *Babylonian Genesis*, 96–97.

originator of divine power."[14] Indeed, they thought that one god fashioned the universe and everything in it. In one New Kingdom hymn we read that the creator-god "brought mankind into being, forming the gods and creating all that exists."[15] The Memphite theology pictures the creator-god Ptah in the same manner: "And so the making of everything and the creation of the gods should be assigned to Ptah. He is Tatenen who produced the gods, from whom everything has come, whether food, divine sustenance or any other good thing. So it has been found and understood that his power is greater than that of the other gods. And then Ptah rested after he had created everything and every divine word."[16]

Some of the images used in the Bible to represent God as the creator resemble those used by the Egyptians of their creator-god (whether Ptah, Khnum, or whomever). An obvious example is the portrayal of the creator-god as a potter crafting the universe.[17] The Hebrews frequently employed this metaphor to describe Yahweh (Isa. 29:16; 45:9). Likewise, in the "Great Hymn to Khnum" the god Khnum is portrayed "forming all on his potter's wheel . . . for the lord of the wheel is their father too, Tatenen who made all that is on their soil. . . . He made mankind, created gods, he fashioned flocks and herds. He made birds, fishes, and reptiles all."[18] The Memphite theology similarly depicts Ptah as a potter creating the universe.[19] Also common to the Egyptian and Hebrew cosmogonies is the concept of the creator-god as a divine metalworker (see p. 64).

The Manner of Creation

In ancient Egyptian literature, no one method of creation was universally accepted. The accounts picture the creator-god forming the universe in a variety of ways.[20] The earliest attempt to describe the method

---

14. R. T. Rundle Clark, *Myth and Symbol in Ancient Egypt* (London: Thames and Hudson, 1959), 44.
15. E. Chassinat, *Le Temple d'Edfou*, 11 vols. (Paris: Mémoires de la mission archéologique française au Caire, 1892–97), 6:16.4.
16. Clark, *Myth and Symbol*, 65.
17. For an extensive study of this imagery see Gordon, "Khnum and El."
18. *AEL* 3:113.
19. W. K. Simpson, ed., *The Literature of Ancient Egypt* (New Haven: Yale University Press, 1973), 262.
20. For excellent surveys of the many Egyptian creation myths, see S. Sauneron and J. Yoyotte, *La Naissance du monde* (Paris: Sources Orientales 1, 1959); B. Menu, "Les Récits de création en Egypte ancienne," *Foi et Vie* 85 (1986): 65–77; and J. P. Allen, *Genesis in Egypt: The Philosophy of Ancient Egyptian Creation Accounts* (New Haven: Yale Egyptological Seminar, 1988). One account on which we will spend little time is the teaching of the Book of the Dead: "Ra it is the creator of the names of his limbs, have come into existence these in the form of the gods who are in the train of Ra" (plate vii—the translation is that of E. A. W. Budge, *The Book of the Dead: The Papyrus of Ani*, vol. 1 [New York:

of creation is to be found in the Pyramid Texts (ca. 2350–2175 B.C.).[21] Here the beginning of creation takes the form of the sudden appearance of a primordial hillock rising up out of a watery void.[22] On that primeval mound Atum then materialized in an act of self-creation. We read in Utterance 587 of the Pyramid Texts:[23]

> Praise to you, Atum!
> Praise to you, Kheprer, who created himself![24]
> You became high in this your name High Ground.[25]
> You created yourself in this your name Kheprer.[26]

Later Egyptian writings echoed the belief that the creator-god was a product of his own creation. Consider, for example, the hieratic Coffin Text 714:[27]

> I (am) Nu[28] the one with no equal.
> I came into being on the

York: Putnam, 1913]). The passage seems to mean that when Re named various parts of his body, gods sprung forth from those parts.

21. The Pyramid Texts were discovered at Saqqara in the tombs of Wenis (Dynasty 5), Teti, Pepy I, Merenre, Pepy II (Dynasty 6), and Ibi (Dynasty 7). The hieroglyphic texts are reproduced in K. Sethe, ed., *Die altägyptischen Pyramidentexten* (Leipzig: J. C. Hinrichs, 1908–22). For a good English translation see R. O. Faulkner, *The Ancient Egyptian Pyramid Texts* (New York: Oxford University Press, 1969). For the role of myth in the Pyramid Texts see R. Anthes, "Remarks on the Pyramid Texts and Early Egyptian Dogma," *JAOS* 74 (1954): 35–39. Out of 759 utterances, 13 refer directly to an act of creation: 222, 301, 484, 486, 506, 527, 558, 571, 587, 600, 609, 660, and 684.

22. H. Kees, "Die Feuerinsel in den Sargtexten und im Totenbuch," *ZAS* 78 (1942): 41; A. A. Saleh, "The So-Called 'Primeval Hill' and Other Elevations in Ancient Egyptian Mythology," *Mitteilungen des deutschen archäologischen Instituts, Kairo* 25 (1969): 110–20.

23. For various translations see Clark, *Myth and Symbol*, 37–38; Faulkner, *Pyramid Texts*, 238–41; and S. A. B. Mercer, *The Pyramid Texts*, 4 vols. (New York: Longmans, Green, 1952), 246–48. Except where noted, the translations of the Egyptian texts are those of the author.

24. Here is a play on words. The Egyptian verb for "to create, to come into being" is *ḫpr*. The name of the god Kheprer is a derivative of that root.

25. Another wordplay is in evidence. The Egyptian word for "High Ground" is *k3*, and that is related to the verb in the sentence—*k3y* ("to be uplifted, raised"). This is a clear reference to the primeval mound upon which the creator-god appeared at creation.

26. The same wordplay occurs here as at n. 24. Here, however, the verb is located before the proper name.

27. The hieroglyphic originals of the Coffin Texts are reproduced in A. de Buck, *The Egyptian Coffin Texts*, 7 vols. (Chicago: University of Chicago Press, 1935–61). For a fine translation and commentary see R. O. Faulkner, *The Ancient Egyptian Coffin Texts*, 3 vols. (Warminster: Aris and Phillips, 1973–77). For specific information on Coffin Text 714, see K. Sethe, *Amun und die acht Urgötter von Hermopolis* (Berlin: APAW, 1929), 29; and Clark, *Myth and Symbol*, 74.

28. A reference to the primeval waters.

Great occasion of the inundation,[29] when I came into being.
I am he[30] who flew, who became *Dbnn*[31]
Who is in his egg.
I am he[32] who began there (in) Nu.
See, the chaos-god came forth from me.

See, I am prosperous.[33]
I created my body in my glory;
I am he who made myself;
I formed myself according to my will and according to my heart.[34]

After his act of self-generation, the creator brought into existence the lesser gods of the cosmos.[35] The theogony was portrayed in different ways in Egyptian literature.[36] One Pyramid Text, Utterance 600, pictures Atum as spitting out of his mouth and thus creating the siblings Shu and Tefnut:[37]

O Atum-Kheprer,[38] you became high on a hill;

---

29. Faulkner, *Ancient Egyptian Coffin Texts*, 2:270, follows de Buck (*Coffin Texts*, 343 n. 3). He argues that there is a corruption here. The text literally reads *nꜣḥt*(?). Faulkner emends it to *nꜣmḥt*. I would rather read *nꜣḥt*.
30. The Egyptian reads *ink*, which literally means "I, me." The repetition is for the purpose of underscoring the claims of deity.
31. Clark translates this as "a circle." The problem is that *Dbnn* is the proper name of a deity, because it carries the seated-god determinative.
32. See n. 30.
33. The word here is *wdꜣ*, which literally means "whole, sound, hearty, prosperous." The idea of prosperity fits the context, since the god has just proclaimed that he produced the chaos-god.
34. Among other ancient Egyptian texts that taught that the creator-god brought himself into existence is the "Sun-Hymn of Haremhab," which says of the creator-god, "Thou art a divine youth, the heir of eternity, who begot thyself and bore thyself" (*ARE* 3:9). In a Leiden papyrus we get the striking image of Amon the creator "joining his seed with his body, to create his egg within his secret self" (A. H. Gardiner, "Hymns to Amon from a Leiden Papyrus," *ZAS* 42 [1905]: 25). Another example is given in Chassinat, *Le Temple d'Edfou*, 2:37: the creator-god "came into being by himself." Similarly, in the Book of the Dead, Spell 85, the creator says, "I came into being of myself in the midst of the primeval waters in this my name of Khopri"; and in Coffin Text, Spell 601, "I am Re-Atum who himself molded himself."
35. Re is portrayed in one text as saying, "Only after I came into being did all that was created come into being." See G. Roeder, *Urkunden zur Religion des alten Ägypten* (Jena: Diedrichs, 1915), 108.
36. For an excellent discussion of theogony in ancient Egypt, see E. Hornung, *Conceptions of God in Ancient Egypt* (Ithaca, N.Y.: Cornell University Press, 1982), 148–51.
37. The hieroglyphic text appears in Sethe, *Pyramidentexten*, 2:372–75. An easily accessible translation is that of J. A. Wilson, "The Creation of Atum," in *ANET*, 3.
38. The creator-god has two names here, a compound of the two phases of the sun, morning and evening. The merism points to the comprehensive, all-embracing character of the deity. The title Atum means "hidden, all in himself." The name Kheprer literally means "the becoming one," which bears the idea of rebirth and renewal.

You rose like the ben-ben stone in the temple of the ben-bird in
   Heliopolis.[39]
You spat out Shu, you spewed out Tefnut.[40]
And you put your arms around them like the arms of a *ka*-sign (so that)
   your *ka*[41] might be in them.
Atum, set your arms around Nefer-ka-Re,[42]
This construction, this pyramid like the arms of a *ka*-sign.
So that the *ka* of Nefer-ka-Re might be in it evermore.

In some later texts spitting out (expectoration) is once again the method by which lesser gods were created.[43] For example, Coffin Text, Spell 76.3–4: "I am this Shu that Atum created when Re was formed himself; I was not formed in a womb or shaped in an egg; I was not conceived by conception, (but) Atum spit me out in the spit of his mouth together with Tefnut."[44]

In the Pyramid Texts there is another method for the birth of the gods: an act of masturbation (onanism) by the creator-god. Since the deity was alone on the primeval hill, and he had no consort to share in the creative act (in contrast to other ancient Near Eastern myths),[45] he used one of the few physical means at his disposal. Utterance 527 gives a concise account:[46]

---

   39. A sanctuary at Heliopolis contained a sacred stone that apparently represented the primeval hillock upon which Atum created the cosmos. Note the consonance in the line: *wbn* ("rose"), *bn-bn* stone, and *bn*-bird.
   40. Shu was the god of the air, and Tefnut the goddess of the atmosphere. Again there is a notable consonance: *ysh* ("spat out") and *shw* ("Shu"), *tfn* ("spewed out") and *tfnt* ("Tefnut").
   41. The first *ka* refers to an ideogram picturing two all-embracing arms (⊔); the second *ka* refers to what the *ka*-sign represents, that is, spirit or essence. For a study of the *ka*-sign, see L. Greven, *Der Ka in Theologie und Königskult der Ägypter des alten Reiches* (Glückstadt-Hamburg: Ägyptologische Forschungen 17, 1952); see also the review by R. O. Faulkner in *JEA* 41 (1955): 141–42. Finally, a brief discussion may be found in A. H. Gardiner, "The Baptism of Pharaoh," *JEA* 36 (1950): 3–12.
   42. A title for Pepy II of Dynasty 6.
   43. Some Egyptian texts also taught that the creator-god spit forth or exhaled the gods from his nostril. In Coffin Text, Spell 75.340, Shu says about the creator: "He created me by his wish, he made me by his power, he exhaled me from his nostril, and I am he whose shape was exhaled." The reader might also consult Coffin Texts, Spells 75.356; 80.36, 40; and 81.44.
   44. For a commentary on the text see J. Zandee, "Sargtexte Spruch 76," *ZÄS* 100 (1973): 60–71; and R. O. Faulkner, "Some Notes on the God Shu," *Jaarbericht "Ex Oriente Lux"* 18 (1964): 266–70.
   45. A procreative act between a male and female deity is suggested in the Mesopotamian creation story. In the opening lines of *Enuma Elish* we read: "Naught but primordial Apsu, their begetter, (and) Mummu-Tiamat, she bore them all, their waters commingling as a single body . . . then it was that the gods were formed within them" (the translation is by E. A. Speiser, in *ANET*, 61).
   46. Another translation and commentary may be found in H. Kees, *Der Götterglaube im alten Ägypten*, 2d ed. (Berlin: Mitteilungen der vorder-asiatisch-ägyptischen Gesellschaft 45, 1956), 219–20.

Atum is this one *(pw)* who was created; now[47] he masturbated[48] in Heliopolis.
He put his phallus in his fist
(so that) he would make sexual pleasure (orgasm) from it.
(Thus) the twins[49] Shu together with Tefnut were born.

The later Coffin Text, Spell 245, alludes to this early myth in a remark of Shu to Atum, the creator-god: "This was the manner of your engendering: you conceived with your mouth and you gave birth from your hand in the pleasure of emission. I am the star that came forth from the two."[50]

It should be noted and stressed at this point that ancient Egyptian theogony was truly cosmogonic, for each of the gods fashioned was a personification of an element of nature.[51] Thus in some of the myths the creator-god produces four children who correspond to the basic structure of the universe: Shu (=air), Tefnut (=atmosphere), Geb (=earth), and Nut (=heavens). They in turn breed another generation of gods who also represent elements of nature (e.g., Seth=storm). So we must in no way think that the Egyptian creation myths describe merely a metaphysical or spiritual creation. Rather, those stories are frankly concerned to explain and detail the physical universe as it appears.

The so-called Memphite theology of the Old Kingdom also produced a document that attempted to describe creation. The Shabaka Stone ascribed the formation of reality to the god Ptah.[52] Indeed, it was he "who made all and brought the gods into being."[53] This clearly polemicized against the Atum cult at Heliopolis. Key here is what the text says about Ptah and his relationship to Atum:

---

47. This is the enclitic particle *yrf*, which serves to emphasize the event.
48. The word here is *msꜣw*. It is clearly related to *msy*, which means "to give birth to, to produce, to create."
49. Most of the hieroglyphics in this section are doubled.
50. The translation is by Clark, *Myth and Symbol*, 44. The hieroglyphic text appears in de Buck, *Egyptian Coffin Texts*, 3:334. Among other texts reporting that method of creation is Spell 77: "I am this soul of Shu which is in the flame of the fiery blast which Atum kindled with his own hand. He created orgasm and fluid fell from his mouth. He spat me out as Shu together with Tefenet" (Faulkner, *Ancient Egyptian Coffin Texts*, 1:80).
51. See J. Currid, "Cosmologies of Myth," in *Building a Christian World View*, ed. W. A. Hoffecker, 2 vols. (Phillipsburg, N.J.: Presbyterian and Reformed, 1986, 1988), 2:9–20.
52. For a remarkable study of the Shabaka Stone see K. Sethe, *Dramatische Texte zu altägyptischen Mysterienspielen* (Leipzig: Untersuchungen zur Geschichte und Altertumskunde Ägyptens 10, 1928). For a partial English translation by J. A. Wilson, see *ANET*, 4–6. See also the basic studies by J. H. Breasted, *The Dawn of Conscience* (New York: Scribner, 1933), 29–42; and "The Philosophy of the Memphite Priest," *ZAS* 39 (1901): 39–54.
53. *ANET*, 5.

The Egyptian and Genesis Cosmogonies 61

> The gods[54] were created from Ptah.[55]
> Ptah is upon the great divine throne . . . who gave birth to the gods.
> Ptah (is) the primeval waters *(Nnw)*, the father of Atum . . . who gave birth to the gods.
> Ptah (is) the lower heaven *(Nnt)*, the mother who gave birth to Atum.
> Ptah (is) great, the heart and tongue[56] of the Ennead.

Ptah is depicted here as the begetter of Atum, indeed as the very primordial waters (Nun) out of which Atum came forth. Ptah, therefore, created Atum and was to be exalted and glorified as the creator-god!

Of utmost importance is the text's emphasis on the totally different ways in which the two gods fashioned the universe:

> Whereas the gods of Atum were created[57] from his semen *(mtwt)* and from his fingers,
> The gods (of Ptah) are the teeth and lips from his mouth, which proclaimed *(mȝt)* the name of everything.
> Shu and Tefnut came forth.

The distinction is explicit: whereas Atum created the Ennead by onanism, Ptah fashioned the lesser gods by lordly speech.[58] The text implicitly criticizes and denigrates Atum's act. He was forced to rely upon "his semen and . . . his fingers." But Ptah is to be acclaimed as the omnipotent creator-god because he formed the cosmos by mere verbal fiat. He commanded with his teeth and lips, and the gods sprung forth.

The description of Ptah's method of creation, otherwise known as the logos doctrine, should immediately remind us of the creative activity of Elohim in Genesis 1. That passage depicts God as creating the universe by the power of his speech: "Then God said, 'Let there be light'; and there was light." In fact, the entire biblical account highlights God's creative effort through the word (Gen. 1:8–11, 14, 20, 22, 24, 26). Other texts further support the Hebrews' belief in God's creation by verbal fiat. For example, Psalm 33:6 reads, "By the word of the LORD the heavens were made, and by the breath of His mouth all their host." Thus in both accounts, the Hebrew and the Memphite, creation takes place by means of the word of the creator-god.

---

54. Here the hieroglyphic sign is repeated three times.
55. Oddly, this phrase lies in a horizontal frame of the relief. The remainder of the text is in vertical columns.
56. This refers to Ptah's creative ability; see n. 58.
57. The text is broken at this point, but the sacred beetle sign *(ḫp)* is discernible.
58. This interpretation is supported later in the text: "Thus all the gods were formed and (Ptah's) Ennead was completed. Indeed, all the divine order really came into being through what the heart thought and the tongue commanded."

Both texts also reflect the ancient idea that all objects are inextricably bound to the spoken word.[59] In fact, many believed that an object took its identity from its name. In other words, things had no being or character unless they had been named. A good example of that belief was the Hebrew practice of giving names that fit individual characters and personalities (Gen. 3:20; 4:2; 25:26). In the two accounts of creation, therefore, the naming of the created objects certified their essence and existence. Without names they had no being. And so we read in ancient Egyptian stories of the time before creation "when the name of anything was not yet named."[60]

Both accounts also articulate a creation divinely fashioned *ex nihilo*, that is, out of nothing. Without a doubt, such was the view of the biblical writers.[61] The perspective of the Memphite theology, however, is less obvious and, therefore, a matter of some debate. At the heart of the issue is the common assumption that Ptah used the preexistent primordial waters (Nun) as the material of creation.[62] Three points can be made in response:

1. Nowhere does the Memphite theology ever represent Ptah as using the primeval waters as the stuff of creation.[63]
2. In fact, the Shabaka Stone portrays Ptah as the primeval waters, and the primeval waters as Ptah. As we have already seen, the text reads: "Ptah is upon the great divine throne. . . . Ptah (is) Nun, the father of Atum. . . . Ptah is Naunet, the mother who gave birth to Atum." The point here for the Memphite theologian was that the preexistent matter which formed the universe was the god Ptah himself. Simply, nothing existed before Ptah.[64]
3. The Memphite theology repeatedly emphasizes that the cosmos came into existence only by means of Ptah's will, desires, and inner being. That is to say, the thoughts of Ptah's heart caused the world. A key passage of the Shabaka Stone says, "Indeed, all

---

59. Morenz, *Egyptian Religion*, 164–65.

60. H. Grapow, "Die Welt vor der Schöpfung," *ZAS* 67 (1931): 36. We know from the first lines of the *Enuma Elish* that the same belief was held in Mesopotamia: "When on high the heaven had not been named, firm ground below had not been called by name . . ." (*ANET*, 60–61).

61. See J. Currid, "A Cosmology of History: From Creation to Consummation," in *Building a Christian World View*, ed. Hoffecker, 2:41–68.

62. In the Berlin "Hymn to Ptah" we read, "What thy mouth produced, what thy hands produced, thou hast taken it out of Nun"; see W. Wolf, "Der berliner Ptah-Hymnus," *ZAS* 64 (1929): 28.

63. Morenz, *Egyptian Religion*, 172.

64. That, of course, was a polemic against the Atum cult. The Atum theology depicted a god who came forth from something else; not so Ptah!

the divine order really came into being through what the heart thought and the tongue commanded."[65]

These points imply that the Memphite theology portrays Ptah, in and of himself, as creating the universe. There is absolutely no indication that any ready-made material was necessary or, for that matter, even available. Instead, the creator merely thought and spoke, and physical objects were generated into existence. That idea appears to be an essential characteristic of both the Memphite and biblical cosmogonies.

Furthermore, the two accounts of creation had a similar purpose in their presentations of how the gods created. Their common presentation of one creator-god who fashioned the universe *ex nihilo* by means of verbal fiat declared to their respective audiences that the deity was all-powerful, incomparable, and sovereign. The authors were proclaiming to the people that here was a god who could create the universe out of nothing. He owed nothing to the agency of another. By fashioning the world through a mere speaking of words this god proved himself a deity above all other deities. Clearly, then, the intent of the writers was, first and foremost, to assert a theological truth. That truth found substance in the climax of the Memphite creation account: "Thus it was discovered and understood that his (Ptah's) strength is greater than (that of the other) gods."[66]

Although we have mentioned only a few examples, the parallels between the Memphite theology and Genesis regarding the method of creation are striking. Actually, the biblical account has greater affinity with the Egyptian texts than with the Mesopotamian. For the main Mesopotamian creation myth *(Enuma Elish)* is oriented toward conflict and violence.[67] The universe came into existence because of a battle between the gods; it was a mere consequence of a war aimed at determining who would be the lord of the gods. Thus we read that after the battle in which Marduk defeated Tiamat,

> He split her open like a mussel into two parts;
> Half of her he set in place and formed the sky (therewith) as a roof.[68]

There is no conflict, on the other hand, in either the biblical or Memphite cosmogony. Creation did not occur as a result of a contest or a struggle. Thus, while much has been written about the Mesopotamian

---

65. *ANET*, 5.
66. Ibid.
67. For a thorough study see Heidel, *Babylonian Genesis*.
68. Ibid., 42.

influences upon or parallels with the biblical text, the Egyptian parallels regarding the means of creation are more substantial.

The Creation

In Genesis 1:1 the biblical author uses the word *bĕrēʾšît* to characterize the time framework of the creation. It is properly translated "in the beginning" or "at the first." Frequently *bĕrēʾšît* or a related form was employed to describe the first phase or step in an event.[69] It is a derivative of the root word *rōʾš*, which in its most basic sense refers to the "human head," but also often signifies "the head or chief" of a group of people, and even the top or peak of a mountain (Gen. 8:5; Exod. 19:20).[70] The Egyptians as well believed that the event of creation had a real beginning. They expressed that idea with the term *sp tpy*, two words that literally meant "time" and "first."[71] One text states that the creator-god "began the earth at the first time *(sp tpy)*."[72] It is striking that the word *tpy* derived from *tp*, a root that literally meant "head."[73] As Abraham Yahuda has correctly pointed out, the terminology of the two accounts is related conceptually, that is, they both reflect the idea that creation took place at the beginning of time.[74]

The biblical authors used a variety of words to represent God's creative activity of forming the universe. The three commonest were *bārāʾ*, *yāṣar*, and *ʿāśāh*. All three terms conveyed the basic idea that God was a master craftsman, one skilled in art who "constructed, shaped, and fashioned" all that there is. Indeed, he was often portrayed as a potter who produced the clay vessel of the cosmos (Isa. 29:16; 45:9; 64:8).[75] The Egyptian words used to refer to the creator-god's work carried the same meaning as did their Hebrew counterparts. Two common words for "creating," *km3* and *nbỉ*, derived from roots that meant "to hammer out of metal, to cast objects from metal."[76] And thus the creator-god was sometimes referred to as the *ḥmww*, the "master craftsman."[77] Furthermore, in Egyptian cosmogony the creator-god

---

69. *BDB*, 912.
70. Ibid., 910.
71. R. O. Faulkner, *A Concise Dictionary of Middle Egyptian* (Oxford: Griffith Institute, 1962), 221; *WAS* 3:435–38.
72. G. Maspéro, *Les Momies royales de Deir el Bahari* (Paris: Mémoires de la mission archéologique française au Caire, 1989), 595. For the idea that *tpy* referred to the first step in an event, see J. H. Breasted, *The Edwin Smith Surgical Papyrus* (Chicago: University of Chicago Press, 1930), 132, 232.
73. *WAS* 5:263–64.
74. Yahuda, *Language of the Pentateuch*, 122–23.
75. *BDB*, 427.
76. Faulkner, *Concise Dictionary*, 129, 278.
77. E.g., in the "Hymn to Ptah"; see Wolf, "Der berliner Ptah-Hymnus," 30–32.

was often depicted as forming parts of the universe upon his potter's wheel.⁷⁸

The Hebrews had no single word to describe the universe. When they wanted to express the concept of all reality, they spoke of "the heavens and the earth" *(haššāmayim wĕʾēt hāʾāreṣ)*. So when Melchizedek blessed Abram in the name of the sovereign God of the universe, he said, "Blessed be Abram of God Most High, possessor of heaven and earth" (Gen. 14:19). The expression "the heavens and the earth" is a merism—two opposites are all-inclusive. Thus when Melchizedek commented that God owned heaven and earth, he meant not only the places of heaven and earth, but also everything in them and on them. Likewise, when the Genesis writer remarked that God created the heavens and the earth, he was saying that God had fashioned the entire universe.

The ancient Egyptians also believed that the creator-god's formative work was comprehensive. In one New Kingdom text, for example, we read that the creator-god "brought mankind into being, forming the gods and creating all that exists."⁷⁹ The so-called Berlin Hymn, which elucidates the results of creation, describes the creator-god as "he who modeled *(nbỉ)*⁸⁰ all the gods, men and animals; he who has created *(ỉrỉ)* all lands and shores and the ocean in his name 'craftsman of the earth.'"⁸¹ Thutmosis IV even dedicated many of his monuments to "the lord who created everything that exists."⁸² The Egyptian belief that the creator-god formed all things is so pervasive in the literature that we can confine ourselves to these few examples.⁸³

Further, the Egyptians, like the Hebrews, commonly described the universe as "heaven and earth" *(p.t* and *t3)*. Thus a hymn to Atum portrays reality as extending "to the height of heaven and to the breadth of earth."⁸⁴ And given that the Egyptians believed in a twofold division of

---

78. The image was especially used in reference to the god Khnum; see Morenz, *Egyptian Religion*, 161.
79. Chassinat, *Le Temple d'Edfou*, 6:16.4.
80. The verb *nb* was usually associated with the craft of metalworking. See *ARE* 1:277, note c; and the review by B. Gunn in *JEA* 6 (1920): 298–302.
81. For text and translation see Wolf, "Der berliner Ptah-Hymnus," 30–32.
82. *Urkunden des ägyptischen Altertums* 4:1540.16.
83. For further study see M. Sandman-Holmberg, *The God Ptah* (Lund: Gleerup, 1946); and E. Drioton, "Les Dédicaces de Ptolémée Evergète III," *ASAE* 44 (1944): 111–62. A fine example comes from the Papyrus of Nesi-Amsu (no. 10188 in the British Museum); the creator-god says, "I was the creator in Khepri. I created the creator of creations, the creator of all creations. Subsequently I created multitudes of creations which came forth from my mouth" (the translation is that of E. A. W. Budge, *From Fetish to God in Ancient Egypt* [New York: Benjamin Blom, 1972], 141). See, in addition, Coffin Text, Spell 306.60.
84. For additional examples see *ARE* 2, texts 139, 288, and 570. The division of the universe into two parts is also reflected in the "Hymn to Amon-Re," who was "the maker of things below, and of things above."

the cosmos, a text that called Khnum "the potter who made the heaven and the earth" meant that he created the entire universe. The same idea is present in the Papyrus of Hu-Nefer, which says of Re, "Thou hast made the heavens and the earth."

Genesis 1:2 pictures the universe, and particularly the earth, as it appeared in the process of being formed.[85] First, we read that the earth was created in a state of *tōhû wābōhû*, that is, a state of "emptiness and wilderness."[86] Twice those words are used together elsewhere in Scripture, Jeremiah 4:23 and Isaiah 34:11, and in both instances the earth is characterized as in a state of turmoil and disorder. In addition, we are told in Genesis 1:2 that darkness *(ḥōšek)* enclosed the entire mass of creation. The picture drawn, then, is a universe in disarray and incomplete.

Archibald Sayce was probably the first to draw a parallel between the chaos in Genesis 1:2 and the primeval chaos in the cosmogony of Hermopolis. Hermopolitan theology maintained that at creation there existed an Octead, that is, four male gods and their consorts. They were called the "chaos gods." "The Octead was composed of a formless deep, an illimitable chaos, darkness, and a breath; the Hebrew cosmogony begins with a formless *(tōhû)* deep, illimitable chaos *(bōhû)*, darkness, and breath."[87]

According to the biblical author, on the first day God broke into the darkness and formlessness of creation (Gen. 1:3). By a mere verbal fiat he called forth a supernatural light *(ʾôr)* that overwhelmed the gloom and the disorder. Evidently, the light was not natural because the sun was not created until day four (v. 16). The Egyptians believed that light was created by the elemental gods as they stood on the primeval hillock. They "created light *(ḳmꜣ šw)*" in order to overcome and subdue chaos.[88] Thus the elemental gods were called "fathers and mothers who made the light *(ỉrỉ šw)*" or "the men and women who created the light *(ḳmꜣ šw)*."[89] Significantly, it was only after that event that the gods "gave birth to the sun-god."[90]

---

85. Hoffmeier makes a puzzling comment: "In Gen 1:2, four cosmic phenomena are mentioned that are apparently present when creation formally begins" ("Some Thoughts on Genesis 1 and 2," 42–43). The idea that God used preexistent matter for creation is dubious at best.

86. *BDB*, 1062.

87. Sayce, "Egyptian Background of Genesis 1," 423; see also R. Kilian, "Gen. 1:2 und die Urgötter von Hermopolis," *VT* 16 (1966): 420–38.

88. Sethe, *Amun und die acht Urgötter*, 96.

89. According to Morenz, *Egyptian Religion*, 176, the elemental gods are also called the ones "who made light as the radiance *(m mꜣwt)* of their hearts." Similarly, in Coffin Text, Spell 76.5–6, Shu lays claim to the creation of light.

90. Sethe, *Amun und die acht Urgötter*, 100.

On the second day of creation, God called forth a *rāqîaʿ* to serve as a divider between the waters above and the waters below (Gen. 1:6). The Hebrews believed that the *rāqîaʿ* was actually a solid mass, as evidenced by certain biblical passages (Ezek. 1:22–25; 10:1; Dan. 12:3; Ps. 19:1), and thus would be able to support the water above itself. Strengthening that idea was the fact that the word derived from the root *rqʿ*, which means "to beat out, to stamp, or to spread out by hammering."[91] (The root also conveyed that sense in Phoenician.) Often the root was used in conjunction with metalworking.[92] So then, the biblical writer employed language and imagery that represented God as the divine metalworker who cast and blocked out the firmament *(rāqîaʿ)* to separate the sky and the earth.

Division of the sky and the earth at creation was frequently mentioned in Egyptian texts. According to the Leiden Stele, for example, Ptah was "the great god who separated the sky from the earth."[93] Coffin Text, Spell 80.39, describes Atum as fashioning the universe "when he separated Geb (the earth-god) from Nut (the sky-goddess)."[94] Ancient Egyptians honored Upwawet of Assiut as the one "who has separated the sky from the earth."[95] In addition, they referred to the deity Khnum as the creator-god who raised up the sky.[96]

It should be noted that the motif of separation played a significant role in both the Hebrew and Egyptian cosmogonies. In Genesis 1 the verb *bādal* ("to separate") is used five times of God's creative activity. He is pictured as dividing the light from darkness (vv. 4, 18), the waters above from the waters below (vv. 6–7), and day from night (v. 14). And although the word *bādal* is not used, the idea of separation is also central to the creation of land on day three. Egyptian literature likewise commonly employed the separation motif to describe the creator-god's work at genesis. A parallel exists here. That is to say, both civilizations believed that the separation of natural phenomena was an expression of the creative act.

After God separated the world from the sky by forming the firmament, he summoned the *yabāšāh* to appear on the third day (Gen. 1:9).

---

91. E. Klein, *A Comprehensive Etymological Dictionary of the Hebrew Language* (New York: Macmillan, 1987), 629.

92. *BDB*, 955–56.

93. E. Otto, *Die biographischen Inschriften der ägyptischen Spätzeit,* Probleme der Ägyptologie 2 (Leiden: Brill, 1954), 187.

94. That this event occurred at the creation is supported by Pyramid Text, Utterance 519.2108 ("when the sky was separated from the earth, when the gods ascended to the sky"), and Coffin Text, Spell 286.36 ("the primeval ones who witnessed the separation of the sky from the earth").

95. P. Munro, "Die beiden Stelen des Wnmj aus Abydos," *ZÄS* 85 (1960): 56–70.

96. Sauneron and Yoyotte, *La Naissance du monde,* 72; for additional references see Sandman-Holmberg, *The God Ptah,* 10; Wolf, "Der berliner Ptah-Hymnus," 20.

This word derived from the root *yābēš*, which means "to be dry, withered, without moisture, drained."[97] *Yabāšāh* thus referred to "dry ground," often in exact opposition to the sea. So in the Exodus story the Israelites walked across the *yabāšāh* through the midst of the Red Sea (Exod. 14:16, 22, 29; see also 4:9 and Josh. 4:22). Once again the act of God specified here involved separation—he ordered the waters into one place, and the dry land became visible in another.

Jan Bergman attempted to find an Egyptian parallel to Genesis 1:9 in the emergence of the primeval hillock out of the flood waters of Nun.[98] The Leiden "Hymn to Amon" speaks of the coming into being of a sacred "creation hill" at Thebes:

> The water and the earth existed at first.
> The sand became arable land, causing its ground to form a hill,
> And thus the land was formed.[99]

On top of that hillock the creator-god brought the universe into being. As in the biblical text, the appearance of the land results from the separation of the waters from the earth.

Scholarship seems to be divided about whether the Egyptians thought that the primeval hillock came into being by itself or was the object of an external act of creation. Some point out that there are no direct references to the formation of land by a creator-god. On that basis the capable scholar Siegfried Morenz concludes, "This primeval hillock took shape by itself, without any creation."[100] On the other hand, some texts indicate that the creator-god was already present in the primordial ocean before the appearance of the hill and the work of creation.[101] In fact, Pyramid Text, Utterance 222.199, may proclaim the god's creation of the primordial mound:

> You stand upon it, this land . . . that came forth from Kheprer!
> You be created upon it, you be high upon it!
> (So) your father might see you, (so) Re might see you![102]

---

97. *BDB*, 386.

98. *TDOT* 1:390.

99. Gardiner's translation ("Hymns to Amon from a Leiden Papyrus," 21) is less fluid: "The water and land were in her on the First Occasion. Sand came to circumscribe(?) the fields, to create her ground upon the highland: thus the earth came into being."

100. Morenz, *Egyptian Religion*, 176.

101. Coffin Text, Spell 80.33–34, quotes Atum as saying, "while I was alone in Nu, in a state of inertness, and I could find no place on which to stand or sit, when Heliopolis had not yet been founded that I might sit on it. . . ."

102. For another translation, see Faulkner, *Ancient Egyptian Pyramid Texts*, 49.

The context here is a ritual in which a king impropriates the image of the god Atum. A priest says to the king, in effect, "Stand as king upon the land, as Atum (Kheprer) did on the primeval hill when he assumed kingship over the world he was creating."[103] The reference to the land that "came forth" from Atum suggests that the primordial hillock came into being and emerged from the watery void because the creator-god willed it to do so.

The third day of God's creative work continued with the command for the earth to sprout forth vegetation (Gen. 1:11). Specifically included in that command were the *dešeʾ*, which literally means "grass,"[104] and the *ʿēṣ pĕrî*, the "fruit trees." Apparently those two terms were used to represent all agricultural and horticultural plant life. One of the significant features of Egyptian cosmogony was that the vegetation of the earth came from the hand of the creator-god. The "Hymn to Khnum," for example, says that "he made plants in the field, he dotted shores with flowers; he made fruit trees bear their fruit."[105] It should be noted that this passage immediately follows a verse that proclaims the greatness of Khnum because "he made mankind, created the gods." It also seems likely that the Egyptians believed that the creation of vegetation occurred prior to the creation of humans. Coffin Text, Spell 680, presents a sequence: "The waters have overflowed for him (the creator-god), the herbage has grown for him, the life of men has come into being."[106]

The creative activity of the fourth and fifth days can be dealt with more briefly. God made the luminaries on the fourth day, including the sun ("the greater light"), the moon ("the lesser light"), and the stars (vv. 14–18). Once again we see the separation motif in God's dividing *(lĕhabdîl)* the day from the night (v. 14). In Egyptian literature the creation of the sun and moon also occurred at the beginning of time and was part of Egyptian theogony. That is to say, when the sun and moon were created at genesis, Re and Thoth came to personify them. The stars also were set in the heavens by the hand of the creator. In the "Great Hymn to Amon" we are told that the creator "put the stars upon his path." The

---

103. Mercer, *Pyramid Texts,* 2:95; see also H. Frankfort, *Kingship and the Gods* (Chicago: University of Chicago Press, 1948), 108.
104. *BDB,* 206; for the literal translation see Deut. 32:2; 2 Sam. 23:4; Job 6:5; 38:27; Prov. 27:25.
105. *AEL* 3:114. In addition, consider the "Hymn to Ptah-tenen": "Thou makest the staff of life (i.e., grain) to flourish, thou makest the grain which cometh forth from thyself in thy name of Nu the Aged. Thou makest fertile . . ." (translation by Budge, *From Fetish to God,* 260).
106. R. O. Faulkner, *The Ancient Egyptian Coffin Texts,* 3 vols. (Warminster: Aris and Phillips, 1973–78), 2:245. See also Coffin Text, Spell 75; and the "Hymn to Amon-Re," which celebrates the creator-god "who created the fruit tree, made herbage" (*ANET,* 365).

"New Hymn" from the temple at Hibis expresses the same idea. There the creator Amon is called the one who "had directed the stars," placing them where they are and controlling what they do.[107]

On the fifth day God made fish and the birds (vv. 20–21; Ps. 8:8). Egyptian literature frequently mentions these two together at creation. The "Great Hymn to Amon" proclaims that the creator-god "made the fish to live in the rivers, and the birds in the sky." Yahuda mentions further examples, such as a text of Merikare that describes Re as having "formed the plants for men and the animals, birds, and fishes for their sustenance."[108] Similarly, Atum created the Nile and called it "the lord of fish and rich in birds." What we have here is a definite parallel, not a fortuitous one.

The sixth day of creation involved the formation of land animals and humankind (Gen. 1:24–28). Likewise, many references in Egyptian writings associate the fashioning of humanity with the fashioning of animals. The "Hymn to Re" (Papyrus of Hu-Nefer) addresses the god: "Thou hast made humankind and the beasts of the field to come into being." In the "Hymn to Aton" we read, "Thou didst create the earth by thy heart, when thou didst exist by thyself, and men and women, and cattle and the beasts of every kind that are on the earth." Another example appears in the "Hymn to Amon," which praises Amon as the "maker of men, creator of animals."[109]

In addition, the Egyptians, like the Hebrews, believed that humans were specifically and specially framed by the creator-god. Many texts speak of that event. The "Great Hymn to Atum" addresses the god as "Atum, who created mankind, who distinguished their nature and made their life."[110] Some texts speak of a potter molding humanity on a wheel or table. In the "Great Hymn to Khnum" the creator-god is pictured "modeling people on his wheel. He has fashioned men."[111] The god Ptah is similarly portrayed as a potter who modeled humanity out of a lump of clay.[112] The "Instruction of Amenemope" declares, "Man is clay and straw, and God is his potter."[113] The Bible also maintains that humanity was originally formed from the elements of the earth (Gen. 2:7; 3:19).

---

107. Morenz, *Egyptian Religion*, 167.
108. Yahuda, *Language of the Pentateuch*, 127.
109. For more examples see the creation texts translated by Budge, *From Fetish to God*, and A. Erman, *The Literature of the Ancient Egyptians* (New York: Dutton, 1927).
110. Erman, *Literature*, 285.
111. *AEL* 3:114. J. H. Breasted, *ARE* 2:81–82, makes mention of a relief at Deir el-Bahari in which Khnum is represented sitting at a potter's wheel and creating two male children. Oddly, one of those male children(!) is Hatshepsut, the future queen of Egypt.
112. A. H. Sayce, *The Religions of Ancient Egypt and Babylonia* (Edinburgh: T. and T. Clark, 1903), 138.
113. Simpson, ed., *Literature of Ancient Egypt*, 262.

According to Genesis 1, humans were created in the image *(ṣelem)* of God. The word *ṣelem* originally meant "something cut from an object," for example, a piece of clay cut from a sculpture.[114] In such a case there was a concrete resemblance between the object and the *ṣelem*. In the Bible *ṣelem* also denotes a statue that a king would erect of himself to serve as a symbol of his sovereignty (Dan. 3). That *ṣelem* was applied to humans at creation indicates that they were God's representative on earth and had a character in keeping with that of the Deity.

The concept of humans' being created in the image of God is likewise found in Egyptian writing. Abraham Yahuda declares that "it was a dominating factor in Egyptian thought throughout and can be traced back to the earliest times. This idea is illustrated in various concrete and metaphorical expressions, not merely in the myths of the gods, in hymns to gods and kings, but also in popular tales, books of wisdom and other writings."[115] As usual, Yahuda dramatically overstates his case. In reality, only a few texts make reference to the concept, among them the "Instruction of King Merikare": "Well directed are men . . . and he (Re) made the air to give life to their nostrils. They are his own images proceeding from his flesh. He arises in heaven at their desire."[116] This passage characterizes humans as the image *(snnw)* of the flesh *(ḥ'w)* of the god. It is noteworthy that *snnw* was often written with a determinative in the shape of a statue.[117]

Another significant aspect of man's creation in the Bible is that God "breathed into his nostrils the breath of life *(wayyipaḥ bĕʾpāyw nišĕmat ḥayyîm)*" (Gen. 2:7). Wilfred Lambert and Alan Millard comment: "The Hebrew account of creation in Genesis 2 explains that God imparted 'the breath of life' into man, and so animation began. The reality of this is that breathing is an essential accompaniment of life, and at death we 'expire.' No similar doctrine is known among the Babylonians or Sumerians."[118] In contrast, an essential characteristic of Egyptian cosmogony was the belief that the creator-god imparted life by giving breath. Explaining human creation, the "Great Hymn to Aton" from the tomb of Ay addresses the creator-god as he "who makes the seed grow in women, who creates people from sperm . . . nurse in the womb, giver of breath. . . . You give breath within to sustain him, when you have made

---

114. Klein, *Etymological Dictionary*, 548.
115. Yahuda, *Language of the Pentateuch*, 142.
116. A. H. Gardiner, "New Literary Works from Ancient Egypt," *JEA* 1 (1914): 34; *ANET*, 417.
117. See Hoffmeier, "Some Thoughts on Genesis 1 and 2," 47, for a discussion of humans as the image of God, a motif evident in the many references in Egyptian literature to the creation of gods and humans together (see *AEL* 3:112).
118. Lambert and Millard, *Atra-hasis*, 22.

him complete."[119] The "Great Hymn to Khnum" states that the creator "knotted the flow of blood to the bones, formed in his (workshop) as his handiwork, so the breath of life is within everything."[120] Furthermore, not only humanity, but all of animate creation was imbued with the breath of the creator. Thus in the Coffin Text, Spell 76.13, Atum is addressed as "you who exhaled the breath which is in the mouth of Shu."[121]

The Egyptian view of the purpose of the creation of humankind is more difficult to pinpoint. The Mesopotamian idea that the gods created humanity to do their labor was clearly foreign to the Egyptians.[122] One suggestion is that humans were fashioned to carry out the creator's procreative purposes.[123] In Genesis 1 that idea is a prominent reason for God's making the human race: "And God blessed them; and God said to them, 'Be fruitful and multiply, and fill the earth . . .'" (v. 28). In addition, the Egyptians likely saw the creation of humans as intended to bring glory, honor, and praise to the creator-god.[124] That this was true of the biblical account of creation goes without saying.

We have seen many points of similarity between the Egyptian and Hebrew accounts of creation. Others could be emphasized.[125] In any event, the fact of the matter is that the magnitude of parallels cannot be by mere chance. We dare not call this situation a freak of antiquity.

While we have stressed the similarities, we must not overlook the differences. First, the Egyptian cosmogony was theogonic, primarily concerned with the creation of the gods as personifications of the elements of nature. The biblical author, on the other hand, was not interested in theogony. He was rigidly monotheistic, as Heidel points out: "The opening chapters of Genesis as well as the Old Testament in general refer to only one Creator and Maintainer of all things, one God who created and transcends all cosmic matter. In the entire Old Testament, there is not a trace of theogony, such as we find, for example, in *Enûma elish* and in Hesiod."[126]

119. *AEL* 2:98.
120. *AEL* 3:112.
121. Faulkner, *Coffin Texts*, 1:78; for other examples see Coffin Texts, Spells 76.4 and 80.38.
122. Regarding the Mesopotamian view see W. R. Mayer, "Ein Mythos von der Erschaffung des Menschen und des Königs," *Orientalia* 56 (1987): 55–68.
123. Morenz, *Egyptian Religion*, 184.
124. The "Great Hymn to Amon" says, "Homage to thee because thou hast created us!" (translation by Budge, *From Fetish to God*, 411).
125. See Gordon, "Khnum and El"; and Hoffmeier, "Some Thoughts on Genesis 1 and 2."
126. Heidel, *Babylonian Genesis*, 97.

Second, the time framework of the Hebrew cosmogony, which is broken down into "days" *(yôm)*, finds no antecedent or parallel in Egypt. Nor is there evidence for the concept of a Sabbath rest in ancient Egypt, as, for instance, appeared in Babylonia.[127] So in seeking parallels with the biblical cosmogony, one must realize that no ancient Near Eastern counterpart matched the biblical account concept for concept.

The dating of the literary contact between Egypt and Genesis is difficult, if not impossible, to determine. Donald Redford has argued that the Joseph pericope should be dated to the Saite–early Persian period (the seventh to fifth centuries B.C.) because Egyptian elements in that Genesis story reflect that period.[128] One could easily assume that other Genesis passages with Egyptian features, for instance, the creation account, also date to that time. The problem here is that the Egyptian elements paralleling the creation account, unlike those of the Joseph narrative, cannot be circumscribed within any one period. For example, the idea of the creator-god's separating the sky from the earth was present in the cosmological literature throughout the entire history of ancient Egypt. The same thing could be said about many of the other Egyptian features in the opening chapters of Genesis. The truth of the matter is that elements found in Genesis 1–2 parallel many centuries of Egyptian cosmogonical thought.

---

127. W. G. Lambert, "A New Look at the Babylonian Background of Genesis," *JTS* 16 (1965): 296–97.

128. D. B. Redford, *A Study of the Biblical Story of Joseph (Genesis 37–50)* (Leiden: Brill, 1970), 242. It should be mentioned, lest the reader be led astray, that Redford's dating of the Joseph story is not here being accepted, but merely used as an example.

4
Potiphar's Standing in Egyptian Society

The position and rank of Potiphar in Egypt and in relation to Pharaoh are mentioned twice in the biblical narratives. Both citations relate to the purchase of the Hebrew patriarch Joseph:

> And the Midianites sold him unto Egypt to Potiphar, the officer of Pharaoh, the chief of the guards. [Gen. 37:36, author's translation]

> And Joseph was brought down to Egypt, and Potiphar, the officer of Pharaoh, the chief of the guards, an Egyptian man, bought him from the hand of the Ishmaelites[1] who brought him down there. [Gen. 39:1, author's translation]

In both verses, Potiphar is called a *sĕrîs parĕ'ōh*, "an/the officer of Pharaoh,"[2] and *śar haṭṭabbāḥîm*, "the chief of the guards." Precisely what these two titles entail has been a matter of debate for some time.[3] Our intention is to reopen the issue of Potiphar's station in the congregation of Egypt, to analyze all relevant data bearing on the inquiry, and to draw appropriate conclusions. We begin with an investigation into the name of the Egyptian official—Potiphar.

---

1. Occasionally the terms *Midianite* and *Ishmaelite* are used interchangeably in the Bible (see Judg. 8:24). Note that Gen. 39:1 adds the information that Potiphar was an Egyptian. Perhaps the addition was to emphasize that Joseph was not purchased by a Hebrew taskmaster.

2. There is no way to determine from the nature of this Hebrew construct whether it signifies a definite or indefinite noun.

3. See, e.g., R. Peter-Contesse, "Was Potiphar a Eunuch?" *Bible Translator* 47.1 (1996): 142–46; and M. Gorg, "Die Amtstitel des Potifar," *BN* 53 (1990): 14–20.

Potiphar

In Egyptian the name Potiphar literally means "He-whom-Re-gives," and most scholars agree that it is an abbreviated form of the Egyptian name *Pꜣ-dỉ-pꜣ-rꜥ*, that is, Potiphera.[4] Elsewhere in the Joseph pericope, the extended name Potiphera is used to identify Joseph's father-in-law, a priest of On (Heliopolis) (Gen. 41:45, 50; 46:20). That the two names are identical is reflected in the Septuagint, where Potiphar and Potiphera are both rendered *Petephrēs*.

The name *Pꜣ-dỉ-pꜣ-rꜥ* appears on inscriptions in Egypt no earlier than Dynasty 21 (eleventh century B.C.).[5] It belongs to an Egyptian group of names that is most common from the tenth century B.C. through the Roman period.[6] Hermann Ranke, in his massive work on Egyptian names, cites 727 personal names beginning with *P*, of which only fifteen date before the New Kingdom. In addition, the combination of *P* and *d* with a divine title occurs 109 times in a personal name, a mere two of which precede the tenth century B.C.[7] A few examples of the exact name *Pꜣ-dỉ-pꜣ-rꜥ* appear in the seventh to third centuries B.C.[8]

Many scholars conclude that the name Potiphar could not have been original to the Joseph story, which is purported to have been written many centuries before the name was commonly used in Egypt. Donald Redford states: "The verses in which the name 'Potiphar' occurs look for all the world like editorial patches with which an earlier text was glossed. . . . This occasional appearance of a personal name is an excellent example of a later attempt to 'personalize' the anonymous figures of a genuine Märchen [fairy tale], and is thus akin to historification."[9] In other words, a later biblical editor, in an attempt to color the Joseph story with Egyptian culture, inserted the names Potiphar and Potiphera into the earlier text. The editor was merely attempting to historify the people and events of the narrative.

For those who hold to a high view of the historicity and unity of the Joseph account such a reconstruction is unacceptable. To posit editorial glossing for the purpose of historicizing a myth is not necessary. Scholars have provided other possible solutions to the problem. Kenneth Kitchen, for instance, argues: "Potiphera may be simply a modernization in Moses' time of the older form *Didi-Rꜥ*, with the same mean-

---

4. R. de Vaux, *The Early History of Israel* (Philadelphia: Westminster, 1978), 308.
5. J. Vergote, *Joseph en Egypte* (Louvain: Publications Universitaires, 1959), 147.
6. D. B. Redford, "Potiphar," in *ABD* 5:426–27.
7. H. Ranke, *Die ägyptischen Personennamen* (Glückstadt: J. J. Augustin, 1935), 1:99–129 (cited in C. F. Aling, *Egypt and Bible History* [Grand Rapids: Baker, 1981], 32).
8. Vergote, *Joseph en Egypte*, 147.
9. D. B. Redford, *A Study of the Biblical Story of Joseph (Genesis 37–50)* (Leiden: Brill, 1970), 136.

ing, of a name-pattern *(Didi-X)* which is particularly common in the Middle Kingdom and Hyksos periods, *i.e.* the patriarchal and Joseph's age (*c.* 2100–1600 BC)."[10] Kitchen is saying that the Mosaic writer updated some of the names in the Joseph story, which had occurred many centuries before it was written down. The reason for converting these names is not stated, although it may have been done for cultural relevancy. This view has some potential, but it needs to be developed to a greater extent.

Y. M. Grintz attempts to explain the difficulty by declaring that Potiphar is not a personal name, but an Egyptian title.[11] In his opinion the term *Potiphar* is a Hebrew transcription of an official title meaning "chief cook." In addition, Grintz proposes that "Potiphar" is a synonym of the Hebrew *śar haṭṭabbāḥîm*, which he defines as "chief of the cooks." Redford adjudges Grintz's proposal to be incorrect: "The recent attempt to derive 'Potiphar' from Egyptian *p3 wdpw wr*, 'the chief cook' (a postulated title), is highly ingenious, but quite unconvincing."[12]

Charles Aling argues along lines similar to those of Grintz. However, he does not claim that Potiphar is a title but a "descriptive epithet."[13] In other words, Potiphar is not a name identifying a specific Egyptian. It is a generic name for any Egyptian. As stated previously, the name Potiphar means "He-whom-Re-gives," which, according to Aling, is a descriptive tag that could be applied to any Egyptian. He further says that this explanation fits with the entire pericope of the Joseph story, which includes very few names. Pharaonic names are not supplied, nor are we given the name of Potiphar's wife. While such an explanation is intriguing, there is a lack of proof for it, especially from Egyptian textual material. If texts could be cited that use Potiphar and Potiphera as broad terms of ethnicity or nationality, then a case might be made. But no such references are known.

Joseph Free contends that the types of Egyptian names found in the Joseph story, such as Potiphera and Asenath (Joseph's Egyptian wife), are not unknown in the "earlier periods" of Egyptian history.[14] He cites T. Eric Peet: "Names of this type are not absolutely wanting in the earlier periods, but they are extremely rare, and it is only in the XXI Dy-

---

10. K. A. Kitchen, "Potiphera," in *New Bible Dictionary*, ed. J. D. Douglas, 2d ed. (Downers Grove, Ill.: InterVarsity, 1982), 951. The reader should also consider Kitchen's significant article "Genesis 12–50 in the Near Eastern World," in *He Swore an Oath*, ed. R. S. Hess et al. (Grand Rapids: Baker, 1994), 67–92.
11. Y. M. Grintz, "Potiphar—The Chief Cook," *Leshonenu* 20 (1965–66): 12–17.
12. Redford, *Biblical Story of Joseph*, 228 n. 2.
13. Aling, *Egypt and Bible History*, 32.
14. J. F. Free, *Archaeology and Bible History*, rev. ed. (Grand Rapids: Zondervan, 1992), 72.

nasty that they begin to be common."[15] Free then concludes that those rare early instances of names like Potiphera and Asenath "provide another piece of evidence that harmonizes with the conservative view, holding to the early writing of the Pentateuch."[16] A few scholars have been convinced.[17] This position, however, does not square with the evidence. As has been stated, Egyptian names that begin with the article *P* (as in *P3-dî-p3-rʿ*) are unknown before the New Kingdom and the introduction of the Late Egyptian dialect.[18]

Several solutions have been presented for the problem of the appearance of the names Potiphar and Potiphera in the Joseph story. None of them are entirely convincing. Therefore, caution is the word of the day. We must simply wait until more material bearing on the issue is made available to us.

Sĕrîs Parĕʿōh

The Hebrew word *sārîs* is found over forty times in the Old Testament. Lexicons provide a variety of definitions: "eunuch," "court official," and "courtier/chamberlain." Each of these meanings finds application in various Old Testament texts.[19] Because of the different shades of meaning, questions are raised when *sārîs* is applied to Potiphar's station in Egypt: What exactly was his status? Was he a eunuch? Did he manage the seraglio? Or was he merely a high official or courtier?

Early versions of the Old Testament do not reflect the varied possible meanings and interpretations of *sārîs* in Genesis 37:36 and 39:1. The Septuagint translates *sārîs* in the former verse with the masculine singular dative noun σπάδοντι, which means "human eunuch." Genesis 39:1 translates *sārîs* with another Greek term, εὐνοῦχος. This is a synonym of σπάδων, although it appears to have a broader application, including animals and fruit (e.g., dates without stones). The Vulgate similarly understands *sārîs* to refer to a eunuch, calling Potiphar *eunuchus Pharaonis* in both Genesis passages. The Old Syriac version renders the Hebrew *sārîs* in both verses with the term *mhymn*, which generally signifies "a faithful, trustworthy person." However, *mhymn* is specifically

---

15. T. E. Peet, *Egypt and the Old Testament* (Liverpool: University Press of Liverpool, 1923), 101.
16. Free, *Archaeology and Bible History*, 72.
17. See, e.g., L. J. Wood and D. O'Brien, *A Survey of Israel's History,* rev. ed. (Grand Rapids: Zondervan, 1986), 59 n. 34.
18. Redford, *Biblical Story of Joseph*, 228.
19. Isa. 56:3–5 joins the word *sārîs* with an inability to procreate; the *sārîs* says, "Behold, I am a dry tree." Clearly *sārîs* is referring to a eunuch in this passage. On the other hand, a verse like 1 Sam. 8:15 uses *sārîs* as a general term for "officers" of the king.

used at times in Syriac to denote a eunuch.[20] One should further note that the Targums' use of the Aramaic word *sārîs* almost always signifies "castration, emasculation." A very few instances occur in which it implies a more general meaning, such as "mediator, manager."[21] The early translations for the most part, then, agree that Potiphar served as a eunuch in Pharaoh's court.

The diverse possible meanings of *sārîs* are manifest in later translations. For instance, William Tyndale calls Potiphar "a lord of Pharaoh"; the King James Version (1611) and John Calvin call him "an officer of Pharaoh." Some renderings, on the other hand, continue to maintain the more specific aspect of the word. The Douay-Rheims translation of 1609 says that Potiphar was "an eunuch of Pharao." John Wycliffe has a very pointed interpretation: "the gelding of Pharaoh"!

Modern translations display confusion over the word *sārîs* in Genesis 37 and 39. While many versions opt for a more generic rendering of this Hebrew word, such as "officer, courtier, or official," a few (e.g., the NEB) yet translate it "eunuch."

The precise meaning of *sārîs* in the Joseph story has been widely examined in scholarly literature. William Albright in an early-twentieth-century article argues that Potiphar was a eunuch. He recognizes, however, that the circumstance was odd since Potiphar was married: "While a eunuch may have a whole harem, and is often blessed with his share of erotic proclivities, it is at least unusual to find a married סריס."[22] Albright's stance has not had much support. A legion of modern interpreters believe that *sārîs* in the Joseph pericope is nothing more than a general term for a court official of Pharaoh.[23] Horst Seebass, on the other hand, reasons that *sārîs* in the generic sense would be superfluous *(überflüssig)* because *śar haṭṭabbāḥîm*, which appears later in both Genesis 37:36 and 39:1, essentially means "court official."[24]

The majority of scholars agree, however, that *sārîs* is a broad Hebrew term identifying a high court functionary in the Egyptian system,

---

20. J. P. Smith, *A Compendious Syriac Dictionary* (Oxford: Clarendon, 1967), 255.

21. M. Jastrow, *A Dictionary of the Targumim, the Talmud Babli and Yerushalmi and the Midrashic Literature*, 2 vols. (New York: Pardes, 1950), 2:1027.

22. W. F. Albright, "Historical and Mythical Elements in the Story of Joseph," *JBL* 37 (1918): 127.

23. See, e.g., G. von Rad, *Das erste Buch Mose: Genesis* (Göttingen: Vandenhoeck and Ruprecht, 1964), 317, who calls Potiphar *ein Kämmerer des Pharao* ("a chamberlain of Pharaoh"). In agreement with von Rad are L. Ruppert, *Die Josephserzählung der Genesis* (Munich: Kösel, 1965), and H.-C. Schmitt, *Die nichtpriesterliche Josephsgeschichte* (Berlin: de Gruyter, 1979). C. Westermann, *Genesis* (Neukirchen-Vluyn: Neukirchener Verlag des Erziehungsvereins, 1982), 3:56–58, renders *sārîs* as *Hofbeamter des Pharao*.

24. H. Seebass, *Geschichtliche Zeit und Theonome Tradition in der Joseph-Erzählung* (Gütersloh: Mohn, 1978), 125.

and nothing more. The etymology and historical development of *sārîs* support this position. It is probably a loanword from the Akkadian *ša-reši*, which generally means "courtier, high official."[25] During the second millennium B.C. the Assyrian word was exclusively used in that generic fashion.[26] By the turn of the millennium, however, *ša-reši* had taken on the specific meaning "eunuch."[27] In Egypt the word appeared only during the Persian domination (the fifth century B.C.), and at that late date it apparently was used of both officers and eunuchs.[28] The point is that *sārîs* as "eunuch" was a late development, and thus such a meaning is problematic for the Joseph story, which presumably occurred sometime during the second millennium B.C.

The biblical usage of *sārîs* reflects a similar evolution in word meaning. Of the forty occurrences of this word in the Hebrew Bible, the only times it without doubt signifies a eunuch are in the late books of Esther and Daniel, and perhaps once in the Book of Isaiah.[29] All other instances of *sārîs* can be dated earlier, and they all can be generally translated "officer, official." So the word *sārîs* seems to have acquired the specific sense of "eunuch" in late Hebrew literature; in early writings, such as the Pentateuch, it signifies a general category of high-ranking leaders in government.[30]

Internal evidence in Egypt also confirms the view that *sārîs* in Genesis should be understood generically. While eunuchs appear frequently in oriental courts (such as Babylon and Persia), thorough study has found that in ancient Egypt eunuchs were not customary.[31] F. Jonck-

---

25. P. Jensen was perhaps the first to make this connection (*ZA* 7 [1892]: 174 n. 1). Albright, however, vigorously disagrees, arguing that *sārîs* actually developed from the Akkadian *sirēšu*, which means "beer." See his "Historical and Mythical Elements," 127 n. 15. Little evidence exists to support Albright's contention.

26. K. A. Kitchen, *Ancient Orient and Old Testament* (Chicago: InterVarsity, 1966), 165.

27. J. Vergote, "'Joseph en Egypte': 25 ans après," in *Pharaonic Egypt: The Bible and Christianity*, ed. S. Israelit-Groll (Jerusalem: Magnes, 1985), 295.

28. Redford, "Potiphar," in *ABD* 5:426–27. For an example of *sārîs* from the period of the Persian domination, see G. Posener, *La Première Domination perse en Egypte* (Cairo: Institut français d'archéologie, 1936), 118.

29. Esth. 1:10, 12, 15; 2:3, 14, 15, 21; 4:4, 5; 6:2, 14; 7:9; Dan. 1:3, 7, 8, 9, 10, 11, 18; and Isa. 56:3–4.

30. Personal communication from K. A. Kitchen, Jan. 1997. It may be more appropriate to discuss whether Nehemiah was a eunuch. See E. Yamauchi, "Was Nehemiah the Cupbearer a Eunuch?" *ZAW* 92.1 (1980): 132–42.

31. For a general study of eunuchs in antiquity, see A. D. Nock, "Eunuchs in Ancient Religion," *Archiv für Religionswissenschaft* 23 (1925): 25–33. There is no evidence that Israelite kings employed eunuchs in their courts. Josephus tells us that the Herodians used them: "There were certain eunuchs which the king (Herod) had, and on account of their beauty was very fond of them; and the care of bringing him drink was entrusted to one of them; of bringing him his supper, to another; and of putting him to bed, to the third, who also managed the principal affairs of the government" (*Antiquities* 16.8.1).

heere, however, attempts to show that eunuchs were more common in Egypt than previously thought.[32] He cites examples of representations of eunuchs in Egyptian art, such as on the sarcophagus of Kaovit, on the tomb walls of Khnoumhotep, and in the temple of Sahoure. Gerald Kadish, however, properly refutes Jonckheere: "It is necessary to insist that the pictorial evidence offers no unambiguous data on the existence of eunuchs and that all the examples offered by Jonckheere can be readily explained on stylistic grounds or some other conventional artistic considerations."[33]

Linguistic evidence for eunuchs in ancient Egypt is similarly slim. The *Wörterbuch der ägyptischen Sprache* lists two instances of the Egyptian word *sḥti*, which is hesitatingly translated *der Verschnittene(?)*, or "the castrated one, the eunuch."[34] Two questionable cases of a word that may signify emasculation are hardly convincing proof that eunuchs existed in ancient Egypt. Even if they did exist, they were of a minimal number and importance.

The foregoing evidence makes it unlikely that Potiphar was a eunuch. The fact that he was married also weighs in favor of that conclusion, although it is not a decisive factor. Married eunuchs are attested in ancient oriental contexts.[35] Potiphar probably held some type of aristocratic office in Pharaoh's court, the precise nature of which we do not know.

Śar Haṭṭabbāḥîm

In Genesis 37:36 and 39:1 a second title is applied to the Egyptian Potiphar: he is called a *śar haṭṭabbāḥîm*. Like *sārîs*, the designation *śar haṭṭabbāḥîm* can mean a variety of things. Not at issue is the word *śar*, which simply means "chief, ruler, captain, or prince"; that is to say, Potiphar was the leader of some group in ancient Egypt.[36] The problem is to identify the group called *haṭṭabbāḥîm*. In the Old Testament, the word *ṭabbāḥ* is used over thirty times, and it can mean "guardsman" (2 Kings 25:8–20—Nebuchadnezzar's "captain of the guard" oversaw the destruction of Jerusalem), "cook" (1 Sam. 9:23–24), or

---

32. F. Jonckheere, "L'Eunuque dans l'Egypte pharaonique," *Revue de l'histoire des sciences* 7 (1954): 139–55.

33. G. E. Kadish, "Eunuchs in Ancient Egypt?" in *Studies in Honor of John A. Wilson*, ed. G. E. Kadish (Chicago: University of Chicago Press, 1969), 59.

34. *WAS* 4:264. Jonckheere's suggestion ("L'Eunuque," 139–55) that "eunuch" is connoted by the Egyptian term *ḥm* has some merit.

35. Kadish, "Eunuchs in Ancient Egypt?" 56. That some seraglio or harem guards in ancient Egypt had wives is attested by records of a harem conspiracy during Dynasty 20 (*ARE* 4:209, 216–17).

36. *BDB*, 978.

"butcher" (Exod. 22:1; Prov. 9:2). We are once again left in a dilemma: what was Potiphar's occupation?

The root ṭbḥ is common in Semitic languages, and it normally carries the meaning "to slaughter."[37] Often it is used in that sense to describe the preparation of animals for a feast (the task of a butcher) or the process of ritual sacrifice. At times ṭbḥ may carry the specialized meaning "to cook." It is not always possible to make a clear distinction between meanings because the art of cooking frequently includes butchering and otherwise preparing animals so they can be eaten. The use of ṭbḥ to denote a guardsman or military figure does not appear outside the Old Testament.

The early versions of Genesis present the varied meanings of ṭbḥ. The Septuagint, for example, calls Potiphar an ἀρχιμάγειρος in both Genesis 37:36 and 39:1, which can signify either a "butcher" or a "cook." Greek, like Semitic languages, does not draw a definite line between those two professions. The Targums agree with the Septuagint that Potiphar was "a meat-dresser, butcher, cook."[38] The Vulgate, on the other hand, translates śar haṭṭabbāḥîm in Genesis as *princeps exercitus,* "chief of the army." The Old Syriac version speaks of Potiphar as "commander of the guard." Thus there is no consensus in the early versions regarding the definition of śar haṭṭabbāḥîm.

Modern translations are almost unanimous in understanding Potiphar's position as a military one. He is called "captain of the guard" (KJV, ASV, RSV, NKJV) or "commander of the guard" (JB) or "chief executioner of the guard" (AMP, LB). Tyndale called Potiphar "the chief marshall," and Wycliffe designated him "the master of chyvalre"!

Unanimity of opinion regarding Potiphar's status in Egypt does not exist in modern scholarly literature. While many do agree with the interpretation of Potiphar as a leader of soldiers, the precise nature of that military position is disputed. Some maintain that he was the captain of the royal bodyguard, that is, the commander of the troops who provided protection to Pharaoh and his court.[39] Others claim that Potiphar's work centered on the exercise of justice against criminals, which would have included imprisonment and capital punishment.[40] Therefore he should be called "chief of executioners." Grintz concludes that śar haṭṭabbāḥîm does not signify a military official, but the office

37. *TDOT* 5:283–87.
38. Jastrow, *Dictionary of the Targumim,* 516.
39. E.g., Westermann, *Genesis,* 3:57.
40. H. G. Stigers, *A Commentary on Genesis* (Grand Rapids: Zondervan, 1976), 282–83; von Rad, *Das erste Buch Mose,* 317, calls Potiphar the *Scharfrichter,* a translation first suggested by H. Gunkel, *Genesis,* 3d ed. (Göttingen: Vandenhoeck and Ruprecht, 1910), 410.

of "chief cook."[41] His stance has not gained widespread approval in the scholarly community.

The fact of the matter is that the designation *śar haṭṭabbāḥîm* is a general phrase in Hebrew that could translate into a number of Egyptian offices. The root *ṭbḥ* can be used in reference to guarding the king (2 Kings 25:8–20), cooking (1 Sam. 9:23–24), and slaughtering animals (Exod. 22:1). It thus appears to be a broad term used to designate officials or courtiers of sundry ranks and titles. Beyond that, we cannot say precisely what Potiphar did for a living or in what capacity he served Pharaoh.

What may we conclude regarding Potiphar's station in Egypt? Frankly, not much. We do know that his name is genuinely Egyptian. However, the time frame for the usage of *P₃-dî-p₃-rʿ* in Egypt is problematic: the name is primarily confined to the first millennium B.C. in inscriptions. If the Joseph story occurred in the second millennium B.C., the appearance of the name *P₃-dî-p₃-rʿ* seems to be an anomaly. We do not possess enough evidence to draw a proper conclusion in the matter. In any event, Potiphar's name provides no insight into his position in Egypt. We can, however, say that he was not a eunuch. For the Hebrew term *sārîs* is mainly employed in the Bible as a general designation for some type of bureaucratic government official. *Śar haṭṭabbāḥîm* is another generic Hebrew title that could be applied to a slew of Egyptian offices. All we can do is specify some positions that Potiphar did *not* occupy in ancient Egypt. Evidently Potiphar was not the chief cook or chief butcher to Pharaoh and his court. What specific role he did have in the land of the Pharaohs remains a question for the ages.

---

41. Grintz, "Potiphar," 12–17; Vergote, "'Joseph en Egypte,'" 290, calls Potiphar *le chef des cuisiniers*.

5
The Egyptian Setting of the Serpent Confrontation

Polemical Parallels in Exodus

Several recent studies into the Egyptian background of the Exodus traditions have focused on the polemical nature of some of the biblical accounts.[1] The principal area of many of these studies has been comparative linguistics and particularly the parallel usages of idiomatic expressions. For instance, ancient Egyptian texts characteristically described Pharaonic power in terms of Pharaoh's "strong hand," his being the "possessor of a strong arm" and "the one who destroys enemies with his arm." The Exodus account ironically assigned the same qualities to Yahweh as he humiliated Pharaoh and Egypt (Exod. 3:19–20; 6:1; 7:4; 15:16, etc.).

An additional example appears in Exodus 5, where both Yahweh and Pharaoh give mandates introduced by the idiom "Thus says . . ." (5:1, 10). The Egyptians were well aware of the use of that expression to preface the commands of a deity. Their own texts, such as the Book of the Dead, frequently introduced the desires of the gods with the words "Thus says. . . ."[2] The ironic use of this idiom by the biblical writer in Exodus 5 sets the stage for the following confrontation between the gods of Egypt (including Pharaoh) and the God of the Hebrews.

---

1. See, e.g., J. K. Hoffmeier, "The Arm of God versus the Arm of Pharaoh in the Exodus Narratives," *Biblica* 67 (1986): 378–87; A. Niccacci, "Yahweh e il Faraone: Teologia biblica ed egiziana a confronto," *BN* 38/39 (1987): 85–102; and D. R. Seely, "The Image of the Hand of God in the Exodus Traditions" (Ph.D. diss., University of Michigan, 1990).
2. See "The Primeval Establishment of Order," in *ANET,* 9–10.

Some scholars see in these parallels a purposeful criticism of Pharaonic sovereignty by the biblical writer: Yahweh is the one who possesses a strong arm; only he can thunder, "Thus says . . ."; and he is all-powerful. As James Hoffmeier comments, "What better way for the Exodus traditions to describe God's victory over Pharaoh, and as a result his superiority, than to use Hebrew derivations or counterparts to Egyptian expressions that symbolized Egyptian royal power?"[3] Such parallels, however, go far beyond mere linguistic affinity.[4] Many of the events in Exodus can be seen as polemics against Egyptian life and culture. The dividing of the Red Sea, for example, may be an ironic, belligerent critique of Egyptian magic and its spells. For the ancient Egyptians in fact had their own account of how a priest had separated a large body of water. The Westcar Papyrus[5] tells of a bored King Snofru who summoned the chief lector and scribe Djadjaemonkh to give him advice on how to find some pleasure.[6] The priest suggested that the Pharaoh travel on a lake in a boat rowed by many beautiful naked women. His heart was happy until one of the rowers dropped her fish-shaped charm into the water. She would accept no substitute, so Snofru called for Djadjaemonkh to solve the problem with his secret arts. Through his magic sayings Djadjaemonkh placed one side of the lake upon the other and found the fish-shaped charm lying on a potsherd. Having returned it to its owner, Djadjaemonkh uttered some more magic sayings that brought the water of the lake back to its original position.

This story is reminiscent of the biblical account of the crossing of the Red Sea. One wonders whether the Hebrew writer may have regarded this event as a polemical parallel. The chief lector priest of Egypt may have divided a lake in search of a valuable charm, but the God of the Hebrews parted the entire Red Sea and caused a nation to pass through on dry ground. Who had the greater power?

In this chapter we will examine another event in the Exodus traditions that drew on the writer's knowledge of Egyptian religion and cul-

---

3. Hoffmeier, "Arm of God," 387.
4. For further study see T. O. Lambdin, "Egyptian Loan Words in the Old Testament," *JAOS* 73 (1953): 145–55; idem, *Loan Words and Transcriptions in the Ancient Semitic Languages* (Baltimore: Johns Hopkins University Press, 1952); and R. J. Williams, "Egypt and Israel," in *The Legacy of Egypt*, ed. J. R. Harris, 2d ed. (Oxford: Clarendon, 1971), 257–90.
5. The Westcar Papyrus is incomplete and dates to the Hyksos period before Dynasty 18 (which began ca. 1550 B.C.). Its composition, however, appears to be as early as Dynasty 12 (ca. 1991–1783 B.C.). See W. K. Simpson, ed., *The Literature of Ancient Egypt* (New Haven: Yale University Press, 1973), 15–30.
6. This is merely one story in a cycle about miracles performed by lector priests at the court of Cheops. These stories were reportedly narrated by Cheops's sons.

ture.⁷ That event is the serpent confrontation of Exodus 7:8–13. Scholars have frequently scrutinized this passage,⁸ yet little study of the Egyptian milieu has been done. We will investigate the Egyptian historical and cultural setting of the serpent contest and then show its usefulness for a proper exegesis of Exodus 7.

The Serpent Confrontation as a Paradigm

When discussing the plagues on Egypt, most scholars omit the serpent confrontation of Exodus 7:8–13. However, a few scholars have diverged, arguing that the pericope should be considered as the first account of a plague.⁹ While the latter position is too extreme because the snake contest did not entail a plague upon the whole of Egypt,¹⁰ the former position is unreasonable because it artificially removes the serpent story from the plague narratives. The fact of the matter is that Exodus 7:8–13 is critical for our understanding of what follows because it is a paradigm of the plague narratives. The serpent confrontation foreshadowed Yahweh's humiliation of Egypt through the plagues and at the Red Sea.¹¹ The incident of the serpents and the crossing of the Red Sea are the boundaries of the entire narrative, reinforcing its singular theme. Supporting that contention is the word *bālaʿ*, which appears in Exodus 7:12 (Aaron's rod "swallowed" the magicians' rods) and in Exodus 15:12 (the Egyptian army was "swallowed" in the Red Sea). In addition, the staff that swallowed the sorcerers' snakes points to the staff that caused the waters to engulf the Egyptian army (Exod. 14:16, 26). Such parallels establish Exodus 7:8–13 as a microcosmic prototype of

---

7. D. B. Redford, "An Egyptological Perspective on the Exodus Narrative," in *Egypt, Israel, Sinai: Archaeological and Historical Relationships in the Biblical Period*, ed. A. F. Rainey (Tel Aviv: Tel Aviv University Press, 1987), argues that only the merest shred of material in the account of the exodus may be considered to be of Egyptian origin: "Now, indeed, there is little Egyptian colouring in the Exodus account, almost wholly toponymic in nature; but the Egyptologist would soon sense that it is anachronistic" (p. 138). Frankly, Redford's assessment is quite hollow in light of advances in research that indicate the exodus story is illuminated by its authentic Egyptian setting. See, e.g., Z. Zevit, "Three Ways to Look at the Ten Plagues," *BR* 6.3 (1990): 16–23, 42. For material on the Egyptian background to other parts of the Pentateuch, see J. D. Currid, "An Examination of the Egyptian Background of the Genesis Cosmogony," *BZ* 35 (1991): 18–40; and J. K. Hoffmeier, "Some Thoughts on Genesis 1 and 2 and Egyptian Cosmology," *JANES* 15 (1983): 39–49.

8. Especially useful are U. Cassuto, *A Commentary on the Book of Exodus* (Jerusalem: Magnes, 1983 reprint), 94–96; and B. S. Childs, *The Book of Exodus* (Philadelphia: Westminster, 1974), 151–53.

9. E.g., D. J. McCarthy, "Moses' Dealings with Pharaoh," *CBQ* 27 (1965): 336–47.

10. The ten plagues had a national extent and consequence—the serpent combat had no such range, except possibly in a symbolic or spiritual sense.

11. T. E. Fretheim, "The Plagues as Ecological Signs of Historical Disaster," *JBL* 110 (1991): 385–96.

the imminent national catastrophe of Egypt. Therefore the plague narratives must be considered in the light of the serpent confrontation.

Exodus 7:8–13 is also paradigmatic in that it defines for the reader the true issue at stake in the entire Exodus struggle. The hostilities were not primarily between Moses and Pharaoh, or between Moses and the Egyptian magicians, or for that matter between Israel and Egypt. What the serpent contest portrays is a heavenly combat—a war between the God of the Hebrews and the deities of Egypt. For the biblical writer the episode was a matter of theology. It was a question of who was the one true God, who was sovereign over the operation of the universe, and whose will was to come to pass in heaven and on earth. The serpent drama introduces us to that theological issue in grand form: Yahweh, God of the Hebrews, engages Pharaoh, a god of Egypt, in a contest of power and will. This theme will be elucidated as we examine Exodus 7:8–13 in detail.

Transmogrification of the Staff of Aaron

When Aaron was ordered by Moses to throw down his staff *(matteh)* before Pharaoh (vv. 9–10), it was transformed into a *tannîn*. One would have expected it to change into a *nāḥāš* because the first sign given to Moses (Exod. 4:2–3) that he was to perform in Egypt was the turning of a *matteh* into a *nāḥāš*. Why is a different Hebrew term used in the two accounts? Many scholars argue that the alteration of terminology is due to the change in scene; they argue that *tannîn* is a crocodile rather than a serpent, and thus more accurately reflects the Egyptian environment.[12] Umberto Cassuto comments: "Instead of the serpent most appropriate to the desert, in which form the sign was transmitted to Moses, comes here the dragon or crocodile most appropriate to the Egyptian milieu."[13] Supporting that position is the fact that the biblical authors often use the word *tannîn* of large reptiles that were more formidable than the simple *nāḥāš* (e.g., Gen. 1:21; Ps. 74:13; 148:7; Isa. 27:1). Other scholars argue that the variation in terms is merely a matter of poetic license. The biblical author was simply trying to make the episode more dramatic and impressive. He was "giving a harmless bit of mystification a sinister cast."[14]

It is doubtful that the Exodus writer meant anything more than that the rods of Aaron and the magicians turned into large snakes. In the

---

12. E.g., W. G. Plaut, *The Torah: A Modern Commentary* (New York: Union of American Hebrew Congregations, 1962), 423.
13. Cassuto, *Exodus*, 94.
14. McCarthy, "Moses' Dealings with Pharaoh," 341.

first place, *tannîn* and *nāḥāš* appear to be used interchangeably in the early chapters of Exodus. Thus, shortly after the serpent contest, God commands Moses, "Go to Pharaoh in the morning as he is going out to the water, and station yourself to meet him on the bank of the Nile; and you shall take in your hand the staff that was turned into a serpent *(nāḥāš)*" (Exod. 7:15). Clearly, the writer is referring here to the immediately preceding story, where the term *tannîn* is employed.

Secondly, the Hebrew poetic literature uses the term *tannîn* in parallel with *peten* (see Deut. 32:33 and Ps. 91:13). *Peten* is a venomous serpent, perhaps a cobra or some type of horned viper (cerastes).[15] A similar parallel is found in the Ugaritic texts.[16] The term *btn*[17] in the Ras Shamra tablets means "serpent" and is used interchangeably with *tnn* ("dragon"). Those parallels suggest that *tannîn* was often used for a serpent rather than for a crocodile or for some type of reptilian monster.

The Septuagint is of little help in this matter. Although it translates *tannîn* into the Greek *drakōn* ("dragon, large reptile"), it also applies *drakōn* to numerous instances of *nāḥāš* (e.g., Job 26:13; Isa. 27:1; Amos 9:3). If anything, the Septuagint supports the idea of the two Hebrew words often being used synonymously.

Finally, the argument that the crocodile was more in keeping with Egyptian culture than was the serpent is fallacious. The cobra, horned viper, and other snake species permeated the land of Egypt, and the figure of the serpent was attested in many more myths, spells, incantations, and narratives than was the crocodile. The venomous snake was truly the symbol or emblem of ancient Egypt.

The Ophidian in Ancient Egypt

The Egyptians were terrified of snakes. Many charms and spells found in the Pyramid Texts and elsewhere confirm their fear of poisonous bites.[18] The danger posed by snakes seems to have been ever present. Pierre Montet states, "Serpents were justly feared throughout Egypt."[19]

---

15. L. Koehler and W. Baumgartner, eds., *Lexicon in Veteris Testamenti libros* (Leiden: Brill, 1985), 789; and *BDB*, 837.
16. C. H. Gordon, *Ugaritic Textbook: Glossary* (Rome: Pontificium Institutum Biblicum, 1965), 33.
17. The shift from *b* to *p* and from *p* to *b* in Hebrew and Ugaritic is well known. See C. H. Gordon, *Ugaritic Textbook: Grammar* (Rome: Pontificium Institutum Biblicum, 1965), 33.
18. E. A. W. Budge, *The Gods of the Egyptians*, 2 vols. (London: Methuen, 1904), 2:376–77.
19. P. Montet, *Egypt and the Bible* (Philadelphia: Fortress, 1968), 92. In Egyptian myths the main enemy of Horus, Re, and Osiris and the personification of evil was Apophis the serpent.

In addition, numerous amulets used to ward off or to charm venomous snakes have been discovered through excavation. Such fear naturally resulted in the worship of many varieties of snakes. Some of these cults were quite ancient, extending back into the late predynastic (ca. 3000 B.C.) and early dynastic (ca. 2920–2575 B.C.) periods. (In fact, the antiquity of snake worship is reflected in hieroglyphics in which the determinative for a goddess is a picture of a cobra.)

On the other hand, many of the snakes of Egypt were harmless, and the Egyptians regarded them as protectors and companions.[20] The friendly guardianship of some snake species is a theme permeating Egyptian mythical literature. For example, an inscription of Amenophis III describes the sacred barge of Amon: "The bows of the barge bear great crowns, whose serpents twine along its two sides; they exercise protection behind them."[21] The serpent Sa-ta was an emblem of resurrection and new life, "ideas suggested by the annual sloughing of the skin by serpents generally."[22] The Book of the Gates describes the sun-god's travels through the underworld and his protection by serpents that spit forth flames into a fiery stream.[23] In the eighth section of that document, a serpent called Kheti preserves Re by belching fire in the direction of the sun-god's enemies. Horus commands Kheti: "Open thy mouth, distend thy jaws, belch forth thy fire against the enemies of my father (Re), burn up their bodies, and consume their souls by the fire which issueth from thy mouth, and by the flames which are in thy body."[24]

So the Egyptians revered the serpent because they feared it for its power and danger, but they also honored the serpent because at times it offered protection. Thus they regarded the snake as both friend and fiend, protector and enemy, and the personification of the sacred and the profane. Some snakes were to be worshiped, others were to be considered incarnations of evil.[25]

---

20. E. A. W. Budge, *From Fetish to God in Ancient Egypt* (New York: Benjamin Blom, 1972), 94–96.
21. *ARE* 2:359.
22. Budge, *From Fetish*, 94.
23. A. Wiedemann, *Religion of the Ancient Egyptians* (London: Grevel, 1897), 99.
24. Translation by E. A. W. Budge, *Osiris and the Egyptian Resurrection*, 2 vols. (London: Medici Society, 1911), 2:233. Among other ancient Egyptian texts that taught that the serpent was the protector of Re or the Pharaoh is chapter 10 of the Book of the Dead, which lists the names of nine serpents that protected the underworld at Saqqara.
25. The dual nature of the snake is in evidence in the "Story of the Shipwrecked Sailor." An island castaway is threatened by a snake-god with death by fire. Later the snake-god turns friendly and helps the castaway. See Simpson, *Literature of Ancient Egypt*, 50–56; and *AEL* 1:212.

Probably the most important serpent worship was the cult of Uraeus centered in the city of Per-Wadjit in the delta.[26] There a temple was built in the early dynastic period in honor of the Uraeus-goddess Wadjet. She personified the cobra and was the tutelary goddess of Lower Egypt.[27] Wadjet served the same function as did the vulture-goddess Nekhbet, the tutelary deity of Upper Egypt. Those two goddesses represented all strength, power, and sovereignty in the two lands of ancient Egypt.

Egyptian textual evidence declares that Pharaoh was able to control all Egypt because he was imbued with the power of the two goddesses. The stele of Tanutamon from Dynasty 25 tells of the king's rise to power:

> In the year one of his coronation as king—his majesty saw a dream by night: two serpents, one upon his right, the other upon his left. Then his majesty awoke and found them not. His majesty said: "Wherefore [has] this [come] to me?" Then they (the two goddesses) answered him, saying: "Thine is the Southland; take for thyself (also) the Northland. The two Goddesses (Wadjet and Nekhbet) shine upon thy brow, the land is given to thee, in its length and its breadth. [No] other divides it with thee."[28]

The two goddesses and the sovereignty they imparted to Pharaoh were physically represented on the front of the king's crown in the form of an enraged female cobra. To the Egyptian the royal diadem was an object "charged with power and was, in fact, not always distinguished from the goddesses themselves."[29] An inanimate object thought to be energized with divine sovereignty and potency, this uraeus came to be considered the emblem of Pharaoh's power.[30]

The Egyptians believed that the serpent-crest would terrorize Pharaoh's enemies just as the common snake instilled fear. A collection of

---

26. The Greek name of the city was Buto. Located at the present site of Tell el-Faraʿin, the remains consist of three mounds, two of which were the town and the third a temple enclosure. The site has undergone some excavation, but it has not revealed remains of great importance.

27. For a unique representation of Wadjet see J. Baines and J. Malek, *Atlas of Ancient Egypt* (New York: Facts on File, 1980), 217. The bronze statue with a lioness head and a cobra on top embodies the goddess's power and ferocious demeanor as portrayed in textual material.

28. *ARE* 4:469.

29. H. Frankfort, *Kingship and the Gods* (Chicago: University of Chicago Press, 1948), 107.

30. Because the Egyptians believed that inanimate objects could be charged with power, it would have been no surprise to them that Moses and Aaron used a staff to perform magical feats. For a text concerning the use of inanimate objects as sources of animate power, see "The God and His Unknown Name of Power," in *ANET*, 12–14.

hymns addressed to his crown give witness to the invincible strength of Pharaoh against his enemies.[31] One such hymn is Pyramid Text 396:

> The *ka*s of Unas[32] are behind him;
> His Hemsut[33] are under his feet;
> His gods are over him;
> His uraeus-serpents are over his head.
> The leading snake of Unas is at his forehead,
> She who perceives the soul (of the enemy),
> She who excels in the force of fire.[34]

From Medinet Habu comes a description of Rameses III (Dynasty 20) in battle against his enemies: "Dreadful is thy serpent-crest among them; the war-mace in thy right hand."[35] A relief at Karnak portrays Shoshenk's (Dynasty 22) defeat of the Asiatics in a similar fashion: "Thy war-mace, it struck down thy foes, the Asiatics of distant countries; thy serpent-crest was mighty among them."[36] According to the Tanis Stele, the monarch Taharqa of Dynasty 25 believed that the serpent-crested diadem protected Egypt and himself: "I had taken the diadems of Re, and I had assumed the double serpent-crest . . . as the protection of my limbs."[37] The dilated hood of the fiery uraeus on the crown of the king was obviously intended to produce fear in the hearts of foes and to protect the divine order against its enemies.[38]

---

31. For an extended discussion of this collection see A. Erman, "Hymnen an das Diadem der Pharaonen," in *Abhandlungen der Preussichen Akademie, Phil.-hist. Klasse* (1911), 1.

32. *Ka* in the plural refers to the impersonal vital spirits of reality. They were simply the life forces of the universe. Wenis (Unas) was an Egyptian king of Dynasty 5 (ca. 2356–2323 B.C.) in whose pyramid this inscription was discovered.

33. Hemsut were female counterparts to the *ka*s.

34. Pyramid Text 396, in K. Sethe, ed., *Die altägyptischen Pyramidentexten* (Leipzig: J. C. Hinrichs, 1908–22).

35. *ARE* 4:77.

36. *ARE* 4:357.

37. *ARE* 4:456. Even the god Re wore two uraei on his forehead for the purpose of protection. The Ennead also wore serpent-crests, as is evident from a statement of Rameses III at his first jubilee: "I mixed for them (the Ennead) ointment for their serpent-crests."

38. See E. Hornung, "The Book of the Divine Cow," *Bulletin de l'institut français d'archéologie orientale* 40 (1941): 58–59; and R. T. Rundle Clark, *Myth and Symbol in Ancient Egypt* (London: Thames and Hudson, 1959), 185. From the time of Sethos II comes a prayer of the high priest Rome to Amon-Re: "Thou didst grant me long life carrying thy image, while my eye beheld the two uraei every day, and my limbs were endued with health." This sounds as if the uraei had not only protective powers but healing powers as well. See G. Léfèbvre, *Inscriptions concernant les grands prêtres d'Amon, Rome-Roy et Amenhotep* (Paris: Geuthner, 1929), 31–39.

The awe that the Egyptians felt for the uraeus of the crown was further charged by their belief that it was also the eye of Horus. A drama from the age of Senwosret I (Dynasty 12) depicts a struggle between the gods Horus and Seth because Seth had killed Horus's father, Osiris. In the battle Seth either wounded or stole Horus's eye, so that the latter was in a weakened condition. Eventually Horus recovered his eye, regained great strength, and defeated Seth. To the Egyptian, the eye of Horus came to symbolize all his power and virtue. Accordingly, "the symbol and seat of royal power, the uraeus of the crown, is called the Eye of Horus."[39] So the serpent-diadem on Pharaoh's forehead not only was imbued with the tenacious and aggressive natures of the two goddesses, but manifested all the power and virility of Horus. A hymn to that effect was recited at the coronation of a new Pharaoh:

> The Great One has borne thee;
> The Exalted One has adorned thee;
> For thou art Horus who hast fought
> For the protection of thine eye.[40]

The ancient Egyptians also thought that the gods had invested great magic in the serpent-crest, and it in turn empowered Pharaoh with magical abilities. In fact, various texts call the goddess of the diadem "The Magician." An example is Pyramid Text 194–95, a coronation hymn addressed to the crown-goddess:

The doors of the Horizon are opened, their bolts are slipped.
He (the king) comes to thee, O Red Crown;[41] he comes to thee, O Fiery One.[42]
He comes to thee, O Great One; he comes to thee, O Magician.
He has purified himself for thee . . .
He comes to thee, O Magician.
It is Horus who has fought to protect his Eye, O Magician.[43]

So the serpent-crested diadem of Pharaoh symbolized all the power, sovereignty, and magic with which the gods endued the king. It was the emblem of his divine force. In recognition of its power the newly enthroned Pharaoh would address the uraeus-crown:

---

39. Frankfort, *Kingship and the Gods*, 126.
40. Ibid., 108.
41. The crown of Lower Egypt.
42. This identifies the goddess as Wadjet, the serpent-goddess of Lower Egypt. Wadjet was frequently portrayed as a snake that spit forth flames as her poison.
43. Frankfort, *Kingship and the Gods*, 107.

> O Red Crown, O Inu, O Great One,
> O Magician, O Fiery Snake!
> Let there be terror of me like the terror of thee.
> Let there be fear of me like the fear of thee.
> Let there be awe of me like the awe of thee.
> Let me rule, a leader of the living.
> Let me be powerful, a leader of spirits.[44]

We should also note here that late biblical texts were aware of the use of serpent symbolism for the power of Pharaoh. Regarding an impending battle between Yahweh and Pharaoh, Ezekiel is told to prophesy, "Thus says the Lord GOD, 'Behold, I am against you, Pharaoh, king of Egypt, the great monster (serpent) *(tannîm)* that lies in the midst of his rivers, that has said, 'My Nile is mine, and I myself have made it'" (Ezek. 29:3; cf. Ps. 74:13).

The Irony in the Serpent Confrontation

Aaron's casting of his staff before Pharaoh and its transformation into a snake was an incident of judicial irony, an extensive polemic against Egyptian thought and practice. In the first place, the textual evidence from the early periods tells us of the Egyptians' pride in their power to manipulate venomous creatures. Moses and Aaron duplicated this feat. However, "this was by no means the only proof which Moses gives that he was versed in the magic of the Egyptians, for, like the sage Aba-aner and King Nectanebus, and all other magicians of the Egypt from time immemorial, he and Aaron possessed a wonderful rod by means of which they worked wonders."[45] The irony is that the two Hebrew leaders chose to humiliate and defeat the Egyptians in areas that traditionally rendered glory to the Egyptians. As Ernst Hengstenberg remarks, "Moses was furnished with power to perform that which the Egyptian magicians most especially gloried in, and by which they most of all supported their authority."[46]

Second, throwing down the staff was a challenge to the power of Egyptian magic as described in numerous mythological texts. Egyptian documents are replete with examples of magicians performing extraordinary feats, including changing inanimate objects into animals. One example is found in the Westcar Papyrus, a cycle of stories detailing the

---

44. Ibid., 108.
45. E. A. W. Budge, *Egyptian Magic* (Evanston, Ill.: University Books, 1958 reprint), 5. See also F. J. Chabas, *Annales du Musée Guimet* (Paris: E. Leroux, 1880), 1:35–48.
46. E. W. Hengstenberg, *Egypt and the Books of Moses* (Edinburgh: Thomas Clark, 1845), 98.

wonders performed by Egyptian lector priests in the days of Cheops.[47] Tale 2 holds great interest for us because it tells of the lector priest Webaoner who fashioned a wax crocodile that came to life when he threw it into a lake. Later Webaoner bent down, picked it up, and it became wax again. That story reminds us of Exodus 4 and 7, where Moses and Aaron do something similar with their staffs, albeit for a higher moral purpose than what is found in the Egyptian tale.[48] The Exodus writer, by narrating a historical event in which a priest actually transformed an inanimate object into an animal, may be subtly pointing to the fictional character of the Egyptian mythological texts. In other words, Exodus 7 is a polemic contending that Moses and Aaron truly did that which Egyptian mythology merely imagined.

Finally, the scene is ironic in that the Hebrew leaders cast before Pharaoh his very emblem. The two tutelary goddesses of Egypt and Horus were represented in the cobra of the crown; they invested all their power, magic, sovereignty, and protection into the uraeus and thereby into Pharaoh. The Egyptians considered him omnipotent because of those imputed powers. He ruled the land as a god, as the incarnation and son of Re, as the Horus, and as a combination of the goddesses of Upper and Lower Egypt. The stele of Sehetep-ib-Re from Abydos enjoins worship of King Ni-Maat-Re (Amenemhat III, 1844–1797 B.C.) as a divinity:

> Worship King Ni-Maat-Re, living forever, within your bodies
> And associate with his majesty in your hearts.
> He is Perception which is in (mer.'s) hearts,
> And his eyes search out every body.
> He is Re, by whose beams one sees,
> He is one who illumines the Two Lands more than the sun disc....
> He who is to be is his creation,
> For he is the Khnum[49] of all bodies.[50]

The Egyptians described Pharaoh as eternal, worthy of worship, and omniscient; he imbued Egypt with existence and power. They taught that he was *ka*, the life force and soul of Egypt. And the serpent-crested coronet symbolized his deification and majesty. When Moses had

---

47. See A. Erman, *The Literature of the Ancient Egyptians* (New York: Dutton, 1927), xxix, lxviii–lxix, 36–49; and Simpson, *Literature of Ancient Egypt*, 15–30.

48. Webaoner made the wax crocodile come to life in order to kill a townsman who was having an affair with his wife. His sole purpose was vengeance.

49. Khnum was one of the creator gods of ancient Egypt. In the "Great Hymn to Khnum" he is portrayed as "forming all on his potter's wheel ... he made mankind, created gods, he fashioned flocks and herds. He made birds, fishes, and reptiles all" (*AEL* 3:113).

50. *ANET*, 431.

Aaron fling the rod-snake before Pharaoh, he was directly assaulting that token of Pharaonic sovereignty—the scene was one of polemical taunting. When Aaron's rod swallowed the staffs of the Egyptian magicians, Pharaonic deity and omnipotence were being denounced and rejected outright. Pharaoh's cobra-crested diadem had no power against Yahweh. Its magic was wanting and weak. It afforded no protection in the face of the reproach of the Hebraic God. Clearly, Yahweh alone was in control of the entire episode.

The Imitative Powers of the Egyptian Magicians

Another evidence of the Egyptian setting of Exodus 7:8–13 is the biblical writer's use of an Egyptian loanword to identify the magicians of Egypt. The Hebrew term ḥarṭōm (v. 11) was certainly borrowed from the Egyptian ḫry-ḥbt.[51] The Egyptian title referred to a chief lector priest, someone who was not only a magician but also a member of the priestly caste and a teacher of wisdom.[52] The biblical borrowing of the term further confirms the Egyptian background and authenticity of the episode.

How the chief lector priests of Egypt were able to transform their staffs into serpents was a matter for conjecture even in the earliest commentaries. Almost all the early scholars agreed that the Egyptian magicians accomplished their feat by a mere sleight of hand—the changing of staffs into snakes was simply an illusion.[53] Ibn Ezra commented that the magicians were "adept in altering the external appearance of things by their arts." Others maintained that the Egyptians were truly able to change rods into serpents because they possessed some sort of evil supernatural power.[54]

In the nineteenth century a new approach was taken. Scholars like Ernst Hengstenberg, Alfred Nevin, and Alan McNeile called attention

---

51. For a good analysis of this linguistic matter see D. B. Redford, *A Study of the Biblical Story of Joseph (Genesis 37–50)* (Leiden: Brill, 1970), 203–4; J. Quaeqebeur, "On the Egyptian Equivalent of Biblical ḤARṬUMMÎN," in *Pharaonic Egypt*, ed. S. Israelit-Groll (Jerusalem: Magnes, 1985), 162–72; and M. Noth, *Exodus* (Philadelphia: Westminster, 1962), 71. For a contrary view see Lambdin, "Egyptian Loan Words," 150–51; and *Loan Words*, 24–25.

52. A. Erman had originally called this position "lector-priest" (*Die Religion der Ägypter* [Berlin: de Gruyter, 1934], 308). Note, however, the pointed correction of Erman by J. Vergote, *Joseph en Egypte* (Louvain: Publications Universitaires, 1959), 67, who says the term actually means "prêtre-lecteur en chef." See also B. Couroyer, "Le 'doigt de Dieu,'" *RB* 63 (1956): 481–95.

53. Josephus, the early rabbinic literature, Philo, Maimonides, and Abrabanel all believed that trickery was involved.

54. For a detailed discussion of this position see J. J. Davis, *Moses and the Gods of Egypt* (Grand Rapids: Baker, 1971), 90–91.

to the Psylli, contemporary Egyptian snake-charmers.⁵⁵ The Psylli were able to put a serpent into a state of catalepsy in which it became rigid and looked like a cane: "When they wish to perform this operation, they spit in the throat of the animal, compel it to shut up its mouth, and lay it down upon the ground. Then, as if in order to give a last command, they lay their hand upon its head, and immediately the serpent, stiff and motionless, falls into a kind of torpor. They wake it up when they wish, seizing it by the tail, and rolling it roughly between the hands."⁵⁶

Archaeological evidence from Egypt suggests that the practice of putting a cobra into a state of catalepsy was commonplace in antiquity. There are, for instance, numerous scarabs depicting a man or a god holding in his hand a snake straight as a rod.⁵⁷ Pierre Montet claims that a scarab from Tanis seems to portray a magician doing his tricks before a divine trio.⁵⁸ Literary evidence also seems to be supportive. A text from Edfu, for instance, speaks of a king driving a herd of cows with a serpent-staff.⁵⁹

Even though serpent charming is a feasible explanation for the incident in Egypt, it is hardly a certainty. The biblical author did not speak definitively about the matter. He expressed no opinion about it. His primary focus seems to have been to demonstrate the superior power of Yahweh over the Egyptians no matter what the source of their power. Be it magic, evil, or illusion, the God of the Hebrews was more powerful. At the end of the episode the writer proves God's sovereignty: Aaron's rod swallowed the rods of the Egyptians.

---

55. Hengstenberg, *Egypt and the Books of Moses*, 98–103; A. Nevin, *Notes, Exegetical, Practical and Devotional on the Book of Exodus* (Philadelphia: Claxton, Remsen, and Haffelfinger, 1873), 90–91; and A. H. McNeile, *The Book of Exodus* (London: Methuen, 1908), 41–42.

56. Hengstenberg, *Egypt and the Books of Moses*, 100. J. Finegan, *Let My People Go* (New York: Harper, 1963), 48, makes a similar observation: "This is still done in Cairo today as a trick of magic. The Egyptian cobra can be paralyzed by putting pressure on a nerve in its neck. At a distance it is readily mistaken for a cane. When the magician throws it on the ground, the jolt causes it to recover, and it crawls away."

57. For illustrations of these scarabs see L. Keimer, "Histoires de serpents dans l'Egypte ancienne et moderne," *Memoires de l'Institute d'Egypte* 50 (1947): 16–17, figs. 14–21.

58. P. Montet, *Tanis: Douze années de fouilles dans une capitale oubliée du delta égyptien* (Paris: Payot, 1942), 219, fig. 63.

59. A. M. Blackman and H. W. Fairman, "The Significance of the Ceremony Ḥwt Bḥsw [The Striking of Calves] in the Temple of Horus at Edfu," *JEA* 35 (1949): 98–112. For other texts that represent magicians rendering scorpions, serpents, and other reptiles motionless see G. Maspéro, *Les Contes populaires de l'Egypte ancienne*, 4th ed. (Paris: E. Guilmoto, 1911), 112.

The Hardening of Pharaoh's Heart

The climax of the serpent contest occurs in verse 13, when Pharaoh gives his final response to Moses and Aaron: "Yet Pharaoh's heart was hardened, and he did not listen to them, as the Lord had said." The concept of the hardening of Pharaoh's heart is a principal motif not only of this narrative, but of the entire conflict between Pharaoh and Yahweh in Exodus 1–15.[60] It is used throughout these chapters to explain Pharaoh's refusal to obey Yahweh's command to release Israel. Three Hebrew terms are used interchangeably throughout the pericope to indicate the state of Pharaoh's heart, his "hardening" toward the situation. The first term, *qāšāh*, which means "to be difficult," refers to the stubbornness of Pharaoh's heart not to let Israel depart. The second word, *ḥāzaq*, which means "to be strong," bears the idea of Pharaoh's maintaining a strong, determined will not to accede to Yahweh. Another example of *ḥāzaq* appears in Joshua 11:20, where Yahweh hardens the hearts of the Canaanites, that is, he gives them a strong will to fight Israel. The final word, *kābēd*, which means "to be heavy," was frequently used to reflect intensity: Pharaoh's desire to keep Israel in chains was overwhelming.[61]

Throughout the Book of Exodus the author specifies that Yahweh is the one who hardened Pharaoh's heart (Exod. 4:21; 7:3; 9:12; 10:1, 20, 27; 14:4, 8). Why did the God of the Hebrews do that to Pharaoh? Critical to our understanding of God's action is the concept of the heart in Egyptian religion.

Ancient Egyptian sacred texts taught that the heart *(ib)* was the essence of the person. The *ib* was to be distinguished from the *ba* ("soul, spirit, body") and the *ka* ("a manifestation of the vital energy"), which were both complex and broad concepts. The *ib* was the inner spiritual center of the self. It was arguably the most important part of the human in ancient Egyptian religion.

As the essence of the person, the heart was the critical component in regard to the afterlife. The Book of the Dead (the Papyrus of Ani) provides a description of future judgment (in text and picture) as taught by the ancient Egyptians during the New Kingdom.[62] In the Papyrus of Ani, the deceased Ani and his wife Tutu are depicted entering the hall

---

60. See J. D. Currid, "Why Did God Harden Pharaoh's Heart?" *BR* 9.6 (1993): 46–51.
61. For an in-depth study of these terms see G. K. Beale, "An Exegetical and Theological Consideration of the Hardening of Pharaoh's Heart in Exodus 4–14 and Romans 9," *Trinity Journal* 5 (1984): 129–54.
62. For colored reproductions of the Papyrus of Ani, see E. A. W. Budge, *The Book of the Dead: The Papyrus of Ani*, vol. 3 (New York: Putnam, 1914); and R. O. Faulkner, *The Egyptian Book of the Dead* (New York: Macmillan, 1972).

of judgment—they are both bowed to demonstrate their attitude of submission and devotion. On one side of the hall the gods of the Ennead (the hierarchical deities of the universe) sit enthroned before a table of offerings. Directly in front of the deceased stands the balance of truth by which the dead are judged. Anubis, the jackal-headed mortuary god, is in charge of the weighing. Behind him stands Thoth, the scribe of the gods, who dutifully records the verdict. At Thoth's back is the frightening goddess Amemit, who waits to devour the condemned sinner. Between Ani and the dreadful seat of judgment are stationed some gods who will testify on Ani's behalf if necessary. For example, the twin goddesses of birth, Rennenit and Meschenit, are there to witness to the circumstances of his birth. In addition, the god Shai, who is the god of destiny and Ani's guardian, stands at the ready. Ani's *ba* ("soul") is also there; in the guise of a falcon with the human head of Ani, it awaits its ultimate fate.

The accompanying text tells us that Anubis calls for the heart of Ani to be weighed against the feather of truth and righteousness. If the heart is too heavy, Ani will be adjudged a sinner and cast to the voracious Amemit; but if the heart achieves balance with the feather, Ani will receive the reward of eternal life. At this most dramatic point Ani addresses his heart:

> O my heart from my mother! O my heart from my mother! O my heart from my different forms![63] Do not stand against me as a witness! Do not oppose me before the Assessors![64] Do not be belligerent to me before the One who keeps the balance![65] You are my *ka*[66] which was in my belly, the protector who strengthened my limbs. Go forth into the joyous place. Do not make my name stink before the officials who make men! Do not speak lies about me in the presence of the god! It is good that you hear![67]

Ani's plea is effective, for he is not judged to be a sinner. Thoth pronounces Ani to be of wholesome character:

---

63. The author of the text includes a mummy determinative here—Ani is probably telling his heart not to desert him even though he is dead and mummified.
64. This is probably a reference to the Ennead, the tribunal of gods waiting to pass judgment on Ani.
65. The ancient mortuary god Anubis.
66. The *ka*-sign represents the spirit or essence of a person. See Currid, "Genesis Cosmogony," 24 n. 31.
67. Book of the Dead, Spell 30B. Other charms from the Book of the Dead were also used to protect the deceased. For instance, Spell 29A: "A spell for not allowing the heart of man to be robbed from him in the Necropolis. You get back, messenger of any god! Have you come to seize my heart which lives? I will not give you my heart which belongs to the living. As I approach, the gods who are pleased for me listen and they fall on their faces . . . facing their own land." (Unless specifically noted, the translations are the author's.)

Thoth, judge of truth, to the great Ennead who are in the presence of Osiris: Hear this speech of notable truth. The heart belonging to Osiris[68] has been weighed, and his soul stands as a witness for him. His deeds are true in the Great Balance. No crime has been found in him. He did not subtract (any) offerings from the temples. He did not damage what he made. He did not go in the lies of deceitful speech while he was on earth.[69]

Because of Ani's virtuous life on earth, the scale of righteousness balances. The Ennead then make the final pronouncement as to whether he is fit for future existence: "No sin is found in him; he has no evil with which we might accuse him. Amemit (the Devouress) shall have no power over him."

Finally, Ani (without his wife) is presented to Osiris, the god of the dead. Osiris is pictured enthroned in a shrine with Isis and Nephthys standing behind him. Directly in front of Osiris and on top of a lotus flower are the four children of Horus, the genii of the dead. Horus, the falcon-god, introduces Ani to Osiris by announcing the righteousness of Ani. Ani prays, kneels, and presents offerings to Osiris. Thus Ani is received into the field of reeds, the Egyptian heaven or abode of the dead.

Obviously the condition of one's heart was the critical factor determining whether one entered the afterlife or not. This was a form of works-righteousness: anyone whose heart was heavy-laden with misdeeds would be annihilated, while anyone whose heart was filled with integrity, truth, and good acts would be escorted to heavenly bliss. To help the deceased on the journey, the New Kingdom Egyptians frequently included with their burials funerary papyri from the Book of the Dead. They were folded into the bandages of the mummy or merely laid upon the chest (near the heart). The Egyptians believed the magical spells of the papyri well equipped the dead to face judgment in the afterlife.

The heart of the dead in ancient Egypt was also thought to be protected by various trinkets. The most important was the scarab, on which were inscribed spells from the Book of the Dead. The scarab was a sculpted model of a dung beetle that was used as an amulet or seal. It was the most popular charm in dynastic Egypt and has been found by the thousands through archaeological excavation.[70] The tomb of

---

68. Actually this statement refers to Ani's heart.
69. Book of the Dead, Spell 30B.
70. See, e.g., W. A. Ward, *Studies on Scarab Seals*, vol. 1 (Warminster: Aris and Phillips, 1978); O. Tufnell, *Studies on Scarab Seals*, vol. 2 (Warminster: Aris and Phillips, 1984); A. Rowe, *A Catalogue of Egyptian Scarabs* (Cairo: L'Institut français d'archéologie orientale, 1936); W. M. F. Petrie, *Scarabs and Cylinders* (London: British School of Archaeology in Egypt, 1917); C. Andrews, *Egyptian Mummies* (Cambridge, Mass.: Harvard University Press, 1984).

King Tutankhamun dramatically displayed the importance of the scarab. Sculpted replicas were attached to the mummy, and dung beetles were also frequently represented in the jewelry of the crypt.[71] Usually the amulet was made out of faience or another hard material, and on its lower surface was inscribed either a text, the name of an official, or some decorative symbol.[72] The scarab was normally one to two inches high.

From earliest times the Egyptians believed the dung beetle to be a sacred creature. That veneration was first displayed in predynastic Egypt where dried beetles in jars were interred with the deceased.[73] Representations have been found in buildings as early as the pyramids; on the walls of the burial chambers King Teti is said to "live like the scarab," and Pepy to be "the son of the scarab."[74] Throughout dynastic times the people believed the beetle to have phenomenal medicinal powers. They applied it externally to stimulate the delivery of a child or to treat burns.[75] The Ebers Papyrus recommended that the Egyptian also use the dung beetle internally. Wallis Budge reported that people in eastern Sudan yet employed dung beetles as an agent of fertility: "For to this day the insect is dried, pounded, and mixed with water, and then drunk by women who believe it to be an unfailing specific for the production of large families."[76]

The Egyptians also revered the dung beetle because its unique behavior of rolling a ball of dung along the ground and then burying it reminded them of the invisible force that rolls the sun across the sky and pushes it under the earth at evening time. So the Egyptians adopted the dung beetle as an earthly model of the sun and its movements. In addition, they observed that at the beginning of life the beetle emerges from the dung ball on its own. Coupling this observation with the apparent lack of gender distinctions, the Egyptians credited self-generation to

---

71. See, e.g., I. E. S. Edwards, *Treasures of Tutankamun* (New York: Ballantine, 1976), nos. 26, 29; H. Carter and A. C. Mace, *The Tomb of Tut-Ankh-Amen,* 3 vols. (New York: Doran, 1923–33); P. Fox, *Tutankhamun's Treasure* (London: Oxford University Press, 1951); A. Piankoff, *The Shrines of Tut-Ankh-Amon* (New York: Pantheon, 1955). A magnificent statue of a sacred dung beetle dating to the reign of Amenophis III was discovered near the sacred lake of the temple of Amon at Karnak; see Baines and Malek, *Atlas,* 91–92.

72. A. H. Gardiner, *Egypt of the Pharaohs* (New York: Oxford University Press, 1961), 44 n. 1. By nature the scarab is black. The ancient Egyptians, however, rarely used black in their reproductions, perhaps because no semiprecious stone of that color is found in Egypt.

73. Petrie, *Scarabs and Cylinders,* 2.

74. Budge, *Egyptian Magic,* 35.

75. W. R. Dawson, "Studies in the Egyptian Medical Texts—XX," *JEA* 20 (1934): 185–88.

76. Budge, *Egyptian Magic,* 35.

the dung beetle. This perception further paralleled the Egyptian sun-god, who was thought to have created himself.[77]

Ancient writers were well aware of the identification of the dung beetle with the sun-god in dynastic Egypt. In his *Natural History* (30.30) Pliny the Elder took note of "the beetle that rolls little pellets. Because of this beetle the greater part of Egypt worships the beetle as one of its deities. Apion, seeking to find an excuse for the religious customs of his race, gives an erudite explanation: he infers that this creature resembles the sun and its revolutions." Plutarch made a similar comment in his *Isis and Osiris* (10 [355A]; 74 [381A]): "As for the scarab-beetle, it is held that there are no females of this species; they are all males. They place their seed in a round pellet of material, which they roll up into a sphere and roll along, pushing it with their hind legs, imitating by their action the course of the sun from east to west."[78] Horapollo added a new twist to the parallel: the scarab "rolls the ball from east to west, looking himself toward the east. Having dug a hole, he buries in it for twenty-eight days; on the twenty-ninth day he opens the ball, and throws it into the water, and from it the scarabaei come forth."[79]

Not surprisingly, the Egyptian word for dung beetle, *kheprer*, was applied to the sun-god as he arose every morning.[80] In addition, *kheprer* was the principal Egyptian word signifying "to come into existence or to become." There is no doubt that the ancient Egyptians perceived a symbiotic relationship between the dung beetle, the sun-god, and the

---

77. In a vignette from the Book of the Dead the scarab is pictured masturbating. That reminds us immediately of the creative activity of the sun-god; see in particular Pyramid Text 527. One needs to be careful, however, not to stretch the parallels too far. Ward suggests that the burrow of the dung beetle has similarities to Old Kingdom mastabas and pyramids, the pupa resembles a mummy, and the emergence of the beetle reflects the rebirth of the dead (*Studies on Scarab Seals*, 1:47). Ward sees a further parallel between the formation of the primeval earth through the creator-god's spittle and the beetle's shaping its dung with its saliva. But no Egyptian textual material supports such grand claims. On the behavior of the scarab beetle see S. I. Bishara, "Biology and Identification of Scarab Beetles," in Ward, *Studies on Scarab Seals*, 1:87–97; Budge, *Egyptian Magic*, 36–38.

78. Other ancient authors who denied the existence of a female scarab include Horapollo, Aelian (*De natura animalium* 10.15), and Porphyry (*De abstinentia* 4.9). For a general discussion see E. A. W. Budge, *The Mummy* (New York: Macmillan, 1972 reprint).

79. Horapollo *Hieroglyphics* 1.1.10. See the discussion of J. H. Fabre, *Souvenirs entomologiques: Etudes sur les instincts et moeurs des insectes*, 5th ser. (Paris: C. Delagrave, 1897). In addition, Horapollo claimed that every scarab had thirty toes corresponding to the thirty days in a month. There is no evidence that the dynastic Egyptians had a similar understanding. Horapollo also said that a scarab represents self-generation because it is self-produced, being unconceived by female.

80. Use of the word *kheprer* for the dung beetle is at least as old as the Pyramid Texts, although some scholars argue for a date as early as predynastic. See Ward, *Studies on Scarab Seals*, 1:44; and Budge, *From Fetish to God*, 98.

concept of coming into existence. In hieroglyphic writing, they used the sign of the scarab for all three.

No wonder the Egyptians considered carved replicas of the dung beetle to be magical. In fact, they believed that the sculpted models were as magical as the bug itself, and that the charms would serve to ensure one's life and its renewal. Just as the dung beetle gave life to its eggs in the ball each day, so, the Egyptians thought, a model would give renewed life and power to them daily. They wore the charms around their necks and elsewhere as protective devices symbolic of invisible powers.

In the New Kingdom (ca. 1550–1070) and succeeding dynasties a new type of sculpted dung beetle appeared in Egypt. Large scarabs were made of green-colored stone, set in gold bands, and encrusted with gold.[81] The flat lower surface was normally engraved with the name of a king or an official, a text, or some type of decoration.[82] Wings were occasionally included in the carving of the dung beetle. Sometimes the scarabs had bases sculpted in the shape of a human heart.

These heart scarabs were essential in the mummification process of the New Kingdom. They were either placed in the wrapping of the deceased or mounted in the mummy's pectoral area. The tomb of Tutankhamun exemplified both practices. One striking specimen is a magnificent scarab pectoral with solar and lunar emblems.[83] Equally impressive is a large heart scarab clearly in evidence on the sarcophagus of the king.[84]

Large scarabs were found frequently in the graves of the New Kingdom because the Egyptians of that time associated the dung beetle with the human heart. To the Egyptians, the heart was the seat of emotion, the center of the intellect and the soul, and the locus of character or personality. They even thought that human physical activity derived from the decisions of the heart. Thus Sinuhe says that at the royal court "my soul departed, my body was powerless, my heart was not in my body, that I might know life from death."[85] And according to a Memphite text, "the action of the arms, the movement of the legs and of every part of the body is dictated by order of the heart."[86]

---

81. A.-P. Leca, *The Egyptian Way of Death* (New York: Doubleday, 1982), 27. Leca suggests that the green color of the heart scarab represented vegetation and thus symbolized rebirth.
82. Gardiner, *Egypt of the Pharaohs,* 44 n. 1. At a later period some of the heart scarabs bore human likenesses of the deceased.
83. Edwards, *Treasures of Tutankamun,* 62 and 137.
84. Ibid., 135.
85. *ANET,* 21.
86. G. Posener, *Dictionary of Egyptian Civilization* (London: Methuen, 1962), 118.

Continuation of life without the heart was unthinkable and impossible. In the early periods of Egyptian mummification the embalmers who eviscerated the corpse often left the heart in the mummy; the heart was needed to ensure survival and renewal in the afterlife. By the time of the New Kingdom, however, the Egyptians believed that the heart actually told harmful tales of the deceased at the last judgment—and thereby prevented one from reaching the afterlife. So the New Kingdom Egyptians removed the heart during embalming and placed it in a canopic jar. In place of the human heart they substituted sculpted dung beetles or heart scarabs. This act invested the deceased with the regenerative powers of the dung beetle so that one would gain the afterlife, the heavenly abode of the dead.

Frequently inscribed on the bases of the heart scarabs of the New Kingdom were sayings from the Book of the Dead.[87] These sayings consisted primarily of funerary magical charms. Combined with the magical powers of the scarab, the incantations were believed to energize the deceased with the potential for regeneration in the judgment.

The assertion of the Exodus writer that Yahweh made Pharaoh's heart heavy has added dimensions for us when we take the Egyptian background into account. Obviously the God of the Hebrews was serving as the judge of Pharaoh. Yahweh was weighing the heart of the Egyptian king, and then proclaiming the result for all to see. Pharaoh was adjudged an imperfect being worthy of condemnation. This is especially striking in light of the ancient Egyptian belief in the purity of Pharaoh. Individuals who approached the king were commanded to prostrate themselves, "smelling the earth, crawling on the ground," while "invoking this perfect god and exalting his beauty." Yahweh's hardening of Pharaoh's heart was a polemic against the prevailing notion that Pharaoh's character was pure and untainted. The two themes of Pharaoh's misdeeds and the hardening of his heart are tied together in Exodus 9:34.

Greg Beale has pointed out that the hardening of Pharaoh's heart was also a polemic against the Egyptian belief that Pharaoh's heart was the all-controlling factor in both history and society.[88] The Memphite theology encapsulated on the Shabaka Stone held that the hearts of the gods Re and Horus were sovereign over everything.[89] Because Pharaoh was an incarnation of those two gods, his heart was thought to be sovereign over creation. Yahweh assaulted the heart of Pharaoh to demon-

---

87. For the original texts see E. A. W. Budge, *The Book of the Dead: The Papyrus of Ani*, vol. 2 (New York: Putnam, 1913).
88. Beale, "Exegetical and Theological Consideration," 149.
89. *ANET*, 54.

strate that only the God of the Hebrews is the sovereign of the universe. That Yahweh controlled the heart of Egypt's king is the basic point of the episode related in Exodus 7:8–13.

The various aspects of Exodus 7:8–13 that we have considered ought to impress upon our minds the authenticity and realistic nature of the serpent contest. The passage is saturated with elements of Egyptian religious and cultural background. Only an author well versed in Egyptian tradition could have composed this poignant piece that reeks of Egypt. And he quite subtly used that knowledge to polemicize against Egyptian practices and thereby demonstrate the truth of the Hebrew religion. He did that not only by employing linguistic parallels (e.g., ḥarṭōm/ḫry-ḥbt), but also by constructing his account of the story as a critique of Egyptian customs. That a passage this short contains such a skillful and profound argument stands as a memorial to the literary genius of the biblical writer.

6

An Exegetical and Historical Consideration of the Ten Plagues of Egypt

The Two Major Positions of Modern Scholarship

In Exodus studies today there is a raging debate regarding the interpretation of the plagues on Egypt (chs. 7–12). Two currents of thought about the issue dominate modern scholarship. The first position maintains that the plagues were natural disasters. In general, this interpretation attempts to explain the plagues of Egypt as typical natural phenomena of antiquity. Various scholars have tried to prove through textual evidence that similar plagues occurred frequently in the ancient Near East.[1] That such events occur even today in Egypt has been used to argue for the historicity of the plagues. In addition, this position holds that the order of the plagues was naturally progressive, that is, each plague was a cause or catalyst of the subsequent plague. They built one upon the other.

Advocacy of this position has a long history. Ernst Hengstenberg, for example, wrote in 1845 that all the plagues "find a foundation in the natural phenomena of Egypt, and stand in close connection with ordinary occurrences." He then cited the English deist Thomas Mor-

---

1. See in particular the recent study by R. Steiglitz, "Ancient Records and the Exodus Plagues," *BAR* 13.6 (1987): 46–49. For good overall summaries of the issues see J. K. Hoffmeier, "Plagues in Egypt," in *ABD* 2:374–78; N. M. Sarna, *Exploring Exodus: The Heritage of Biblical Israel* (New York: Schocken, 1986); and David Livingstone, "The Plagues and the Exodus," *Archaeology and Biblical Research* 4.1 (1991): 4–14.

gan as proof that this point "has already long ago been said."[2] Flinders Petrie popularized the position, and with the publication of his *Egypt and Israel* it became the dominant understanding of the plagues. Petrie took the issue a step further by claiming that the plagues were not only a natural sequence, but also the consequences of seasonal changes. In particular, they followed the cycle of the inundation of the Nile River:

> The river turned to blood, with the fish dying, was the unwholesome stagnant Nile just at the lowest before the inundation, when it is red and swarming with organisms. The Egyptians have to resort to wells and cisterns at this time in the early part of June. The frogs abound after the inundation has come in July. The plagues of insects, murrain, and boils, belong to the hot summer and damp unwholesome autumn. The hail and rain came in January. This is closely fixed by the effect on the crops. The barley must have been up early for the wheat to be yet "hidden" or hardly sprouting. This would show it was planted early in November, in ear by the middle of January, and ripe early in March. The flax has like seasons, and the wheat is a month later. The locusts come in the spring, over the green crops about February. The sand storms bring a thick darkness that may be felt, in March, at the break of the hot winds. And the last plague, the death of the first-born, was at the Exodus in April.... The intervals are about a month apart; from the middle of January to mid April the time agrees to the months.[3]

According to Petrie's calculations, then, the plagues upon Egypt were natural events occurring in less than a twelve-month period.

The most scholarly and detailed attempt to present the plagues as natural disasters was by Greta Hort in the 1950s.[4] According to her study, the first six plagues clearly reflected the ecosystem of ancient Egypt. The first plague was the result of a high inundation that made the river red with sediment (causing it to look like blood). Concurrent excessive precipitation brought flagellates and their bacteria from mountain lakes and streams, resulting in animal death in the river. The death of the fish polluted the water habitat, a disaster which forced the frogs from the river onto dry land. The frogs died, and soon thereafter mosquitoes (or lice) and flies multiplied off the dead amphibians. The insects in turn carried disease (probably anthrax) to the land animals and eventually to humans.

---

2. E. W. Hengstenberg, *Egypt and the Books of Moses* (Edinburgh: Thomas Clark, 1845), 95, 104.

3. W. M. F. Petrie, *Egypt and Israel* (London: Society for Promoting Christian Knowledge, 1911), 35–36.

4. G. Hort, "The Plagues of Egypt," ZAW 69 (1957): 84–103; 70 (1958): 48–59.

Plagues seven through nine were not related sequentially, but they had in common their origination in the atmosphere. Hort emphasized the naturalistic character of these plagues, detailing frequent similar occurrences in Egypt. The final plague may have been merely a reflection of the high infant-mortality rate of ancient Egypt.

Those scholars who hold that the plagues were natural disasters are generally of two camps. Some believe that the fact that the plagues can be explained as natural phenomena actually serves as confirmation of the supernatural.[5] In other words, if the biblical material detailing the natural phenomena is true, then it follows that the entire narrative, including the supernatural elements, is accurate. Most interpreters, however, argue that the commonplace occurrence of phenomena akin to the plagues of Egypt actually explains away the miraculous. The divine or theological elements in the text are merely the author's attempt to dress up a simple naturalistic account. Present-day scholars overwhelmingly adhere to the latter position.

The interpretation of the plagues as natural disasters has obvious weaknesses and breaks down under careful scrutiny. First of all, nowhere in the six chapters detailing the plagues is there any hint of one plague's having been the source of another plague. Only by mere speculation can one argue from the text that the frogs were infected with anthrax, and that the disease was passed on to land animals by lice. Second, the ecological sequence crumbles after the sixth plague because the hailstones of the seventh plague had no relation to the anthrax of plague six. In addition, plagues seven through nine had no chronological connection with one another even though there was a conceptional relationship. And the tenth plague had absolutely no link with the previous plagues.[6] Finally, the argument that plagues one and ten were simply natural phenomena is difficult to defend. The theory that the first plague was symbolic—the water did not turn into blood but merely looked like it—cannot be supported by the text.[7] In no way does the Book of Exodus present that plague as having been metaphorical in nature; rather, it relates the disaster as direct historical narrative. The bib-

---

5. See the discussion in Hengstenberg, *Egypt and the Books of Moses*, 95–98; and A. H. McNeile, *The Book of Exodus* (London: Methuen, 1908), 43.
6. For these criticisms see Z. Zevit, "Three Ways to Look at the Ten Plagues," *BR* 6.3 (1990): 16–23, 42.
7. See C. F. Keil and F. Delitzsch, *The Pentateuch*, vol. 1 of *Commentary on the Old Testament* (Peabody, Mass.: Hendrickson, 1989 reprint), 478, where Keil comments: "The changing of the water into blood is to be interpreted in the same sense as in Joel iii. 4 [2:31], where the moon is said to be turned into blood; that is to say, not as a chemical change into real blood, but as a change in the colour, which caused it to assume the appearance of blood (2 Kings iii. 22)."

lical writer does often relate events phenomenologically, but there are no indicators or clues that he is doing so in this case. In addition, if the plague had been the result of a natural disaster involving only the Nile, why then were even the waters of the pools and reservoirs of Egypt turned to blood? Similarly weak is the theory that the final plague was natural, merely the reflection of a severe infant-mortality rate in ancient Egypt.[8]

The second major position held by scholars today, and one that is gaining more and more support, views the plagues as literary creations. This explanation was pointedly espoused in a 1906 publication by Eduard Meyer, in which he said that the plagues were the free creations of the author of Exodus.[9] More recent authors have built upon the foundations of Meyer's work. J. Coert Rylaarsdam, for instance, has claimed that the account of the ten plagues was artificially assembled by different authors—in this instance, J, E, and P—because no tradition contained all ten plagues. He noted further that "modern scholars have sought to provide a natural explanation at least for the core of each sign. . . . This is a highly dubious and conjectural procedure. . . . Some of them probably rest on actual events that facilitated the escape of the Israelites, and in which they saw the hand of God. But the text now presents a series of piously decorated accounts. . . . The significance and value of this total complex is symbolic rather than historical."[10] This explanation admits that there may be a bare kernel of historical truth: the account of "some of the plagues" may contain a vestige of a bygone historical reality. That truth, however, was only a remembrance or reminiscence of a much later generation.

Some modern commentators have taken the view that the plagues were literary creations to an extreme, but logical, end. The conclusion of the radical Old Testament scholar John Van Seters on this issue serves as a prime example:

> Consequently, there is no mystery about the form and history of the plagues tradition. The Yahwist [J author] created it. . . . In other words, the plagues narrative is a literary creation by the Yahwist that made use of varied traditions of Hebrew prophecy. . . . There is no primary and secondary material, no ancient oral tradition behind the text. The

---

8. For this theory see P. Montet, *Egypt and the Bible* (Philadelphia: Fortress, 1968), 97–98.

9. E. Meyer, *Die Israeliten und ihre Nachbarstämme* (Halle: Max Niemeyer, 1906), 31.

10. J. C. Rylaarsdam, "The Book of Exodus: Introduction and Exegesis," in *Interpreter's Bible* (New York: Abingdon, 1952), 1:839. That position appears to be supported by D. Irvin and T. L. Thompson, "The Joseph and Moses Narratives," in *Israelite and Judaean History*, ed. J. H. Hayes and J. M. Miller (Philadelphia: Westminster, 1977), 149–212 (esp. 198–200).

plagues narrative did not exist as a specific tradition before the Yahwist's work and is, therefore, no older than the exilic period.[11]

The title of Van Seters's article asks the crucial question: "The Plagues of Egypt: Ancient Tradition or Literary Invention?" His answer is plain: the plague narrative is the fabrication of a postexilic author.

Such a position is difficult, if not impossible, to sustain in light of the overall historical credibility of the Exodus record. Van Seters's stance is pure hypothesis. It simply has no valid historical proof. Ironically, he is guilty of the same charge he levels against those who hold to the historical reliability of the plagues account: he indulges in speculation. To give credence to such a radical, out-of-hand reconstruction (or should we say deconstruction?) of history would be harmful and dangerous.

Neither of the widely held interpretations of the plagues provides satisfactory explanations of the meaning and significance of the account. They leave too many unanswered questions. But if the plagues were not simply natural disasters and they were not literary creations, then how are they to be understood?

The Plagues as a Polemic

Some scholars have suggested that the ten plagues were directed by the God of the Hebrews against particular Egyptian deities.[12] There should be no question that the biblical authors understood the plagues in that manner.[13] The Book of Numbers, for example, reports: "The Egyptians were burying all their first-born whom the LORD had struck down among them. The LORD had also executed judgments on their gods" (33:4). In

---

11. J. Van Seters, "The Plagues of Egypt: Ancient Tradition or Literary Invention?" *ZAW* 98 (1986): 31–39. Z. Zevit, "The Priestly Redaction and Interpretation of the Plague Narrative in Exodus," *Jewish Quarterly Review* 66 (1976): 193–211, seems to agree with Van Seters. Zevit argues that the pattern of ten plagues was an original creation of the redactor-compiler rather than "a reflection of any single tradition in his sources" (p. 193). See also A. M. Cartun, "'Who Knows Ten?' The Structural and Symbolic Use of Numbers in the Ten Plagues: Exodus 7:14–13:16," *Union Seminary Quarterly Review* 45 (1991): 65–119.

12. See, e.g., C. Aling, *Egypt and Bible History* (Grand Rapids: Baker, 1981), 103–10; J. J. Davis, *Moses and the Gods of Egypt*, 2d ed. (Grand Rapids: Baker, 1986), 98–153; G. A. F. Knight, *Theology as Narration* (Grand Rapids: Eerdmans, 1976), 62–79; and Sarna, *Exploring Exodus*, 78–80.

13. It is curious that some recent commentators deny the relationship between the plagues and the Egyptian gods. V. P. Hamilton, *Handbook on the Pentateuch* (Grand Rapids: Baker, 1982), 166, says: "It needs to be pointed out that the biblical text gives no indication that the plagues are to be associated with Egyptian religion and deities. The similarities may, therefore, be only coincidental." See also J. H. Sailhamer, *The Pentateuch as Narrative* (Grand Rapids: Zondervan, 1992), 252–53.

fact, the plague account itself contains similar wording: "For I will go through the land of Egypt on that night, and will strike down all the first-born in the land of Egypt, both man and beast; and against all the gods of Egypt I will execute judgments—I am the LORD" (Exod. 12:12). The idea that the disasters that Egypt experienced were a mockery of that land and its customs is unmistakable. The Scriptures even use the term *mockery (ʿālal)* for God's judgment upon Egypt (Exod. 10:2).

Intertestamental literature subscribed to the interpretation of the plagues as a polemic against the gods of Egypt. For example, the author of the Wisdom of Solomon records: "For through those animal deities at whom they (the Egyptians) were indignant by reason of their own suffering, punished by means of those very creatures whom they deemed gods, they came to recognize the true God, perceiving him whom they had formerly denied knowing. Thus did the utter limit of judgment descend upon them."[14]

The apocryphal Book of Jubilees (48:5) also teaches that the plagues were a mockery of the pagan gods of Egypt:

> And the Lord executed a great vengeance on them for Israel's sake, and smote them through (the plagues of) blood and frogs, lice and dog-flies, and malignant boils breaking forth in blains; and their cattle by death; and by hail-stones, thereby He destroyed everything that grew for them; and by locusts which devoured the residue which had been left by the hail; and by darkness; and by (the death of) the first-born of men and animals, and on all their idols the Lord took vengeance and burned them with fire.[15]

One can account for most of the ten plagues in this manner. The opening disaster (Exod. 7:15–25) was clearly directed against the Nile River, which in its inundation was deified and personified as the Egyptian god Hapi. In fact, as early as the Pyramid Texts the Egyptians called the Nile River by the divine name Hapi *(hʿpi)*.[16] They often portrayed the god as a bearded man with female breasts and a hanging stomach (pregnant?), all of which reflect the concept of fertility. And, indeed, Egyptian writings spoke of Hapi as the one who kept Egypt alive. The "Hymn to the Nile," for example, taught that life in Egypt

---

14. *The Wisdom of Solomon*, trans. D. Winston, Anchor Bible (Garden City, N.Y.: Doubleday, 1979), 245. For additional material see E. G. Clark, *The Wisdom of Solomon* (Cambridge: Cambridge University Press, 1973); and J. Geyer, *The Wisdom of Solomon* (London: SCM, 1963).

15. R. H. Charles, *The Book of Jubilees or The Little Genesis* (Jerusalem: Makor, 1972), 205.

16. See S. A. B. Mercer, *The Pyramid Texts*, 4 vols. (New York: Longmans, Green, 1952), 4:65.

came from the Nile: "O all men who uphold the Ennead, fear ye the majesty which his son, the All-Lord, has made, (by) making verdant the two banks. So it is 'Verdant art thou!' So it is 'Verdant art thou!' So it is 'O Nile, verdant art thou, who makest man and cattle to live!'"[17]

A major consequence of the Nile's turning to blood was the death of the fish, a staple of the Egyptian diet.[18] The people were unable to eat or drink from the river.[19] The river and its god could no longer supply the people's needs. This disaster was a demonstration that true sustenance came only from the hand of Yahweh and not from a false pagan deity of the Egyptians.

The second plague (Exod. 8:1-6) also appears to be a contest between deities. The Egyptians regarded the frog as a symbol of divine power and a representation of fertility. One of the main goddesses of Egypt was Hekhet, who was depicted as a human female with a frog's head. She was the spouse of the creator-god Khnum. He fashioned human bodies on his potter's wheel, and then Hekhet blew the breath of life into them and assisted as midwife at their births. Hekhet also had the responsibility to control the multiplication of frogs in ancient Egypt by protecting the frog-eating crocodiles.[20] But Yahweh overwhelmed Hekhet and caused her to be impotent in her task. She could not repel or resist Yahweh's overpowering regeneration of frogs. It was the Hebrew God who really bestowed fertility; he rapidly produced frogs so that they would be a curse upon Egypt. The theme is the sovereignty of God over fertility, over Egypt, over her deities, and over all things.

The third and fourth plagues (Exod. 8:16-24) both involved flying insects as divine judgments against Egypt. The third plague was *kinnim*, a Hebrew term that is not clear in meaning although it likely refers to gnats. Other suggestions are that the *kinnim* were vermin, lice, or maggots.[21] The fourth plague came in the form of *ʿārōb*, which is commonly understood to be a stinging fly, possibly even a mosquito.[22] These

---

17. *ANET*, 372-73. The "Hymn to the Nile" occurs on four papyri: Papyrus Sallier II, Papyrus Anastasi VII, Papyrus Chester Beatty V, and a papyrus in Turin. For a good translation see A. Erman, *The Literature of the Ancient Egyptians* (New York: Dutton, 1927), 146-49.

18. Egypt, of course, had numerous fish deities such as Hat-mehit from the town of Mendes in the delta. She was a minor fish-goddess who was represented as a woman with a fish on her head.

19. The Egyptians believed that blood was a creative power, an efflux or emanation of their gods. That Yahweh could turn the Nile River into blood demonstrated his creative potency.

20. Knight, *Theology as Narration*, 62.

21. L. Koehler and W. Baumgartner, eds., *Lexicon in Veteris Testamenti libros* (Leiden: Brill, 1985), 443.

22. *BDB*, 787.

plagues may have been directed against the Egyptian self-generated god of resurrection, Kheprer, who was symbolized by the flying beetle.[23]

Plague five was the pestilence on the domesticated animals of Egypt (Exod. 9:1–7). Bull cults, of course, are known to have flourished throughout the land in antiquity. Ancient Egyptians viewed the bull as a fertility figure, the great inseminator imbued with the potency and vitality of life. Apis was the most important of the Egyptian sacred bulls. Other bull cults included Buchis (sacred bull of Hermonthis) and Mneuis (Heliopolis). In addition, bulls were understood as embodiments of the great Egyptian gods Ptah and Re.[24] Numerous important female deities were pictured as livestock animals: Isis, queen of the gods, bore cow's horns on her head; Hathor was given a bovine head for her task of protecting the king. The livestock animals provided necessities to the people—in the form of food, milk, clothing, transportation— and they were destroyed in the fifth plague. The biblical author is again demonstrating that Yahweh was sovereign over and in control of all things. The Egyptian gods were imposters.

The subsequent plague of boils (or possibly smallpox) has been identified as a polemic against Imhotep, the vizier of Dynasty 3 who was later deified as a god of medicine and healing.[25] His chapel at Saqqara was used as a sanatorium where cripples flocked from all over Egypt during the Egyptian Late Period (ca. 712–343 B.C.). The problem with this identification is that Imhotep was deified and revered at a much later date than the exodus. Therefore, the sixth plague is incorrectly connected with him. Instead, the malady may have been directed against the Egyptian goddess Sekhmet, the lion-headed deity of plagues. She was responsible for epidemics in ancient Egypt, but ironically she also had the power to heal those who were visited by pestilence. The priests of Sekhmet, one of the oldest medical fraternities in antiquity, included both doctors and veterinary surgeons.[26] Other gods regarded as divine physicians and healers included the Theban god Amon-Re, whom a text from Dynasty 19 describes as "he who dissolves evils and dispels ailments; a physician who heals the eye without having remedies, opening the eyes and driving away the squint . . . Amon. Rescuing whom he desires . . . he makes a lifetime long or shortens it."[27]

23. Knight, *Theology as Narration*, 62–64.
24. G. A. F. Knight, *Nile and Jordan* (London: J. Clarke, 1921), 160.
25. Livingstone, "Plagues and the Exodus," 10.
26. G. Posener, *Dictionary of Egyptian Civilization* (London: Methuen, 1962), 256; and M. Bunson, *The Encyclopedia of Ancient Egypt* (New York: Facts on File, 1991), 239.
27. *ANET*, 369.

The catastrophe of the hail was a mockery of the Egyptian heavenly deities, including Nut (the female representative of the sky and personification of the vault of heaven), Shu (the supporter of the heavens who holds up the sky), and Tefnut (the goddess of moisture).

Locusts were a particularly nasty problem in ancient Egypt. On account of that danger, the ancient Egyptians worshiped the god Senehem, who was the divine protector against ravages from pests.[28] An identification problem exists because Senehem appears to have been a minor deity in dynastic Egypt. Why Yahweh would have concerned himself to mock a subordinate deity is a problem. Perhaps protecting against grasshopper attack was a function not merely of one god, but of the gods in general. A hint of that possibility appears in the Tanis Stele from the reign of Taharqa (Dynasty 25), which speaks of "a fine field, which the gods protected against grasshoppers."[29]

The ancient Egyptians regarded Amon-Re, the personification of the sun, as their chief deity. They believed that Amon-Re in his rising in the east symbolized new life and resurrection—in fact, they considered him to be the creator-god. Papyrus Boulaq 17 ("Hymn to Amon-Re") reflects the universal reverence the ancient Egyptians paid to the sun-god:

> The goodly beloved youth to whom the gods give praise,
> Who made what is below and what is above,
> Who illuminates the Two Lands
> And crosses the heavens in peace:
> The King of Upper and Lower Egypt: Ra, the triumphant,
> Chief of the Two Lands,
> Great of strength, lord of reverence,
> The chief one, who made the entire earth.
> More distinguished than any (other) god. . . .[30]

But when Amon-Re sank in the west, he represented something different and antithetical; he symbolized death and the underworld. When Yahweh so willed (Exod. 10:21–29), the sun was darkened, and Amon-Re was hidden and unable to shine upon his worshipers. During the ninth plague Amon-Re did not rise again and did not give life; his realm was death, judgment, and hopelessness.

The Hebrew writers were quite familiar with the cult of Re in Egypt. In certain pentateuchal texts, for example, the biblical author employed obvious wordplays on the name of the Egyptian god Re and the Hebrew

---

28. *WAS* 3:461 translates the word *snḥm* as *die Heuschrecke* ("locust"), and tentatively parallels it with the Hebrew *sāl'ām*, "an edible, winged locust."
29. *ARE* 4:456.
30. *ANET*, 365.

concept of *ra^c* ("evil"). Apparent allusions are found in Exodus 5:19; 10:10; 32:12, 22; Numbers 11:1; 20:5; and Deuteronomy 9:18. These double entendres were for the purpose of ridiculing the chief deity of Egypt.[31]

The final plague was primarily directed against Pharaoh as a god of Egypt and against the Pharaonic succession.

In summary, the pestilences, Yahweh's conquest of Egypt, and the humiliation of Pharaoh constitute a history of severe contempt for the gods of Egypt. A later parallel can be found in the prophet Jeremiah, when he speaks of contemporary judgment on Egypt: "The LORD of hosts, the God of Israel, says, 'Behold, I am going to punish Amon of Thebes, and Pharaoh, and Egypt along with her gods and her kings, even Pharaoh and those who trust in him'" (Jer. 46:25).

Mockery of Egyptian polytheism found expression in other ways in the Exodus narrative. Exodus 11:7, for example, states that during the final plague "against any of the sons of Israel a dog shall not even sharpen its tongue, whether against man or beast, that you may understand how the LORD makes a distinction between Egypt and Israel." An arguable point is that the author is making a subtle reference here to the impotence of Anubis, the god of the dead and embalming. Anubis, who had a canine form, had no power of life or death over the Israelites, who were protected by Yahweh. The inability of the Egyptian magicians to reproduce most of the plagues pointed to the lack of power of the Egyptian gods whom they represented.[32]

The Plagues as De-Creation

Many scholars have pointed out that Exodus 1–15 owes much of its structure, language, and theology to the Genesis creation account.[33] As Warren Gage states, "the exodus-eisodus history of the hexateuch is so structured as to be a redemptive reenactment of creation."[34] In other words, the account of the deliverance of Israel out of the oppression of Egypt through the plagues and the crossing of the Red Sea reflects the narrative of the original creation. Although the creation theme is reflected in many passages of Exodus, we will take time to consider only three of them.

First of all, in the introductory section of the Book of Exodus there are clear-cut indications that the author was familiar with the Book of

---

31. For a detailed study of these wordplays see G. A. Rendsburg, "The Egyptian Sun-God Ra in the Pentateuch," *Henoch* 10 (1988): 3–15.
32. Sarna, *Exploring Exodus*, 80.
33. See in particular M. G. Kline, *Images of the Spirit* (Grand Rapids: Baker, 1980), 13–42.
34. W. A. Gage, *The Gospel of Genesis* (Winona Lake, Ind.: Carpenter Books, 1984), 20.

Genesis. The first five verses, for instance, show awareness of the Genesis tradition of the seventy persons descended from the patriarch Jacob (Gen. 46:26–27). Most importantly, the biblical writer describes the *Sitz im Leben* of Israel in terms of the cultural mandate of Genesis 1:28: "But the sons of Israel were fruitful and increased greatly, and multiplied, and became exceedingly mighty, so that the land was filled with them" (Exod. 1:7). The Hebrews were fulfilling the command of God given at creation. In addition, Pharaoh's response to the increase of the Hebrews probably reflects the story of Babel in Genesis 11.[35] The author was casting the beginning of the Exodus event as a second creation account.

Second, the water ordeal Moses underwent is reminiscent of the redemption of Noah in Genesis 6–8. After the birth of Moses, his mother Jochebed could not hide him for more than three months, so she placed him in a *gōmeʾ tēbāh* ("wicker basket"; Exod. 2:3). The first term, *gōmeʾ*, is an Egyptian word that means "papyrus."[36] *Tēbāh*, an Egyptian word which means "chest, coffin," is also used in reference to Noah's ark. One should observe as well that in Exodus 2:3 Jochebed covers the wicker basket with "tar and pitch" as Noah did the ark (Gen. 6:14). The deliverance of Noah can be viewed as a re-creation because God directs the cultural mandate of Genesis 1:28 to Noah and his offspring: "And God blessed Noah and his sons and said to them, 'Be fruitful and multiply, and fill the earth'" (Gen. 9:1). That command is the same decree that the Hebrews were fulfilling in Exodus 1 as they multiplied and increased in Egypt. So the deliverance of Israel out of Egypt is being cast by the biblical writer as a re-creation.

Finally, that the exodus is a second act of creation is evident in Exodus 13–15; the Genesis creation account served as the paradigm for Israel's deliverance at the sea. That is to say, "the redemptive creation of Israel at the sea is cast in the same narrative style of original creation as the pillar of divine presence brings light into darkness (Exod. 13:21, cf. the first creative day), the waters are divided (Exod. 14:21, cf. the second creative day), and the dry land emerges (Exod. 14:29, cf. the third creative day)."[37] In Deuteronomy 32:11 God's tender care of Israel after she had passed through the sea is likened to an eagle's hovering over and protecting its newborn. The Hebrew term *rāḥap* ("hovers") used here also occurs in Genesis 1:2, where the Spirit of God "hovered" over the infantile universe. Those are the only two occurrences of *rāḥap* in the Pentateuch. That the biblical author is drawing a parallel be-

---

35. In Gen. 11:3–4 the rulers of Babel have an attitude similar to that of Pharaoh, "Come, let us . . ." (cf. Exod. 1:10–11). Also, like the people of Babel the Egyptians built cities out of bricks (Gen. 11:4).

36. The Egyptians were known to use vessels made of long reeds (see Isa. 18:1–2).

37. Gage, *Gospel of Genesis*, 20–21.

tween the original creation account and the Exodus narrative is further confirmed by his use of the Hebrew term *tōhû* to describe the wilderness (Deut. 32:10). He also used this word to characterize the conditions at the original creation (Gen. 1:2). As with *rāḥap*, *tōhû* also appears nowhere else in the Pentateuch.[38]

The scriptural writer understood and described the exodus as a second creation. It was a new conquest of chaos, another prevailing over the waters of the deep, and a redemptive creation of the people of Israel. This view has found its way into the literature of biblical studies. What has not often been recognized is that the preceding plague account is an ironic undoing or destruction of the creation order in the land of Egypt. God took the creation order of Genesis 1 and reversed it in Exodus 7–12 for the purposes of reducing order to chaos and bringing judgment upon Egypt.[39] The biblical writer conveys this theme in his account of each of the plagues.

Figure 3. **The Plagues as De-Creation**

Creation Day	Creation Description	Plague on Egypt	Plague Description
Day 1 Gen. 1:1–5	Light created out of darkness	Plague 9 Exod. 10:21–29	Darkness prevailing over light
Day 2 Gen. 1:6–8	Ordering and separation of the waters	Plague 1 Exod. 7:15–25	Chaos and destruction brought by the changing of water into blood
Day 3 Gen. 1:9–13	Appearance of dry land and creation of vegetation	Plagues 7–8 Exod. 9:18–10:20	Destruction of vegetation by hail and locusts
Day 4 Gen. 1:14–19	Creation of luminaries	Plague 9 Exod. 10:21–29	Darkening of luminaries
Day 5 Gen. 1:20–23	Creation of birds, fish, and swarming creatures in the sea	Plagues 1–2 Exod. 7:15–8:15	Death of fish; multiplication and death of frogs
Day 6 Gen. 1:24–31	Creation of land animals and humans	Plagues 3–4 Exod. 8:16–24 Plague 5 Exod. 9:1–7 Plague 6 Exod. 9:8–17 Plague 10 Exod. 11–12	Pestilence of insects; anthrax; boils on beasts and humans; destruction of firstborn

---

38. Kline, *Images of the Spirit*, 14–15.
39. The groundbreaking work in this area is Zevit, "Three Ways."

The first day of creation, described in Genesis 1:1–5, consisted of God's bringing forth light out of darkness in order to overcome the *tōhû wābōhû* ("emptiness and wilderness"). That event in Genesis, of course, was a major step in Yahweh's bringing order out of chaos. In Egypt, Yahweh accomplished the opposite by causing the darkness to prevail over the light. He thus reduced order to chaos. Yet the darkness was not completely dominant: Israel had light. That contrast underscores the point of the plague account: Yahweh was re-creating in his establishment of Israel, and he was "de-creating" in his destruction of Egypt.

The second and third days of creation (Gen. 1:6–13) included the separation and gathering of the waters on the earth. Thus God brought the creation into order. With the opening plague in Egypt (Exod. 7:15–25), however, Yahweh begins his destruction of Egypt by changing the waters to blood. Confirmation of the connection between these two events comes from the use of the word *miqĕwēh* in Exodus 7:19: "Then the LORD said to Moses, 'Say to Aaron, "Take your staff and stretch out your hand over the waters of Egypt, over their rivers, over their streams, and over their pools, and over all their reservoirs *(miqĕwēh)* of water, that they may become blood."'" The term *miqĕwēh* was first employed in the Scriptures in Genesis 1:10: "God called the dry land earth, and the gathering *(miqĕwēh)* He called seas; and God saw that it was good." What was originally good for the earth and humanity at creation has now ironically turned into curse and judgment upon the pagan Egyptians.

Genesis 1:9–13 relates the third day of creation: dry land appeared and vegetation sprouted upon it. According to verse 11, three of the principal categories of verdure that became visible were *ʿēśeb* ("herbs"), *pĕrî* ("fruit"), and *ʿēṣ* ("trees"). These three divisions of vegetation were precisely the ones destroyed by the plagues of hail and locusts in Exodus 9:18–10:20. (For the desolation of the *ʿēśeb*, see Exod. 9:22, 25; 10:12, 15; for the *pĕrî*, Exod. 10:15; and for the *ʿēṣ*, Exod. 9:25; and 10:5, 15.)

The purpose of the creation of the luminaries on day four was "to separate the day from the night, and . . . for signs, and for seasons, and for days and years . . . and to separate the light from the darkness" (Gen. 1:14, 18). On that day God not only set the sun, moon, and stars in the sky, but he also established the order of the daily cycle and the calendar. This provided humans with a temporal framework in which to live and work. The ninth plague was a divine darkening of the sun in Egypt, "even a darkness that may be felt" (Exod. 10:21). The natural order established by God at creation was briefly suspended in Egypt—although not for Israel ("all the sons of Israel had light in their dwellings" [Exod. 10:23]).

The fifth day of creation focused on the generation of the birds, fish, and swarming creatures of the sea (Gen. 1:20–23). "Then God said, 'Let the waters teem with swarms of living creatures. . . .'" The Hebrew verb and noun forms used for "teem" and "swarms" in Genesis 1 derive from the root *šrṣ*, which is employed in Exodus 8:3 in regard to the pestilence of the frogs: "And the Nile will swarm with frogs, which will come up and go into your house and into your bedroom and on your bed, and into the houses of your servants and on your people, and into your ovens and into your kneading bowls." So whereas in Genesis 1 God created an ordered process of generation for amphibians, in Exodus 8 he throws that procreative process into chaos by causing frogs to multiply monstrously and to overwhelm the Egyptians. Again Yahweh has taken the uniformity of nature that he established at creation and plunged it into disarray in the land of Egypt.

Also on the fifth day God created the *tannînim* ("great sea monsters"). That same word is used in Exodus 7 in an ironic fashion to point to the destruction of Pharaoh and Egypt at the hands of Yahweh as Aaron hurls a *tannîn* before the king of Egypt. Pharaoh's magicians also throw down *tannînim* in the contest, but Yahweh's *tannîn* swallows the *tannînim* of the Egyptians. Yahweh alone is sovereign and can truly create a *tannîn*. Ironically, some of the later prophets refer to Pharaoh as a *tannîn* (e.g., Ezek. 29:3).

The final day of active creation produced the land animals and humankind (Gen. 1:24–31). One of the principal orders of animals created at that time was the *běhēmāh*, a term frequently translated "cattle." In Exodus this class of beast is particularly devastated in the plague of insects (Exod. 8:17–18), the plague of boils (Exod. 9:9–10), the plague of hail (Exod. 9:19, 22, 25), and the plague of the death of the firstborn (Exod. 11:5; 12:12). In addition, the Hebrew word *ʾādām*, used for the creation of humankind in Genesis 1:26–28, is employed in Exodus for the people ravaged and destroyed by the plagues of boils (Exod. 9:9–10), hail (Exod. 9:19, 22, 25), and the death of the firstborn (Exod. 12:12).

In summary, the principal objects of the six-day creation as related in Genesis 1 were assaulted and thrown into confusion in Egypt by the Lord's onslaught with the plagues as related in Exodus 7–12. In addition, each of the ten plagues was directed against the natural order of creation. This was no mere coincidence. Yahweh was hurling order into chaos. It may be argued that a weakness of this interpretation is that the plagues do not follow the sequence of the days of creation. But that is the point—chaos, not order, reigned in Egypt.

The Concept of *Maʾat*

As we have seen, the plagues on Egypt were an ironic reversal of the created order as understood by the Hebrews and recorded in Genesis 1. It is important to recognize also that the ten pestilences of Exodus 7–12 were a polemic against the Egyptian concept of the created order denoted by the hieroglyphic term *maʾat*. That is to say, Yahweh's attack on the Egyptians in the plagues was an assault not only on their deities and Pharaoh, but on Egypt's very ideas of creation, order, and harmony in the universe.[40]

Much of the literature concerning ancient Egypt conceives of and translates *maʾat* as "truth" or "justice" or "right."[41] In reality, these terms cover only three aspects of *maʾat; maʾat* was an even more general and foundational concept of the universe. It was, as Georges Posener notes, "the equilibrium of the whole universe, the harmonious co-existence of its elements, and the essential cohesion, indispensable for maintaining the created forms."[42] *Maʾat* was the "cosmic force of harmony, order, stability, and security . . . and the organizing quality of created phenomena."[43] It may be simply defined as universal order.

Maʾat was a result of the first creation and part of the inherent structure of creation. *Maʾat* held order together. *Maʾat*, therefore, was the antithesis of chaos. It was a dynamic force not limited to the initial structure of creation, but always necessary because "the voracity of the forces of chaos continued to menace the very existence of the created world."[44] Consequently, the Egyptians strove to maintain *maʾat* in their earthly existence. *Maʾat* was not merely an ideal concept removed from daily living, but the model for human behavior. Humans had to struggle to preserve *maʾat* and to keep cosmic balance upon the earth. "Strict adherence to *maʾat* allowed the Egyptians to feel secure with the world and with the divine plan for all creation . . . *maʾat* was the true essence of creation."[45]

The idea of order was critically important in the Egyptian conception of eternal happiness. When a person died, the heart was weighed against the feather of truth and righteousness—actually the feather of *maʾat*—to determine one's fitness for heavenly bliss (see pp. 96–98). Even in death there had to be harmony, stability, and order.

---

40. For this understanding of the plagues see J. K. Hoffmeier, "Egypt, Plagues in," in *ABD* 2:374–78.
41. *WAS* 2:18–19.
42. Posener, *Dictionary*, 155. For a contrasting view see M. V. Fox, "World Order and Maʾat: A Crooked Parallel," *JANES* 23 (1995): 37–48.
43. J. A. Wilson, *The Burden of Egypt* (Chicago: University of Chicago Press, 1951), 48.
44. Posener, *Dictionary*, 155.
45. Bunson, *Encyclopedia of Ancient Egypt*, 152.

In ancient Egypt, the king had the duty to maintain *ma'at;* he was considered the personification of universal order.[46] Thus, in the "Instruction for King Meri-ka-Re," the Pharaoh is advised by his father to "do *ma'at* whilst thou endurest upon earth."[47] The "Prophecy of Neferti" presents the picture of Egypt in chaos: "The land is completely perished, (so that) no remainder exists, (so that) not (even) the black of the nail survives from what was fated. This land is (so) damaged (that) there is no one who is concerned with it, no one who speaks, no eye that weeps. . . . The sun disc is covered over. . . . The rivers of Egypt are empty. . . . This land is helter-skelter."[48] But the promise of a new king (probably Amenemhat I) gives hope to the beleaguered land: "(Then) it is that a king will come, belonging to the south, Ameni, the triumphant, his name. . . . And justice *(ma'at)* shall come again to its place, and iniquity/chaos, it is cast out."

Every Pharaoh had the obligation to reestablish and reaffirm *ma'at* upon accession to the throne. The forces of chaos could upset *ma'at*, so at the advent of a new king, order had to be restored. "The means by which the king established *ma'at* were his 'Authoritative Utterance' and his 'Understanding.'"[49] A primary responsibility of Pharaoh was to confirm and consolidate the status quo of *ma'at* and to maintain the order of creation throughout his reign. Accordingly, Vizier Ptah-hetep (Dynasty 5) could proclaim: "*Ma'at* is great, its value enduring. It has not been disturbed since the days of him who created it."

The importance of *ma'at* for Egyptian kingship should not be underestimated. The idea of *ma'at* played a central role in the king's identification with the god Horus. In the Pyramid Texts, Snofru is called "Lord of *ma'at*" and Userkaf named "Performer of *ma'at*." Restoring and maintaining this harmony were imperatives for the Egyptian king, expectations that befit his office as the son of Re and the god-king.

When Yahweh assailed Egypt with the ten plagues, he was casting the universal order of creation *(ma'at)* into chaos. This was a direct challenge to the power and sovereignty of Pharaoh: could he maintain *ma'at* or not? Could he by divine utterance ("Thus says Pharaoh," Exod. 5:10) hold together the universe and hold off the onslaught of Yahweh? That he could not underscores the main purpose of the plague account: "to challenge this basic concept [*ma'at*] by showing that the Pharaoh was powerless before the God of the covenant, Yahweh (Exod. 12:12)."[50] The plague account was an unmasking of Pharaoh. He was

---

46. C. Aldred, *The Egyptians* (London: Thames and Hudson, 1961), 161.
47. Wilson, *Burden*, 119.
48. *ANET*, 445.
49. Aldred, *The Egyptians*, 161.
50. Sailhamer, *Pentateuch as Narrative*, 252.

not a deity, and he certainly did not control the operation of the universe. Yahweh is sovereign.

We have seen that the plague account of Exodus 7–12 had a variety of purposes. In general, it portrayed the pestilences as an attack against many of the deities of Egypt. Theological, historical, linguistic, and exegetical considerations clearly support such an interpretation. The account, however, had a more specific and pointed aim: the plagues were an overwhelming assault on Pharaoh and his status as a god in Egypt. That he was the main object of Yahweh's attack is fully confirmed by the account of the serpent confrontation in Exodus 7 and by a study of the concept of *ma'at* in Egyptian history. Ultimately, the principal aim of the plagues was the glorification of Yahweh and the recognition of his sovereignty over all. The text itself underscores that purpose: "And the Egyptians shall know that I am the Lord, when I stretch out My hand on Egypt and bring out the sons of Israel from their midst" (Exod. 7:5; see also 7:17; 8:19, 22; 10:7; 14:4, 18, 25).

7
The Travel Itinerary of the Hebrews from Egypt

The record of Israel's journey from Egypt to Canaan is found in various places in the Pentateuch, including Exodus 12–19, Numbers 11–12, and Deuteronomy 10. However, the principal account detailing the route of the escape from Egypt, the wilderness wanderings, and the final approach to Palestine is Numbers 33:1–49. This passage appears to be a uniform, consistent, complete itinerary written early on.[1] Those who hold to the common view in biblical scholarship disagree, maintaining that Numbers 33 is a composite document consisting of various sources and editorial glosses.[2] But there is no reason to date the piece to postexilic times and describe it as a very late compilation of a priestly author.[3] More reasonable are the conclusions of Jacob Milgrom: "It is hardly likely that this chapter [Numbers 33] is a composite of place-names drawn from other Pentateuchal sources. To the contrary, it is more logical to assume that since so many names in Numbers 33 are

---

1. See the important discussion by G. I. Davies in "The Wilderness Itineraries: A Comparative Study," *Tyndale Bulletin* 25 (1974): 46–81; idem, *The Way of the Wilderness* (Cambridge: Cambridge University Press, 1979), 58–61.
2. See in particular the study of J. de Vaulx, *Les Nombres* (Paris: J. Gabalda, 1972), 372–82.
3. See, e.g., P. J. Budd, *Numbers*, Word Biblical Commentary, vol. 5 (Waco: Word, 1984), 350–57; M. Noth, *Numbers: A Commentary* (Philadelphia: Westminster, 1968), 242–46; and, especially, G. B. Gray, *A Critical and Exegetical Commentary on Numbers*, International Critical Commentary (Edinburgh: T. and T. Clark, 1903), xxix–xxx. The perspective that the chapter is a unit from Moses' time may be found in T. R. Ashley, *The Book of Numbers*, New International Commentary on the Old Testament (Grand Rapids: Eerdmans, 1993), 624–25; and R. B. Allen, "Numbers," in *Expositor's Bible Commentary*, ed. F. E. Gaebelein, vol. 2 (Grand Rapids: Zondervan, 1990), 983–92.

unattested anywhere else, it represents the master list for the other sources. In other words, the chapter is not a composite text but, in the main, an authentic unified itinerary."[4]

That Numbers 33 is an original and true account of the Hebrews' wilderness journey is supported by the fact that the military itinerary is a widely attested literary genre in the ancient Near East.[5] In Mesopotamian literature the expeditions of Tiglath-pileser I (ca. 1114–1076 B.C.), Shalmaneser III (ca. 858–824 B.C.), and Sennacherib (ca. 704–681 B.C.) are cases in point.[6] Itineraries frequently appear in Egyptian texts as well. Beginning with Thutmosis III (ca. 1479–1425 B.C.) campaign journals were recorded. Amenophis II (ca. 1427–1401 B.C.), Sethos I (ca. 1306–1290 B.C.), and Shishak are among numerous Egyptian kings who left written accounts of their expeditions.[7]

One might argue that Numbers 33 does not record a military campaign and therefore is not of the same literary style or form as the ancient Near Eastern documents we have mentioned. However, Numbers 33 was in fact designed according to the form of a military itinerary. For example, verse 1, which sets the context for the wilderness journey, states that the Israelites were leaving Egypt according to their ṣibĕʾōt ("hosts, armies"), a term that almost always has military overtones. In addition, verse 3 describes Israel as leaving Egypt *yād rāmāh* (lit., "with a high hand"). When these words are employed together in the Old Testament, they symbolize military might (Deut. 32:27; Mic. 5:8).[8] Further, military matters circumscribe and bracket Numbers 33. At the beginning of the account Israel (vv. 3–4) is marching forth out of Egypt in military array after the great victory of Yahweh over Egypt and her gods. Immediately after the account the Lord speaks to the Hebrews about driving the inhabitants of Canaan out of their land (Num. 33:50–56). The overarching tenor of this chapter is combat, which points to the conclusion that Numbers 33 is an ancient Near Eastern campaign itinerary.

Numbers 33:2 notes that Moses wrote down the itinerary: "Moses recorded their starting places according to their journeys by the command of the Lord." That statement has much force because it is the only place in Numbers where Moses is specifically designated as a chroni-

---

4. J. Milgrom, *Numbers*, JPS Torah Commentary (Philadelphia: Jewish Publication Society, 1990), 497.
5. This subject has been explored in great detail by Davies, "Wilderness Itineraries," 52–78.
6. *ANET*, 274–87.
7. *ANET*, 234–64 passim.
8. The phrase is also used of Yahweh's power in battle during the hostilities of the day of the Lord (see, e.g., Isa. 26:11).

cler or recorder of events. There is nothing in the text to lead one to doubt the authenticity of the claim of Mosaic authorship of the itinerary.[9]

The problem that scholars face when studying Numbers 33 is that so few sites can be identified with any certainty. Of the fifty-one geographical stations mentioned in the passage, at best only about ten of the sites or topographical features are known. In Sinai, very few of the names of the exodus itinerary have been preserved in Arab nomenclature.[10] In addition, no physical remains have been uncovered in the Sinai that would indicate the route of the Hebrews. Evidence may be there, but little archaeological work has been attempted in this regard.[11] To make the matter of tracking the Hebrews' travels even more difficult, some of the names in Numbers 33 reflect noteworthy events that occurred to the Hebrews at the time and thus would not be expected to survive outside their literature.[12] No wonder scholars disagree widely regarding the route of Israel from Egypt to the Promised Land. Much of it remains conjectural. Nahum Sarna asserts that "it is easier to delineate the route that the fleeing Israelites avoided than to chart the course they actually took to their destination, the land of Canaan."[13] With this caveat in mind, we will yet attempt to use current scholarly research to reconstruct the route of the exodus.

From Egypt to the Wilderness (Num. 33:3–8)

The biblical writer structured the itinerary of Numbers 33 according to Israel's *môṣāʾêhem*, literally "their goings out" (v. 2). This Hebrew term, a derivative of the verb *yṣʾ*, normally denoted source, origin, or beginning.[14] The vein that yields silver (Job 28:1), the spring that gives rise to water (2 Chron. 32:30; Ps. 107:33–35), and the bud from which the flower derives (Job 38:27) were each called *môṣāʾ* in the Hebrew Bible.

---

9. Milgrom, *Numbers*, 498.
10. See the discussion by K. A. Kitchen, "Wilderness," in *Illustrated Bible Dictionary*, ed. J. D. Douglas, 3 vols. (Leicester: Inter-Varsity, 1980), 3:1644–45.
11. A basic assumption has been that nomads leave behind few physical remains and, therefore, one should expect no evidence of the Hebrews' travels in Sinai. The argument is flawed because nomads do in fact leave plenty of remains, some of which have been dated as early as the Early Bronze Age (ca. 3000 B.C.). See S. A. Rosen, "Finding Evidence of Ancient Nomads," *BAR* 14.5 (1988): 46–53, 58–59.
12. E.g., Kibroth-hattaavah (Num. 33:17) was given its name because of the greed of the people (Num. 11:31–35). Marah (Num. 33:9) received its name because of the bitter waters encountered there (Exod. 15:23–27).
13. N. M. Sarna, *Exploring Exodus: The Heritage of Biblical Israel* (New York: Schocken, 1986), 103.
14. *TDOT* 6:225–50; and R. L. Harris, G. L. Archer, and B. K. Waltke, *Theological Wordbook of the Old Testament* (Chicago: Moody, 1980), 1:393–94.

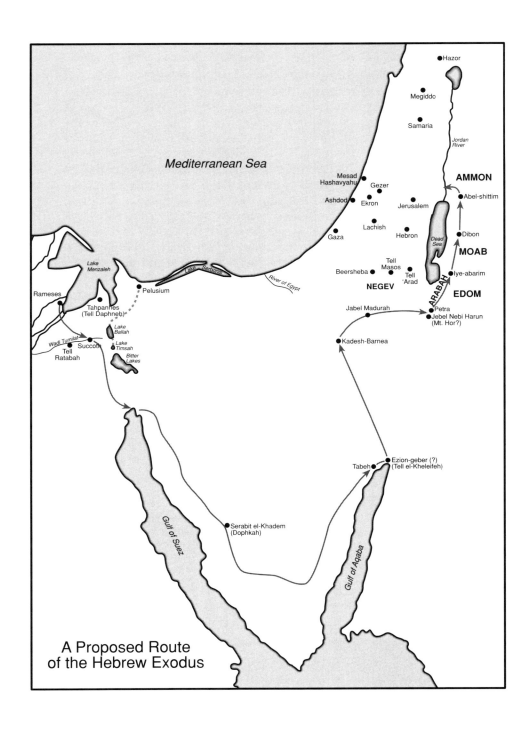

The word also signified the place of a journey's commencement, whether it be the position of the sun at dawn (Ps. 19:6; Hos. 6:3) or the exit from the sanctuary (Ezek. 42:11; 43:11; 44:5). Simply put, *môṣāʾ* denoted a starting point or a place of departure. The sites listed in Numbers 33, then, were not merely geographical markers for the Israelites as they passed through various regions, but places of actual encampment and departure.[15]

Confirmation that Numbers 33 served as an encampment itinerary appears in the text itself. The Hebrew verb *ḥānāh*, "to camp," appears forty-two times in a space of forty-five verses. *Ḥānāh* bears the basic meaning "to bend, curve," and when it is applied to settlement areas, it perhaps reflects the circular configuration of an encampment. Recent studies by Israel Finkelstein have demonstrated that the Hebrews probably camped in an elliptical pattern during the wilderness wanderings.[16] Later, the Israelites designed their first settlements in Canaan in an ovate form.

The author of Numbers identifies the first departure site of the Hebrews as the Egyptian city of Rameses (vv. 3, 5, "and they journeyed from Rameses"). That town appears to have been a home base for the Hebrews in Egypt. According to Exodus 1:11, the Israelites had constructed a storage city at Rameses: "And they built for Pharaoh storage cities, Pithom and Raamses." The location of Rameses has been a matter of debate for a long time. Some early documents, including the Palestinian Targum, Pseudo-Jonathan (Targum Yerushalmi I), and Josephus, place Rameses at the site of Pelusium (Tell el-Farama) on the edge of the Mediterranean Sea just west of Lake Serbonis.[17] Some scholars have agreed with that identification.[18] Other researchers have looked farther south for the location of Rameses, such as at Phacusa or Memphis.[19] All these sites, however, have proven to be archaeologically, historically, or geographically incompatible with the evidence for the location of Rameses.

---

15. The NIV translation of *môṣāʾ* as "stage" misses the sense of way station that the word carries. Among the versions that properly translate the term as "starting point" are the NASB, NKJV, NRSV, and NJB.

16. I. Finkelstein, *The Archaeology of the Israelite Settlement* (Jerusalem: Israel Exploration Society, 1988); idem, "Searching for Israelite Origins," *BAR* 14.5 (1988): 34–45, 58.

17. Davies, *Way of the Wilderness*, 19.

18. A. Mallon, *Les Hébreux en Egypte* (Rome: Pontificium Institutum Biblicum, 1922); and A. H. Gardiner, "The Geography of the Exodus," in *Recueil d'études égyptologiques dediées à la mémoire de Jean-François Champollion* (Paris: E. Champion, 1922), 213–14.

19. See the discussion of C. deWit, *The Date and Route of the Exodus* (London: Tyndale, 1960), 13–16.

One of the principal issues in the discussion is the fact that Egyptian sources designate a variety of towns as Rameses.[20] Most of these cities are to be referred to the reign of Rameses II (ca. 1290–1224 B.C.), although a few may be referred to the time of Rameses III (ca. 1194–1163 B.C.). M. A. el-Maqsoud has uncovered one of these "Rameses" sites at Tell Haboua.[21] The name "Rameses" also appears on occasion to signify a region, as it does in Genesis 47:11.

Another problem in attempting to identify Rameses was outlined by Donald Redford in 1963.[22] He argued that the biblical Rameses could not be the delta capital of the Ramessides because the latter was called Pr-Rameses in Egyptian texts: "But is Raamses to be equated with Ramses II's new capital? The latter during the late New Kingdom bore the name Pr Rꜥ-mś-św whence we should expect a Hebrew פי־רעמסס. Biblical Raamses and Pr Rꜥ-mś-św, apart from the personal name, seem to have nothing in common."[23] Manfred Bietak has adequately answered Redford's challenge by demonstrating, on the basis of earlier work by Alan Gardiner and Wolfgang Helck, that the Pr of Pr Rꜥ-mś-św does drop off in various grammatical situations. The abbreviated form could have easily transferred to another language.[24]

Most investigators have situated Rameses either at Tanis (San el-Hagar) or at Qantir (Tell el-Dabꜥa). Tanis has been the more popular of the two identifications.[25] But, as Edward Wente has pointed out, little belonging to the Ramesside periods is *in situ* at the town.[26] None of the buildings at Tanis appear to have been erected before Psusennes I of Dynasty 21. Many of the Ramesside blocks and monuments were robbed from other towns and brought to Tanis as building material. Qantir was one of the Ramesside sites plundered by kings of Dynasties 21 and 22 in order to build Tanis, which was not a very important town during the Ramesside dynasties (19–20).

---

20. A. H. Gardiner, "The Delta Residence of the Ramessides," *JEA* 5 (1918): 127–38, 179–200, 242–71; and K. A. Kitchen, "The Exodus," in *ABD* 2:700–708.

21. M. A. el-Maqsoud, "Un monument du roi 'Aa-sḥ-r' Nḥsy à Tell Haboua (Sinaï nord)," *ASAE* 69 (1983): 3–5; idem, "Une nouvelle forteresse sur la route d'Horus: Tell Heboua 1986 (Nord-Sinaï)," *Papyrologie et l'Egyptologie de Lille* 9 (1987): 13–16.

22. D. B. Redford, "Exodus I 11," *VT* 13 (1963): 401–18. One needs to be careful with this article because it contains some misinformation. See the response by W. Helck, "Tkw und die Ramses-stadt," *VT* 15 (1965): 35–48.

23. Redford, "Exodus I 11," 409–10.

24. M. Bietak, "Comments on Exodus," in *Egypt, Israel, and Sinai*, ed. A. F. Rainey (Tel Aviv: Tel Aviv University Press, 1987), 163–71.

25. See, e.g., H. Brugsch, *L'Exode et les monuments égyptiens* (Leipzig: J. C. Hinrichs, 1875); deWit, *Date and Route of the Exodus*, 13.

26. E. F. Wente, "Rameses," in *ABD* 5:617–18.

A few writers have concluded that the Bible itself mistakenly sites Rameses at the town of Tanis (Heb., Zoan). Bietak, for instance, claims that "according to Psalm 78 [vv. 12, 43], which is of post-exilic date, the site of Ramesses clearly is located at Tanis."[27] He further argues that Rameses is actually to be identified with Qantir, and therefore the Bible must be incorrect in this matter. In like manner Redford regards Numbers 13:22 as being in error because it identifies Tanis (Zoan) with Rameses: "Early excavators, such as P. Montet, mistakenly identified Zoʿan with Pi-Ramesses and Avaris, an identification now universally abandoned *(cf. Num 13:22 for a similar mistake)*."[28]

There is difficulty, however, in seeing how either Psalm 78 or Numbers 13 can be understood to identify Rameses with the city of Tanis. Psalm 78 never mentions Tanis, but in verses 12 and 43 identifies the area of the plagues merely as *śĕdēh ṣōʿan*, "the field of Zoan." The Hebrew term *śdh* often broadly designates a region, an area, or even a country (e.g., Gen. 25:27; Exod. 10:15; 22:30; and Deut. 21:1). Consider also that in both verses the expression "the field of Zoan" is in poetic parallel with "the land of Egypt." "The field of Zoan" is merely another way to identify the land of Egypt—they are one and the same. Take note as well that the word "Rameses" is not found in this psalm.

To argue that the Bible identifies Rameses with Tanis in Numbers 13:22 is equally dubious. The text says parenthetically, "Now Hebron was built seven years before Zoan in Egypt." How that passage can be used to determine the site of Rameses is perplexing, to say the least. The purpose of the statement is to establish the date of the founding of Hebron by relating it to a known date—the founding of Tanis. Tanis appears to have been founded in the early second millennium. Recent excavations at Tell Hebron indicate that the first fortified city dates to the Middle Bronze II period (ca. 2000–1750 B.C.).[29] The correspondence in dating is striking.

Widely accepted today is the belief that Rameses is located at Qantir (Tell el-Dabʿa), about seventeen miles southwest of Tanis. Excavations of the site in the last twenty-five years have confirmed that identification.[30] Qantir was an important city in the eastern Nile delta during the second millennium B.C. In the Second Intermediate Period (ca. 1640–

---

27. Bietak, "Comments on Exodus," 166.
28. D. B. Redford, "Zoan," in *ABD* 6:1106–7 (italics added).
29. A. Ofer, "Hebron," in *NEAEHL* 2:606–9.
30. See M. Bietak, *Tell el-Dabʿa*, vol. 2 (Vienna: Oesterreichische Akademie der Wissenschaften, 1975); idem, *Avaris and Piramesse* (Oxford: British Academy, 1979); idem, "Avaris and Piramesse," *Proceedings of the British Academy* 65 (1979): 225–89; E. P. Uphill, "Pithom and Raamses: Their Location and Significance," *JNES* 27 (1968): 291–316 and 28 (1969): 15–39.

1532 B.C.) the city witnessed a massive influx of foreigners, and it probably served as the capital of the Hyksos (Dynasty 15).[31] So a foreign Asiatic influence was dominant at Qantir in this time period:

> The period has recently become better known through systematic excavations by an Austrian expedition at Tell ed Debaa, near the site of Qantir in the eastern Delta. Here a temple and burial site have been brought to light. . . . The non-Egyptian pottery and grave goods are identical to those of the Middle Bronze Age in Palestine. Archeologically it is as if the site were actually in Palestine. The characteristic pottery ware is the so-called Tell el Yahudiyeh juglet.[32]

Following a hiatus during Dynasty 18, Haremhab and the Ramessides rebuilt Qantir. Rameses II appears to have done most of the planning for and construction at the site. To the north of the mound, excavators uncovered what seems to have been a factory that produced decorated glazed tiles for architectural ornament.[33] The tiles, painted with beautiful floral designs, were made especially for Pharaonic palaces. The names of kings, for example, Sethos I and Rameses II, have been found on a few of the tiles. Some ostraca discovered in the factory bear the name Rameses.[34]

The Ramessides constructed buildings and monuments in the delta by employing foreign labor, most of which consisted of slaves. The Egyptian document Papyrus Leiden 348 informs us that a group called the ʿapiru were engaged in "hauling stones to the great pylon" of one of Pi-Rameses' temples.[35] A term that means "fugitives, refugees," ʿapiru was applied in antiquity to people who were present all over the ancient Near East in the second millennium B.C.[36] To equate the Hebrews with the ʿapiru is a mistake, although perhaps the Israelites were a segment of the larger social grouping called ʿapiru. In any event, Qantir seems to be the first departure point for the Hebrews on their journey to Canaan.

Although Pithom is not mentioned in the Numbers 33 itinerary, we will discuss its location briefly because the site is mentioned in connection with "Raamses" in Exodus 1:11. Most scholars appear to favor Tell

---

31. It was known as Avaris in this early period.
32. W. W. Hallo and W. K. Simpson, *The Ancient Near East: A History* (New York: Harcourt Brace Jovanovich, 1971), 251.
33. W. C. Hayes, *Glazed Tiles from a Palace of Ramesses at Kantir* (New York: Metropolitan Museum of Art, 1937).
34. Bietak, *Tell el-Dabʿa*, 2:28–43.
35. A. H. Gardiner, *Late-Egyptian Miscellanies* (Brussels: Fondation égyptologique de la reine Elisabeth, 1937), 132–37.
36. J. Bottéro, *Le Problème des Ḫabiru à la 4e rencontre assyriologique internationale* (Paris: Cahiers de la société asiatique, 1954), 160–61.

el-Maskhuta, near the eastern end of the Wadi Tumilat, as the location of biblical Pithom. Edouard Naville, the nineteenth-century excavator of Tell el-Maskhuta, first proposed this identification.[37] Naville had uncovered a number of monuments from the period of the Ramessides and Dynasties 21–22 (eleventh and tenth centuries B.C.). Two of them bear inscriptions that make reference to a place called Per-Atum ("house of Atum"), the Egyptian way of saying Pithom.[38] On that basis, Naville believed he had uncovered the biblical city, and numerous scholars have since concurred with his identification.[39]

Recent excavations at Tell el-Maskhuta have revealed, however, "absolutely no evidence for a New Kingdom or 19th Dynasty occupation at the site."[40] Pottery and other dating factors indicate that Tell el-Maskhuta was not a city prior to the Saite period (seventh and sixth centuries B.C.), when it was called Per-Atum or Pithom. John Holladay concludes that this point destroys the integrity of Exodus 1:11: the verse "is an anachronistic gloss to the developing literature of the Passover Haggadah by Judean refugees."[41] On the other hand, there is no a priori reason that biblical Pithom must be located at Tell el-Maskhuta. It is, first of all, a poor assumption to say that biblical Pithom must be located near Rameses (Qantir) in the eastern Nile delta. The biblical text does not presuppose that location. It is likely that the reason Pithom is not mentioned in the escape itinerary of the Hebrews is that it was not in the same area as Rameses and Succoth. In fact, there were many sites throughout Egypt, primarily temple estates, that bore the name Per-Atum.[42] Biblical Pithom must be sited at a location other than Tell el-Maskhuta.

---

37. E. Naville, *The Store-City of Pithom and the Route of the Exodus* (London: Trubner, 1885).

38. Redford, "Exodus I 11," 403–8.

39. E.g., P. Montet, *Egypt and the Bible* (Philadelphia: Fortress, 1968), 57; T. E. Peet, *Egypt and the Old Testament* (Liverpool: University Press of Liverpool, 1923), 85–87; and H. H. Rowley, *From Joseph to Joshua* (London: British Academy, 1950), 3.

40. J. S. Holladay, Jr., "Maskhuta, Tell el-," in *ABD* 4:590. For the excavation reports see idem, *Cities of the Delta,* part 3, *Tell el-Maskhuta* (Malibu, Calif.: Undena, 1982); idem, "The Wadi Tumilat Project—1977 and 1978 Seasons," *Qadmoniot* 12 (1979): 85–90 (in Hebrew); and idem, "The Wadi Tumilat Project: Tell el-Maskhuta," *Canadian Mediterranean Institute Bulletin* 7.2 (1987): 1–7.

41. Holladay, in *ABD* 4:591; see also idem, "A Biblical/Archaeological Whodunit," *Canadian Mediterranean Institute Bulletin* 8.2 (1988): 6–8.

42. *AEL* 2:57–58; Redford, "Exodus I 11," 403. A letter from Dynasty 19, for example, mentions the place-name Per-Atum: "We have finished passing the tribes of the Shasu of Edom through the Fortress of Merneptah-Hotephirma . . . in Theku, to the pools of Pithom, of Merneptah-Hotephirma in Theku" (*ARE* 3:273). Although Pithom in this passage is not a city, the reference yet demonstrates the common use of the name in ancient Egypt.

Some scholars have argued that Tell Ratabah, located in the Wadi Tumilat about eight miles to the west of Tell el-Maskhuta, is the site of biblical Pithom.[43] This theory has not met with wide acceptance in the academic community. E. P. Uphill is convinced that biblical Pithom sits at Heliopolis (Tell Hisn at the southernmost extreme of the delta), where numerous buildings from the New Kingdom era have been found, including a large temple of the god Re along with several lesser-known temples. Uphill's identification may in fact be correct.[44]

The first station recorded in Numbers 33 is Succoth (v. 5). Exodus 12:37 chronicles the same information: "Now the sons of Israel journeyed from Rameses to Succoth." Some researchers propose that Succoth is to be found at Tell el-Maskhuta.[45] The name Succoth, apparently derived from the Egyptian *tkw* (Tjeku), has been discovered on numerous monuments at Tell el-Maskhuta. The same problem exists for this identification, however, as for the attempt to locate Pithom at Tell el-Maskhuta: urban occupation did not begin at Tell el-Maskhuta until the seventh and sixth centuries B.C. E. L. Bleiberg has attempted to solve this problem by asserting that Tjeku (Succoth) was originally a region in the Wadi Tumilat area of Egypt and was later located specifically at Tell el-Maskhuta.[46] He is probably correct in this regard.

Papyrus Anastasi V, an Egyptian text from the end of the thirteenth century B.C., may help in determining the Hebrew route within Egypt. The text, in the form of a letter written by a chief bowman from a place called Tjeku, tells of the pursuit of two slaves fleeing from Egypt into Asia. Three place-names are mentioned: "I reached the enclosure wall of Tjeku on the third month of the third season . . . to the south . . . . When I reached *htm*, they told me that the scout had come from the desert [saying that] they had passed the walled place north of Migdol."[47] Let us suppose that Tjeku is a regional name for the Wadi Tumilat. The slaves headed south from there to *htm*, which may correspond to biblical Etham (at least it is a phonetic possibility). The slaves then ran to Migdol, which appears to have been located on the edge of the desert. The order of escape, Succoth-Etham-Migdol, is similar to the account

---

43. Gardiner, "Delta Residence," 127–38, 179–200, 242–71; and K. A. Kitchen, "Exodus," in *Zondervan Pictorial Encyclopedia of the Bible*, ed. M. C. Tenney, 5 vols. (Grand Rapids: Zondervan, 1975), 2:428–36.
44. Uphill, "Pithom and Raamses," *JNES* 27 and 28.
45. Kitchen, "Exodus," in *ABD* 2:700–708; idem, "Exodus," in *Zondervan Pictorial Encyclopedia*, 2:429; Y. Aharoni, *The Land of the Bible* (Philadelphia: Westminster, 1967), 179; B. Beitzel, *The Moody Atlas of Bible Lands* (Chicago: Moody, 1985), 86.
46. E. L. Bleiberg, "The Location of Pithom and Succoth," *Ancient World* 6 (1983): 21–27.
47. *ANET*, 259.

of the Hebrews' departure in Numbers 33:6–7: "And they journeyed from Succoth, and camped in Etham, which is on the edge of the wilderness. And they journeyed from Etham, and turned back to Pi-hahiroth, which faces Baal-zephon; and they camped before Migdol." The Egyptian papyrus raises the possibility that the Israelites fled Egypt on a common escape route into the wilderness. Some scholars vehemently disagree with that reconstruction, however.[48]

Perhaps the fugitives fled south before attempting to cross into the Sinai wilderness because the eastern boundary of Egypt was protected by a huge canal that appears to have run from Pelusium on the Mediterranean Sea to Lake Timsah just to the east of the Wadi Tumilat.[49] The canal measured twenty meters wide at the bottom and seventy meters wide at water level. Diagonal irrigation trenches can be seen in the northern sections of the canal, an indication that it was used to some extent for irrigation. Its primary function, however, seems to have been for defense and containment—to keep Asiatics out and slaves in. The canal was probably built either during the First Intermediate Period (ca. 2134–2040 B.C.) or during the Middle Kingdom (ca. 2040–1640 B.C.) when Asiatics were particularly troublesome to Egypt.[50]

The Wadi Tumilat is known to have had ancient canal systems, but most of these were erected later than the New Kingdom period and thus would have posed no threat to fugitives fleeing to the south prior to that time.[51] In our reconstruction, then, the Hebrews would have left Succoth, the region of the Wadi Tumilat, and traveled south towards Etham and Migdol, looking for an eastern passage into the Sinai wilderness. Etham has not been identified. Migdol, originally a Semitic term meaning "tower/fortress,"[52] was borrowed by the Egyptians, who from the New Kingdom on used it as a place-name for numerous sites.[53] A network of Egyptian fortresses lined the eastern border of Egypt during the New Kingdom, and any one of them could have gone by the name Migdol.

Numbers 33:7 states that on their way from Etham to Migdol the Hebrews passed by Baal-zephon. Baal-zephon was the name of an im-

---

48. A. H. Gardiner, "The Ancient Military Road between Egypt and Palestine," *JEA* 6 (1920): 109.

49. See A. Sneh, T. Weissbrod, and I. Perath, "Evidence for an Ancient Egyptian Frontier Canal," *American Scientist* 63 (1975): 542–48; and W. H. Shea, "A Date for the Recently Discovered Eastern Canal of Egypt," *BASOR* 226 (1977): 31–38.

50. Shea, "Eastern Canal of Egypt," 35.

51. See the critical study of C. A. Redmount, "The Wadi Tumilat and the 'Canal of the Pharaohs,'" *JNES* 54.2 (1995): 127–35.

52. See the important contribution of E. D. Oren, "Migdol: A New Fortress on the Edge of the Eastern Nile Delta," *BASOR* 256 (1984): 7–44.

53. Gardiner, "Ancient Military Road," 107–9.

portant Canaanite deity well known from the Ugaritic texts. During the second millennium, worship of Semitic gods had penetrated into Egypt, and the ritual tied to Baal-zephon was prominent. Three sanctuaries are known to have been dedicated to him: at Memphis, Tell Daphneh, and Casium (located at modern Ras Kasrun).[54] Excavators have found a possible fourth sanctuary at Tell el-Dabʿa.[55]

Three major proposals have been offered regarding the location of Baal-zephon. Numerous scholars identify it with Tell Daphneh (Tahpanhes), about ten miles west of el-Qantara.[56] They give great weight to a sixth-century B.C. letter sent from Tell Daphneh to Memphis: "To Arishot, daughter of Eshmun-ya[ton]. Say to my sister Arishot: Your sister Bisha said: Are things well with you? They are also well with me! I wish you blessings from Baal-Zaphon and from all the gods of Tahpanhes. May they further your welfare. I wish I had the silver that you sent me!"[57] However, there is nothing in the passage that would indicate that Baal-zephon and Tahpanhes are identical. The text mentions merely that the god Baal-zephon was worshiped at Tahpanhes, and, as we have seen, numerous other sites were dedicated to his worship. In addition, the principal occupation of Tell Daphneh seems to have been during the Saite period (seventh and sixth centuries B.C.). Only a few remains have been found from the Ramessides. The Old Testament itself does not support the northerly route supposed by this proposal: "Now it came about when Pharaoh had let the people go, that God did not lead them by the way of the land of the Philistines, even though it was near. . . . Hence God led the people around by the way of the wilderness to the Red Sea" (Exod. 13:17–18).

Another reconstruction locates Baal-zephon in the vicinity of the Bitter Lakes, about twelve miles to the southeast of Tell el-Maskhuta.[58] G. I. Davies comments, "From the point of view of the distribution of the stages of the itinerary over the distance from Egypt to the southern mountains a location in the region of the Bitter Lakes appears most satisfactory."[59] Those who hold this view properly see

---

54. P. R. Raabe, "Baal-zephon," in *ABD* 1:554–55.

55. Bietak, *Avaris and Piramesse*, 253.

56. W. F. Albright, "Baal-Zephon," in *Festschrift Alfred Bertholet zum 80. Geburtstag*, ed. W. Baumgartner et al. (Tübingen: Mohr, 1950), 1–14; Sarna, *Exploring Exodus*, 109; Kitchen, "Exodus," in *Zondervan Pictorial Encyclopedia*, 2:430; G. E. Wright, *Biblical Archaeology* (Philadelphia: Westminster, 1962), 62.

57. W. Beyerlin, ed., *Near Eastern Religious Texts Relating to the Old Testament* (Philadelphia: Westminster, 1978), 253–54. In addition, see A. Dupont-Sommer, "Note on a Phoenician Papyrus from Saqqara," *PEQ* 81 (1949): 52–57.

58. J. Simons, *The Geographical and Topographical Texts of the Old Testament* (Leiden: Brill, 1959), 247–48.

59. Davies, *Way of the Wilderness*, 82.

the Hebrews traveling south from Rameses and Etham toward Baal-zephon and Migdol. However, these scholars also argue that, given the time constraints and small number of recorded encampments, the Israelites could not have gotten much farther south than the Bitter Lakes region. They rule out a more southern siting of Baal-zephon, Migdol, and the crossing of the Red Sea because "the beginning of the journey is fixed so far north by the locations adopted for Rameses and Succoth."[60]

This second reconstruction assumes that the itinerary of Numbers 33 is exhaustive, listing each and every Hebrew encampment on the journey to Palestine. This is clearly not the case. First of all, statements like "they . . . camped in the Wilderness of Sin" (v. 11) and "they . . . camped in the wilderness of Sinai" (v. 15) point to the broad geographical nature of the itinerary. Furthermore, several encampments named elsewhere (e.g., Num. 12:16; 21:12, 18–20) do not appear in Numbers 33. Numbers 33 does not record every stop or encampment of the Hebrews after they departed Egypt; consequently, we cannot determine their route solely on the basis of that passage.

A third possibility is that Baal-zephon lies near the head of the Gulf of Suez on the Red Sea.[61] This view is partially dependent on the location of the *yam sûph* (see pp. 134–36).[62]

A place called Pi-hahiroth is mentioned in the itinerary as facing or near Baal-zephon (v. 7). Although there have been numerous attempts to locate this site, its identity is still uncertain. Some have suggested that Pi-hahiroth is a Hebraized form of the Egyptian Pi(Per)-Hathor, "house of Hathor," and that it lay in the eastern delta between Tanis (San el-Hagar) and Bubastis (Tell Basta).[63] Others argue that the closest linguistic approximation puts the site at Pa(Per)-Kherta, a town dedicated to the goddess Tefnut and located somewhere in the eastern delta close to the wilderness.[64] Kenneth Kitchen contends that Pi-hahiroth is

60. Ibid.
61. See A. Servin, "La Tradition judéo-chrétienne de l'exode," *Bulletin de l'Institut d'Egypte* 31 (1948–49): 315–55.
62. Others have suggested an extreme northern route for the exodus. See O. Eissfeldt, *Baal Zaphon, Zeus Kasios und der Durchzug der Israeliten durchs Meer*, Beiträge zur Religionsgeschichte des Altertums 1 (Halle: Niemeyer, 1932). Eissfeldt located Baal-zephon at Mount Casios near Lake Serbonis. His identification of Mount Casios was mistaken, however; see the correction by H. Cazelles, "Les Localisations de l'exode et la critique littéraire," *RB* 62 (1955): 321–64. Aharoni, *Land of the Bible*, 179, subscribes to the northerly route.
63. Gardiner, "Geography of the Exodus," 213–14; and Sarna, *Exploring Exodus*, 108.
64. D. B. Redford, "Pi-hahiroth," in *ABD* 5:371. On the other hand, Peet, *Egypt and the Old Testament*, 136, says that "the identification of Pi-hahiroth with Pi-keheret is philologically impossible."

perhaps to be equated with Pa-hir, "the Hir-waters," which he would locate "somewhere in the region of the present Lake Ballah."[65] All of these candidates, however, have both linguistic and geographical problems and, therefore, the location of the site remains uncertain.

One clue to the location of Pi-hahiroth may derive from the meaning of the city's name. As written in Numbers 33, the name appears to be a Hebraized form of the original Akkadian *Pi-hiriti*, which literally means "the mouth or the opening of the canal."[66] As mentioned earlier, the eastern delta had a defensive canal from the Mediterranean Sea to at least the area of the Bitter Lakes and perhaps farther south. One may suggest that Pi-hahiroth was an opening or break in the canal system that allowed entrance into the wilderness of the Sinai Peninsula. It would probably have been located near the Gulf of Suez. J. Simons states that while we cannot closely identify the location of Pi-hahiroth, we do have "the general impression that the Israelite camp was at some point on the even ground east of *ğebel abu ḥaṣah*."[67] Of course, such a reconstruction is conjecture, although it is an intriguing possibility.

After Pi-hahiroth, the Hebrews "passed through the midst of the sea into the wilderness." Throughout the parallel accounts of the crossing, the water is often referred to as the *yam sûph* (Exod. 15:4; Deut. 11:4; Josh. 2:10; 4:23; 24:6; Ps. 106:7, 9, 22; 136:13, 15). Many modern scholars translate *yam sûph* as "Sea of Reeds/Papyrus" because the term *sûph* is used in the Old Testament to refer to the reeds growing along the side of the Nile River (see Exod. 2:3). Furthermore, we are told that *sûph* may in fact be related to the Egyptian word *twf(y)*, "marsh plant."[68] Since papyrus does not grow along the Red Sea/Gulf of Suez, scholars conclude that the *yam sûph* is one of the marshy lakes in the eastern delta region north of the Red Sea. Barry Beitzel explains:

> Now for two reasons it appears likely to me that the body of water at which the miracle occurred was one of the marshy lakes situated east of the delta area. First, papyrus does not grow in the deep waters of the Gulfs; second, a New Kingdom text speaks of the area between Tanis/Ra'amses and a line created by the intermittent marshes from Lake Menzaleh to Lake Timsah as "the land of papyrus par excellence." (The traditional rendition "Red Sea" in English Bibles ultimately derives

---

65. Kitchen, "Exodus," in *Zondervan Pictorial Encyclopedia*, 2:430.
66. Redford, "Pi-hahiroth," 371.
67. Simons, *Geographical and Topographical Texts*, 249.
68. W. A. Ward, "The Semitic Biconsonantal Root *sp* and the Common Origin of Egyptian *čwf* and Hebrew *sûp:* 'Marsh(-Plant),'" *VT* 24 (1974): 339–49.

from the Septuagint via the Latin Vulgate.) . . . Based on all the foregoing considerations . . . it seems reasonable to suggest that the divine event occurred at or near Lake Timsah.[69]

Some allege that the Egyptian text Papyrus Anastasi III tells of a "papyrus/marsh lake" not far from the city of Rameses, and this body of water should be identified with *yam sûph*. The text reads: "The papyrus-swamps *(p3-twfy)* come to it with papyrus, and Shihor with rushes."[70] Alan Gardiner was so convinced of the identification that he said it was "beyond dispute."[71] This reconstruction has become almost credal in modern scholarship.[72]

Recent studies by Bernard Batto have demonstrated, however, that this common view cannot be sustained by the evidence, but in fact *yam sûph* does refer to the Red Sea/Gulf of Suez.[73] In the first place, every certain reference to *yam sûph* in the Bible refers to the Red Sea or its northern extensions in the Gulfs of Aqaba and Suez (e.g., 1 Kings 9:26; Jer. 49:21). Second, the parallel drawn between Egyptian *p3-twfy* and *yam sûph* is not without its problems. Whereas *yam sûph* refers to a body of water, that is not true of *p3-twfy*. Egyptian *p3* is a demonstrative pronoun meaning "this," and in later Egyptian came to be used as the definite article "the."[74] The term *twfy* is properly translated "papyrus, papyrus thicket," and sometimes designated a region or district where papyrus grows.[75] Nowhere in Egyptian texts does *p3-twfy* refer to a body of water; it means "the land/area of papyrus."

Batto has also demonstrated that the word *sûph* in Hebrew is not related to the Egyptian *twfy*, but derives instead from the Semitic root *sôph*, which means "end."[76] Therefore the Hebrew place-name *yam sûph*, literally meaning "the sea of the end," refers to the waters to the

---

69. Beitzel, *Moody Atlas of Bible Lands*, 90.
70. See also the translation of A. Erman, *The Literature of the Ancient Egyptians* (New York: Dutton, 1927), 207.
71. A. H. Gardiner, *Ancient Egyptian Onomastica* (Oxford: Oxford University Press, 1947), 201–2.
72. J. Bright, *A History of Israel*, 3d ed. (Philadelphia: Westminster, 1981), 122–23; Wright, *Biblical Archaeology*, 60–62; G. Cornfeld, *Archaeology of the Bible: Book by Book* (New York: Harper and Row, 1976), 39–40; Kitchen, "Exodus," in *Zondervan Pictorial Encyclopedia*, 2:430; and D. W. Searle and B. C. Chapman, "Red Sea," in E. M. Blaiklock and R. K. Harrison, eds., *The New International Dictionary of Biblical Archaeology* (Grand Rapids: Zondervan, 1983), 386.
73. B. Batto, "The Reed Sea: *Requiescat in Pace*," *JBL* 102.1 (1983): 27–35; idem, "Red Sea or Reed Sea?" *BAR* 10.4 (1984): 57–63.
74. *WAS* 1:492.
75. Ibid., 5:359.
76. First suggested by N. Snaith, "יַם־סוּף: The Sea of Reeds: The Red Sea," *VT* 15 (1965): 397–98.

far south, the waters at the end of the land. And that, of course, would be the Red Sea.

From Sinai to the Land of Edom (Num. 33:9–40)

The initial stages of Israel's escape from Egypt had followed a southerly direction, beginning at Rameses (Tell el-Dabʿa) and concluding at the Gulf of Suez. At the Red Sea, the Hebrews turned eastward, crossed through the waters, and entered into the Sinai Peninsula.

Although almost no sites in this area can be identified with any certainty, the general direction of the Hebrews' march appears to be clear. After the Israelites crossed the Red Sea, they likely turned south-southeast, and journeyed down the western coast of the Sinai Peninsula along the Red Sea/Gulf of Suez. That course is confirmed by Numbers 33:10, which records that after Israel had passed through the *yam sûph* and had encamped at Marah and Elim, they then returned to camp by the *yam sûph* (Red Sea). In other words, the Hebrews had passed through the northern part of the Gulf of Suez, made two encampments and departures, and then camped at a more southerly place on the Red Sea. This southern route was a primary road for Egyptian mining expeditions during the Middle and New Kingdoms (ca. the twentieth to the twelfth centuries B.C.).[77] Semites worked in these mines, and perhaps they participated in the Egyptian expeditions to the digs. Most assuredly, the Hebrews, who had been in Egypt for a long time, would have known this route, possibly in a firsthand way. Fortunately, a clash between the Hebrews and Egyptians was not inevitable on this route. The Egyptian expeditions used the road primarily during the months of January through March,[78] while the Israelites would not have traversed the territory until some time after April.[79]

A site named Dophkah is mentioned in Numbers 33:12–13. Some scholars have understood the name to mean "smelter," and they have identified it with the mining center of Serabit el-Khadem.[80] Although no specific and concrete evidence exists for the identification, the name does support the belief that the Hebrews passed through a mining area of the Sinai.

---

77. I. Beit-Arieh, "Serabit el-Khadim: New Metallurgical and Chronological Aspects," *Levant* 17 (1985): 89–116.
78. W. M. F. Petrie, *Researches in Sinai* (London: Murray, 1906), 169.
79. Kitchen, "Wilderness," 3:1643–47. According to Exod. 13:4, Israel left Egypt during the month of Abib (ca. March) and then departed from Elim (Exod. 16:1) about a month later (ca. April).
80. Wright, *Biblical Archaeology*, 64.

In an intriguing article Itzhaq Beit-Arieh argues that the Israelites traveled the southern route because "this region is ecologically better adapted to the sustenance of life" than are the other parts of the Sinai Peninsula. He claims that the south-central Sinai had "a reasonably adequate water supply and a relatively comfortable climate that makes it possible to maintain a daily lifestyle suitably adapted to the conditions of the desert. . . . It is covered by assorted vegetation consisting of acacia and palm trees and a fairly dense growth of perennial bushes, along with a seasonal cover of grasses and weeds suitable for pasturing sheep and goats." In addition, south-central Sinai was geographically isolated and outside the control of Egyptian sovereignty: "ancient Egyptian hegemony never extended into south central Sinai."[81]

On the other hand, an attempted escape through northern Sinai would have placed the Hebrews in harm's way because the primary roads in that region were guarded by a series of Egyptian forts.[82] Regardless of the possibilities, the Bible explicitly states that the Israelites did not traverse the northern route: "Now it came about when Pharaoh had let the people go, that God did not lead them by the way of the land of the Philistines, even though it was near; for God said, 'Lest the people change their minds when they see war, and they return to Egypt'" (Exod. 13:17).

The Hebrew encampment at Mount Sinai is not mentioned in the Numbers 33 itinerary. Its precise location is unknown, although many suggestions have been presented. We will not take the time to review them.[83]

In Numbers 33:35 we read that the Hebrews having traversed the Sinai Peninsula arrived at the site of Ezion-geber on the northern coast of the Gulf of Aqaba/Red Sea. Many scholars on the basis of the excavations of Nelson Glueck have located Ezion-geber at the mound of Tell el-Kheleifeh.[84] A recent reevaluation of the archaeological remains uncovered by Glueck has demonstrated that this siting is highly questionable. Gary Pratico concludes, "Tell el-Kheleifeh provides no clear archaeological evidence, either ceramic or architectural, for its

---

81. I. Beit-Arieh, "The Route through Sinai: Why the Israelites Fleeing Egypt Went South," *BAR* 14.3 (1988): 36.

82. Gardiner, "Ancient Military Road," 99–116; T. Dothan, *Deir el-Balah* (Jerusalem: Hebrew University, 1978); idem, "Gaza Sands Yield Lost Outpost of the Egyptian Empire," *National Geographic* 162.6 (1982): 738–69.

83. See Beit-Arieh, "Route through Sinai," 28–37, for an adequate survey of the leading proposed locations of Mount Sinai.

84. N. Glueck, "The First Campaign at Tell el-Kheleifeh (Ezion-geber)," *BASOR* 71 (1938): 3–17; idem, "The Second Campaign at Tell el-Kheleifeh (Ezion-geber: Elath)," *BASOR* 75 (1939): 8–22; and idem, "The Third Season of Excavation at Tell el-Kheleifeh," *BASOR* 79 (1940): 2–18.

identification with the Ezion-Geber of Israel's wilderness traditions."[85] The earliest material remains from Tell el-Kheleifeh come from the ninth century B.C., and Israel was securely in Canaan by that date. The Bible does provide a general location for Ezion-geber: "King Solomon also built a fleet of ships in Ezion-geber, which is near Eloth on the shore of the Red Sea, in the land of Edom" (1 Kings 9:26). On the basis of this passage we are justified in looking for Ezion-geber in the general vicinity of the northern shore of the Gulf of Aqaba, but we do not know precisely where it was situated.

The site of Jotbathah, which is recorded in Numbers 33:34 as the second station before Ezion-geber, may be located at Tabeh, about seven miles south of Tell el-Kheleifeh on the western shore of the Gulf of Aqaba.[86] The identification is hardly certain, however, since it primarily rests on the similarity of the two names, Jotbathah and Tabeh.

From Ezion-geber the Hebrews traveled to Kadesh, which is "in the wilderness of Zin" (Num. 33:36). Kadesh, or Kadesh-Barnea, is sometimes identified with 'Ain Qedeis, an oasis that lies about fifty miles southwest of Beersheba on the Wadi Qedeis in northeastern Sinai.[87] In support of the identification is the name of the tell, which appears to preserve the name of the station Kadesh, and there is a water supply at the site. Many scholars remain unconvinced of this siting, however, because they feel the water supply is insignificant. A majority of researchers today place Kadesh at 'Ain Qudeirat, which sits about five miles northwest of 'Ain Qedeis next to the Wadi el-ʿAin.[88] It appears to be a more ecologically suitable location: significantly more vegetation and water are found here than at 'Ain Qedeis.[89]

Excavations at 'Ain Qudeirat have revealed no remains prior to the tenth century B.C.[90] Nothing has been uncovered at the site that might indicate the presence of the Hebrews in the second millennium B.C. The identification of Kadesh-Barnea with 'Ain Qudeirat is, in fact, rather

---

85. G. Pratico, "Where Is Ezion-Geber? A Reappraisal of the Site Archaeologist Nelson Glueck Identified as King Solomon's Red Sea Port," *BAR* 12.5 (1986): 24–35. For a more in-depth study see idem, *Nelson Glueck's 1938–1940 Excavations at Tell el-Kheleifeh: A Reappraisal* (Atlanta: Scholars, 1993); idem, "Nelson Glueck's 1938–1940 Excavations at Tell el-Kheleifeh: A Reappraisal," *BASOR* 259 (1985): 1–32.

86. Aharoni, *Land of the Bible*, 183.

87. C. H. J. De Geus, "Kadesh Barnea: Some Geographical and Historical Remarks," in *Instruction and Interpretation*, ed. H. A. Brongers et al. (Leiden: Brill, 1977), 66: "There is no convincing reason why Kadesh Barnea should not be identified with 'Ain Qdeis."

88. First suggested by N. Schmidt, "Kadesh Barnea," *JBL* 29 (1910): 61–76.

89. Archaeologists have estimated that the spring produces forty cubic meters of water per hour. See M. Dothan, "The Fortress at Kadesh-Barnea," *IEJ* 15.3 (1965): 134–51.

90. R. Cohen, "Excavations at Kadesh-barnea, 1976–1978," *BA* 44 (1981): 93–107; see also the various excavation summaries in *IEJ* 26.4 (1976): 201–2; 30.3–4 (1980): 235–36; 32.1 (1982): 70–71; 32.4 (1982): 266–67.

flimsy. No inscriptional evidence establishes that it was the ancient site. Even the excavator admits that "identification of the site is not absolutely certain."[91] Yohanan Aharoni has a balanced approach: "one may surmise that the whole region was called Kadesh-barnea," and that no remains of the traveling Hebrews have as yet been found.[92]

The Hebrews were unable to penetrate the land of Canaan from Kadesh-Barnea in the south because of hostile Canaanite groups (see Num. 20:14–21:4). So they journeyed eastward to Mount Hor "at the edge of the land of Edom" (Num. 33:37). Here Aaron died (Num. 33:38–39). The location of Mount Hor is uncertain. For centuries tradition has placed it at Jebel Nebi Harun near the Nabatean site of Petra. That siting is incorrect because Jebel Nebi Harun is in the middle of the land of Edom, and the biblical text tells us that Mount Hor was at the edge or border of Edom. Some scholars have suggested that Mount Hor lies at Jabel Madurah, about fifteen miles northeast of 'Ain Qudeirat, but this is mere guesswork.[93]

Travels in Transjordan:
From Edom to the Plains of Moab

On the basis of the surface surveys of Nelson Glueck in Transjordan during the 1930s, many scholars have been convinced that there was an occupational gap in Moab and Edom from the twentieth to the thirteenth centuries B.C.[94] Because of that hiatus, they believe that the Hebrews could not have traveled through Transjordan before the thirteenth century B.C.: how could they have faced the Amorites and Bashanites (Num. 21) if people were not living in Transjordan? Some researchers say that this gap in habitation proves that the Hebrew itinerary through Transjordan is a fabrication.[95] However, more recent archaeological work, including excavation and surface survey, has discredited the idea that there was a clear occupational break in Transjordan in the second millennium.[96] People did inhabit these ar-

91. R. Cohen, "Did I Excavate Kadesh-Barnea?" *BAR* 7.3 (1981): 20–33.
92. Aharoni, *Land of the Bible*, 65.
93. R. L. Roth, "Hor," in *ABD* 3:287.
94. N. Glueck, *Explorations in Eastern Palestine*, vols. 1–4=*AASOR* 14 (1934), 15 (1935), 18–19 (1939), and 25–28 (1951).
95. See the discussions of Sh. Yeivin, *The Israelite Conquest of Canaan* (Istanbul: Nederlands Historisch-Archaeologisch Instituut, 1971), 67; and M. Weippert, *Settlement of the Israelite Tribes in Palestine* (Naperville, Ill.: Allenson, 1971), 60–62.
96. J. M. Miller, "Archaeological Survey of Central Moab: 1978," *BASOR* 234 (1979): 43–52; idem, "Recent Archaeological Developments Relevant to Ancient Moab," in *Studies in the History and Archaeology of Jordan* (Amman: Department of Antiquities, Jordan, 1982): 2:169–73; S. Mittmann, *Beiträge zur Siedlungs- und Territorialgeschichte des nördlichen Ostjordanlandes* (Wiesbaden: Harrassowitz, 1970).

eas, and they certainly could have been a menace and danger to a nomadic group attempting to cross through their land.

The specific itinerary through Transjordan recorded in Numbers 33 covers Zalmonah to Punon to Oboth to Iye-abarim (Iyim) to Dibon(-gad) to Almon(-diblathaim) to the mountains of Abarim and to the Plains of Moab by the Jordan River as far as Abel-shittim. Some scholars question, in particular, the listing of Dibon because "no Late Bronze Age strata were found at the tell of Dhiban (Dibon). Remains from ca. 1200–1100 were found on the summit of the tell, but a city did not exist before the ninth century BCE."[97] How could Numbers 33 be accurate if a city did not appear at this site until several centuries after the exodus event?

Charles Krahmalkov has demonstrated that the Transjordanian route of the Hebrews was a traditional road used by the Egyptians throughout the Late Bronze Age.[98] Three Egyptian topographical lists—from the reigns of Thutmosis III (ca. 1479–1425 B.C.), Amenophis III (ca. 1391–1353 B.C.), and Rameses II (ca. 1290–1224 B.C.)—provide a description of a route from the Arabah to the Plains of Moab at the Jordan River. The earliest list, sometimes referred to as the Palestine List, chronicles sites in Transjordan from Iyyin to Dibon to Abel to Jordan. Those place-names are four of the Transjordanian stations listed in the Israelite itinerary in Numbers 33. All three Egyptian lists mention Dibon, and therefore "we have irrefutable primary historical evidence for the existence of the city of Dibon in the Late Bronze Age."[99] Krahmalkov sums up: "In short, the Biblical story of the invasion of Transjordan that set the stage for the conquest of all Palestine is told against a background that is historically accurate. The Israelite invasion route described in Numbers 33:45b–50 was in fact an official, heavily trafficked Egyptian road through the Transjordan in the Late Bronze Age. And the city of Dibon was in fact a station on that road in

---

97. G. W. Ahlström, *The History of Ancient Palestine* (Minneapolis: Fortress, 1993), 416.

98. C. R. Krahmalkov, "Exodus Itinerary Confirmed by Egyptian Evidence," *BAR* 20.5 (1994): 54–62.

99. Ibid., 58. Some scholars question whether Dibon actually appears in the list of Rameses II. For a reading of *t-b-n-i* as a reference to Dibon, see K. A. Kitchen, "Some New Light on the Asiatic Wars of Rameses II," *JEA* 50 (1964): 47–50. Others find Kitchen's reading to be suspect: see S. Ahituv, "Did Rameses II Conquer Dibon?" *IEJ* 22 (1972): 141–42; and G. W. Ahlström, *Royal Administration and National Religion in Ancient Palestine* (Leiden: Brill, 1982), 17 n. 44. Although the appearance of Dibon is questionable in the topographical list of Rameses II, it is almost universally held that it does appear in the earlier records of Thutmosis III and Amenophis III. See D. B. Redford, "A Bronze Age Itinerary in Transjordan," *Journal of the Society for the Study of Egyptian Antiquities* 12 (1982): 55–74.

the Late Bronze Age."[100] Having traveled that route and now encamped next to the Jordan River, the Hebrews plotted their strategy for the invasion of Canaan.

Numbers 33 is a coherent, uniform early text that presents the route of the Hebrew exodus out of Egypt. It is in the form of an ancient Near Eastern military itinerary, a genre very common in the second millennium B.C. It is, then, "not a composite of the itinerary segments presented earlier in the Exodus-Numbers narrative,"[101] but a description of actual routes that were used in the second millennium B.C., in particular, an escape route for slaves out of Egypt, a mining road through southwestern Sinai, and a well-worn military road through Transjordan.

The precise route of the Israelite itinerary is tentative because few sites can be identified with any certainty. However, a general course of travel emerges from the evidence available. Leaving the delta region of Egypt, the Hebrews traveled in a southerly direction toward the Gulf of Suez. There they turned east and crossed through a northern portion of the *yam sûph*. The Hebrews then took a south-southeast route along the shore of the Red Sea in the Sinai Peninsula. They proceeded to the northern point of the Gulf of Aqaba and from there traveled the military road to the Plains of Moab and the Jordan River.

The current crop of historical revisionists argue that "it is quite clear that the biblical writers knew nothing about events in Palestine before the tenth century BCE" and "do not provide any basic information about the emergence of the people or nation Israel."[102] Many of these researchers outright deny the historical nature of the exodus as recorded in the Bible. We have seen, to the contrary, that the backdrop to the biblical story of the exodus out of Egypt, the travel through Sinai, and the invasion of Transjordan is accurate. The writer knew the geography and topography of Egypt, Sinai, and Transjordan; he understood the ecology of those areas; and he was well acquainted with the road system that was in use in the second millennium B.C.

---

100. Krahmalkov, "Exodus Itinerary Confirmed," 58.
101. J. M. Miller, "The Israelite Journey through (around) Moab and Moabite Toponymy," *JBL* 108.4 (1989): 577–95.
102. Ahlström, *History of Ancient Palestine*, 44–45. Scholars such as R. B. Coote, T. L. Thompson, and P. R. Davies may be included in this group.

The Egyptian Complexion of the Bronze Serpent

The image of a bronze serpent appears twice in the Old Testament. The first occasion is in Numbers 21:4–9, where the biblical author explains why the command was given to create such a figure. The second reference relates the destruction of the bronze snake at the hands of King Hezekiah during his religious reform in Jerusalem (2 Kings 18:4). The authenticity of the Numbers 21 pericope has been a matter of serious scholarly focus and debate for decades. Many interpreters have argued that the passage was merely a literary creation to explain the cult of the bronze serpent in Jerusalem at the time of Hezekiah. H. H. Rowley declared: "The undeniable fact that Nehushtan was in the Temple, however, called for some explanation, and hence the aetiological story of Numbers 21:8f. was created to legitimate its presence there."[1] Other scholars, such as Martin Noth, disagreed, claiming that Numbers 21 "provides no aetiology of Nehushtan" in 2 Kings 18:4.[2] H. R. Hall went as far as to pronounce the absolute historicity of the incident on the grounds that the Israelites had brought the bronze serpent with them out of Egypt.[3] Most commentaries have also concentrated on the question of the historical accuracy of Numbers 21.[4]

---

1. H. H. Rowley, "Zadok and Nehushtan," *JBL* 58 (1939): 138. G. W. Coats, *Rebellion in the Wilderness* (Nashville: Abingdon, 1968), wholeheartedly agrees with Rowley's assessment.
2. M. Noth, *Numbers: A Commentary* (Philadelphia: Westminster, 1968), 155–58.
3. H. R. Hall, *Ancient History of the Near East,* 7th ed. (London: Methuen, 1927), 485.
4. E.g., A. Dillmann, *Die Bücher Numeri, Deuteronomium und Josua* (Leipzig: Hirzel, 1886); G. B. Gray, *A Critical and Exegetical Commentary on Numbers* (Edinburgh: T. and T. Clark, 1903); C. F. Keil, *Numbers and Deuteronomy,* vol. 3 of *Commentary on the Old Testament* (Peabody, Mass.: Hendrickson, 1989 reprint); P. J. Budd, *Numbers* (Waco: Word, 1984); A. H. McNeile, *The Book of Numbers* (Cambridge: Cambridge University Press,

Because of the centralization of scholarly debate on textual and source criticisms of Numbers 21, very little work has been done on the ancient Near Eastern background of the event. In particular, little attention has been given to Egyptian customs, iconography, and motifs that may, in fact, lie at the heart of the story. None of the major commentaries even mentions the slightest possibility of Egyptian influence on the episode.[5] Yet the Egyptian background is critical to a proper understanding of Numbers 21. To gain that understanding, we must first place the passage in its context.

Geographical Context

To say that the precise route of the Hebrew exodus from Egypt is difficult to establish is an obvious understatement.[6] Out of the fifty-one sites mentioned in Numbers 33, only about ten can be identified with any certainty.[7] In general, the same difficulty holds for the geographical context of Numbers 21:4–9: the sites are hard to identify with any precision. In the opening verse of Numbers 21, for instance, we are told that the Israelites fought against the king of Arad. Most scholars have identified Arad with Tell 'Arad, which lies about twenty miles east-northeast of Beersheba. However, no remains have been found at Tell 'Arad from the Middle or Late Bronze Ages.[8] Scholars have presented numerous ingenious interpretations to solve the problem. Benjamin Mazar argued that Canaanite Arad was a district and not a city. The king of Arad in Numbers 21 actually resided at Hormah (v. 3), where the battle is said to have taken place. Mazar identified Hormah with Tell

---

1911); N. H. Snaith, *Leviticus and Numbers* (Greenwood, S.C.: Attic, 1977 reprint); and J. Sturdy, *Numbers* (New York: Cambridge University Press, 1976).

5. The most important studies that argue for Egyptian influence are K. R. Joines, "Winged Serpents in Isaiah's Inaugural Vision," *JBL* 86 (1967): 410–15; and idem, *Serpent Symbolism in the Old Testament* (Haddonfield, N.J.: Haddonfield House, 1974). The reader should also consult T. E. Fretheim, "Life in the Wilderness," *Dialog* 17 (1978): 266–72; and R. S. Boraas, "Of Serpents and Gods," *Dialog* 17 (1978): 273–79.

6. The literature on the subject is vast. For a recent survey see I. Beit-Arieh, "The Route through Sinai," *BAR* 14.2 (1988): 28–37. Another helpful piece, although dated, is A. H. Gardiner, "The Geography of the Exodus," in *Recueil d'études égyptologiques dediées à la mémoire de Jean-François Champollion* (Paris: E. Champion, 1922), 213–14. Of course, some scholars today question whether there even was an exodus, or they maintain that if there was one, it was quite small. See especially N. K. Gottwald, *The Tribes of Yahweh* (Maryknoll, N.Y.: Orbis, 1979), 35–41; S. Herrmann, *Israel in Egypt* (Naperville, Ill.: Allenson, 1973), 38–50; and G. E. Mendenhall, "The Hebrew Conquest of Palestine," *BA* 25 (1962): 66–87.

7. The identification of Rameses, the starting point of the exodus (Num. 33:3, 5), with Qantir is beyond reasonable doubt (see pp. 127–28).

8. M. Aharoni, "Arad," in *NEAEHL* 1:75–87.

Malhata, which has significant remains from the Bronze Age.⁹ Nadav Na'aman agreed with Mazar regarding Arad, but he located Hormah in the western Negev at the site of Tell Halif.¹⁰ Yohanan Aharoni proposed, on the contrary, that Canaanite Arad should be identified with Tell Malhata, and Hormah should be equated with the modern mound of Tell Masos.¹¹ The truth is that we do not know where these sites were.

The biblical writer relates that the Hebrews were journeying along the *derek hāʾăthārîm* when they encountered the king of Arad (Num. 21:1). Some have said that Atharim was a specific site or region. However, the phrase *derek hāʾăthārîm* should be translated the "way of the spies." It refers to Numbers 13:21–22, where the Hebrew spies traveled through the Negev to Hebron. The Hebrews were attempting to penetrate Canaan by traveling the same route that their spies had originally gone. That interpretation lends support to the idea that the episode of the serpent took place somewhere in the northern Negev near the site of Tell ʿArad.

After the battle of Hormah, the Hebrews understood a northern penetration to be too difficult, so they marched eastward to Edom. A problem arises in the text: the writer tells us that the Hebrews went to Edom by way of the *yam sûph*. The term *yam sûph* is primarily used in the Bible to refer to the Gulf of Suez and the exodus (Exod. 13:18; Num. 33:10–11). However, the biblical writers also employed *yam sûph* as a designation for the Gulf of Aqaba: "King Solomon also built a fleet of ships in Ezion-geber, which is near Eloth on the shore of the *yam sûph*, in the land of Edom" (1 Kings 9:26; cf. Num. 14:25). Evidently, the Gulf of Aqaba is what the author of Numbers had in view.

Even with all the geographical problems noted, it is clear that the biblical author is describing the northern Negev as the location of the incident of the bronze serpent. He is well versed in the geography of that land, whether by tradition or firsthand exposure, and that knowledge is obvious in the text.

Egypt and the Murmuring Motif

Numbers 21:4–9 recounts an episode of the Israelites' murmuring, a motif that characterized the wilderness wanderings. Murmuring is a

---

9. B. Mazar, "The Sanctuary of Arad and the Family of Hobab the Kenite," *JNES* 24 (1965): 297–303.

10. N. Na'aman, "Arad in the Topographical List of Shishak," *TA* 12 (1985): 91–92.

11. Y. Aharoni, "Nothing Early and Nothing Late: Re-Writing Israel's Conquest," *BA* 39 (1976): 55–76. However, V. Fritz, "The Israelite 'Conquest' in the Light of Recent Excavations at Khirbet el-Meshâsh," *BASOR* 241 (1981): 61, contends that the excavations at Tell Masos argue against Aharoni: "The long gap in the history of the settlement from the middle of the 10th century until the second half of the 7th century is evidence against Y. Aharoni's identification of it with Hormah."

dominant negative theme found repeatedly throughout the books of Exodus and Numbers (see, e.g., Exod. 14:11; 15:23–26; 16:2–3; 17:2–3; Num. 11:4–6; 14:1–4; 16:11–14; 20:2–5). George Coats specifies the nature of this murmuring: "A form-critical study of the relevant texts reveals that the murmuring motif is not designed to express a disgruntled complaint. Quite the contrary, it describes an open rebellion. . . . In the wilderness theme the murmuring motif characterizes a basic tradition about the rebellion of Israel."[12] The biblical writers see it as the antithesis of Yahweh's grace and favor to the people; the alternation of Yahweh's long-suffering patience with Israel's complaints and demands is all too obvious.

What is not frequently noticed in regard to the murmuring motif is how commonly Egypt is mentioned in the texts. For example, the Hebrews complained: "Is it because there were no graves in Egypt that you have taken us away to die in the wilderness? Why have you dealt with us in this way, bringing us out of Egypt? Is this not the word that we spoke to you in Egypt, saying, 'Leave us alone that we may serve the Egyptians'? For it would have been better for us to serve the Egyptians than to die in the wilderness" (Exod. 14:11–12; see also Exod. 16:3; 17:3; Num. 11:5; 14:2–4; 16:13; 20:5). The groaning began already in Egypt (Exod. 5:21). In fact, whenever the Hebrews complained, they mentioned Egypt.

Because Egypt was inevitably mentioned when the Israelites murmured, one would not be surprised to find some Egyptian elements, both literary and cultural, in those stories. And that is certainly the case. In each grumbling incident is at least one motif or object that reflects Egyptian influence. Note, for example, the irony in the passage we have just quoted. The phrase "no graves in Egypt" borders on the humorous because Egypt was the land of graves, death, and preoccupation with the afterlife.

Consider also Numbers 11:5–6, where the Hebrews complain: "We remember the fish which we used to eat free in Egypt, the cucumbers and the melons and the leeks and the onions and the garlic, but now our appetite is gone. There is nothing at all to look at except this manna." The Hebrews' remembrance of the culinary staples of Egypt was quite accurate. Papyrus Anastasi III celebrates the glories of the new capital of Rameses: "Its granaries are (so) full of barley and emmer (that) they come near to the sky. Onions and leeks are *for food*, and lettuce of the *garden*, pomegranates, apples, and olives, figs of the orchard, . . . red *wedj*-fish of the canal of the Residence City, *which* live on lotus-flowers, *bedin*-fish of the *Hari*-waters (numerous other types of fish species fol-

---

12. Coats, *Rebellion in the Wilderness*, 249.

low). . . ."¹³ Among the other examples that could be cited is Numbers 21:4–9, which mirrors Egypt far more strongly than has previously been recognized.¹⁴

Fiery Serpents

Reacting to the last grumbling incident before the Hebrews reached the Promised Land, God sent *hannĕḥāšîm haśśĕrāphîm* ("fiery serpents") upon them because of their unfaithfulness. The *nĕḥāšîm* bit many of the Hebrews and some died. Yahweh then ordered Moses to fashion a *śārāph* and set it on a standard or pole in the middle of the Israelite camp. So Moses crafted a *nĕḥaš nĕḥōšet* ("bronze serpent"), and whoever had been bitten needed only to look at the image to be healed.

The Hebrew word *śārāph* appears only seven times in the Old Testament, and each occurrence signifies some type of snake. Deuteronomy 8:15 speaks of Yahweh's protecting hand in the wilderness: "he led you through the great and terrible wilderness, with its fiery serpents *(nāḥāš śārāph)* and scorpions and thirsty ground."¹⁵ Apparently the *nāḥāš śārāph* was a common creature in the desert areas of the Sinai. Isaiah 6 represents the attendants of Yahweh as *śĕrāphîm* with six wings, and elsewhere the prophet speaks of *śārāph mĕʿôpēp* ("a fiery flying one").¹⁶ By definition, "a saraph is a serpent, and for Isaiah it may have wings, as is the case with the seraphim of Isaiah 6."¹⁷

Scholars disagree as to why the serpents in these accounts are called "fiery." According to some, "fiery" refers to the bite of the

---

13. *ANET*, 471. For an extended discussion of all the agricultural products mentioned in Numbers 11 and of their abundance in ancient and nineteenth-century Egypt, see E. W. Hengstenberg, *Egypt and the Books of Moses* (Edinburgh: Thomas Clark, 1845), 208–14.

14. The Hebrews complain in Num. 16:13 that Moses has brought them "out of a land flowing with milk and honey," a designation normally reserved for the land of Canaan. The truth is that Egypt was well known in antiquity for both of these products; their being mentioned here is an ironic twist.

15. *Nāḥāš śārāph* is to be understood as a collective here, a common construction to designate animal species in the Hebrew Old Testament. The only appearances of *śārāph* in the plural are in Num. 21 and Isa. 6.

16. Isa. 14:29 and 30:6. There is no uncertainty that the prophet has a snake in view because *śārāph mĕʿôpēp* is parallel with "viper" in both of these instances. A similar parallel is found in the later writings of Herodotus: "Vipers are found in all parts of the world, but the winged serpents are nowhere seen except in Arabia, where they are all congregated together. This makes them appear so numerous" (*History* 3.109). Herodotus also connects flying serpents to Egypt: "The trees which bear the frankincense are guarded by winged serpents, small in size and of varied colors, whereof vast numbers hang about every tree. They are of the same kind as the serpents which invade Egypt, and there is nothing but the smoke of styrax which will drive them from the trees" (*History* 3.107). For further explanation see D. J. Wiseman, "Flying Serpents," *Tyndale Bulletin* 23 (1972): 108–10.

17. Joines, "Winged Serpents in Isaiah's Inaugural Vision," 411.

snakes and the resulting inflammation and pain.[18] Coats disagrees, arguing that the word is a description of the creatures themselves; they looked shiny or bright.[19] Although either one of those understandings may be correct, the real importance of śārāph is that it was originally an Egyptian word. The hieroglyphic noun ⌈☙⌹ (srf) means "warm, hot," and derives from the verb meaning "to heat up, inflame."[20] The concept of the śĕrāphîm, then, was borrowed from Egypt by the Hebrew writer.

Another point worth noting is that the Hebrew word nĕḥōšet ("bronze") was originally the Egyptian word ṯḥśt, which is frequently translated "copper." Hieroglyphic ṯḥśt represented "a variety of copper that came from Asia"; in Egypt it often referred to the mountings on a flagpole or a standard.[21] This linguistic affinity points to Egypt and suggests that Numbers 21 bears a strong Egyptian flavor historically and culturally.

The fiery serpents are to be understood in light of Egyptian symbolism and belief which we explored in chapter 5. We saw that the ancient Egyptians revered the serpent for both the danger and protection it presented. On the front of the king's crown was the form of an enraged female cobra that, imbued with the power of the gods, would instill terror in Pharaoh's enemies. Parts of two texts that we quoted earlier (pp. 90, 92) are worth repeating here:

> O Red Crown, O Inu, O Great One,
> O Magician, O Fiery Snake!
> Let there be terror of me like the terror of thee.[22]

> His uraeus-serpents are over his head.
> The leading snake of Unas is at his forehead,
> She who perceives the soul (of the enemy),
> She who excels in the force of fire.[23]

It is clear that the uraeus was a fiery snake which the Egyptians believed would protect the Pharaoh by spitting forth fire on his enemies.

The mythological literature of Egypt frequently mentions the figure of the fiery serpent. For example, in the eighth section of the Book of

18. Budd, *Numbers*, 234; and Gray, *Numbers*, 277.
19. Coats, *Rebellion in the Wilderness*, 117 n. 51.
20. *WAS* 3:463.
21. *WAS* 10 Lfrg., 396.
22. H. Frankfort, *Kingship and the Gods* (Chicago: University of Chicago Press, 1948), 108.
23. Pyramid Text 396, in K. Sethe, ed., *Die altägyptischen Pyramidentexten* (Leipzig: J. C. Hinrichs, 1908–22).

the Gates the sun-god Re, as he travels through the underworld, is protected by a serpent named Kheti. The snake spits fire into the faces of the enemy.[24] In the tomb of Sethos I a copy of the Book of Am Duat was found. The ninth section depicts twelve uraei spitting forth fire to light the path of the sun-god in the underworld and strike down his enemies. As soon as the god passes by, the uraei consume the flames in order to spit them out again the next day.[25] A New Kingdom story explains how Isis magically created a poisonous snake that tortured the sun-god through fire.[26] The "Story of the Shipwrecked Sailor" tells of a castaway on an island whom a snake threatens with fiery death.[27]

The serpent as an emblem of ancient Egyptian sovereignty and power appears in a vast array of archaeological remains as well. It was common in the long friezes of the temples and belched fire at enemies in the royal tombs.[28]

Clearly, then, the biblical writer employed Egyptian background material and motifs when recording the Numbers 21 incident. But this raises a difficult question: Why the Egyptian symbol of a bronze serpent? First of all, this episode is an example of sympathetic magic, that is, "controlling an adversary through manipulation of a replication."[29] Moses and the Israelites attempted to change curse into blessing by manipulating an image of the very thing bringing the curse.[30] The ancient Egyptians were well known for techniques of sympathetic magic; they frequently defended themselves against scorpions, crocodiles, and serpents by manipulating images of them.[31] Sympathetic magic was especially common in dealing with snake bites—the Egyptians believed they could be healed by an image of a snake. Karen Joines argues that sympathetic magic in relation to serpents is found only in Egypt. There is "no evidence for it in ancient Palestine and Mesopotamia."[32] The

---

24. See E. A. W. Budge, *Osiris and the Egyptian Resurrection*, 2 vols. (London: Medici Society, 1911), 2:233.

25. A. Wiedemann, *Religion of the Ancient Egyptians* (London: Grevel, 1897), 86.

26. E. Hornung, *Conceptions of God in Ancient Egypt* (Ithaca, N.Y.: Cornell University Press, 1982), 86–88.

27. See the translations in W. K. Simpson, ed., *The Literature of Ancient Egypt* (New Haven: Yale University Press, 1973), 52; and *AEL* 1:212.

28. G. Posener, *Dictionary of Egyptian Civilization* (New York: Tudor, 1959), 291; for more on serpent symbolism see K. R. Joines, *Serpent Symbolism*, "Winged Serpents," and "The Bronze Serpent in the Israelite Cult," *JBL* 87 (1968): 245–56.

29. Fretheim, "Life in the Wilderness," 267; see also Boraas, "Of Serpents and Gods."

30. R. J. Burns, "Jesus and the Bronze Serpent," *The Bible Today* 28 (1990): 84–89.

31. For a discussion of this practice and of Egyptian magic in general, see A. H. Gardiner, "Magic (Egyptian)," in *Encyclopaedia of Religion and Ethics*, ed. J. Hastings, 13 vols. (Edinburgh: T. and T. Clark, 1908–26), 8:262–69. For examples of archaeological remnants of such images, see W. M. F. Petrie, *Amulets* (London: Constable, 1914).

32. Joines, "Bronze Serpent," 251.

bronze serpent, then, reflects Egyptian customs and verifies that the setting of Numbers 21 is the recent escape from Egypt.[33]

The raising up of the bronze serpent on a standard may also be a symbol of Yahweh's vanquishing Egypt. The Egyptians fashioned images of threatening forces in order to demolish those forces. Alan Gardiner explains that "sometimes it is the hostile power to be destroyed that is thus counterfeited and done to death."[34] So the replication of snakes, scorpions, crocodiles, and the like not only served to protect whoever made use of such an image, but on occasion functioned as a force of destruction against the object represented. Since the serpent was the emblem of ancient Egyptian sacral and regal sovereignty,[35] Yahweh's command in Numbers 21 to fashion a model of a serpent was a sign of his conquering that nation. This point would have been especially clear to those Hebrews who desired to return to Egypt and who believed that their security and deliverance rested in Pharaoh and his people. Yahweh was proclaiming the annihilation of Egypt. Egypt could in no way liberate Israel. Salvation came only from the hand of Yahweh.

In summary, the construction of the bronze serpent signified blessing and curse. Those Hebrews who were bitten by the fiery serpents needed only to look to the bronze serpent and they would be healed. That was the blessing. However, the brass image also symbolized the destruction of Egypt (which had occurred during the Exodus plagues) and of those who wished to return to Egypt and her ways. That was the curse.

Standards

The Hebrew term used for standard *(nēs)* in Numbers 21:8–9 appears twenty times in the Hebrew Bible; it is variously translated "banner, ensign, pole, sail, sign, pennon, and standard."[36] It is not certain whether *nēs* derives from the verbal root *nāsas* ("to lift up as an ensign"—see Isa. 10:18; Zech. 9:16) or *nûs* ("to lift up as an ensign"—see Isa. 59:19). It is

---

33. The designation of the material used in the fashioning of the serpent also mirrors Egyptian magical practices: in Egypt "the materials of which such images and amulets should be made are nearly always specified, and it is evident that this was considered a matter of vital importance," what is often called the Egyptian doctrine of properties (Gardiner, "Magic [Egyptian]," 266).

34. Gardiner, "Magic (Egyptian)," 266.

35. The gods often bore the symbol of a serpent on their crowns. For a unique representation of the goddess Wadjet wearing a serpent-crested diadem, see J. Baines and J. Malek, *Atlas of Ancient Egypt* (New York: Facts on File, 1980), 217. This bronze statue of Wadjet with a lioness head and cobra on top embodies the goddess's power and ferocious demeanor as portrayed in textual material.

36. *BDB*, 651; and L. Koehler and W. Baumgartner, eds., *Lexicon in Veteris Testamenti libros* (Leiden: Brill, 1985), 619.

The Narmer Palette: An Egyptian King Hitting an Asiatic. *Courtesy of the Egyptian Museum, Cairo.*

important to note, however, that the first occurrence of *nēs* in the Hebrew Bible is Numbers 21:8–9, where the context is Israel's escape from Egypt. That observation is critical because the use of the standard reflects Egyptian beliefs and practices.

The literature of the time indicates that the use of standards was commonplace in ancient Egypt. The principal purpose of the standards was to serve as a physical repository of the power of the gods. That is to say, these poles were empowered with the divine force. In reality, the gods were thought to be embodied in the standards, and so the Egyptian word for standard (𓏏𓊨𓏤) is usually accompanied by an ideogram for a particular god; for example, *t͗t Mnw* ("standard of Min") and *t͗t Ḥ͗* ("standard of Ha"). Egyptian texts so identify the poles with the deities that they often use the words *standards* and *gods* interchangeably. Thus the texts of the Min Feast of Rameses II call the standards "the gods who (habitually) follow the god."[37]

The concept of a physical object being empowered by the gods was foundational to Egyptian religion. For example, the various royal crowns of the Pharaohs were considered to be sacred objects invested with divine powers. The rods that the Pharaoh and his magicians used were also endued with divine character. Even temple furniture was venerated as a great god.[38] Similarly the ancient Egyptians truly believed that standards were imbued with the magic and power of the gods. They "are obviously symbols of gods, but we must allow the word 'symbol' more weight than we would normally ascribe to it. The symbols . . . partake of the power which they represent. They are true fetishes, replete with power."[39]

This idea of deified standards was present in Egypt as early as the late predynastic period. The Battlefield Palette from Abydos pictures standards with birds at their tops and with arms which are holding on to captives. The standards are actual agents of the enemies' misery. The so-named Lion Palette, which probably dates earlier than the Battlefield Palette in the predynastic period, portrays a man holding a standard. The Narmer Palette from Hierakonpolis in the late predynastic period shows four men holding standards at the top of which are various animals that represent gods.[40]

Throughout dynastic Egypt, the standards of the gods are found so often that we must limit ourselves to providing only a few examples. Thutmosis I (Dynasty 18) commanded that statues be made of the gods

---

37. Frankfort, *Kingship and the Gods*, 91.
38. A. Erman, *A Handbook of Egyptian Religion* (Boston: Longwood, 1977 reprint), 75.
39. Frankfort, *Kingship and the Gods*, 91.
40. For illustrations of all three palettes see K. Michalowski, *Art of Ancient Egypt* (New York: Abrams, 1969), figs. 56, 57, and 181.

and placed on standards. "The standards thereof were of electrum, more excellent than their predecessors; more splendid were they than that which is in heaven."[41] An inscription commemorating the coronation of Thutmosis III at Karnak reads:

> His own titulary was affixed for me.[42]
> He fixed my Horus upon the standard;[43]
> He made me mighty as a mighty bull.
> He caused that I should shine in the midst of Thebes.[44]

In the inscription of the Speos Artemidos, Thutmosis III's queen, calling for the restoration of Egypt after the terrible desolation brought by the Hyksos, says, "I have commanded that my [titulary] abide like the mountains; when the sun shines, (its) rays are bright upon the titulary of my majesty; my Horus is high upon the standard . . . forever."[45] A limestone relief of Rameses I (Dynasty 19) making an offering to Osiris depicts two standards with the god Mendes (ram-god) on top. Holding the standards at the bottom is the symbol of life (the ankh sign) with human arms.[46] A scene on the exterior north side and west end of Rameses III's funerary temple at Medinet Habu pictures the king going into battle on his chariot. Before him is a chariot bearing the standard of Amon. An inscription over the standard reads: "Utterance of Amon-Re, king of gods: 'Lo, I am before thee, my son, lord of the Two Lands, Usermare-Meriamon, I give [to thee] all [might and power] among the Nine Bows.'"[47] Most important for our purposes are the frequent depictions of a serpent on top of a standard. For example, a relief from the temple of Mentuhotep I (Dynasty 11) at Deir el-Bahari pictures the king victorious in battle, and near him is a standard with a uraeus on its top.

From the examples provided, it is clear that the ancient Egyptians believed that the deific standards produced both blessing and curse. On the one hand, the poles were viewed as the means of judgment against enemies. Reliefs show them being carried into battle and conquering, binding, and tormenting the foe. Consequently, deific standards were symbols of wrath against Egypt's enemies. On the other hand, the an-

---

41. *ARE* 2:39.
42. The god Re's titulary was given to Thutmosis III.
43. The Horus hawk surmounted the standard or banner bearing the Horus name of the king.
44. *ARE* 2:61–62.
45. *ARE* 2:125–26.
46. W. C. Hayes, *The Scepter of Egypt*, 2 vols. (New York: Metropolitan Museum of Art, 1959), 2:331.
47. *ARE* 4:27.

The Narmer Palette: Standard Bearers and Long-necked Lions.
Courtesy of the Egyptian Museum, Cairo.

cient Egyptians believed the standards to be edifying for Egypt. They were endowed with the power of the gods, and they were actual agents of divine protection for Egypt and especially for her king. Standards played a significant role in the coronation rituals and Sed Festivals of the Pharaohs. A relief at Abydos from the reign of Sethos I (1306–1290 B.C.) demonstrates the importance of standards for Egyptian royalty. The picture presents a number of animated symbols—representing such things as life, welfare, truth—carrying standards. Next to the standards are texts explaining their relationship to the king. One reads, for example, "He gives an eternity of peaceful years to King Men-maat-re (Sethos I)"; this is a spell "spoken by the gods upon their standards."[48] Standards, then, served as mediums of the gods' blessings upon Egypt.

How does this understanding of Egyptian standards affect the interpretation of Numbers 21:4–9? Very simply, the standard (with the bronze serpent affixed to it) in the middle of the Israelite camp had a function and purpose similar to that of Egyptian standards. It symbolized that Yahweh had invested his power in the standard in much the same way that the gods of Egypt did in theirs. Yahweh did so primarily in order to protect and heal the Israelites. The standard was a means of great blessing, sanctification, and defense for the Hebrews. But the standard also served as an agent of judgment against the enemies of Yahweh, especially against Egypt and those who wanted to return there. Thus the standard symbolized blessing and curse, friend and fiend, the sacred and the profane.

The most basic conclusion we may draw is that Numbers 21:4–9 should be understood in the light of Egyptian culture and beliefs. All the physical elements of the account—the geography, bronze serpent, and standard—point to Egypt as foundational to the story. The linguistic evidence, especially parallels in word usage, also underscores the Egyptian character of Numbers 21. In reality, apart from the Egyptian background and setting of the event, a proper interpretation of Numbers 21 would be elusive and difficult, if not impossible.

Many stories in Exodus are critical of Egyptian culture. Episodes such as the dividing of the Red Sea and the serpent confrontation were ironic critiques of similar accounts in Egyptian literature. Moreover, the biblical writer often used a parallel idiom as a polemic against Egypt—for example, the description of Yahweh as humiliating and destroying Pharaoh and Egypt with a "strong arm" (Exod. 3:19–20; 6:1; 7:4; 15:16, etc.). Ancient Egyptian texts characteristically described Pharaonic power in terms of Pharaoh's "strong hand"; he was the "pos-

---

48. Frankfort, *Kingship and the Gods*, 92.

sessor of a strong arm" and "the one who destroys enemies with his arm."[49] Likewise, Numbers 21 is a scene of polemical taunting against Egypt. Both the serpent and the standard were emblems of the power and sovereignty of the gods of Egypt. But in Numbers 21 they actually reflect the omnipotence of Yahweh alone. Only he can protect and heal the people—and the symbols of serpent and standard demonstrate that truth. Even though many Israelites desire to return to Egypt, the Egyptian gods can do nothing for the Hebrews.

Finally, the biblical author of Numbers 21 was evidently well versed in Egyptian practices and beliefs. The Egyptian *Sitz im Leben* is simply there. That is to say, the qualities and temper of the episode direct us to Egypt and nowhere else. In addition, the account does not appear to be anachronistic, but it properly reflects ancient Egyptian customs, particularly those in vogue during the New Kingdom period. The biblical author constructed this poignant and profound piece as a critique of contemporary Egyptian dogma and practice and as a demonstration of the truth of the power of Yahweh.

---

49. For an in-depth study of this parallel see J. K. Hoffmeier, "The Arm of God versus the Arm of Pharaoh in the Exodus Narratives," *Biblica* 67 (1986): 378–87; and D. R. Seely, "The Image of the Hand of God in the Exodus Traditions" (Ph.D. diss., University of Michigan, 1990).

Part 3
Contacts between Israel and Egypt in the Historical Books

9
Egyptian Influence on the United Monarchy

In light of the current atmosphere of revisionism in ancient Near Eastern studies, it is not surprising to find scholars who reject outright the validity of any investigation into the united monarchy of Israel and its relationship with Egypt. Many of these researchers deny that there is actually much history in the biblical materials purporting to describe the period of the united monarchy. Thomas L. Thompson condescendingly proclaims that there is an "already established historical conclusion that the bible's stories about a united monarchy are a late fictional reflection on a 'golden age,' much like the legends of Arthur."[1] A cornerstone of this ahistoric view is that no extrabiblical data exist that men named David and Solomon actually sat upon the throne of Israel. As Donald Redford points out, "Not even the names 'David' and 'Solomon' appear, either in West Semitic or Egyptian inscriptions."[2] These scholars draw the conclusion that the Bible contains little historically reliable information regarding the periods before the exile. The biblical description of the united monarchy, therefore, is principally fabrication.[3]

---

1. T. L. Thompson, "'House of David': An Eponymic Referent to Yahweh as Godfather," *SJOT* 9 (1995): 60.
2. D. B. Redford, *Egypt, Canaan, and Israel in Ancient Times* (Princeton, N.J.: Princeton University Press, 1992), 309.
3. See, in particular, the studies by G. Garbini, *History and Ideology in Ancient Israel* (London: SCM, 1988); D. W. Jamieson-Drake, *Scribes and Schools in Monarchic Judah: A Socio-archaeological Approach* (Sheffield: Almond, 1991); D. V. Edelman, ed., *The Fabric of History* (Sheffield: JSOT, 1991); and G. J. Wightman, "The Myth of Solomon," *BASOR* 278 (1990): 5–22.

Avraham Biran and Joseph Naveh reported in 1993, however, that an inscription with the word *bytdwd* had been found at the site of Tell Dan in northern Palestine.[4] They convincingly argued that the word means "house of David" and dates to the ninth century B.C. This recent discovery has thrown the deconstructionist camp into mass confusion.[5] Some of the revisionists have attempted to explain away the inscription by asserting that *bytdwd* is either a place-name in northern Palestine or a designation for the temple of a deity *(dwd?)*.[6] A few of the skeptics have even called into question Biran's excavation technique, arguing that the fragment was "hardly likely to have been found *in situ* or in the way that Biran has claimed."[7] Having visited the excavation three times during 1994–95 and having reviewed all available evidence regarding the discovery, I am thoroughly convinced of the accuracy of Biran's fieldwork. The inscription had been sealed off by a later Assyrian destruction layer, firmly dated to 733/732 B.C. An ash layer is an archaeologist's dream. Anything sealed beneath it must be dated earlier *(terminus ad quem)*, because there was no possibility of intrusion. Pottery beneath the destruction level dates to the ninth–early eighth century B.C., and from this period the so-called House of David inscription must have come. All the revisionist attacks have been to no avail.[8] The House of David inscription refers to what it claims to refer: the house or lineage of David, the second king of the united monarchy and arguably the most significant ruler in the history of Israel. Additional evidence is the likely appearance of the term *bytdwd* on the Mesha Stele, which dates to the ninth century B.C.[9]

---

4. A. Biran and J. Naveh, "An Aramaic Stele Fragment from Tel Dan," *IEJ* 43.2–3 (1993): 81–98; and idem, "The Tel Dan Inscription: A New Fragment," *IEJ* 45.1 (1995): 1–18.

5. The ink spilled over the interpretation of this fragment is immense. The reader ought to consider the following pieces: P. R. Davies, "'House of David' Built on Sand," *BAR* 20.4 (1994): 54–55; A. F. Rainey, "The 'House of David' and the House of the Deconstructionists," *BAR* 20.6 (1994): 47; E. Puech, "La Stèle araméenne de Dan: Bar Hadad II et la coalition des Omrides et de la maison de David," *RB* 101 (1994): 215–41; N. P. Lemche and T. L. Thompson, "Did Biran Kill David? The Bible in the Light of Archaeology," *JSOT* 64 (1994): 3–22; H. Shanks, "'David' Found at Dan," *BAR* 20.2 (1994): 26–39; F. H. Cryer, "On the Recently Discovered 'House of David' Inscription," *SJOT* 8 (1994): 3–19; idem, "A *'Betdawd'* Miscellany: *Dwd, Dwd', or Dwdh?*" *SJOT* 9 (1995): 52–58; T. Muraoka, "Linguistic Notes on the Aramaic Inscription from Tel Dan," *IEJ* 45.1 (1995): 19–21; G. A. Rendsburg, "On the Writing *bytdwd* in the Aramaic Inscription from Tel Dan," *IEJ* 45.1 (1995): 22–25; and D. N. Freedman and J. C. Geoghegan, "'House of David' Is There!" *BAR* 21.2 (1995): 78–79.

6. Thompson, "'House of David,'" 59–60.

7. Ibid., 59.

8. Rainey, "'House of David,'" 47, comments that "their view that nothing in Biblical tradition is earlier than the Persian period, especially their denial of the existence of a United Monarchy, is a figment of their vain imagination."

9. A. Lemaire, "'House of David' Restored in Moabite Inscription," *BAR* 20.3 (1994): 30–37.

Other archaeological evidence supports the existence of the united monarchy in Israel during the tenth century B.C. For instance, 1 Kings 9:15 records that Solomon fortified the cities of Hazor, Megiddo, and Gezer. The fortification of these three sites in the tenth century B.C. has been dramatically confirmed through excavation and the research of Yigael Yadin.[10] Gates and defensive walls are not the only remains there that can be identified with the united monarchy. Inner structures, such as lavish palaces, have also been uncovered that may be associated with the building activity of the united monarchy.[11]

Not surprisingly, the scholarly skepticism about the united monarchy extends to all material regarding its relationship with Egypt. Redford, for example, concludes that any Egyptian material found in biblical descriptions of the united monarchy is not concrete history but merely "plausible" history. And because Egyptian elements, such as Solomon's marrying Pharaoh's daughter (1 Kings 3:1), are only vague possibilities, "it seems foolhardy in the extreme (and at the very least pretentious) to go on writing about these things . . . these must remain themes for midrash or fictional treatment."[12]

Such suspicion of the biblical text is unreasonable. If the Bible claims a connection between an element of Egyptian culture or history and the united monarchy, and Egyptian evidence and other extrabiblical data lend support to the claim, why would we not take the Bible at face value? For example, the Bible reports that Solomon bought horses from Egypt: "Also Solomon's import of horses was from Egypt and Kue, and the king's merchants procured them from Kue for a price. And a chariot was imported from Egypt for 600 shekels of silver . . ." (1 Kings 10:28–29a). Now ancient Egypt was well known for its mastery of the horse and chariot, at least from the beginning of Dynasty 18.[13] Further, a recent study has demonstrated that the Egyptians during the New Kingdom traded horses and chariots to western Asia.[14] Such considerations take the biblical report from being plausible to highly likely. In

---

10. See Y. Yadin, "New Light on Solomon's Megiddo," *BA* 23 (1960): 62 1–68; idem, "Megiddo of the Kings of Israel," *BA* 33 (1970): 85; Y. Aharoni, "The Building Activities of David and Solomon," *IEJ* 24 (1974): 13–16; idem, "The Stratification of Israelite Megiddo," *JNES* 31 (1972): 308; and J. Currid, "The Re-Stratification of Megiddo during the United Monarchy," *ZDPV* 107 (1991): 28–38.
11. D. Ussishkin, "King Solomon's Palaces," *BA* 36 (1973): 78–105.
12. Redford, *Egypt, Canaan, and Israel*, 311.
13. See A. R. Schulman, "Egyptian Representations of Horsemen and Riding in the New Kingdom," *JNES* 16 (1957): 263–71; idem, "Chariots, Chariotry, and the Hyksos," *JSSEA* 10 (1979): 105–53; and J. Van Seters, *The Hyksos: A New Investigation* (New Haven: Yale University Press, 1966), 184–85.
14. Y. Ikeda, "Solomon's Trade in Horses and Chariots in Its International Setting," in *Studies in the Period of David and Solomon and Other Essays*, ed. T. Ishida (Winona Lake, Ind.: Eisenbrauns, 1982), 215–38.

this chapter we will consider several connecting points between Egypt and the Hebrew united monarchy. Our purpose is not to be exhaustive, but merely to provide the reader with a taste of the issues.

Solomon's Marriage to Pharaoh's Daughter

The Bible mentions Solomon's Egyptian wife, a daughter of Pharaoh, six times: 1 Kings 3:1; 7:8; 9:16; 9:24; 11:1–2; 2 Chronicles 8:11. The first reference informs us that Solomon became a son-in-law of Pharaoh through a marriage alliance, and that he housed his wife in the city of David until he finished his monumental building projects in Jerusalem. The second passage notes that one of these architectural projects was a palace for his Egyptian bride, a palace that resembled his own. First Kings 9:24 records her move from the city of David into her own palace. The writer of Chronicles tells us why Solomon moved his Egyptian wife out of the city of David, a point not mentioned by the author of 1 Kings. Thus four of the six texts deal with the living quarters of Pharaoh's daughter after her marriage to Solomon. The remaining two texts treat other aspects of the marriage alliance. First Kings 9:16 tells us that Pharaoh destroyed the city of Gezer, annihilating its inhabitants, and then presented the town as a dowry to his daughter for her marriage to Solomon. Finally, 1 Kings 11:1–2 analyzes Solomon's marriages to Pharaoh's daughter and to other foreign women: they caused him to forsake and abandon the God of Israel.[15]

Since those six texts constitute all the material we have regarding Solomon's marriage alliance with Egypt, we are left with many unanswered questions. The first problem is to identify the Pharaoh who made a treaty with Solomon. His name is not given in the text.[16] A general consensus among scholars has been that this Egyptian king is Siamun, the next-to-last pharaoh of Dynasty 21 (ca. 978–959 B.C.).[17] Of par-

---

15. For a detailed exegesis of these six passages, see S. J. D. Cohen, "Solomon and the Daughter of Pharaoh: Inter-marriage, Conversion, and the Impurity of Women," *JANES* 16–17 (1984–85): 23–37.

16. It is common in the Old Testament not to identify the Pharaoh by name; in the accounts of Abraham's confrontation with an Egyptian king (Gen. 12:10–20), of Joseph, and of the oppression and exodus no specific Pharaonic name is mentioned. Not until the reign of Rehoboam in the late tenth century B.C. is a Pharaoh specifically identified: "Shishak the king of Egypt" (1 Kings 14:25).

17. A. R. Green, "Solomon and Siamun: A Synchronism between Early Dynastic Israel and the Twenty-First Dynasty of Egypt," *JBL* 97 (1978): 353–67; S. H. Horn, "Who Was Solomon's Egyptian Father-in-Law?" *Biblical Research* 12 (1967): 3–17; K. A. Kitchen, *The Third Intermediate Period in Egypt (1100–650 B.C.)* (Warminster: Aris and Phillips, 1973), 280–82; A. Malamat, "Aspects of the Foreign Policies of David and Solomon," *JNES* 22 (1963): 1–17; and A. R. Schulman, "Diplomatic Marriage in the Egyptian New Kingdom," *JNES* 38 (1979): 177–93.

amount importance to this identification is a relief found at Tanis by Pierre Montet that purportedly portrays Siamun carrying out a military campaign against Philistia.[18] The relief is believed to depict Siamun killing an enemy whose body is only partly in view. The enemy appears to be holding a double axe in one of his hands. According to Montet, this type of weapon was used by the Philistines. Consequently, Montet and others connect this raid into Philistia with the conquest of Gezer, the city mentioned in 1 Kings 9:16 as a dowry for the Pharaoh's daughter.

H. Darrell Lance has called into question Montet's interpretation. Lance concludes that the Siamun relief "must be eliminated from discussion" of the identity of Solomon's Egyptian father-in-law because the double axe "bears no resemblance to any weapon which can be connected with the Philistines."[19] Raphael Giveon questions whether the object in the relief is even an axe.[20] His criticism has no merit because the object obviously is an axe; however, none of the Sea Peoples (including the Philistines) are represented with a double axe.[21] Consequently, there is no real evidence that Siamun conquered the Philistines or, specifically, destroyed the city of Gezer. Thus the identity of the Pharaoh in treaty with Solomon remains open to question.

Trying to answer the question on the basis of the chronology of the kings of Israel is similarly fraught with problems. Even though we can demonstrate that Solomon married Pharaoh's daughter between the fourth and eleventh years of his reign,[22] we are yet stymied in our attempt to determine precise dates; we simply do not know when Solomon's reign began and ended. Many scholars assume that his rule began between 970 and 960 and ended between 930 and 920 B.C., but these dates are approximations based upon circumstantial evidence.[23] The most we can say is that the Egyptian king of 1 Kings 9:16 was one

---

18. P. Montet, *Le Drame d'Avaris* (Paris: P. Geuthner, 1941), 196; idem, *Egypt and the Bible* (Philadelphia: Fortress, 1968), 37.

19. H. D. Lance, "Solomon, Siamun, and the Double-Ax," in *Magnalia Dei, the Mighty Acts of God,* ed. F. M. Cross et al. (Garden City, N.Y.: Doubleday, 1976), 209–23.

20. R. Giveon, "An Egyptian Official at Gezer?" *IEJ* 22 (1972): 143–44.

21. Horn's examples of double axes are concentrated in Phoenicia and Crete ("Who Was Solomon's Father-in-Law?" 14–15). In addition, these double axes are not battle-axes—they are much too small—but tools used for cutting down trees. See *ANEP*, no. 331. The axe found by Macalister at Gezer measures a mere 4-1/2 inches long, hardly the size of a weapon; see R. A. S. Macalister, *The Excavation of Gezer,* 3 vols. (London: Palestine Exploration Fund, 1912), 2:343.

22. Solomon's marriage to Pharaoh's daughter almost certainly occurred sometime during that period, for he had not yet completed any of his major building projects in Jerusalem; see Lance, "Solomon, Siamun, and the Double-Ax," 210.

23. One should note that E. Thiele in his major works on the chronology of the Hebrew kings does not tackle the dating of the united monarchy. See his *The Mysterious Numbers of the Hebrew Kings* (Grand Rapids: Zondervan, 1983), and *A Chronology of the Hebrew Kings* (Grand Rapids: Zondervan, 1977).

of the last rulers of Dynasty 21: either Amenemope (ca. 984–978 B.C.), Siamun (ca. 978–959 B.C.), or Psusennes II (ca. 959–945 B.C.).[24]

Despite the difficulties just described, that Solomon married Pharaoh's daughter by treaty has an authentic ring to it. First of all, that she is mentioned in six different places in the Bible leads us to believe that the event was historical and highly significant. In addition, during this period compacts between nations were frequently ratified by marriages between royal houses. The wedding of Solomon to the daughter of Pharaoh would have a privileged place among all those royal intermarriages.

Abraham Malamat has argued that this marriage alliance is an "absolutely unique event in the annals of not only Israel but Egypt as well."[25] His point has found its way into much of the literature.[26] Although the marriage between Solomon and Pharaoh's daughter is the only example of such an agreement *between* Israel and Egypt, the fact is that both Israel and Egypt did participate in diplomatic marriages in the first millennium B.C. That Israel participated is clear (see 2 Sam. 3:3; 1 Kings 11:1; 14:21); the situation in Egypt needs to be dealt with more extensively.[27]

In an important study Alan Schulman has provided numerous examples of Egyptian diplomatic marriages during the New Kingdom period.[28] For instance, a certain queen of Egypt, who had recently been widowed (probably by the death of Tutankhamun), sent envoys with a letter to the Hittite king Suppiluliumas to set up a marriage: "My husband died and I have no son. People say that you have many sons. If you were to send me one of your sons, he might become my husband. I am loath to take a servant of mine and make him my husband."[29] The catalyst of this attempt at a diplomatic marriage was the attack of the Hittite army on the country of Amqa to the north of Lebanon. Also worth noting are the marriages of Princess Tany and Princess Herit to the Hyksos king Apopi.[30]

---

24. The belief that Solomon wed a daughter of Shishak (Shoshenk I) is unwarranted according to the biblical evidence; see the bibliography given by Horn, "Who Was Solomon's Father-in-Law?" 4–5.
25. Malamat, "Aspects of the Foreign Policies," 10.
26. E.g., Kitchen, *Third Intermediate Period,* 282, says that "a marriage of an Egyptian princess to a foreign potentate was unthinkable in the New Kingdom or Empire period."
27. Despite abundant textual evidence from ancient Egypt, we know very little about how the Egyptians chose marriage partners. For a good discussion of this point see G. Pinch, "Private Life in Ancient Egypt," in *Civilizations of the Ancient Near East,* ed. J. M. Sasson (New York: Scribner, 1995), 1:363–81.
28. Schulman, "Diplomatic Marriage," 177–93.
29. *ANET,* 319.
30. W. K. Simpson, "The Hyksos Princess Tany," *Chronique d'Egypte* 34.68 (1959): 233–39; and H. Carter, "Report on the Tomb of Zeser-Ka-Ra Amen-Hetep I, Discovered by the Earl of Carnarvon in 1914," *JEA* 3 (1916): 152. Kenneth Kitchen has made me aware of twin door jambs recently uncovered at Tell el-Dabʿa that indicate that Tany was not

But then how does one understand the statement of Amenophis III to the Babylonian monarch Kadasman-Enlil I that "from old, the daughter of an Egyptian king has not been given in marriage to anyone"?[31] The context of the statement is revealing. Apparently the Pharaoh is rejecting a Babylonian request for a marriage treaty with Egypt; Amenophis III seems to be denying that petition in an insulting, boasting, and derogatory fashion. Schulman argues that Pharaoh's statement is "bombastic exaggeration"; it does not represent fixed policy.[32] In fact, royal diplomatic marriages, under certain conditions, were quite characteristic of Egyptian foreign relations.

A noteworthy aspect of Egyptian marriage treaties is that they forged alliances between rulers but not between their states. Thus, when one of the rulers died or was ousted from power, the political relationship was no longer binding. That practice is evidenced in the biblical account of the diplomatic marriage between Solomon and Pharaoh's daughter. During his reign there appears to have been peace between Egypt and Israel. However, soon after Solomon's death, Shoshenk I attacked Israel and Judah. The alliance that Solomon had made with a previous pharaoh was no longer in effect. Shoshenk I was not bound by the marriage alliance of a predecessor.

The facts are these: both Israel and Egypt participated in royal diplomatic marriages throughout their histories; there appears to have been peace between these two nations throughout the tenth century B.C.; a marriage between Solomon and Pharaoh's daughter is mentioned six times in the Bible in various contexts; and Shoshenk I attacked Israel only after the death of Solomon. All this makes it likely that such a marriage covenant did take place, though we have no absolute proof. We are yet to find an inscription that reads: "I Pharaoh present my daughter to Solomon, king of Israel, for a wife."

Solomon's Taxation System

Some scholars contend that Solomon's apportioning of his kingdom into twelve districts for the purposes of taxation and the monthly provision of supplies for his household (1 Kings 4) is similar to a system

---

an Egyptian princess but of Hyksos royalty. See M. Bietak, *Avaris: The Capital of the Hyksos* (London: British Museum, 1996), fig. 54. Even so, I am not convinced that this invalidates the thesis that Egypt participated in royal diplomatic marriages.

31. O. Weber and E. Ebeling, *Die El-Amarna Tafeln,* 2 vols. (Leipzig: Hinrichs, 1908, 1915), 2:4–21.

32. Schulman, "Diplomatic Marriage," 180.

employed by Shoshenk I in Egypt.[33] A stele discovered in the temple of Arsaphes in Herakleopolis describes Shoshenk I's restoration of daily sacrifices in the sanctuary. According to the text, Shoshenk I instituted a levy upon the population of the Herakleopolitan nome to pay for the sacrifices. It was divided into twelve monthly portions; the text specifies the amount of each portion as well as the officials and towns responsible for collecting it. Solomon's system of provisioning his court is strikingly similar: 1 Kings 4 sets forth a twelve-month levy system for the people of Israel. Included are the names of the officials and many of the towns responsible. In addition, the amount of the levy for each month is specified (vv. 21–22).

Numerous scholars have agreed that there is a connection here between Israel and Egypt.[34] The only question has been where the system originated. Did it originate in Egypt or in Israel? Most scholars have assumed that the system began in Egypt and was adopted in Israel. Redford believes it "highly likely that Solomon was consciously using this common Egyptian means of taxation for supplying the organs of central government with sustenance. Whether he was directly inspired by contemporary Egyptian practice, or whether he derived it indirectly through the former Egyptian Empire in Canaan, is a moot point."[35] Alberto Green has proposed, however, that the borrowing actually went the other way: Shoshenk I modeled his levy system after that of Solomon.[36] Green's view has not been widely accepted.[37]

Kenneth Kitchen, on the other hand, has vigorously attacked the position that Solomon's and Shoshenk I's taxation systems had any relationship. He finds it "entirely unjustified to derive one from the other in either direction" because there is only one real parallel, that is, twelve monthly levies per annum.[38] But as we have seen, there are more paral-

---

33. For the best treatment see D. B. Redford, "Studies in Relations between Palestine and Egypt during the First Millennium B.C.: I. The Taxation System of Solomon," in J. W. Wevers and D. B. Redford, eds., *Studies on the Ancient Palestinian World* (Toronto: University of Toronto Press, 1972), 141–56.

34. E. W. Heaton, *Solomon's New Men* (London: Thames and Hudson, 1974), 51, says, "The king's bureaucrats were equal to the situation and simply adopted a system of taxation which had proved efficient in Egypt."

35. Redford, "Studies in Relations," 156.

36. A. R. Green, "Israelite Influence at Shishak's Court," *BASOR* 233 (1979): 59–62. According to Green, Shoshenk learned the system from Jeroboam, who had fled Solomon's vengeance.

37. K. A. Kitchen, "Egypt and Israel during the First Millennium B.C.," in *Congress Volume: 1988* (SVT), ed. J. A. Emerton (Leiden: Brill, 1988), 116, labels Green's work a "farfetched hypothesis." In this instance, the influence could have gone either way. We will have to wait until further relevant material is uncovered. We should at the same time recognize that scholars are frequently too quick to assume Israelite dependence on other cultures.

38. Kitchen, "Egypt and Israel," 116.

lels than Kitchen acknowledges. The listing of officials, the amounts of the levy, and even the types of materials to be provided are important similarities between the two. There was, then, an institutional connection between the provisioning systems of Egypt and Solomonic Israel, although who influenced whom is a debatable point.

Administrative Structures

The parallels between the administrative structures of Egypt and the united monarchy of Israel have been dealt with so extensively in the modern literature that only a few remarks are necessary.[39] In an important article from the first half of the twentieth century, Roland de Vaux maintained that elements of the administrative structure of monarchic Israel were based on Egyptian models.[40] He claimed that two high offices of the Davidic and Solomonic court, the *sôpēr* and the *mazĕkîr*, were based respectively on the Egyptian *sš nsw* and *wḥmw*. Other offices in the Hebrew court were also adopted from Egyptian governmental structures. Aelred Cody added to de Vaux's work by claiming that the high Hebrew office of royal scribe *(šîšā᾽)* reflected the Egyptian office of document scribe *(sš š᾽t)*.[41] On the basis of these studies, numerous scholars are convinced of solid connections between the administrative structures of Egypt and those of Israel during the united monarchy.

Redford has correctly maintained, on the other hand, that there is no need to invoke Egyptian influence on these high Hebrew court offices, except possibly regarding the title *mazĕkîr*. These offices were "not in mimicry of Egyptian ways, but in fulfilment of the ordinary, day-to-day needs of the administration."[42] Kitchen convincingly argues specifically against Cody's thesis.[43] Redford and others, however, do find resemblances between the lower administrative spheres of the two kingdoms.

With regard to the highest level of government, Gerhard von Rad contended in 1947 that there was Egyptian influence on the Judean coronation ritual, and pointed especially to 2 Kings 11:12: "Then he brought the king's son out and put the crown on him, and gave him the testimony *(ʿēdût)*; and they made him king and anointed him, and they clapped their hands and said, 'Long live the king!'" Von Rad compared the Hebrew *ʿēdût* to the Egyptian concept of *nekhbet*, which is under-

---

39. See, e.g., Heaton, *Solomon's New Men*, 47–60.
40. R. de Vaux, "Titres et fonctionnaires égyptiens à la cour de David et de Salomon," *RB* 48 (1939): 394–405.
41. A. Cody, "Le titre égyptien et le nom propre du scribe de David," *RB* 72 (1965): 381–93.
42. Redford, "Studies in Relations," 144.
43. Kitchen, "Egypt and Israel," 112–13.

stood as a formal adoption by the gods and presentation of a titulary.[44] De Vaux expanded von Rad's position by tracing the anointing recorded in 2 Kings 11:12 to the Egyptian custom of anointing vassal rulers.[45] Although the alleged parallels have been supported by much scholarship, Kitchen has argued to the contrary that *ēdût* and *nekhbet* are two entirely distinct things, and thus "the evidence for Egyptian influence on Judaean coronation-ritual simply evaporates."[46] That most kings in the ancient Near East were crowned and anointed would seem to lessen the possibility of any direct connection between the Egyptian and Israelite rituals.

More likely is the possibility of a direct Egyptian influence on the coregency between David and Solomon. As E. Ball states, "the co-regency into which David took his son Solomon could well have been based on the Egyptian model."[47] It was common throughout the history of ancient Egypt for Pharaoh to exalt his son to co-kingship. Ball cites numerous examples from the Old Kingdom, the Middle Kingdom, the New Kingdom, and the Third Intermediate Period.[48] In other ancient Near Eastern cultures such a practice was either rare or nonexistent, as in Hatti and Canaan. Among the similarities in Egypt and Israel is that in both kingdoms, once a son had been crowned as coregent, no further coronation was required when he became sole ruler. In addition, coregency frequently took place in Egypt when the father was too old to fulfil his duties as king. That, of course, is just like the coregency of David and Solomon in 1 Kings 1.

To sum up our findings: the Egyptian imprint on the court and administration of the Hebrew united monarchy was considerable. Though we cannot say how extensive the influence was nor whether it came to Israel directly from Egypt, it was probably greater than many today acknowledge.

Miscellaneous Parallels

Finally, we will look at some apparent parallels between Egypt and the Hebrew united monarchy that have been proposed but not dealt with

---

44. G. von Rad, "Das judäische Königsritual," *TLZ* 72 (1947): 211–16. For a development of this parallel see G. Cooke, "The Israelite King as Son of God," *ZAW* 73 (1961): 202–25.
45. R. de Vaux, *Bible et Orient* (Paris: Editions du Cerf, 1967), 287–301.
46. K. A. Kitchen, *Ancient Orient and Old Testament* (Chicago: InterVarsity, 1966), 106–11.
47. E. Ball, "The Co-Regency of David and Solomon (1 Kings 1)," *VT* 27 (1977): 268–79.
48. Ibid., 272–78. For more detail on Egyptian coregencies, see the classic work of W. J. Murnane, *Ancient Egyptian Coregencies*, Studies in Ancient Oriental Civilizations (Chicago: Oriental Institute, 1977).

to any great extent in the literature. Some scholars argue that they are merely minor possibilities. In some cases, however, further investigation and research may be warranted.

It has been suggested that the description of Solomon's throne in 1 Kings 10:18–20 reflects a throne design found in Ugarit and Phoenicia that in turn is based on an Egyptian prototype of the New Kingdom period.[49] The evidence certainly has some merit, although more thorough study is needed. Hellmut Brunner adds to the discussion by suggesting that the very form of the Egyptian throne is reflected in Hebrew theological literature.[50] He says that the Egyptian throne was mounted on a pedestal in the shape of the hieroglyphic character *ma'at,* which means "righteousness, truth" (see pp. 118–20). He then connects that form with Hebrew phrases such as "righteousness and justice are the foundation of Thy throne" (Ps. 89:14). The proposal is ingenious, but it also may be a little far-fetched.

Another suggested point of contact is that Solomon's shipping enterprise on the Red Sea (1 Kings 9:26) "follows an Egyptian precedent even older than the famous expedition of Queen Hatshepsut to Punt in the first half of the fifteenth century B.C., and one which was still being maintained, as the Great Harris Papyrus records, in the reign of Ramesses III."[51] It is further maintained that Solomon's relations with Tyre, especially his purchasing of timber, reflect earlier imperial policies of Egypt. The relations between Egypt and Tyre are concretely described in the "Journey of Wenamon" from the reign of Rameses XI (ca. 1100–1070 B.C.). Whether there was a direct Egyptian influence on Israel in the area of commerce is difficult to detect. Maybe Tyre was simply the place where ancient Near Eastern countries got their timber because it had a lot of trees. And Solomon may have had ships at Ezion-geber on the Red Sea because the Hebrews had no other port for seafaring. One needs to be careful in seeing parallels merely on the basis of similar activity.

K. Elliger has proposed that David's coterie of thirty men described in 2 Samuel 23:13–39 was based upon the Egyptian *m'b yt,* a high tribunal of thirty leaders.[52] Objections to this hypothesis have been strongly voiced by some scholars.[53] The principal problem is that David's men

---

49. F. Canciani and G. Pettinato, "Salomos Thron: Philologische und archäologische Erwägungen," *ZDPV* 81 (1965): 88–108.

50. H. Brunner, "Gerechtigkeit als Fundament des Thrones," *VT* 8 (1958): 426–28. For the information regarding thrones we are dependent on the work of R. J. Williams, "A People Come Out of Egypt," *SVT* 28 (1975): 231–52.

51. Heaton, *Solomon's New Men,* 28.

52. K. Elliger, "Die dreissig Helden Davids," *Palästina-Jahrbuch* 31 (1935): 29–75.

53. B. Mazar, "The Military Elite of King David," *VT* 13 (1963): 310–20; and Redford, "Studies in Relations," 141–42.

are military leaders in Israel, whereas the Egyptian group is administrative. Although this alleged parallel is frequently cited, it ought once and for all to be laid to rest.

The claims that Egyptian architectural forms influenced the building styles of the Hebrew united monarchy have also encountered great suspicion.[54] For Levantine archetypes appear to have had the major impact on the building projects at the royal cities of the early monarchy. However, we must be careful in this matter because to deny any Egyptian influence on Israelite architecture would be unjust. In fact, the dimensions of the gates at the Solomonic royal cities of Gezer, Hazor, and Megiddo are based on the Egyptian common cubit.[55] This led R. B. Y. Scott to suggest that the architect of the fortifications at the Hebrew royal cities was Egyptian.[56] Although that conclusion is unfounded, the use of Egyptian measurements by Solomon's royal engineers underscores the impact of Egyptian culture on the united monarchy.

One definite example of an Egyptian import into Israel is the use of hieratic numerals. The Egyptian numbering system appears in Hebrew written materials from Samaria, Tell Arad, Wadi Murabbaʿat, Lachish, Mesad Hashavyahu, and elsewhere.[57] Yohanan Aharoni concludes "that hieratic numerals were used in the royal administration both in Israel and in Judah. This furnishes striking evidence for the influence of Egyptian prototypes in the Israelite administration."[58]

We have seen that there was a direct and strong Egyptian influence on the early monarchy of Israel. Many Israelite activities of that period as described in the Bible or discovered through archaeology are clearly connected to previous Egyptian practices. As Ronald Williams says, "the evidence is overwhelming that Israel drank deeply at the wells of Egypt."[59] Yet the extent of the Egyptian imprint on Israel is uncertain. We need to be careful, on the one hand, of a pan-Egyptianism that views every feature of the united monarchy as in some way related to Egypt. The Hebrews were not Egyptians. And, of course, the Israelites

---

54. Redford, "Studies in Relations," 144, leads the outcry against these claims.
55. Y. Yadin, "Solomon's City Wall and Gate at Gezer," *IEJ* 8 (1958): 80–86.
56. R. B. Y. Scott, "Weights and Measures of the Bible," *BA* 22.2 (1959): 26. We really should not be surprised that architectural parallels exist between Egypt and monarchic Israel. On the possibility of the discovery of an Israelite house in Egypt see M. Bietak, "An Iron Age Four-Room House in Ramesside Egypt," *EI* 23 (1992): 10–12.
57. Y. Aharoni, "The Use of Hieratic Numerals in Hebrew Ostraca and the Shekel Weights," *BASOR* 184 (1966): 13–19.
58. Ibid., 19.
59. Williams, "A People Come Out of Egypt," 252.

were greatly influenced, for good and ill, by the peoples of Mesopotamia, Canaan, and elsewhere. But, on the other hand, a non-Egyptianism that holds that Egypt had little or no impact on Israelite customs is equally mistaken. The latter appears to be more common in today's scholarship, and it needs to be avoided.

10
Shishak's Invasion of Palestine at the Beginning of the Divided Monarchy

Some recent studies in Old Testament literature argue that ancient Israel produced few, if any, reliable historical records.[1] The narrative in the books of Kings, Chronicles, and elsewhere in the Bible is to be understood as history by invention. In other words, it was created by postexilic authors who had no access to real historical sources. Consequently, biblical history is mere fabrication, an artificial construction that has no grounding in events that truly happened. The history of Israel, in many scholars' estimation, is really nothing more than a Judaic *Iliad, Odyssey,* or even *Winnie-the-Pooh.* One is not hard-pressed to find this perspective in recent literature about the Old Testament.[2] Con-

---

1. See in particular John Van Seters, *Abraham in History and Tradition* (New Haven: Yale University Press, 1975); idem, *In Search of History: Historiography in the Ancient World and the Origins of Biblical History* (New Haven: Yale University Press, 1983); idem, *Prologue to History: The Yahwist as Historian in Genesis* (Louisville: Westminster/John Knox, 1992); and T. L. Thompson, *Early History of the Israelite People: From the Written and Archaeological Sources* (Leiden: Brill, 1992); idem, *The Historicity of the Patriarchal Narratives: The Quest for the Historical Abraham* (Berlin: de Gruyter, 1974); idem, *The Origin Tradition of Ancient Israel* (Sheffield: JSOT, 1987). In the last-mentioned work, Thompson arrogantly announces that his studies have "systematically destroyed the premises on which so much early scholarship had proceeded, especially the assumption that archaeological and extra-biblical historical data was relevant to an understanding of traditional tales" (p. 22). In other words, if the biblical material is a literary creation of radically late date, how can archaeology and ancient Near Eastern written materials shed light on it? The two subjects are simply nonsynchronous.

2. Typical are the works of J. H. Hayes and J. M. Miller: *Israelite and Judaean History* (Philadelphia: Westminster, 1977); and *A History of Ancient Israel and Judah* (Philadelphia: Westminster, 1986). See also P. R. Davies, *In Search of 'Ancient Israel'* (Sheffield: JSOT, 1992), which argues that the origins of biblical historical literature date to the Persian period (400–200 B.C.).

sider, for example, the conclusion of Thomas L. Thompson: "We have seen that the biblical chronologies are not grounded on historical memory, but are rather based on a very late theological schema that presupposes a very unhistorical world-view. Those efforts to use the biblical narratives for a reconstruction of the history of the Near East, in a manner comparable to the use of the archives of Mari and similar finds, can justly be dismissed as fundamentalist."[3]

In light of secure historical connections between the Bible and other ancient Near Eastern documents, however, the modernist approach is difficult, if not downright impossible, to defend. That the biblical authors set incidents like the invasions of Sennacherib (2 Kings 18:13; 19:16, 20; 2 Chron. 32:1–22) and Nebuchadnezzar (2 Kings 24:1–10; 1 Chron. 6:15) in their proper chronological framework and setting is confirmed by contemporary ancient Near Eastern texts—the Prism of Sennacherib for the former campaign[4] and the Lachish Letters for the latter.[5] Moreover, excavations at Lachish and Jerusalem furnish positive evidence of the historical accuracy of the biblical account of those events.[6] If the books of Kings and Chronicles were free literary creations by late and disparate authors, how could they have placed so many events in their "right time and pew"?[7]

One of the strongest connections between the Bible and other ancient Near Eastern evidences is its presentation of the invasion of Judah and Israel by the forces of Pharaoh Shishak of Egypt. First Kings 14:25–26 gives a synopsis of the Egyptian campaign: "It came about in the fifth year of King Rehoboam, that Shishak the king of Egypt came up against Jerusalem. And he took away the treasures of the house of the LORD and the treasures of the king's house, and he took everything, even taking all

---

3. Thompson, *Historicity of the Patriarchal Narratives*, 315. Thompson's choice of the term *fundamentalist* is unfortunate and, frankly, unconscionable. It evokes images of a narrow-mindedness that hardly befits the character of many who disagree with him. Such language is name-calling at its worst.

4. *ANET*, 287–88. The prism mentions Judean King Hezekiah by name, and its historical content fits well with the biblical narratives.

5. *ANET*, 321–22.

6. See D. Ussishkin, "Excavations at Tel Lachish—1973–1977, Preliminary Report," *TA* 5 (1978): 1–97; idem, "Excavations at Tel Lachish—1978–1983, Second Preliminary Report," *TA* 10 (1983): 97–175; N. Avigad, *Discovering Jerusalem* (Nashville: Nelson, 1983), 23–60; M. Ben-Dov, *In the Shadow of the Temple* (Jerusalem: Keter, 1982), 31–55; B. Mazar, *The Mountain of the Lord* (Garden City, N.Y.: Doubleday, 1975); and Y. Shiloh, *Excavations at the City of David*, vol. 1 (Jerusalem: Hebrew University, 1984).

7. At a recent Society of Biblical Literature meeting, J. M. Miller asked this question of Van Seters in regard to the historical accuracy of the invasion of Pharaoh Shishak. For an interesting insight into the current debate, see R. E. Friedman, review of *Prologue to History*, by J. Van Seters, *BR* 9.6 (1993): 12–16; Van Seters's response in *BR* 10.4 (1994): 42–43, 54; and Friedman's rejoinder (p. 44).

the shields of gold which Solomon had made." Second Chronicles 12:2–4 adds a few details: "It came about in King Rehoboam's fifth year, because they had been unfaithful to the Lord, that Shishak king of Egypt came up against Jerusalem with 1,200 chariots and 60,000 horsemen. And the people who came with him from Egypt were without number: the Lubim, Sukkiim, and the Ethiopians. And he captured the fortified towns of Judah and came as far as Jerusalem."

Unfortunately, there is no Egyptian document of the time that describes the campaign of Shishak in narrative form. However, we do possess a monumental triumphal relief on the Bubastite Portal of the main temple of Amon at Karnak that catalogues, town by town, Shishak's military incursion.[8] The Karnak relief provides a striking verification of the biblical account that cannot be ignored by the revisionists. This chapter will take a close look at the issue. Our study will be divided into four parts: (1) an overview of Shishak's reign in Egypt; (2) a general look at the construction and date of the Bubastite Portal at Karnak; (3) an evaluation of the information set forth on the relief; and (4) a discussion of the reasons for Shishak's incursion into Israel and Judah. An appendix examines in more detail the individual entries on the relief. As we proceed, the stunning historical accuracy of the biblical account will be confirmed.

Reign of Shoshenk I

By coincidence in 1973 both Donald Redford[9] and Kenneth Kitchen[10] produced masterful studies detailing the rule of Shoshenk I.[11] Here we

---

8. The best reproductions of this relief are found in *Reliefs and Inscriptions at Karnak*, vol. 3, *The Bubastite Portal* (Chicago: Oriental Institute, 1954); for more readily available photographs see K. A. Kitchen, "Shishak's Military Campaign in Israel Confirmed," *BAR* 15.3 (1989): 32–33.

9. D. B. Redford, "Studies in Relations between Palestine and Egypt during the First Millennium B.C.: II. The Twenty-Second Dynasty," *JAOS* 93 (1973): 3–17. Redford's handling of Egyptian material here is superb, but his work in regard to the Bible is not. He states, for example: "It is no counsel of despair nor negative approach to state that the only traditions we can associate with the name of Solomon are his marriage, his building programme at Jerusalem and elsewhere, his commercial adventures, and, probably, the establishment of a grid of tax districts. But to characterize his reign as one of literary activity is, in the present state of our knowledge, pure imagination" (p. 6). For Redford, the Bible is always suspect.

10. K. A. Kitchen, *The Third Intermediate Period in Egypt (1100–650 B.C.)* (Warminster: Aris and Phillips, 1973), 287–302.

11. This is the probable Egyptian spelling and pronunciation of the king's name. It is doubtless identical with the biblical Shishak. The ruler is also called Sheshonk after the Greek form *Sesōnchis*. See S. Herrmann, *A History of Israel in Old Testament Times* (Philadelphia: Fortress, 1975), 196.

will review only some of the highlights of Shoshenk I's reign and, in particular, those events that have a direct bearing on our understanding of his invasion of Palestine.

The family history of Shoshenk is not well documented, although a few inscriptions are helpful.[12] Shoshenk was a Libyan from the tribe of Meshwesh and therefore not of royal Egyptian blood. His parents were referred to in Egyptian texts simply as "Chief of Me and God's Father, Nimlot, and God's Mother, Tentsepeh."[13] They were not commoners, but appear to have had great power and influence over the thrones of the later part of Dynasty 21. A family monument at Abydos, for instance, pictures Shoshenk gaining favors from the reigning Pharaoh (probably Psusennes II) for his father's cult.[14] In the text the king describes Shoshenk as "the great chief of the Meshwesh . . . chief of chiefs, my chief officer," and then refers to "all those who are loyal to thee, and thine army likewise."[15] It seems that prior to his accession to the throne of Egypt, Shoshenk was a power (rival?) behind the throne of Psusennes II, for he controlled an independent army and occupied a prominent office in the Egyptian government.

That the Egyptian sovereigns at Tanis and the Libyan chiefs shared power during the closing decades of Dynasty 21 is confirmed by evidence of marriage alliances between them. For example, it is likely that a certain Shedsunefertem was married to Tentsepeh, a daughter of Pharaoh Psusennes II, *and* to Mehtenweskhet, a sister of Shoshenk I. Thus Shedsunefertem was a brother-in-law of Shoshenk I and a son-in-law of Psusennes II at the same time. These very high level intermarriages are evidence that the Tanite rulers recognized the increasing and formidable power of the Libyans.[16]

The enthronement of Shoshenk I marked the first time in several hundred years (not since the Hyksos rulers of the seventeenth and sixteenth centuries B.C.) that a foreigner had been on the throne of Egypt. Probably because of Shoshenk's alien status, the first few years of his reign were dominated by questions of the validity of his authority over Egypt. For example, at Thebes in these early years the populace did not recognize him as full pharaoh, but referred to him simply by the old title "Great Chief of the Me." Theban texts employed no cartouches or Pharaonic titles for Shoshenk at this time, but adorned his name with

---

12. See *ARE* 4:325–33.
13. M. G. Daressy, "Fragments deux cercueils, Saqqara," *ASAE* 17 (1917): 17.
14. A. M. Blackman, "Stela of Shoshenk: Great Chief of the Meshwesh," *JEA* 27 (1941): 83–95.
15. Ibid., plate x, as quoted in Redford, "Studies in Relations," 8.
16. Kitchen, *Third Intermediate Period*, 111–16. Kitchen's genealogical chart on the bottom of p. 115 should read Psusennes II rather than Psusennes I.

the throw-stick determinative which symbolized a foreigner. Elsewhere in Egypt in this period there appear to have been warfare and turmoil; the oasis of Dakhla was "in a state of rebellion."[17] The evidence we have suggests that Egypt was somewhat floundering, unstable, and weak at the beginning of Shoshenk I's reign.

Shoshenk's early years of rule were spent consolidating his power, securing his throne, and bringing political unity to Egypt. This is confirmed by the title that declares him to be the one "to unite the Two Lands." Also, in many texts he is pictured wearing the double crown of Egypt (the sign of the unification of Upper and Lower Egypt), and he is called the one "Appearing in the Double Crown," "King of Upper and Lower Egypt," and "Lord of the Two Lands." Shoshenk's methods of unification and centralization of power took many forms. He dealt with his lack of royal recognition at Thebes by appointing his son Yewepet as high priest of Amon at Thebes, "thus at last interrupting the hereditary succession to that office, and securing the control of the priestly principality of Thebes for his own family."[18] By the fifth year of his rule the Thebans recognized Shoshenk I as pharaoh in toto. That change is fully confirmed by inscriptions on the bandages of royal mummies at Deir el-Bahari (the site of the Theban mortuary temples). These inscriptions from the fifth, tenth, and eleventh years of his reign proclaim Shoshenk I

> King of Upper and Lower Egypt, Lord of the Two Lands,
> Kheperhezre-Setepnere; Son of Re,
> Lord of Diadems, Meriamon-Sheshonk I.[19]

To consolidate his rule, Shoshenk frequently appointed his sons and grandsons to high positions.[20] For example, his son Namlot was given command of the armed forces in the region of Herakleopolis, and he was called "general of the army of Herakleopolis."[21] Shoshenk I also used ethnic ties to his political advantage. To deal with the rebellion at the oasis of Dakhla, he assigned the Libyan Wayeheset to the governorship of the area and charged him to bring order. A stele found at the oasis by H. G. Lyons in 1894 preserves the mandate: "when Pharaoh . . . sent him to organize the land of the oasis, after it had been found to be in a state

---

17. *ARE* 4:360.
18. *ARE* 4:344.
19. Ibid.
20. A. H. Gardiner, *Egypt of the Pharaohs* (New York: Oxford University Press, 1961), 327: "Several sons of the new ruler are known and he seems to have assigned to them such positions as would be most likely to secure the permanence of his regime."
21. For other examples see Redford, "Studies in Relations," 8–9.

of rebellion, and desolate, on the day of arrival to inspect the wells and cisterns . . ."[22] Through appointments like these, Shoshenk I dominated all aspects of Egyptian life, and the political, military, and religious realms in particular.

Another means of consolidating control of Egypt was marriage alliances. A well-known diplomatic marriage occurred between Shoshenk I's son Osorkon (the future Pharaoh Osorkon I) and Maatkare, daughter of Psusennes II, the last ruler of Dynasty 21.[23] This provided at least a semblance of political continuity between the two dynasties and demonstrated Shoshenk I's willingness to acknowledge and pay homage to Egyptian history.

Shoshenk I further established a continuum with the past by selecting as his prenomen[24] *Hedjkheperre setepnere* ("chosen of the god Re"), which had originally belonged to Smendes, the first pharaoh of Dynasty 21. Why Smendes? The major reason is probably that Smendes was undisputed pharaoh of all Egypt—and that, of course, was a goal of Shoshenk I. In addition, there may have been a conscious attempt to underscore the similarities of the two pharaohs as the founders of new dynasties and as the most powerful monarchs of those dynasties.[25] The tie between the two was also solidified by Shoshenk's establishing Tanis as his delta capital. Smendes hailed from Tanis, which had become the central capital during his rulership.

Not much is known about the domestic reign of Shoshenk I after his consolidation of power. We are aware from inscriptions, however, of land and water disputes during his regime.[26] Shoshenk I did some building, although to what extent remains a mystery. He did erect a temple to Amon at El Hibeh, but unfortunately little of it remains.[27] He added sections to some temples at Tanis and Karnak. Kitchen mentions building activity at Bubastis, Tell el-Maskhuta, Memphis, and elsewhere.[28] Most of these remains are mere fragments, widely dispersed blocks bearing the name of Shoshenk I. The meager remains suggest that Shoshenk's reign was more focused on other issues (such as unification) and possibly that the monarchy was somewhat frail domestically.

---

22. *ARE* 4:360.
23. H. Gauthier, *Le Livre des rois d'Egypte* (Cairo: L'Institut français d'archéologie orientale du Caire, 1914), 3:299.
24. A principal name for the king most commonly found within a cartouche. See A. H. Gardiner, *Egyptian Grammar* (London: Oxford University Press, 1957), 71–76.
25. Kitchen, *Third Intermediate Period,* 287.
26. A. H. Gardiner, "The Dakhleh Stela," *JEA* 19 (1933): 19–30.
27. See B. Porter and R. L. B. Moss, *Topographical Bibliography of Ancient Egyptian Hieroglyphic Texts, Reliefs, and Paintings,* 7 vols. (Oxford: Oxford University Press, 1927–64), 4:124.
28. Kitchen, *Third Intermediate Period,* 291.

Foreign affairs under Shoshenk I gained increased prominence over Dynasty 21. Shoshenk I established an aggressive policy of external relations in two basic ways. First, he renewed economic and trade links with Byblos on the Phoenician coast of the Mediterranean Sea.[29] The link between the two kingdoms is confirmed by the discovery of a seated statue of Shoshenk I at Byblos. The second plank of his foreign policy was military incursion. Although the evidence is much debated, it appears likely that Shoshenk I conquered Nubia in the south to obtain tribute from the area and to open up trade relations with regions still farther south. An inscription on a chamber wall of the great temple of Karnak pictures Shoshenk I addressing the god Amon:

> [Year] —— under the majesty of King Sheshonk (I) —— [in] "The-House-of-Millions-of-Years-of-King-Kheperhezre-Setepnere,-Son-of-Re,-Meriamon-Sheshonk-I,-Which-Is-in-Memphis" —— O Amon, thou maker of the land of the Negro —— tribute of the land of Syria[30] —— I bring it to thee from the land of the Negro ——red cattle, thy firstlings —— thy gazelles, thy panther-skins.[31]

Our knowledge of the relationship that Shoshenk I had with the Hebrews, both during the united monarchy under Solomon and during the division under Jeroboam and Rehoboam, is sketchy. As we noted earlier (pp. 165–68), some scholars see a great Egyptian influence upon the courts of David and Solomon;[32] in particular, they argue that the

---

29. During the reign of Rameses II (ca. 1290–1224 B.C.), Byblos was under the control of the Egyptians. It received independent status after his death, and the ties between Egypt and Phoenicia were almost severed. The weakness of Egypt in its relations with Byblos at this time is underscored by the story of the "Journey of Wenamon." In about 1065 B.C. an Egyptian official named Wenamon traveled to Byblos to purchase lumber. He was treated rudely and harshly by the ruler of Byblos. That incident symbolizes Phoenicia's new attitude toward Egypt. See W. A. Ward, "Egyptian Relations with Canaan," in *ABD* 2:399–408; and J. Leclant, "Les Relations entre l'Egypte et la Phénicie du voyage d'Ounamon à l'expédition d'Alexandre," in *The Role of the Phoenicians in the Interaction of Mediterranean Civilizations*, ed. W. A. Ward (Beirut: American University of Beirut Press, 1968), 9–31.

30. The mention of Syria in this context is an anomaly. Does it possibly suggest that Shoshenk I invaded Syria to the north as well as Nubia to the south?

31. *ARE* 4:358. Kitchen, *Third Intermediate Period*, 575, has concluded that there was no Nubian campaign by Shoshenk I.

32. See A. Malamat, "Aspects of the Foreign Policies of David and Solomon," *JNES* 22 (1963): 1–17; idem, "The Kingdom of David and Solomon in Its Contact with Egypt and Aram Naharaim," *BA* 21 (1958): 96–102; E. Ball, "The Co-Regency of David and Solomon," *VT* 27 (1977): 268–87; R. de Vaux, "Titres et fonctionnaires égyptiens à la cour de David et de Salomon," *RB* 48 (1939): 395–405; J. Begrich, "Sofer und Mazkir: Ein Beitrag zur inneren Geschichte des davidisch-salomonischen Grossreiches und des Königreiches Juda," *ZAW* 58 (1940): 1–29; and T. N. D. Mettinger, *Solomonic State Officials* (Lund: Gleerup, 1971).

court offices mentioned in 2 Samuel 8:16–18; 20:23–26; and 1 Kings 4:2–6 were modeled after the administration of Shoshenk I and his predecessors. In addition, these scholars suggest that Solomon's tax system and the titles of functionaries and dignitaries were adapted from Egypt. Other investigators disagree, arguing, for example, that Shoshenk I borrowed Solomon's taxation system. There is, however, no concrete evidence to prove which culture borrowed from the other.

Then, too, there is the matter of Solomon's marriage to an Egyptian princess. We saw in chapter 9 that this alliance probably occurred in the early part of Solomon's reign. So his Egyptian father-in-law was not Shoshenk I, who ruled during the later part of Solomon's monarchy, but probably either Siamun (ca. 978–959) or Psusennes II (ca. 959–945).[33] In addition, that an Egyptian princess was given in marriage to a foreign king was an indication that Egypt was weak.[34] Such an admission would not have taken place during the reign of Shoshenk I. Another indication of the feebleness of Egypt in Dynasty 21 was the handing over of the city of Gezer as a dowry for the marriage to Solomon (1 Kings 9:16). This was also a keen act of diplomacy on the part of the Egyptians.[35]

The accession of Shoshenk I to the throne of Egypt evidently brought a shift in the Egyptian policy of yielding to the formidable strength of the Hebrews. Hostility and rivalry soon came to the forefront. A salient event was the flight of the prominent Hebrew official Jeroboam to Egypt. Jeroboam had become a competitor for Solomon's throne, and he was eventually forced to flee for his life. We read in 1 Kings 11:40: "Solomon sought therefore to put Jeroboam to death; but Jeroboam arose and fled to Egypt to Shishak king of Egypt, and he was in Egypt until the death of Solomon." Jeroboam appears to have been well received by Shoshenk I, and his "arrival at the Egyptian court may have signaled to the Pharaoh that the Solomonic monarchy was not too stable."[36] Shoshenk I's protection of Jeroboam reflects a willingness to incur the displeasure of Solomon. It may also signify a shift of power from Israel to Egypt that was later confirmed by Shoshenk's attack on Palestine.

The death of Solomon and the division of his kingdom into Israel and Judah were the defining events of the transition of power from united Israel to Egypt. Shoshenk I became bolder and more aggressive

33. A. R. Green, "Solomon and Siamun: A Synchronism between Early Dynastic Israel and the Twenty-First Dynasty of Egypt," *JBL* 97 (1978): 353–67.

34. A. R. Schulman, "Diplomatic Marriage in the Egyptian New Kingdom," *JNES* 38 (1979): 177–93.

35. Herrmann, *History of Israel*, 175; G. W. Ahlström, *The History of Ancient Palestine* (Minneapolis: Fortress, 1993), 519–20; and Malamat, "Aspects of the Foreign Policies," 8–17.

36. Ahlström, *History of Ancient Palestine*, 545.

towards his northeastern neighbors. In fact, the Pharaoh sought a reason to attack. He appears to have found the catalyst in an apparently minor border skirmish recorded in Hall K at Karnak:

> Said his majesty to the court: "—— the evil things which they have done." Said they: —— his horses after him, while they knew (it) not. Lo —— His majesty made a great slaughter among them —— he ——ed them upon the [dyke] of the shore of Kemwer.[37] He it was ——.[38]

It was soon after the division of the Hebrew kingdom ("in the fifth year of King Rehoboam," 1 Kings 14:25) that Shoshenk I launched a full-scale invasion of Palestine. The record of that campaign is inscribed on the walls of the temple at Karnak.

The Bubastite Portal at Karnak

Construction and Date

The Bubastite Portal is a large imposing entrance in the southern end of the first court of the great temple of Amon at Karnak.[39] According to the epigraphic investigators, the portal was originally a separate entity, although it is now part of an outer wall of the temple.[40] Evidently the wall was a later addition. That should be no surprise since the great temple of Amon was the work of many pharaohs for over a thousand years, beginning with Thutmosis I. It was erected, added to, pulled down, restored, and enlarged in the course of its construction.

Shoshenk I probably planned and constructed the entire enclosure of the court, including the Bubastite Portal. A stele set up in the Silsileh quarries by Haremsaf, the overseer of Shoshenk I's building programs, attests that "it was his majesty who gave directions to build a very great pylon . . . , to illumine Thebes by erecting its double door of millions of cubits, to make a festival court for the house of his father Amon-Re, king of the gods, and to surround it with statues and a colonnade."[41] That his reliefs are the earliest carved on the edifice is further confirmation that Shoshenk built the portal.[42]

---

37. Literally "the big black," Kemwer refers to the northern part of the Red Sea. It is also mentioned in the "Story of Sinuhe" as a geographic designation on the way to Byblos (*AEL* 1:224).
38. *ARE* 4:358.
39. The name of the gate reflects Manetho's tradition that Dynasty 22 originated at the site of Bubastis in the delta region of Lower Egypt. The temple of Amon at Karnak "was ideally and economically the most important temple establishment in the whole of Egypt" (J. Baines and J. Malek, *Atlas of Ancient Egypt* [New York: Facts on File, 1980], 90).
40. *Bubastite Portal*, vii.
41. R. A. Caminos, "Gebel es-Silsilah no. 100," *JEA* 38 (1952): 46–61.
42. *Bubastite Portal*, vii.

The Bubasite Portal at Karnak. *Courtesy of The Oriental Institute of The University of Chicago.*

The Silsileh Inscription provides a date for the command to quarry stones for use at Karnak: the second month of the twenty-first year of Shoshenk I. Because Manetho gives twenty-one years as the length of Shoshenk I's reign, William Albright concluded that the pharaoh's reliefs on the portal must have been carved at the end of his rule.[43] Moreover, Albright argued that this "makes certain that the list of towns of Judah, Edom, and Israel, included in the reliefs, must reflect a campaign of the last few years of the king's reign."[44] Numerous scholars have followed Albright's interpretation.[45]

---

43. W. F. Albright, "New Light from Egypt on the Chronology and History of Israel and Judah," *BASOR* 130 (1953): 4–11.
44. Ibid., 7.
45. E.g., Malamat, "Kingdom of David and Solomon," 99, says that Shoshenk I's Palestinian campaign was "undertaken not long before Pharaoh's death"; H. Tadmor, "The Period of the First Temple, the Babylonian Exile, and the Restoration," in *A History of the Jewish People*, ed. H. H. Ben-Sasson (Cambridge, Mass.: Harvard University Press, 1976), 116; and E. P. Uphill, "The Date of Osorkon II's Sed-Festival," *JNES* 26 (1967): 61–62.

Donald Redford and Edward Wente have pointed out a number of problems with Albright's chronology. Shoshenk I may have reigned for thirty-three years rather than the twenty-one claimed by Manetho.[46] If that be true, then the construction work at Karnak was undertaken in the middle of Shoshenk I's reign rather than at the end. In addition, the Karnak relief describes the Palestinian expedition as the Pharaoh's "first victorious [campaign]"; Redford contends that such a designation would be singularly peculiar at the end of a pharaoh's reign.[47] Thus it is likely that Shoshenk I's campaign against Palestine was early in his rule, the construction at Karnak in the middle, and the carving of the reliefs somewhat later.

Some scholars argue that the figure of Shoshenk I was left unfinished on the relief, a defect that reflects the death of the king prior to completion of the relief.[48] In actual fact, the incised figure of the king was not left unfinished, but was dealt with differently from the rest of the relief. George Hughes of the epigraphic survey noted that "the king's figure was very delicately modelled, at least in outline, in a thin coat of gypsum plaster applied to the stone . . . at many points the modelling impinged upon the stone beneath."[49] The linguistic team believed Shoshenk I's figure to be complete, but specially carved and painted to show striking contrast between Pharaoh and the remainder of the relief. The distinct portrayal made Shoshenk I the focus. This technique is not unique at Karnak.[50] So the nature of his figure does not support late dates for Shoshenk's campaign into Palestine, the additions to the temple at Karnak, and the carving of the reliefs on the Bubastite Portal.

The reliefs on the Bubastite Portal were incised in three (possibly four) stages. Shoshenk I had the first reliefs carved; they were uniformly well incised to a great depth and "admirably executed."[51] The

---

46. E. F. Wente, review of *The Third Intermediate Period in Egypt*, by K. A. Kitchen, *JNES* 35 (1976): 275–78, points out that the Book of Sothis assigns a reign of thirty-four years to Shoshenk I and that he celebrated a second jubilee at Karnak. This is an emendation of Wente's earlier view that Shoshenk ruled for twenty-one years ("On the Chronology of the Twenty-First Dynasty," *JNES* 26 [1967]: 155–76). K. Baer had also originally agreed with the Manethonian chronology ("The Libyan and Nubian Kings of Egypt," *JNES* 32 [1973]: 4–25), but later altered his position on the basis of Wente's study.

47. Redford, "Studies in Relations between Palestine and Egypt II," 10.

48. J. Simons, *Handbook for the Study of Egyptian Topographical Lists Relating to Western Asia* (Leiden: Brill, 1937), 89. W. F. Albright, "Recent Books on Archaeology and Ancient History," *BASOR* 139 (1955): 20, states that the "monument was not finished until after Shishak's death." He assumes that the royal figure was painted in by Shoshenk's son Osorkon I, and then later scraped away so that Osorkon could replace it with his own likeness, an intention that was never carried out.

49. *Bubastite Portal*, ix.

50. Redford, "Studies in Relations between Palestine and Egypt II," 10 n. 63.

51. *Bubastite Portal*, viii.

second series was the work of Shoshenk I's son Osorkon I. The final group was commissioned by the high priest of Amon, Osorkon son of Takelot II.

The Basic Form of the Relief

Shoshenk I's invasion of Palestine is recorded on the southern side of the Bubastite Portal. The record consists of a series of tiers or rows containing the names of various sites on the route(s) of the campaign. Whether or not each place-name denotes a site destroyed by Shoshenk I is debatable. Syro-Palestinian archaeologists tend to be overzealous in this regard, declaring almost every Palestinian site evidencing a destruction layer from the tenth century B.C. to be a result of Shoshenk I's campaign.[52] But there is no indication that the list is a catalogue of sites razed to the ground by the Egyptians. On the other hand, it is not merely a set of itineraries taken from military daybooks, as some have suggested.[53] The towns on the relief were certainly captured and subjugated, as is evident in the fact that each town is represented as being led captive by a slave-rope of the gods. But to say that each city on the list was destroyed by Shoshenk I goes beyond the present evidence.

Each town is pictured as a human figure with the abdominal area serving as a name-ring. The representations are not uniform, but many of the figures are distinct. Most appear to have beards, long hair, and headbands—obvious signs of Asiatic foreigners. Most, if not all, are bound by a rope around the elbow, and they are also tied to one another by a rope around the neck. They are led to Shoshenk I by the gods Amon and Wast.

It appears that there are eleven rows of village names in the relief.[54] The towns in tiers 1–5 are represented as being led captive to the figure of Shoshenk I by the god Amon. There are thirteen captive towns in each tier for a total of sixty-five. The goddess Wast has six ropes in her

---

52. According to *NEAEHL* 1–4, archaeological investigators believe that Shoshenk I destroyed Tell Abu Huwam, Aphek, Arad, Tell Batash, Beersheba, Tell Beit Mirsim, Beth Shemesh, Tell el-Farʿah, Tell Gerisa, Gezer, and Tell el-Kheleifeh. A. Mazar, *Archaeology of the Land of the Bible* (New York: Doubleday, 1990), 398, adds the following sites to the list: Tell el-Mazar, Tell el-Hama, Tell el-Saʾidiyeh, Megiddo, Tell Mevorakh, Tell Michal, and Tell Qasile. Many other sites could be added to the catalogue; see R. Cohen, "Excavations at Kadesh-barnea, 1976–1978," *BA* 44 (1981): 93–104; and E. D. Oren, "Ziklag— A Biblical City on the Edge of the Negev," *BA* 45 (1982): 155–66.

53. S. Herrmann, "Operationen Pharao Schoschenks I. im östlichen Ephraim," *ZDPV* 80 (1964): 57; Redford, "Studies in Relations between Palestine and Egypt II," 11 n. 74, agrees, adding that the sites listed were towns Shoshenk I's army "visited" on the campaign.

54. Many early commentators recognized only ten rows; see Simons, *Egyptian Topographical Lists*, 90.

hand, and tiers 6–10 have seventeen captives apiece for a total of eighty-five. Most of the eleventh tier has been destroyed, but on the very right of the bottom of the relief are five name-rings.[55] Up to thirty-two name-rings may be missing from the last tier. Originally, then, the relief in its entirety included approximately 187 name-rings.

Some of the name-rings are totally obliterated, and many are partially destroyed. One of the blocks (105–8) was removed by Karl Lepsius and taken to the Egyptian Museum in Berlin.[56] The state of preservation of the relief makes it difficult to determine whether the carving provides definite travel routes, what precisely they might be, and specifically what regions may have been subjugated.

Evaluation of the Evidence on the Relief

The veracity of the triumphal relief of Shoshenk I has frequently been called into question. The principal argument against its reliability stems from some scholars' belief that many of the towns were copied from older texts.[57] For example, the cities of the Esdraelon Plain closely conform to invasion lists of Sethos I (ca. 1306–1290 B.C.) and Rameses II (ca. 1290–1224 B.C.).[58] In addition, Shoshenk I introduces the relief by declaring before Amon: "I have subjected for you the Asiatics of the armies of Mitanni." The problem is that Mitanni had ceased to be a nation by the time of Shoshenk I's reign. Furthermore, the argument goes, some of the sites had been destroyed and abandoned before Shoshenk I's invasion, among them Yaham, Beth-Shean, and Rehob.[59]

We must admit that the text may be partly invention or partly plagiarism from earlier inscriptions. However, for the most part it appears to be original, containing many names found nowhere else and being "rivalled in this respect only by the great list of Tuthmosis III and the exotic Kom el-Hetan lists of Amenophis III."[60] The form and presentation of the relief also set it apart as a unique representation in ancient Egypt.

There is no question that Shoshenk I invaded Israel and Judah. Remains of the Shishak Stele discovered at Megiddo provide concrete ev-

---

55. We know that Tier 11 is not a continuation of Tier 10, for the hieroglyphs of the two rows face in different directions. On the other hand, the need to account for the sixth rope of Wast suggests that there is some connection.

56. For a concise history of the copying of the document, see Simons, *Egyptian Topographical Lists*, 89–102.

57. W. F. Albright, "Egypt and the Early History of the Negeb," *JPOS* 4 (1924): 131–61. Albright's suspicions have found their way into much of the recent literature.

58. *ANET*, 253–58.

59. While this argument is probably not true, it would not be a problem even if it were. For, as stated earlier (p. 183), it is an unwarranted assumption that the relief lists only sites destroyed by Shoshenk I.

60. Kitchen, *Third Intermediate Period*, 432 n. 49.

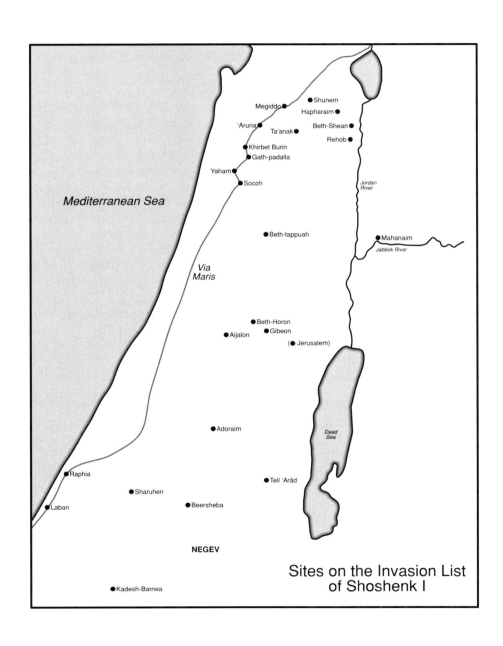

idence.[61] Though fragmented, it contains two important cartouches:

	Cartouche 1	Cartouche 2
nfr ntr	*hdhprr*	*stpnr ssnk*
"good god"	"white is the existence of Re"	"chosen of Re, Shoshenk (I)"

These are common designations for Shoshenk I. So this stele reflects an Egyptian presence at Megiddo during his reign, and its erection probably coincides with the invasion recorded at Karnak and in the Bible.

The route of Shoshenk I's military campaign has received much scholarly attention, and various interpretations have been presented.[62] We will not spend much time discussing them. We should note, however, that Benjamin Mazar's interpretation (after Bernhard Grdseloff) that the relief should be read boustrophedon is very unlikely.[63] Not only are there no examples of this technique in all Egyptian literature, but the very form and positioning of the name-rings deny its viability: all of the hieroglyphs in the top ten tiers are facing to the right, which indicates a right-to-left reading of the text. The five name-rings of the concluding tier face in the opposite direction, so they are to be read from left to right.

Identification of the towns in the list is less certain than many scholars suppose. (For more-detailed analysis see the appendix on pp. 189–202.) Of the approximately 178 name-rings (not including the Nine Bows in tier 1) of the original inscription, we are assured of the location of only about twenty-seven (14, 15, 16, 17, 18, 19, 22, 23, 24, 26, 27, 32, 33, 34, 35, 38, 39, 66, 69, 70, 97, 102, 108–9, 124, 125, 2a, 3a). That is a very low percentage (ca. 15 percent) by which to try to reconstruct the route of the army. Much of the journey, therefore, remains a mystery.

The first assured location is the town of Taʿanak (14) in the southwest Jezreel Valley. The early name-rings (10–13), then, likely are sites on the way from Egypt to the Jezreel Valley. From Taʿanak the army crossed the Jezreel to the northeast to Shunem (15). From there they probably traversed the Harod Valley to the city of Beth-Shean (16), located in the northern Beth-Shean Valley. Heading south, the force struck Rehob (17) in the middle of the valley. In order to secure the region, it appears that the army veered six miles to the northwest of Beth-Shean to the city of Hapharaim (18). An Egyptian detachment possibly

---

61. R. S. Lamon and G. M. Shipton, *Megiddo I* (Chicago: University of Chicago Press, 1939), 60–61.

62. For a summary see Kitchen, *Third Intermediate Period*, 442–46.

63. B. Mazar, "The Campaign of Pharaoh Shishak to Palestine," *VTS* 4 (1957): 60. Boustrophedon means that the lines of a text are read alternately from left to right and right to left.

continued east across the Jordan River, penetrating as far as Mahanaim on the Jabbok River (22).

The next section (23–26) covers an Egyptian incursion into the hill country northwest of Jerusalem. The cities of Gibeon, Beth-Horon, and Aijalon can be identified. Whether this is the same military force that penetrated east to the Beth-Shean Valley is unknown.

The next site mentioned is Megiddo (27), located back in the Jezreel Valley, which may give justification to Siegfried Herrmann's argument that the Egyptian army was headquartered in the Jezreel Valley.[64] The army marched southwest of Megiddo by way of the Nahal 'Iron to 'Aruna (32) on a major leg of the Via Maris. From there the journey continued south on the Via Maris, and the Egyptians subjugated a series of towns from north to south: Khirbet Burin (33), Gath-padalla (34), Yaham (35), and Socoh (38). Apparently a force penetrated the Israelite hill country, beginning at Beth-tappuah (39) in Ephraim. At that point we lose the route of the invasion until the Negev.

The identifiable sites in tiers 6–10 all lie in the Negev region of Palestine. Sites 66, 69, and 70 are located in the general area of Beersheba, 97 and 125 in the western Negev, and 108–9 in the eastern Negev. This southern quarter of Palestine seems to have received the brunt of the Egyptian attack, if one may draw such a conclusion from the number of sites.

Tier 11 contains two known sites, Raphia and Laban. Their location along the Mediterranean coast verifies that the Egyptian army was returning to Egypt at the conclusion of the campaign.

One obvious conclusion we may draw from this reconstruction of the route is that Shoshenk I's invasion was leveled against both Judah and Israel. Scholars once believed that Judah was the only target of the attack, but that view is incorrect.[65] While Philistia and Transjordan may also have suffered some of the assaults, the raid was actually directed at the two Hebrew kingdoms.[66]

---

64. Herrmann, "Operationen Pharao Schoschenks I.," 58–60, contends that Shoshenk I sent forth "flying-columns" from Megiddo into Transjordan, the hill country, and the Negev. The destruction of layer VA–IVB of Megiddo may be associated with the campaign of Shoshenk I. For an in-depth analysis of the archaeological correspondences, see J. D. Currid, "The Re-Stratification of Megiddo during the United Monarchy," *ZDPV* 107 (1991): 28–38.

65. Albright, "Egypt and the Early History of the Negeb," 146. The reason why the Bible mentions attacks only against the cities of Judah (2 Chron. 12:4) is that the author was interested only in the situation in Judah and, particularly, in Jerusalem.

66. Ironically, Jerusalem does not appear on Shoshenk I's relief at Karnak. The name-ring may have been destroyed. But it is more likely that Jerusalem does not appear because it was not captured. Rehoboam eluded Jerusalem's capture by paying heavy tribute to the Egyptians (1 Kings 14:25–26).

Reasons for the Invasion

Scholars have proposed many theories regarding the reasons why Shoshenk I attacked Palestine. Some have merit, and some are fanciful.[67] Martin Noth provided two suggestions regarding the Egyptian campaign. First, Pharaoh was mainly interested in the booty and tribute he could collect from the subjugated regions.[68] There is some merit to this idea because in 1 Kings 14 Rehoboam pays off the Egyptian forces so that Jerusalem will not be captured. In addition, plunder appears to have been a primary objective of Shoshenk I's invasion of Nubia earlier in his reign. However, if that was Shoshenk I's purpose for the attack on Palestine, it is peculiar that he left no lasting Egyptian presence there. If Pharaoh had desired tributary states, one would expect to see some type of tributary system. But the invasion "did not have any lasting results" of that nature.[69]

Noth's second suggestion is that Shoshenk I "undertook an expedition to Palestine, evidently in order to renew the tradition of the great Pharaohs of the New Kingdom who had for a time possessed the whole of Syria and Palestine."[70] As we have already seen, Shoshenk I had a longing and zeal to be as powerful as the kings of the earlier New Kingdom dynasties. That aspiration served as a catalyst in his choice of a prenomen, in his uniting Upper and Lower Egypt, and possibly in his carving the triumphal relief at Karnak next to the temple of Rameses III. It is not clear, however, that a longing to rival his predecessors was enough of a motivation for a major attack on Palestine.

A third suggestion is that the campaign was intended to set up a buffer zone between Egypt and the rising power of Assyria in the east.[71] If that be the case, however, why was there no Egyptian military presence in Palestine after the campaign?

It seems more likely that the principal reason for the Egyptian expedition was to reestablish Egyptian trade routes and economic activity in Palestine. Dynasty 21 had been weak, with minimal trade contact

---

67. Among the fanciful theories is that of T. H. Robinson, *A History of Israel* (Oxford: Clarendon, 1932), 275—the towns destroyed in Israel were actually in the hands of Rehoboam, king of Judah. Shoshenk I as the benefactor of Jeroboam, king of Israel, was rescuing Israel from the aggression of Rehoboam.

68. M. Noth, *The History of Israel*, 2d ed. (New York: Harper and Row, 1960), 240. This position is also held by N. Na'aman, "Israel, Edom, and Egypt in the 10th Century B.C.," *TA* 19 (1992): 81.

69. Herrmann, *History of Israel*, 197.

70. Noth, *History of Israel*, 239.

71. Albright, "Egypt and the Early History of the Negeb," 146. Indeed, Ashur-dan II, who ruled Assyria at that time (ca. 932–910 B.C.), can be credited with re-establishing its economic and military might. See the discussion of G. Roux, *Ancient Iraq* (Baltimore: Penguin, 1964), 256–71.

with neighboring areas. In addition, Solomon appears to have had almost a monopoly on business traffic throughout the Near East. He controlled the northern coastal areas and the Jezreel Valley, thus dominating critical portions of the Via Maris. The Red Sea was also under Solomonic hegemony, affording the Hebrews access to Arabian trade and to parts farther east. With the rise of Dynasty 22 and the death of Solomon, power shifted to the Egyptians. Shoshenk I took advantage by attacking the recently divided Hebrew kingdoms, destroying the Israelite economic dominion, and opening up trade routes for Egypt. The identifiable sites on the relief at Karnak confirm this hypothesis: the Egyptians captured numerous sites on the Via Maris which had been under Israelite sovereignty (e.g., Megiddo), and they subjugated numerous sites in the Negev that provided access to the Red Sea. The trade network created by Solomon never recovered.

There is no doubt that Shoshenk I was interested in expanding trade for Egypt. He renewed trade contacts with Byblos. He also opened up the way to Nubia and points south in order to secure "all manner of products for Amun at Karnak."[72] No doubt he attacked Palestine for the same reason: to open and secure major trade routes in that region.

Appendix: Commentary on the Bubastite Portal

Numerous works were consulted in the preparation of this analysis of the individual entries on the Bubastite Portal. The following are frequently referred to in the commentary:

Aharoni, Y. *The Land of the Bible: A Historical Geography.* 2d ed. Philadelphia: Westminster, 1979.
Albright, W. F. "Egypt and the Early History of the Negeb." *JPOS* 4 (1924): 131–61.
Breasted, J. H. *Ancient Records of Egypt.* London: Histories and Mysteries of Man, 1988 reprint. 4:344–58.
Herrmann, S. "Operationen Pharao Schoschenks I. im östlichen Ephraim." *ZDPV* 80 (1964): 55–79.
Kitchen, K. A. *The Third Intermediate Period in Egypt (1100–650 B.C.).* Warminster: Aris and Phillips, 1973.
Mazar, B. "The Campaign of Pharaoh Shishak to Palestine." *VTS* 4 (1957): 57–66.
Müller, W. M. *Asia und Europa nach altägyptischen Denkmalern.* Leipzig: Engelmann, 1893.
Noth, M. "Die Wege der Pharonenheere in Palästina und Syrien. IV. Die Schoschenkliste." *ZDPV* 61 (1938): 227–304.
Simons, J. *Handbook for the Study of Egyptian Topographical Lists Relating to Western Asia.* Leiden: Brill, 1937.

---

72. Kitchen, *Third Intermediate Period,* 293.

Tier 1

7	6	5	4	3	2	1
←	BOWS	←	NINE	←	THE	←

13	12	11	10	9	8
rbꜣt	mꜣ...	gꜣ...	mı̓tt...	←	←

1–9
- a. Nine Bows is an ancient sign denoting subdued enemies. Worn on Pharaoh's slippers, it is a symbol of the Egyptian empire's trampling its foes.
- b. Another example is the Beth-Shean Stele of Sethos I (1306–1290), which uses "Repelling the Nine Bows" as an epithet in the list of the king's names.

10
- a. *mı̓tt* literally means "likeness." The name-ring is partially destroyed.
- b. G. Maspéro (*Etudes de mythologie et d'archéologie égyptiennes* 5 [1911]: 88) argues that this name-ring is a comprehensive title for the following list. He reconstructs the destroyed part and reads the ring as "copy of Asiatic names." Kitchen agrees (433–35).
- c. Maspéro's reconstruction is a reach. All that clearly appears at the bottom of the name-ring is ≈, the determinative for "foreign land." It is likely that what we have here is the first town in the list.

11
- a. Simons (180) adds phonetic *m* ("The Owl") after *gꜣ*. It is not evident in the inscription.
- b. Müller (166–72) identifies the site as Gaza. Kitchen (435) and Mazar (60) agree.
- c. Breasted (350) claims that the inscription is too mutilated for recognition. To say the site is Gaza is, at best, a guess.

12
- a. Early scholars such as Maspéro (*Etudes*, 50, 88) identified the site as Megiddo. However, site 27 is certainly Megiddo, a reading with which the letters of name-ring 12 hardly fit.
- b. Simons (181) suggests the reading ꜣꜣr with determinative. (Actually, the bird is an owl rather than a vulture.)
- c. Mazar (60) and Aharoni (285–86) believe this site is Gezer. Mazar says, "As a fact the two last names in the first line are Gezer (No. 12) and Rubuti (No. 13)." This is a poor reading. Cf. Herrmann (59).
- d. Kitchen's (435) rendering of Makkedah seems unwarranted.
- e. Herrmann (*History of Israel*, 196) appears to accept the site as Megiddo.

13
- a. Mazar (60) and Noth (287) say this site is Rubuti.
- b. Aharoni (355) and Kitchen (435) opt for Rabbah, a site southeast of Gezer at Khirbet Ḥamîdeh. That identification fails if site 12 is not Gezer.
- c. Breasted (350) declares site 13 to be Rabbith, a town in the Kishon Valley north of Megiddo. If site 12 is not Megiddo, the identification fails.

Tier 2

20	19	18	17	16	15	14
...	ỉdrm	ḥpwrmꜣ	rḥbꜣ	bꜣtšnrꜣ	šnmꜣ	tꜥnkꜣ

26	25	24	23	22	21
ỉywrn	kꜣdtm	bꜣtḥꜣrn	ḳbꜣꜥnꜣ	mḥꜣnm	šwꜣd

14
  a. There is common agreement that this site is Taʿanak: Kitchen (435); Aharoni (325); Breasted (350); Simons (98); Noth (282).
  b. Twenty-six towns in the list end in ꜣ: 14–18, 40, 56, 59, 66, 68–69, 71, 77, 79–80, 88, 95–96, 100, 103, 108(?), 110(?), 118, 119, 121, and 127. Breasted (352 n. f) concludes it is a feminine ending. Müller (170–71) explains it as a *status emphaticus*. Oddly, Kitchen does not deal with it. In reality, the element is, as Simons says (100), "an unsolved mystery."

15
  a. This is consistently held to be Shunem: Kitchen (435); Aharoni (325); Breasted (350); Simons (98); Noth (282).

16
  a. This is consistently held to be Beth-Shean: Kitchen (435); Aharoni (325); Breasted (350); Simons (98); Noth (282).

17
  a. There is general agreement that the site is Rehob (Tell es-Sarem): Kitchen (435); Aharoni (325); Breasted (350); Simons (98); Noth (282); Mazar (60); Herrmann (59).

18
  a. The inscription is to be read Hapharaim.
  b. Mazar (62) identifies the site with Tell Saʿidiye (Ephron on the Jordan).
  c. Citing Joshua 19:19, Noth (283) insists it is et-Taiyiba in Issachar. This is probably correct.

19
  a. Note that the letter 𓏲 is inverted.
  b. This is probably the city of Adoraim in Judah: Aharoni (325); Breasted (350 n. f); Mazar (60).

20
  a. The inscription is destroyed.
  b. Mazar (62) deems the site to be Zaphon at Tell Qos on the Wadi Jadur. How he draws that conclusion from this name-ring is unclear.

21
  a. This is an unknown site.

22
  a. There is general agreement that the site is Mahanaim.
  b. Mazar (60) identifies it with Tulul edh-Dhahab on the Jabbok River. If true, it reflects a penetration of Shoshenk I into Transjordan.

23
   a. The site is commonly held to be Gibeon, which is in Benjamin northwest of Jerusalem: Kitchen (436); Aharoni (325); Breasted (350); Noth (284); Mazar (60); Herrmann (60).
24
   a. The site is Beth-Horon, located on the border between the tribes of Ephraim and Benjamin: Kitchen (435); Aharoni (352); Breasted (350–51); Noth (284); Mazar (60).
25
   a. The site is unknown.
   b. Mazar (61) and Aharoni (326 n. 11) agree with B. Grdseloff's suggestion that the Egyptian scribe misread hieratic *r* as a *d*. Thus this site is Kiriathaim (a highly questionable interpretation).
26
   a. The site is generally agreed to be Aijalon: Kitchen (435); Aharoni (325); Breasted (351); Noth (284); Mazar (60); Herrmann (59).
   b. A letter in Egyptian corresponds to the Hebrew *l* (there is no *l* in Egyptian).

Tier 3

33	32	31	30	29	28	27
bꜣrm	ꜥrnꜣ	ḫꜣnm	...rt	ywdhmrwk	idr	mkdiw

39	38	37	36	35	34
bꜣ(t)tpw	šiwk	kkiry	bꜣtꜥrm	ywḥm	ddptr

27
   a. The site is Megiddo: Kitchen (436); Aharoni (325); Breasted (351); Noth (281); Mazar (60); Herrmann (58).
   b. An unstratified piece of a "Shishak" stele was found on the mound of Megiddo; see C. S. Fisher, *The Excavation of Armageddon* (Chicago: University of Chicago Press, 1929), 16, figs. 7–9.
28
   a. The site is unknown.
   b. Breasted (351) says it is Adar in Judah. This is a problem because site 27 is in the north, in the Jezreel Valley.
   c. Sh. Yeiven (*JEA* 48 [1962]: 75–80) believes it is Idalah in the tribal allotment of Zebulun (Josh. 19:15).
29
   a. Some early Egyptologists believed this inscription to mean "the king or kingdom of Judah." The *h* would thus be understood as the Hebrew article. However, the Egyptian scribe of the Shoshenk I relief always translates the Hebrew article into the Egyptian article; he never transliterates it (cf. 71, 77, 87, 90, 92, and 94). See W. M. Müller, "The Supposed Name of Judah in the List of Shoshenq," *Proceedings of the Society of Biblical Archaeology* 10 (1888): 81–83.

30

b. The inscription literally means "hand of the king"; *yd* may also mean "monument" (*BDB*, 390) and, therefore, the term may refer to a stele of the king (Kitchen [437]; Aharoni [325]).

c. Mazar (62) goes too far by suggesting "a royal monument which stood at the entrance to the Wadi ʿArah."

30

a. The inscription is fragmentary.

b. Kitchen (437) restores it to *[Ḥb]rt* and suggests it possibly refers to Ḥebel ("border" in Josh. 19:29). Such a reconstruction is unlikely.

c. Sh. Yeivin (*JEA* 48 [1962]: 78–79) identifies the site as Tell Abu Hawam (also highly unlikely).

31

a. The reading is obscure.

b. Mazar (60) says it is Honim, "a resting place for the caravans in the Wadi ʿArah" (another improbable identification).

32

a. The site is generally agreed to be ʿAruna, located at Khirbet ʿAra in the Wadi ʿĀra: Kitchen (436); Breasted (351); Mazar (60); Noth (285).

b. The annals of Thutmosis III (line 32) mention this site as a place he passed on his march to Megiddo.

33

a. The site is probably Khirbet Burin: Kitchen (436); Aharoni (325); Mazar (60); Noth (285).

b. Note the inverted 𓏴.

34

a. Gath-padalla was an important site in the northern Sharon Valley on the Via Maris. It is Tell Jatt.

b. The site is mentioned in the Amarna Letters (no. 250). See W. F. Albright, *BASOR* 104 (1946): 25–26; Sh. Yeivin, *JEA* 36 (1950): 58ff.

c. Breasted (351) proposes that the name refers to a city of central Palestine. This is unlikely.

35

a. This is probably Yaham, located at Khirbet Yemma (Tell Yaham) on the Via Maris: Noth (285); Kitchen (436); Aharoni (325); Mazar (60).

b. The site is mentioned in the Annals of Thutmosis III; cf. site 32.

36

a. Beth-Olam; the location is unknown.

37

a. The reading is obscure.

38

a. This is certainly to be identified as Socoh, sited at Khirbet Shuweiket er-Ras in the Sharon Valley on the Via Maris: Kitchen (436); Mazar (60).

b. Breasted (351) mistakenly argues that the reference is to Socoh in Judah: "phonetically exactly equivalent to Socoh . . . and it would carry us into Judah." However, this is neither the Socoh in southern Judah nor the Socoh in the Shephelah.

39
   a. This is Beth-tappuah, located at Ain Tuba near to the Via Maris (in Ephraim, eighteen miles from Socoh): Noth (286 n. 5); Kitchen (436 n. 68); Mazar (60).

Tier 4

46	45	44	43	42	41	40
kk...	btd̠ȝbỉ(ȝ)	...	...	...	...	ỉbrȝ

52	51	50	49	48	47
...	...ss̠d...	...	...	...	...

40
   a. This is likely the first part of one of the many "Abel"-names in ancient Palestine. It is probably to be read in combination with 41, which has been destroyed (Simons [181]).
   b. Breasted (352) reads "Abel" as "meadow."
41–44
   a. The readings have been destroyed.
45
   a. Beth-Ṣoba, an unknown site. In Hebrew the names of many sites begin with *Beth* ("house of") (Kitchen [437]; Mazar [60]).
46
   a. The reading is obscure.
   b. Mazar's (61) reading *ḳkrt* is a guess.
47–50
   a. The readings have been destroyed.
51
   a. The inscription is obscure.
52
   a. The reading has been destroyed.

Tier 5

59	58	57	56	55	54	53
rdȝ	...dr	d̠mrm	ỉdmȝ	p(nds)ktt	ḥds̆t	(p)...nw(?)ỉr

65	64	63	62	61	60
pʿmḳ	...pȝpn	...	...	...	...nȝr

53
   a. The reading is partially destroyed. Müller was the first to restore the opening *p* (168), and reads Penuel. Kitchen agrees (438) because a pseudodeterminative of an animal skin appears here, and "practically guarantees" the *p*-restoration.
   b. The location is unknown. Mazar (60) suggests the reference is to Tell el-Ḥamma on the Jabbok River, but this is highly questionable.

54
   a. The reading literally means "New (town)" (Kitchen [438]).
   b. Aharoni (325) identifies the site as Kedesh; Mazar (61) proposes it to be Qodeš, a sacred site near Penuel (this is unlikely).

55
   a. This is possibly Pꜣ-n-Skt, "the one of Succoth." The multiconsonantal sign nds is to be reduced to n; cf. reading 85, where ns symbolizes n (Kitchen [438]).
   b. Simons (182) deems the site to be ʿAin Berqit.
   c. Mazar (60) says it is Tell Deir ʿAlla near the Jordan River.

56
   a. Some scholars argue that the reference is to Edom: Breasted (352). A problem is that no countries appear in the list.
   b. The site is probably to be identified as Adamah (Khirbet Tell Edh-Damiye) at the confluence of the Jordan and Jabbok Rivers: Kitchen (438); Mazar (60).

57
   a. The top of the name-ring is broken.
   b. Some scholars suggest that the site is Zemaraim in the tribal territory of Benjamin (Josh. 18:22): Simons (182); Kitchen (438); Mazar (60).
   c. Breasted (352) incorrectly says that the reading means "rocks."

58
   a. The top is broken.
   b. The reference is generally understood as a "migdol"-name ("tower" in Hebrew): Kitchen (438); Simons (178); Aharoni (325); Mazar (60).

59
   a. The first letter is apparently missing.
   b. The site is possibly Tirzah at Tell el-Farʿah: Kitchen (438); Aharoni (325); Mazar (60).
   c. Breasted (352) identifies it as Yerazaʿ, which is mentioned in the Annals of Thutmosis III and located in northwestern Judah.
   d. Simons (183) restores the first letter as y; it is actually obscure.

60
   a. The inscription is broken.
   b. Simons (183) misreads it.

61–63
   a. The readings have been destroyed.

64
   a. The top is broken.
   b. Aharoni (325) incorrectly reconstructs the reading as [Go]phnah.
   c. Kitchen (439) restores an h at the beginning. But cf. reading 31, where the h symbol reaches down to the right of the vulture; this is not clear in 64.

65
   a. Literally, "the valley," the reading is possibly the name of a town or a valley; see Judg. 1:19; 5:15.
   b. Mazar (60) and Aharoni (325) argue that the reference is to the Valley of Beth-Shean, but there is no evidence.

c. Kitchen (439) says it is the valley par excellence of Palestine, that is, the Jezreel Valley, but again there is no evidence.

Tier 6

71	70	69	68	67	66
pꜣḥkrꜣ	ỉrhrr	ftywšꜣ	pꜣḥkꜣrꜣ	ỉnꜣrỉ	ꜥꜣdmꜣ

77	76	75	74	73	72
pꜣḥkrꜣ	wꜣrkyt	šbrt	ngbry	šbrt	ỉbrm

82	81	80	79	78
tꜣ(p?)...	m...	dpkꜣ	...dd...ꜣ	nꜥdyt

66
  a. This is ʿEṣem at Umm el-ʿazam near Beersheba: Albright (146).
  b. Simons (183) and Breasted (352) believe that this name-ring is compounded with name-ring 65 and should read "valley of the trees."

67
  a. The site is unknown.
  b. Noth (301) and Simons (183) both misread the name as ꜣnmr. They mix up the owl (m) and the vulture (ꜣ). Noth suggests that the site is to be identified with the Wadi Namala, thirteen miles north of Petra.

68
  a. The reading literally means "the Fort." pꜣ is the Egyptian article, followed by the noun ḥkr: Noth (295–300).
  b. Simons (99), Breasted (352), and Albright (146) disagree, arguing that the term is Semitic ḥql, "field." Albright further argues that this "suggests that Shishak's scribes swelled the list by noting down names of meadows and pastures, in order to impress their master, who may not have accompanied his army at all"; this reasoning is ungrounded.
  c. When joined with the following reading (69), what we have here is the beginning of a compound name-ring, "the Fort of . . . ." Nine names on the list are compounds introduced by the element "Fort."

69
  a. The site is probably Khirbet Futeis (Tell el-ʿUṣeifer), ten miles northwest of Beersheba: Aharoni (328); Albright (146). Iron Age remains have been found here.

70
  a. Albright (146) suggests that the site is Yehallel-el, which is connected with Ziph in 1 Chronicles 4:16. Kitchen (439) agrees.
  b. It is located in the area southeast of Beersheba.

71
  a. This is the beginning of a compound name-ring.

72
  a. Coupled with the preceding reading, this is the "Fort of Abram"; it cannot be identified.

b. On the basis of "sacred traditions" Aharoni (*BA* 35 [1972]: 114–15) believes it to be Tell es-Sebaʿ.
c. For a lengthy discussion see Noth, 291–92.

73
a. Albright (146) says that the site is Khirbet Zubâlah (Greek *Sobila*).
b. Others see here the Hebrew שִׁבֹּלֶת, "stream of," and thus the beginning of a compound name-ring: Breasted (352); Kitchen (439).

74
a. The opening *n* is the genitival construction "of."
b. Mazar (65) claims that the reading should remind us of Ezion-geber on the Gulf of Aqaba.

75
a. Like reading 73, this is the beginning of a compound name-ring.

76
a. The site cannot be identified.

77
a. See reading 68.

78
a. The *n* is a genitival construction.
b. The reading is obscure.

79
a. The reading is obscure.

80
a. Kitchen (439) believes that this may be the Sapek mentioned in 1 Samuel 30:28. The argument is based on Noth, 301, and Mazar, 65.

81
a. Most of the inscription has been destroyed.

82
a. Aharoni (328) argues for a reading of "Tappuah." The inscription is too damaged to draw such a conclusion. The partial letter read as *p* is highly questionable.

Tier 7

88	87	86	85	84	83
šnꜣyꜣ	pꜣḥḳꜣr(t)	tꜣ(š)dn(w)	ʿdꜣ...t	pꜣnꜣgbw	gꜣnꜣtỉ

94	93	92	91	90	89
pꜣḥgry	ỉšḥt	pꜣnꜣgbw	wꜣḥtrwk...	pꜣnꜣgb(w)	hꜣkꜣ...

99	98	97	96	95
ḫꜣnꜣy	ỉdꜣmt	ỉrḳꜣd	pꜣḥgrꜣ	ḫꜣnnꜣ

83
a. Kitchen (440) speculates that this "could be any Gath/Ginti." Gath is a stretch, for it is difficult to explain the *n*.
b. The site is unknown.

84
  a. Literally, "the Negev" (the south country); pȝ is the Egyptian article.
  b. This is probably the first element of a compound name; see also readings 90 and 92.

85
  a. Kitchen (440 n. 91) reads the missing letter as the tongue *ns*, with the value of *n*. He agrees with Aharoni (328) that there is a connection with the clan name Negev of the Eznites (2 Sam. 23:8; cf. 1 Sam. 27:10 and 30:14).
  b. The proposal is dubious. Although the term *Negev* is used of various regions in the Bible, it is never employed in conjunction with the Eznites.
  c. It may also be too much to assume that the Shoshenk list catalogues regions.

86
  a. The reading is obscure.

87
  a. Like reading 68, this is the beginning of a compound name: "Fort of . . . ."

88
  a. Aharoni's reconstruction (328) *šnt* (or *šnm*) is incorrect.
  b. Kitchen (440) suggests that the name may be philologically related to the two Judean places called Ashna (Josh. 15:33, 43). However, he also acknowledges that these sites may be too far north to fit the list here.

89
  a. The site is unidentifiable.
  b. Simons (184) deems *h* to be the Hebrew article. This is doubtful because the Egyptian scribes of this list did not transliterate but translated articles.

90
  a. Like reading 84, this is the beginning of a compound name.

91
  a. The reading is obscure.

92
  a. Like reading 84, this is the beginning of a compound name.

93
  a. This inscription may refer to the clan of Shuhathites (1 Chron. 4:11): Kitchen (440); Mazar (64); Aharoni (328). Or, perhaps, it may refer to the Sucathites (1 Chron. 2:55).

94
  a. Like reading 68, this is the beginning of a compound name: "Fort of . . . ."

95
  a. This is possibly a reference to the clan of Ben-Hanan (1 Chron. 4:20): Mazar (64–65); Aharoni (328); Kitchen (440).

96
  a. Like reading 68, this is the beginning of a compound name: "Fort of . . . ."

97
  a. This is probably Hazer-Gaddeh in the western Negev: Mazar (65); Aharoni (328); Kitchen (440).

98
  a. Note that the ⸗ is *not* inverted.
  b. Although some have argued that this is Edom, that identification is unlikely; see Noth, 295.
99
  a. See reading 95.

Tier 8

105	104	103	102	101	100
...y...	šrnrỉm	ḥydbꜣ	trwꜣn	pꜣḥgr	ỉdrꜣ

111	110	109	108	107	106
nbptt	ꜥrdꜣy	rbt	ꜥrdꜣt	ḥꜣkrm	dywꜣt

116	115	114	113	112
ỉd...ꜣ...	...	...	...ỉ	ywrḥm

100
  a. This is an ꜥAdar in Palestine.
  b. Breasted (353) places it in Judah.
  c. Kitchen (440) suggests ꜥAin Qedais (Hazar-Addar), a few miles east of Kadesh-Barnea.
101
  a. Though slightly broken, this inscription is probably the beginning of a compound name: "Fort of . . . ."
102
  a. This is generally agreed to be "the Fort of Tilon" (1 Chron. 4:20): Mazar (64–65); Aharoni (328); Kitchen (440).
103
  a. The site is unknown.
  b. The suggestion that this is Mount Horeb is a fallacious identification.
  c. Simons (185) reckons the term to be the same as reading 105, "apparently a generic word . . . but its Semitic equivalent is unknown."
104
  a. The inscription is obscure.
105
  a. The reading has been mostly destroyed.
106
  a. The inscription is obscure.
107
  a. The plural "forts," this inscription is probably to be combined with the next five name-rings (108–9, 110–12).
108–9
  a. A compound name meaning "Great Arad," this reading is to be identified with Tell ꜥArâd: Noth (294); Aharoni (328); Kitchen (440).

b. Albright (146) separates the two rings: the first is ʿArad, the second Leba'ot. The suggestion is unlikely.

110–12
a. This is a tricompound name—"Arad of the House of Jeroham."
b. The *n* is a genitival construction.
c. Kitchen (440) suggests the site is Tell Malhata.

113–15
a. The readings have been destroyed.

116
a. The inscription is obscure.

Tier 9

122	121	120	119	118	117
ỉbr	frtmỉꜣ	...ꜣrywk	ḫgỉꜣ	byỉꜣ	ỉdr...

128	127	126	125	124	123
ỉdmm	grnỉꜣ	ỉrmʿtn	šrḥ(n)	btʿnt	(b)pỉrrdꜣ

133	132	131	130	129
ywr(ḏw)	ỉrr...	mʿr...	...rỉ	...rḫt

117
a. Though the reading is not found in *Bubastite Portal*, Müller had restored it.
b. Kitchen (441) says that the site is Adar.

118
a. Though the reading is not found in *Bubastite Portal*, Müller had restored it.
b. Breasted (354 n. b) says that the site is Tell esh-Shehab in the Hauran region of Transjordan. This interpretation is questionable.

119
a. The inscription is broken and unreadable.

120
a. The inscription is unreadable.

121
a. The inscription may relate to the clan Peleth (1 Chron. 2:33): Mazar (65); Kitchen (441).

122
a. This is likely the first part of one of the many "Abel"-names in ancient Palestine. It is probably to be read in combination with 123.

123
a. The inscription is obscure. The first letter is unreadable, but may be a *b*.

124
a. The site is Beth-Anath.

b. Breasted declares that the inscription may refer to either Beth-Anath in Naphtali (Josh. 19:38; Judg. 1:33) or Beth-Anath in Judah (Josh. 15:59). The latter is the better possibility.

125
   a. This is probably Sharuhen in the western Negev.
   b. Noth (290 n. 1) erroneously restores the last letter as *t3w*.
   c. Albright (146) incorrectly identifies the site as Šilḥim at Tell el-Ḥuweilfeh.

126
   a. The site is unknown.
   b. Kitchen (441) says it may be El-mat(t)an in Ephraim (related to Mattanah in Num. 21:18–19).

127
   a. The site of Goren is unknown.

128
   a. The site of Adamam is unknown.

129–31
   a. The inscriptions are broken and obscure.

132
   a. The inscription is broken.
   b. Kitchen (441) restores it to El-ra[m] (see 1 Chron. 2:9, 27).
   c. Mazar (65–66) suggests Elroi, a sacred site of the Ishmaelites; this is doubtful.

133
   a. Kitchen (441) says that the site is "certainly Yurza south of Gaza." Mazar (65) and Aharoni (328) locate it at Tell Jemmeh.
   b. This is not so clear because the last two letters are broken.

Tier 10

139 ywrḥm	138 ...	137 ...	136 ...	135 ...	134 ...
145 mʿk...	144 ...	143 ...	142 ꜣ...g	141 ...	140 ꜣwnn
150 ywrdn	149 ...	148 ...	147 ...	146 ...ἰd...	

134–38
   a. The readings have been destroyed.

139
   a. This may be a reference to the clan Yeroham (cf. "Jerahmeel" in 1 Chron. 2:9): Aharoni (328).

140
   a. This may be a reference to the clan Onam (cf. 1 Chron. 2:26): Mazar (65).

141–44
   a. The readings have been lost.

145
  a. Aharoni (328) sees here the clan name Maacah (cf. 1 Chron. 2:48).
146–49
  a. The readings have been lost.
150
  a. This may be a reference to the Jordan.
  b. Mazar (66) says that the site is Yorda on the southern border of Judah; this is possible.

Tier 11

1a	2a	3a	4a	5a
šrdd	rpḥ	rwbn	ʿngrn	hȝm

1a
  a. The reading is obscure.
2a
  a. There is general agreement that the site is Raphia: Albright (146); Kitchen (441); Aharoni (329).
3a
  a. The site is probably Laban, which was south of Raphia at Tell Abu Seleimeh: Aharoni (329).
4a
  a. The site is unknown.
5a
  a. The site is unknown.

Part 4
Egyptian Wisdom Literature and the Poetical Books

11
The "Instruction of Amenemope" and the Book of Proverbs

A commonly held view is that Egyptian literature had a direct impact upon Israelite wisdom writings.[1] Ronald Clements says, "The influence of Egyptian intellectual and literary pursuits, broadly related to wisdom, was at one period quite strong."[2] Similarities in theme, tone, and sometimes even vocabulary appear to reflect a relationship between the two wisdom literatures. The concept of *ma'at* dominates these writings, at least according to some scholars.[3] A majority believe that the prevailing direction of influence was from Egypt to Israel, and not vice versa. And thus, when considering Hebrew wisdom literature, they understand it to be largely a product of Egyptian origination and impetus.

The Book of Proverbs has been a particular focus of this viewpoint. Scholars have long believed that there is a strong connection between

---

1. Scholarly material analyzing this relationship is vast. See especially G. E. Bryce, *A Legacy of Wisdom: The Egyptian Contribution to the Wisdom of Israel* (Lewisburg, Pa.: Bucknell University Press, 1979); L. G. Perdue, *Wisdom and Cult* (Missoula, Mont.: Scholars, 1977); E. Wurthwein, "Egyptian Wisdom and the Old Testament," in *Studies in Ancient Israelite Wisdom*, ed. J. L. Crenshaw (New York: Ktav, 1976); J. Blenkinsopp, *Wisdom and Law in the Old Testament* (Oxford: Oxford University Press, 1983); and R. N. Whybray, "Wisdom Literature in the Reigns of David and Solomon," in *Studies in the Period of David and Solomon and Other Essays*, ed. T. Ishida (Winona Lake, Ind.: Eisenbrauns, 1982), 13–26.
2. R. E. Clements, *Wisdom in Theology* (Grand Rapids: Eerdmans, 1992), 94.
3. Ibid., 94–96. For a detailed account of *ma'at* parallels, see Perdue, *Wisdom and Cult*, 19–28.

Limestone Statue of an Unidentified Scribe (Dynasty 6). *Courtesy of the Egyptian Museum, Cairo.*

the form and content of Hebrew proverbial sayings and Egyptian instruction texts.[4] For example, the Egyptian instructions are in poetic style as are the Israelite proverbs. They both employ assonance, alliter-

4. Included in this literary category would be texts like the "Instructions of Ptahhotep," "Instruction for King Meri-ka-Re," "Instructions of King Amen-em-het," "Wisdom of Ani," and "Instruction of Amenemope." These documents are to be found, translated into English, in *ANET*, 412–25.

ation, similes, and metaphors.[5] Synthetic, synonymous, and antithetical parallelisms are found frequently in both collections.[6] In regard to content, "no real difference is discernible between the fundamental ideas and aims of the discourses [i.e., Proverbs] and those of the Egyptian instructions. Both were composed for use in the same kind of scribal school, an institution which the Israelites had borrowed, together with its curriculum, from the Egyptians."[7]

Recent scholarship tends to agree: Egyptian influence on Hebrew wisdom literature goes beyond mere form and content, for the institutional sphere was also involved. Some writers argue that the instruction texts of Egypt and the proverbial sayings of Israel both arose out of a school tradition. Since Egypt's school tradition was earlier, it served as a model for Israel's school of wisdom. Nili Shupak's summation is incisive: "Semantic equivalents . . . confirm the existence of a link between the world of the Hebrew sage and the Egyptian school. It should seem reasonable to assume, therefore, that the first schools in Israel were inspired by an Egyptian prototype; and that the Book of Proverbs served as a text book in such schools."[8] Although this direct connection between schools in Egypt and Israel is hardly certain, the literary influence of Egypt in the area of wisdom appears to have been quite strong and persistent.

Amenemope

Much of the scholarly interest in the wisdom genre has focused on the similarity between the Egyptian "Instruction of Amenemope" and the Israelite Book of Proverbs.[9] The Egyptian document was first published

---

5. See J. M. Thompson, *The Form and Function of Proverbs in Ancient Israel* (Paris: Mouton, 1974), 37–41.

6. For further correspondences see P. Humbert, *Recherches sur les sources égyptiennes de la littérature sapientiale d'Israel* (Neuchatel: Secretariat de l'Université, 1929), 64–66. G. E. Bryce, "'Better'-Proverbs: An Historical and Structural Study," in *SBL Seminar Papers*, Los Angeles, 1972, 343–54, makes a good case that the "better"-form of proverb originated in Egypt and was then employed by Hebrew writers.

7. R. N. Whybray, *Wisdom in Proverbs* (London: SCM, 1965), 71.

8. N. Shupak, "The 'Sitz im Leben' of the Book of Proverbs in the Light of a Comparison of Biblical and Egyptian Wisdom Literature," *RB* 94 (1987): 98. For a detailed study of Egyptian school writings, see R. J. Williams, "Scribal Training in Ancient Egypt," *JAOS* 92 (1972): 216–21; idem, "The Sages of Egypt in Recent Study," *JAOS* 101 (1981): 1–19; and L. G. Perdue and J. G. Gammie, eds., *The Sage in Israel and the Ancient Near East* (Winona Lake, Ind.: Eisenbrauns, 1989).

9. So much ink has been spilled attempting to define the nature of the relationship between "Amenemope" and Proverbs that the modern researcher may be overwhelmed by the amount of material available. A basic bibliography of works that treat the issue in detail will give the reader a solid point of departure for further study:
   Alden, R. L. *Proverbs: A Commentary on an Ancient Book of Timeless Advice.* Grand Rapids: Baker, 1983.

in 1923 by E. A. Wallis Budge.[10] He provided an English translation and then mentioned two parallels with the Book of Proverbs.[11] A fragment

---

Alt, A. "Zur literarischen Analyse der Weisheit des Amenemope." In *Wisdom in Israel and in the Ancient Near East,* ed. M. Noth and D. W. Thomas, 16–25. Leiden: Brill, 1969.
Anthes, R. "Die Funktion des vierten Kapitels in der Lehre des Amenemope." In *Archäologie und Altes Testament,* ed. A. Kuschke and E. Kutsch, 9–18. Tübingen: Mohr, 1970.
Budge, E. A. W. *Facsimiles of Egyptian Hieratic Papyri in the British Museum.* 2d series. London: British Museum, 1923.
———. *The Teaching of Amen-em-apt, Son of Kanekht.* London: Martin Hopkinson, 1924.
Couroyer, B. "L'Origine égyptienne de la Sagesse d'Aménemopé." *RB* 70 (1963): 208–24.
DeVries, C. E. "The Bearing of Current Egyptian Studies on the Old Testament." In *New Perspectives on the Old Testament,* ed. J. B. Payne, 25–36. Waco: Word, 1970.
Drioton, E. "Une Colonie israélite en moyenne Egypte à la fin du vii siècle AV. J.-C." In *A la rencontre de Dieu,* ed. A. Baruco et al., 181–91. Le Puy: Xavier Mappus, 1961.
———. "Le Livre des Proverbes et la Sagessa d'Aménemopé." *Sacra Pagina* 1 (1959): 229–41.
———. "Un Livre hébreu sous couverture égyptienne." *La Table Ronde* 154 (1960): 81–91.
———. "Sur la Sagesse d'Aménemopé." *Mélanges bibliques rédigés en l'honneur d'André Robert* (Paris: Bloud and Gay, 1957), 3:25–280.
Dunsmore, M. H. "An Egyptian Contribution to the Book of Proverbs." *JR* 5.3 (1925): 300–308.
Erman, A. "Eine ägyptische Quelle der Sprüche Salomos." *Philosophische-historische Klasse* (1924): 86–93.
Gressmann, H. "Die neugefundene Lehre des Amen-em-ope und die vorexilische Spruchdichtung Israels." *ZAW* 42 (1924): 272–96.
Griffith, F. L. "The Teaching of Amenophis, the Son of Kanakht." *JEA* 12 (1926): 191–231.
Grumach, I. *Untersuchungen zur Lebenslehre des Amenemope.* Munich: Deutscher Kunstverlag, 1972.
Herzog, D. "Die Sprüche des Amen-em-ope und Proverbien Kapp. 22,17–24,35." *Zeitschrift für Semitistik und verwandte Gebiete* 7 (1929): 124–60.
Kevin, R. O. "The Wisdom of Amen-Em-Apt and Its Possible Dependence upon the Hebrew Book of Proverbs." *JSOR* 14 (1930): 115–57.
Kidner, D. *Proverbs.* Tyndale Old Testament Commentaries. Downers Grove, Ill.: InterVarsity, 1964.
Kitchen, K. A. *Ancient Orient and Old Testament.* Chicago: InterVarsity, 1966.
Lange, H. O. *Das Weisheitsbuch des Amenemope aus dem Papyrus 10.474 des British Museum.* Copenhagen: A. F. Høst, 1925.
McCown, C. C. "Hebrew and Egyptian Apocalyptic Literature." *HTR* 18 (1925): 357–411.
McKane, W. *Proverbs.* Philadelphia: Westminster, 1970.
Oesterley, W. O. E. *The Wisdom of Egypt and the Old Testament in the Light of the Newly Discovered 'Teaching of Amen-em-ope.'* London: S.P.C.K., 1927.
Peterson, B. J. "A New Fragment of the Wisdom of Amenemope." *JEA* 52 (1966): 120–28.
Posener, G. "Quatre tablettes scolaires de basse époque (Amenemope et Hardjedef)." *Revue d'Egyptologie* 18 (1966): 45–65.
Ruffle, J. "The Teaching of Amenemope and Its Connection with the Book of Proverbs." *Tyndale Bulletin* 28 (1977): 29–68.
Simpson, D. C. "The Hebrew Book of Proverbs and the Teaching of Amenophis." *JEA* 12 (1926): 232–39.
Whybray, R. N. *Proverbs.* New Century Bible Commentary. Grand Rapids: Eerdmans, 1994.
Williams, R. J. "The Alleged Semitic Original of the Wisdom of Amenemope." *JEA* 47 (1961): 100–106.

10. Budge, *Facsimiles,* plates 1–14.
11. One of the parallels was "Amenemope" 9.7–8 and Prov. 15:16–17. In the subsequent literature there is confusion regarding which verse from Prov. 15, verse 16 or 17, actually parallels the Egyptian passage. For a difference of opinion, see Erman, "Eine ägyptische Quelle," 86–87, and Gressmann, "Die neugefundene Lehre," 278. For another early English translation of "Amenemope," see Griffith, "Teaching of Amenophis," 191–231. For later (and better) translations see *ANET,* 421–25; and *AEL* 2:146–63. Especially useful is W. K. Simpson, ed., *The Literature of Ancient Egypt* (New Haven: Yale University Press, 1973), 241–65.

of another copy of the "Instruction of Amenemope" was discovered and published in the 1960s.[12] Portions of the document are also known from writing boards housed in the Turin Museum, the Pushkin Museum in Moscow, and the Louvre.[13]

The papyrus published by Budge was discovered inside a wooden statue of Osiris in a tomb in western Thebes. The consensus of scholarship is that it dates no earlier than Dynasty 21 (ca. 1070–945 B.C.). The fragment discovered on an ostracon in Cairo in the 1960s also appears to date to Dynasty 21. However, the language of the piece resembles the "Wisdom of Ani," which comes from Dynasty 18 or 19 (ca. 1300 B.C.). "Amenemope" likely dates to that earlier period as well.[14] Modern scholarship, then, places the original composition of the "Instruction" sometime during the New Kingdom.

Amenemope, called "the superintendent of the land," was an administrator of royal estates. His work consisted of managing food production, setting grain taxes, and overseeing the documents of his master. He resided in the Panapolite nome to the north of the city of Abydos. Amenemope wrote the "Instruction" for his son Hor-em-maa-kheru, a young priestly scribe. In the introduction he states his purpose in writing the document:

> The beginning of the instruction about life,
> The guide for well-being,
> All the principles of official procedure,
> The duties of the courtiers;
> To know how to refute the accusation of one who made it,
> And to send back a reply to the one who wrote;
> To set one straight on the paths of life,
> And make him prosper on earth;
> To let his heart settle down in its chapel,
> As one who steers him clear of evil;
> To save him from the talk of others,
> As one who is respected in the speech of men.[15]

Following this purpose statement and a brief autobiography Amenemope presents thirty chapters of moral instructions for his son.

While Budge made only minimal mention of parallels between the Book of Proverbs and the "Instruction of Amenemope," an article published by Adolf Erman quickly drew attention to the similarities between

12. Peterson, "A New Fragment," 120–28; Posener, "Quatre tablettes," 45–65.
13. Simpson, *Literature*, 241.
14. Williams, "Alleged Semitic Original," 100–106.
15. Simpson, *Literature*, 242.

the two documents.[16] Erman concluded that the Hebrew writer of Proverbs borrowed materials from the "Instruction of Amenemope." He argued that during the Saite or Persian periods a Hebrew in Egypt translated the "Instruction" into either Hebrew or Aramaic. Excerpts from that translation were inserted into the Book of Proverbs. Scholars in the 1920s generally accepted Hebrew borrowing as the reason for the parallels between the two documents. Hugo Gressmann, in fact, claimed that parts of Proverbs were taken almost verbatim from "Amenemope."[17] Direct Hebrew dependence is still held in some quarters today.[18]

In an article published in 1926 D. C. Simpson added a new twist to the discussion by suggesting that perhaps the Hebrews did not borrow directly from "Amenemope," but that both writings were dependent on an earlier common source.[19] W. O. E. Oesterley concurred with this theory,[20] but it did not find much acceptance in the scholarly community. However, it was later revived in Irene Grumach's major study *Untersuchungen zur Lebenslehre des Amenemope*. She provides an important translation, textual examination, and commentary for the "Instruction of Amenemope." She postulates that both Proverbs and "Amenemope" drew materials from an Egyptian book of maxims from the late eighteenth dynasty. Grumach tries to reconstruct the original book of maxims, but the problem, of course, is that no such book is known to have existed in antiquity.

By the close of the 1920s several scholars were rejecting outright the notion of Hebrew dependence. D. Herzog and Georges Posener are noteworthy in this regard.[21] R. O. Kevin went as far as to argue that the Egyptian author of "Amenemope" borrowed from the Book of Proverbs.[22] Almost thirty years later, Etienne Drioton published a series of articles proposing that "Amenemope" was an Egyptian translation of a Hebrew original composed by Jews in Egypt.[23] He dates the Hebrew

---

16. Erman, "Eine ägyptische Quelle," 86–93.
17. Gressmann, "Die neugefundene Lehre," 272–96, provides a list of parallels between the two ancient pieces.
18. Kidner, *Proverbs*, 24; and D. K. Berry, *An Introduction to Wisdom and Poetry* (Nashville: Broadman and Holman, 1995), 33: "Numerous duplicated proverbs indicate dependence by the later author of the passage in Proverbs."
19. Simpson, "Hebrew Book of Proverbs," 232–39.
20. Oesterley, *Wisdom of Egypt*.
21. Herzog, "Die Sprüche des Amen-em-ope," 124–60; G. Posener, review of *Recherches sur les sources égyptiennes de la littérature sapientiale d'Israel*, by P. Humbert, *Revue des études juives* 8 (1929): 97–101.
22. Kevin, "Wisdom of Amen-Em-Apt," 154–57.
23. Drioton, "Le Livre des Proverbes," 229–41; idem, "Un Livre hébreu," 81–91; idem, "Une Colonie israélite," 181–91; idem, "Sur la Sagesse," 25–280; idem, "L'Apologue des deux arbres," *Mélanges V. V. Struve* (1962): 76–80.

work to the time of Josiah's reform, and says that "Amenemope" was derived from it during the Persian period.

Drioton's position has been thoroughly discredited by Ronald Williams and B. Couroyer.[24] They demonstrate that "Amenemope" was composed many centuries before the Persian period. Key evidence here was the discovery of portions of "Amenemope" on the broken ostracon from Dynasty 21. In addition, Williams argues that the language of "Amenemope" is Egyptian and not Semitic, and that fact lends "strong support for an original Egyptian text."

More-recent writers have been hesitant to acknowledge a direct connection between the two works. Carl DeVries reflects the cautious and judicious approach that characterizes present scholarship: the question is not settled as to "the direction of the theoretical relationship between Amenemope and Proverbs . . . the existence of historical literary connection between the two cannot be demonstrated, though it is often assumed. . . . It may well be that with respect to possible connections between Amenemope and Proverbs the relationships are neither as many nor as close as has been thought."[25] Kenneth Kitchen similarly concludes that "careful study of both books in their full Near Eastern context has shown how inadequate are the grounds for relationship offered hitherto."[26]

The debate regarding dependence rages today, essentially focusing on the section of Proverbs most frequently cited as having an Egyptian connection, 22:17–24:22.[27] Scholars see many linguistic, thematic, and structural parallels. Our purpose is not to list and discuss each and every parallel, but to present a detailed discussion of the key text in the debate, the introductory passage of Proverbs 22:17–25.[28]

---

24. Williams, "Alleged Semitic Original," 100–106; Couroyer, "L'Origine égyptienne," 208–24.

25. DeVries, "Bearing of Current Egyptian Studies," 32.

26. Kitchen, *Ancient Orient*, 88 n. 3. For qualification or outright rejection of a direct connection between Proverbs and "Amenemope" see Ruffle, "Teaching of Amenemope," 29–68; and J. Krispenz, *Spruchkompositionen im Buch Proverbia* (Frankfurt am Main: Peter Lang, 1989), 129–31.

27. D. C. Snell, *Twice-Told Proverbs and the Composition of the Book of Proverbs* (Winona Lake, Ind.: Eisenbrauns, 1993), 3, labels Prov. 22:17–24:22 "a selection of sayings loosely translated from the Egyptian *Instruction of Amenemope* . . . [a] work more closely connected to the Bible than any other ancient Near Eastern composition."

28. For a list of the parallels see Simpson, "Hebrew Book of Proverbs," 232–39; and Gressmann, "Die neugefundene Lehre," 272–96. For a quick reference chart of the parallels see J. L. Crenshaw, "Proverbs, Book of," in *ABD* 5:516. For general points of connection see Ruffle, "Teaching of Amenemope," 36–52.

Proverbs 22 and *Amenemope*

We will begin our analysis with a translation of Proverbs 22:17–25 and then consider the proposed parallels verse by verse:

> 17. Turn your ear and hear the words of the sages,
> Set your heart on my knowledge.
> 18. For (it is) pleasant if you keep them in your inmost soul;
> They will be firm all at once upon your lips.
> 19. So that your confidence may be in Yahweh,
> I cause you to know today, indeed you!
> 20. Did I not write to you previously
> regarding counsels and knowledge,
> 21. To cause you to know truth, (that is) sayings of truth;
> To cause sayings of truth to return to those who sent you?
> 22. Do not rob the poor because he is poor,
> And do not crush the afflicted in the gate.
> 23. For Yahweh will contend (for) their dispute,
> And he will rob their robbers (of) life.
> 24. Do not associate with a master of anger,
> And with a man of wrath do not go,
> 25. Lest you learn his ways,
> And you find a trap for your soul.

Verses 17–18. Several writers observe some significant similarities between the opening verses and the beginning of "Amenemope" (1.3.9–16):

> (9) Give your ears, and listen to what is said,
> (10) Give your mind to interpreting them.
> (11) It is profitable to put them in your heart.
> (12) Woe to him who neglects them!
> (13) Let them rest in the casket of your belly,
> (14) May they be a lock in your heart.
> (15) When there arises a storm of words,
> (16) They will be a mooring-post for your tongue.

While there are some general similarities between the two passages, there are also major differences. For example, lines 12–15 of "Amenemope" appear nowhere in the Proverbs pericope. The Egyptian uses the dual form for "ears" in line 9, whereas the Hebrew (v. 17) employs a singular. The same verse in the Hebrew includes "the words of the sages," which the Egyptian line omits.[29]

Some scholars have been so convinced of Hebrew dependence in this section that they have gone to creative lengths to emend the He-

---

29. Ruffle, "Teaching of Amenemope," 53–54, discusses the distinctions at length.

brew text and force it to correspond to the Egyptian model. P. Humbert's *Recherches sur les sources égyptiennes de la littérature sapientiale d'Israel* is extreme in this regard. But the Hebrew text flows smoothly and makes perfect sense on its own. No emendations are needed either for grammatical purposes or for meaning. One should also note that other documents from the ancient Near East likewise begin with injunctions to take heed to the teachings about to be given, most notably the "Instructions of Ptah-hotep" and Psalm 78.[30] Proverbs 22:17–18 and "Amenemope" 1.3.9–16 may reflect a common introductory formula in the ancient Near East.[31]

Verse 19. "Amenemope" 1.7 reads, "To direct him on the paths of life." The argument that this text relates to Proverbs 22:19 is difficult to justify in terms of linguistics or interpretation. The reference to Yahweh in the Hebrew text appears to confirm the originality of the verse in the Old Testament.[32]

Verse 20. Erman ingeniously suggested that the word שִׁלְשׁוֹם in the Masoretic text should be repointed to שְׁלֹשִׁים, which means "thirty."[33] He then saw a parallel between the thirty chapters of "Amenemope" and thirty sayings in the Book of Proverbs. Numerous problems plague Erman's reconstruction. First of all, Erman's rendering is not a certain translation, but only a possibility. Depending upon how the word is pointed, it can mean "a third set" (שְׁלִשִׁים), "thirty" (שְׁלֹשִׁים), "previously, heretofore" (שִׁלְשׁוֹם), or a number of other renderings.[34] Second, the structure of Proverbs 22:17–24:22 does not easily divide into thirty parts. Some scholars have tried to force thirty divisions onto the Hebrew text.[35] Third, sayings that seem to correspond occur in a different sequence in the two works. Finally, the content of the thirty chapters of "Amenemope" and the so-called thirty sayings of Proverbs only partially correspond. There may be general thematic similarities, but not much more than that.

---

30. Ibid., 38.
31. There really is no basis for Ruffle's argument ("Teaching of Amenemope," 54) that the Hebrew passage is a free rendering by someone who was generally acquainted with "Amenemope."
32. The New American Bible replaces the phrase "indeed you" with the name Amenemope. This is highly speculative and uncalled for.
33. Erman, "Eine ägyptische Quelle," 89.
34. *BDB*, 1026.
35. See, in particular, Gressmann, "Die neugefundene Lehre," 272–96. Miriam Lichtheim's statement (*AEL* 2:147) that "it can hardly be doubted that the author of Proverbs was acquainted with the Egyptian work and borrowed from it, for in addition to the similarities in thought and expression—especially close and striking in Proverbs xxii and xxiii—the line in xxii,20: 'Have I not written for you thirty sayings of admonition and knowledge' derives its meaning from the author's acquaintance with the 'thirty' chapters of Amenemope," demonstrates an uncritical judgment.

Verse 21. The "Amenemope" prologue (1.5–6) reads, "To know how to refute the accusation of one who made it, and to send back a reply to the one who wrote." The two passages have only a single aspect in common: something is to be sent back to someone. But that is as far as it goes. Proverbs focuses on the learning of truth, which will be relayed to those who inquire about it. Truth is not even mentioned in "Amenemope." How these two passages might be related is difficult to see.

Verse 22. Proverbs now relates specific activities that the reader is not to do: one is not to steal from the poor or oppress the needy. This teaching has often been compared to "Amenemope" 2.4.4–5:

> Beware of robbing an oppressed man
> And of attacking the crippled.

The idea of the two passages is certainly the same. However, the prohibition of harming the afflicted is such a common idea in ancient Near Eastern literature that to argue for a direct parallel between "Amenemope" and Proverbs is wishful thinking at best. As well, the teaching that the needy must not be persecuted at the gate, that is, before the elders and judges of a city, is not found in the Egyptian text. That particular instruction appears to be a singularly Hebrew concept, at least in this context.

Verse 23. No parallel exists in the Egyptian document. The teaching that Yahweh will fight for the indigent, and that he will do so with dramatic irony—that is, those who are robbers will themselves be robbed of life by Yahweh—is foreign to the "Instruction of Amenemope."

Verse 24. "Amenemope" 9.11.13–14 commands, "Do not associate with a hot-tempered man, and do not approach him for conversation." The two passages are quite similar, and some have argued that the chiastic Hebrew verse may be a close translation of the Egyptian text.[36] But again, we need to recognize that the mandate to keep away from virulent men is found in much ancient Near Eastern wisdom literature. Similar exhortations are seen elsewhere in the Book of Proverbs and in Hebrew wisdom literature in general.

Verse 25. Scholars see a parallel with "Amenemope" 9.11.17–18: "Do not let him cast words to trap you, and do not be loose in your answers." The sole basis of the proposed parallel is the metaphor of the trap. Yet the agent of entrapment in "Amenemope" is the malicious man's words, whereas in the Hebrew the man who associates with such a person sets a trap for himself. In addition, as John Ruffle points out, there is no teaching in the Egyptian passage that one will become a man of wrath

---

36. Simpson, "Hebrew Book of Proverbs," 237–39.

if he listens to another's angry words, as is clearly the main instruction of the Hebrew text.[37]

From our brief comparative study it is evident that there are only vague similarities between Proverbs 22:17–25 and the "Instruction of Amenemope." Some general themes and foundational ideas correspond. Likewise, similar broad concepts are found throughout the entire section of Proverbs 22:17–24:22 and "Amenemope." But does that mean there is a necessary and direct connection between the two pieces of literature? And because the Egyptian text appeared earlier in time, does that mean the Hebrew writing was dependent upon it?

Most scholars take one of three positions: (1) the Hebrew text relied upon the Egyptian text; (2) "Amenemope" was based upon the Hebrew writing; or (3) both texts rested on an earlier source that is unknown to us.[38] Yet there does exist another position that a few scholars have propounded, namely, there is no direct connection between "Amenemope" and Proverbs. The evidence appears to support that view. First of all, the correspondences between the two pieces are by nature shallow and vague. And in most places the content is only partially similar. Second, many of the parallel themes are common in the various writings of the ancient Near East. Much of the correspondence could be a mark of universal ideas or universally accepted images. Third, the seemingly parallel passages in the two works are arranged in a different sequence. They are out of order. Fourth, many of the proverbs in "Amenemope" are not found in Proverbs 22:17–24:22, and vice versa. If there was dependence, it must have been very selective and fragmented. Lastly, any attempt to divide the Hebrew text into thirty sayings is artificial. Moreover, Proverbs 22:17–24:22 is likely not a single, unitary composition but part of a broader literary structure.[39] Such problems are difficult to overcome when one argues a case for direct dependence, one way or the other.

How then does one explain the affinities that do exist between Proverbs and "Amenemope"? Ruffle reasons that "the relationship that can be demonstrated can be adequately explained by the suggestion that this passage was contributed by an Egyptian scribe working at the court of Solomon based on his memories of a text that he had heard and, maybe, used in his scribal training."[40] This is mere conjecture. There is no evidence at all. Yet the writer of Proverbs obviously did have a gen-

---

37. Ruffle, "Teaching of Amenemope," 58.
38. Whybray, *Proverbs*, 323.
39. See the discussion of A. Niccacci, "Proverbi 22:17–23:11," *Studii Biblici Franciscani* 29 (1979): 42–72.
40. Ruffle, "Teaching of Amenemope," 65.

eral familiarity with the genre of Egyptian wisdom literature. This, however, did not have a direct and detailed influence on the Hebrew writer of Proverbs. The impact was of an indirect nature and of the broadest strokes. The Hebrew author was not guilty of crass plagiarism—on all accounts Proverbs is a thoroughly Hebrew document.

Part 5
Egyptian and Israelite Prophecy

12
Knowing the Divine Will: The Art of Divination in Ancient Egypt

> The practice of divining from a sacrificed victim has come from Egypt. It would seem too that the Egyptians were the first people to establish solemn assemblies, and processions, and services; the Greeks learned all this from them. I hold this proved, because the Egyptian ceremonies are manifestly very ancient, and the Greek are of late origin.

This is part of Herodotus's account (2.56) of the beginning of divination practices in Greece. He relates that they originated in Egypt and were conveyed to Greece and elsewhere by two Theban priestesses who had been kidnapped by Phoenician sailors and sold abroad. There is no need to discuss the merits of Herodotus's story because he was merely relaying hearsay, and there is no evidence to support it. What is important to note, however, is that Herodotus (and others of his day) believed that divination, the human art of finding out a god's mind, began in ancient Egypt. To him, the land of the Pharaohs was the epicenter from which other parts of the ancient world received their magical arts.

Herodotus considered Egypt to be strange and mysterious: "As the Egyptians have a climate peculiar to themselves and their river is different in its nature from all other rivers, so have they made all their customs and laws of a kind contrary for the most part to those of all other men" (2.35). Such a view of ancient Egypt persists today. "To a certain type of mind, Egypt is beyond doubt the land of dreamlike ghostliness."[1] And like Herodotus, many today have the impression of ancient Egypt as peculiar because of its divining arts, which included practices such as written communication with the dead, astrology, and lecanomancy. But how accurate is that picture?

Before we begin to answer that question, it is necessary that we provide a working definition of divination. Divination is the attempt to forecast the future or discover the will of the gods through any one of a variety of methods.[2] It is a process that is usually originated by humans (often the priesthood) and then responded to by a deity. Gods may reveal themselves without prompting, but that appears to be rare in antiquity, especially in Egypt.

The types of divination in ancient Egypt were surprisingly limited. Apparently there was, contra Herodotus, no extispicy (inspection of the liver of an animal to discern the future), nor was there libanomancy (reading smoke from a censer), practices that were common in ancient Mesopotamia.[3] In fact, the Egyptians did not employ as many forms of divination as did other peoples of the ancient Near East, a fact to be kept in mind as we consider the Egyptian practices.

Oracles

The primary form of divination in Egypt was oracular.[4] The consultation normally began with a written or oral question. This was followed by a deific response that could arrive in a variety of ways. Audible voices from chapels or statues (probably emanating from priests) often affirmed or denied a request. At Deir el-Medinah priests carried the gods

---

1. J. D. Ray, "Ancient Egypt," in *Oracles and Divination,* ed. M. Loewe and C. Blacker (London: Allen and Unwin, 1981), 175.

2. For a general study of divination in antiquity see M. W. Meyer and P. A. Mirecki, eds., *Ancient Magic and Ritual Power* (Leiden: Brill, 1995); for the Syro-Palestinian sphere in particular, the reader should examine A. Jeffers, *Magic and Divination in Ancient Palestine and Syria* (Leiden: Brill, 1996); for Egypt see J. F. Borghouts, *Ancient Egyptian Magical Texts* (Leiden: Brill, 1978); R. K. Ritner, *The Mechanics of Ancient Egyptian Magical Practice,* Studies in Ancient Oriental Civilization (Chicago: Oriental Institute, 1992); and, for an older study, F. Lexa, *La Magie dans l'Egypte antique de l'ancien empire jusqu'à l'époque copte,* 3 vols. (Paris: P. Geuthner, 1925).

3. For a good popular presentation and excellent bibliography of Mesopotamian divination see W. Farber, "Witchcraft, Magic, and Divination in Ancient Mesopotamia," in *Civilizations of the Ancient Near East,* ed. J. M. Sasson (New York: Scribner, 1995), 3:1895–1909.

4. The literature on ancient Egyptian oracles is vast. See, e.g., A. M. Blackman, "Oracles in Ancient Egypt," *JEA* 11 (1925): 249–55 and *JEA* 12 (1926): 176–85; A. Barucq, "Oracle et Divination," *Dictionnaire de la Bible,* supp. 6 (1960): 761–65; J. Cerny, "Egyptian Oracles," in *A Saite Oracle Papyrus,* ed. R. A. Parker (Providence: Brown University Press, 1962), 35–48; O. Kaiser, "Das Orakel als Mittel der Rechtsfindung im alten Ägypten," *ZRG* 10.3 (1958): 193–208; and G. Roeder, *Kulte, Orakel und Naturverehrung im alten Ägypten* (Zurich: Artemis, 1960).

of the community on their shoulders as portable shrines. Questions were put to a god—if it moved forward, it was giving an affirmative reply; if it went backward, it was answering negatively. All sorts of questions dealing with daily activities were handled in this manner.[5]

The context of most oracles was not in a temple, because the sacred shrines were denied to the general populace.[6] Oracles were usually found at festivals where the divine image was mobile. However, even in that more secular environment the presence of the priesthood was essential, for in ancient Egypt they were the seat of oracular power.

Oracles prior to the New Kingdom have not been discovered. Allusions to pre–New Kingdom oracles are made by later texts, but none of the originals have survived. Oracular consultation had a long history in Egypt, persisting until the seventh century A.D.

Frederick Cryer has argued for a thematic evolution of oracles in ancient Egypt.[7] The focus of consultation in the first half of the New Kingdom was the throne and military matters. The life of Pharaoh and the royal court were the dominant subjects of oracular divination in the early centuries. Later in the New Kingdom, oracles at Amarna dealt with judiciary and legal matters. Finally, by the Greco-Roman period they applied to all areas of ordinary life. This theory of development appears to be generally sound.

Astrology

Astrology may be defined as the forecasting of events on the basis of celestial phenomena. This form of divination began in Mesopotamia and was influential throughout the history of that land.[8] But astrology is poorly attested in ancient Egypt, and it appeared there quite late. According to Franz Cumont, "astrology was unknown in ancient Egypt; it was not until the Persian period . . . that it began to be cultivated there."[9] The art was likely transmitted from Mesopotamia to Egypt between the fifth and third centuries B.C. The examples of celestial divination in Egypt at that time clearly show Babylonian influence.[10] Most as-

---

5. J. F. Borghouts, "Divine Intervention in Ancient Egypt and Its Manifestation," in *Gleanings from Deir el Medîna*, ed. R. J. Demarée and J. J. Janssen (Leiden: Nederlands Instituut voor het Nabije Oosten, 1982).

6. F. H. Cryer, *Divination in Ancient Israel and Its Near Eastern Environment* (Sheffield: JSOT, 1994), 217.

7. Ibid., 217–20.

8. Farber, "Witchcraft, Magic, and Divination," 1907–8.

9. F. V. M. Cumont, *Astrology and Religion among the Greeks and Romans* (New York: Dover, 1960), 43.

10. R. A. Parker, *A Vienna Demotic Papyrus on Eclipse-and-Lunar Omina* (Providence: Brown University Press, 1959).

trological divination texts from Egypt fall within the first half of the first century A.D.[11]

Communication with the Dead

Given their particular regard for the dead, it is not surprising that the ancient Egyptians expected them to intervene in the affairs of this world. Such a belief appears in letters written to dead relatives.[12] These letters often ask for assistance with matters of everyday life. In one letter the departed is asked to mediate a family dispute; in another, to assist a widow and orphans who were being victimized by unscrupulous relatives.[13] Requests like these are quite common.

Letters to the dead were not understood to be one-way communications. Many expected a response through dreams or other forms of deific revelation. Consider, for example, a letter from Merertifi to the deceased Nebetyotef:

> I am your beloved upon earth. Fight on my behalf and intercede on behalf of my name. I have not garbled a spell before you when I perpetuated your name upon earth. Remove the infirmity of my body. Please become a spirit before my eyes, so that I may see you fighting for me in a dream. Then I will deposit offerings for you.[14]

Some of the letters to the dead, then, were a form of necromancy, an attempt to know or manipulate the future.

Lecanomancy

The Greek word *lekanē* means "dish," and thus lecanomancy refers to divining the future by looking into a dish. In Egypt, a dish would be filled with oil or water, and a medium—usually a young boy—would gaze into the liquid and have a vision. Others could then question the lad, who would "tell you about everything you ask him."[15] Our knowl-

---

11. O. Neugebauer, "Two Demotic Horoscopes," *JAOS* 63 (1943): 115–27. The Merneptah Victory Stele from Dynasty 19 describes a Libyan chieftain's retreating from an attack on Egypt because "the observers of their stars and all those who know their spells from looking at the winds" predicted defeat (*ANET*, 377). This, however, is not an example of Egyptian but foreign divination.

12. A. H. Gardiner and K. Sethe, *Egyptian Letters to the Dead* (London: Egyptian Exploration Society, 1928); and E. F. Wente, "A Misplaced Letter to the Dead," *Orientalia lovaniensia periodica* 6–7 (1976): 595–600.

13. H. Frankfort, *Kingship and the Gods* (Chicago: University of Chicago Press, 1948), 362.

14. Wente, "A Misplaced Letter," 595–96.

15. F. Ll. Griffith and H. Thompson, *The Demotic Magical Papyrus of London and Leiden* (London: H. Grevel, 1904), 8–22.

edge about this divining art comes from a papyrus of the Roman period and is archaeologically attested by numerous statuettes.[16]

Lecanomancy appeared very late in Egyptian history, no earlier than the third century A.D. The practice was probably adopted from Mesopotamia, where it had developed centuries earlier.[17]

Prophecy

One's view of whether prophecy existed in ancient Egypt depends on how one defines the term. To some, prophecy means predicting the future; to others, it signifies social critique; and to still others, it refers to divine revelation.[18] For our purposes here, prophecy is otherwise inaccessible information given by a god and communicated to others by a human speaker. The prophet may initiate the giving of the divine information, although normally it begins with divine power. This definition of prophecy as a proclamation of divine messages by inspiration also applies to ancient Israel.

Ancient Egypt offers very little evidence of prophets as inspired speakers of divine oracles. Some have suggested that the Middle Egyptian document "The Admonitions of Ipu-wer" may be a good example of Egyptian prophecy.[19] And yet while this text shows a certain Ipu-wer standing before Pharaoh and criticizing the current social and economic situation, there is no mention of Ipu-wer's having received his words from a deity. Thus Ipu-wer was preaching, but certainly not prophesying (at least not according to our working definition). The same problem exists with the view that "The Prophecy of Neferti" from Dynasty 18 is prophetic. This text tells the tale of a prophet who foretold to King Snofru (Dynasty 4) the decline and fall of the Old Kingdom. He further related that the greatness of Egypt would be restored by a coming king: Amenemhat I, the first king of Dynasty 12 (ca. 1991–1962 B.C.).[20] Of course, this document was only a "fictional creation designed

---

16. J. Capart, "Les Anciens Egyptiens pratiquaient-ils la lecanomancie?" *Chronique d'Egypte* 37 (1944).

17. Cryer, *Divination in Ancient Israel*, 222.

18. For a general discussion of the prophecy of the ancient Near East as it relates to Israel, see J. Blenkinsopp, *A History of Prophecy in Israel* (Philadelphia: Westminster, 1983); R. Coggins, A. Phillips, and M. Knibb, eds., *Israel's Prophetic Tradition* (New York: Cambridge University Press, 1982); J. A. Emerton, ed., *Prophecy* (Berlin: W. de Gruyter, 1980); B. Lang, *Monotheism and the Prophetic Minority* (Sheffield: Almond, 1983); and J. Lindblom, *Prophecy in Ancient Israel* (Philadelphia: Fortress, 1962). A good study of Israelite prophecy and Egypt is S. Herrmann, "Prophetie in Israel und Ägypten: Recht und Grenze eines Vergleiches," *VTS* 9 (1962): 47–65.

19. *ANET*, 441.

20. *ANET*, 444–46.

to serve the cause of propaganda."[21] Further, there is no hint of divine impetus or revelation to the human speaker Neferti.

Gunter Lanczkowski attempts to demonstrate that the Middle Kingdom "Protests of the Eloquent Peasant" is an example of ancient Egyptian prophecy.[22] The peasant protests the social injustice of his time, much in the manner of an Old Testament prophet. Also, Lanczkowski sees prophetic activity in that some of the peasant's proclamations were uttered in the temple precinct. That should remind us of many Old Testament prophets, such as Jeremiah and Amos, who prophesied and preached in a cultic environment.[23] However, the essential elements of prophecy that we described above are missing.

Not until the Greco-Roman period did texts appear that reflect our definition of prophecy.[24] Works like "The Demotic Chronicle," "Bocchoris and the Lamb," and "The Potter's Oracle" are to be included in the prophetic genre. These documents differ from earlier so-called prophetic texts in that each one involves a supernatural revelation, whether by a god (such as Amon) or by a mediate supernatural being (such as an angel). This type of literature is often called apocalyptic, although it really does not differ greatly from prophetic literature as we have defined it.

Dreams and Dream Interpretation

One of the earliest mediums through which the Egyptians received communications from the gods was dreams. Our first evidence is in a series of Middle Kingdom letters written to the dead.[25] Kings often received commands from a deity through dreams. According to a New Kingdom temple inscription from Karnak, a statue of Ptah appeared to Merneptah in his sleep, extended his sword to him, and commanded him to be courageous against the Libyan foe.[26] The stele of Tanutamon (Dynasty 25) tells of a dream revelation to the king. He saw two serpents, one on his right and one on his left. This was symbolic of the double diadem of Egypt (uraeus), and its appearance in the dream signified that the king was to unite Upper and Lower Egypt.[27] A document of

21. Ray, "Ancient Egypt," 182.
22. G. Lanczkowski, *Altägyptischer Prophetismus* (Wiesbaden: O. Harrassowitz, 1960).
23. H. Ringgren, "Prophecy in the Ancient Near East," in Coggins et al., eds., *Israel's Prophetic Tradition*, 1–2.
24. J. C. VanderKam, "Prophecy and Apocalyptics in the Ancient Near East," in *Civilizations of the Ancient Near East*, ed. Sasson, 3:2086–88.
25. Gardiner and Sethe, *Egyptian Letters to the Dead*.
26. *ARE* 3:245.
27. *ARE* 4:469.

Thutmosis IV tells of how he fell asleep in front of the Sphinx and then in a dream had a conversation with it.[28] This is an example of incubation: a person slept in the presence of a god, normally in a temple precinct, and the god responded in dreams and provided counsel.

Perhaps the most famous passage where dreams seem to be regarded as revelations from the gods so that humans might know the future is found in the "Instruction for King Meri-ka-Re" from about 2100 B.C. In describing what the deity has provided for humans, the anonymous author says in line 137:

> He made for them magic as weapons to ward off (evil) events;
> Dreams *(rswt)* also by night and day.[29]

That this text actually refers to communication through dreams has been called into question by Walter Federn.[30] He first points out that "dreams" is an inappropriate translation of *rswt*, because there are no signs reflecting the plural after the word. Second, the expression "by night and day" is usually found in connection with terms denoting watchfulness rather than dreams. And, finally, he convincingly argues that *rswt* derives from the root *rsỉ*, which means "to watch out."[31] Consequently, line 137 is better translated:

> He has made for them magic to be weapons to ward off what may happen.
> Be watchful over it by night as by day.[32]

Most scholars agree with Federn's reconstruction.[33]

Be that as it may, in ancient Egypt dream omens were an important source for knowing the divine will. In support of that contention is that, unlike the Mesopotamians, the ancient Egyptians collected omens in only one category: dream omina.[34] The most important collection of dream omens is the Chester Beatty Papyrus III, which comes from Dynasty 19. Alan Gardiner maintains that the style and language of the document may be dated as early as Dynasty 12 (ca. 1991–1783 B.C.). The

---

28. Roeder, *Kulte, Orakel und Naturverehrung*, 191–272.
29. An early translation by A. H. Gardiner, "New Literary Works from Ancient Egypt," *JEA* 1 (1914): 20–36. *ANET*, 417, basically agrees; see also Ray, "Ancient Egypt," 179.
30. W. Federn, "The 'Transformations' in the Coffin Texts: A New Approach," *JNES* 19.4 (1960): 241–57.
31. *WÄS* 2:452.
32. Translated by R. O. Faulkner in *The Literature of Ancient Egypt*, ed. W. K. Simpson (New Haven: Yale University Press, 1973), 191.
33. See, e.g., *AEL* 1:106.
34. Cryer, *Divination in Ancient Israel*, 220.

earliest extant collection of dreams, it may well date to the twelfth dynasty, though this cannot be proved.[35]

The manuscript is divided into dreams experienced by the Sons of Seth and the Sons of Horus. Over columns listing various dreams are written the words, "If a man sees himself in a dream." Adjoining columns provide interpretations. For example:

If a man sees himself in a dream:
Seeing a large cat—   Good: it means a large harvest will come to him
Seeing his face in a mirror—   Bad: it means another wife[36]

These two dreams with their interpretations reflect some of the characteristics of the Beatty papyrus:

1. In each dream the dreamer sees himself doing something.
2. The dreams have oracular power, that is, they can predict the future.
3. The dreams are allegorical. Thus the cat in the first example symbolizes a large agricultural harvest.
4. "Very commonly the principle of similars is used, either similars of sound, that is, puns, or similars of situation."[37] For instance, the Egyptian term for "large cat" sounds like the Egyptian for "large harvest."

Another collection of dream omina is a demotic text from the second century A.D.[38] Leo Oppenheim, in his major study on dream omens in the ancient Near East, has conclusively demonstrated that what we have in this text was greatly influenced by Mesopotamian ideas.[39] On the other hand, Mesopotamia contributed little to the earlier dream omina of the Beatty papyrus, which he believes to be essentially an independent Egyptian production. Others disagree, seeing a definite Mesopotamian tradition in that document along with some Egyptian adaptations.[40] Dream collections were common throughout the history of

---

35. A. H. Gardiner, *Hieratic Papyri in the British Museum* (London: British Museum, 1935), 8. For an excellent exegetical commentary on the Beatty papyrus, see S. Israelit-Groll, "A Ramesside Grammar Book of a Technical Language of Dream Interpretation," in *Pharaonic Egypt*, ed. S. Israelit-Groll (Jerusalem: Magnes, 1985), 71–118.
36. *ANET*, 495.
37. Ibid.
38. A. Volten, *Demotische Traumdeutung* (Copenhagen: E. Munksgaard, 1942).
39. A. L. Oppenheim, "The Interpretation of Dreams in the Ancient Near East," *TAPS* 46.3 (1956): 179–353.
40. Cryer, *Divination in Ancient Israel*, 222.

Mesopotamia, but whether they influenced the Beatty papyrus is a moot point: there simply is no way to make a conclusive judgment on the matter.

Regardless of whether they bear Mesopotamian influence, dream omens in ancient Egypt were a means of receiving information from the next world. Though not as all-pervasive as the oracle, they were yet widely employed as a means of knowing the divine will.

Joseph and Dream Interpretation

Comparison of the Egyptian collections of dream omens with the biblical story of Joseph reveals significant parallels. In fact, the foundational elements present in the Chester Beatty Papyrus III are also essential characteristics of the dream sequences in Genesis 40–41:

1. *The dreamer sees himself doing something.* In all four dreams in Genesis 40–41 the dreamer is an active participant. The chief cupbearer views himself grasping and squeezing a cluster of grapes (40:11); the chief baker dreams that he is carrying three baskets on his head (40:16); Pharaoh sees himself "standing by the Nile" (41:1).

2. *The dreams possess oracular power.* Joseph's interpretations of the four dreams all come to pass: "and it came about that just as he interpreted for us, so it happened" (41:13). Thus the Genesis story, like the Egyptian texts, teaches that dreams can foretell the future.

3. *The dreams are allegorical.* In the Egyptian dream omina a large cat symbolizes a large harvest, whereas in Pharaoh's first dream a fat cow represents a large harvest. The similar symbolism is obvious.

4. *The principle of similars is used.* Similars of situation are a common feature of the Genesis episode. For example, the chief baker dreams that birds are eating baked goods out of a basket on his head; Pharaoh would soon chop off the baker's head, and birds would eat his flesh.

We should not hesitate to see the implications of the parallels between the Joseph account and the Beatty papyrus. J. D. Ray asserts, "Joseph owes his success to dream-interpretation, and it is tempting to think that he is really defeating the Egyptians on their own ground."[41] When Pharaoh wanted his dreams interpreted, he purposely turned first to his own diviners who were skilled in the arts of dream interpretation. The result was less than desirable, however: "He sent and called for all the magicians of Egypt, and all its wise men. And Pharaoh told them his dreams, but there was no one who could interpret them to Pharaoh" (Gen. 41:8). Joseph, on the other hand, was able to provide

---

41. Ray, "Ancient Egypt," 177.

the meanings of the dreams because "interpretations belong to God" (Gen. 40:8).

A variety of forms of divination are known to have been employed by the ancient Egyptians. Most of these methods (astrology and lecanomancy, for instance) were used only in later periods of Egyptian history, from the Persian period onward. Their appearance in Egypt was for the most part a result of Mesopotamian influence and corresponded with the increasing political, cultural, and military penetration of foreign powers into Egypt at a late date.[42] Prior to the Persian period, the two principal genres of divination in Egypt were oracles and dream interpretation. Examination of these phenomena, especially the latter, provides insightful and penetrating background material for a proper understanding of the biblical story of Joseph.

Was ancient Egypt the land of the strange? Certainly to our modern minds it is shrouded in mystery. However, the land of the Pharaohs was no more enigmatic than the other societies of the ancient Near East. And, frankly, when dealing with the divining arts, it was less peculiar than Mesopotamia and Ugarit.

---

42. Cryer, *Divination in Ancient Israel*, 223.

13

Hebrew Prophecies against Egypt: The Nile Curse Passages

Egypt is a common target of the curses uttered by the prophets of Israel and Judah. Principal among these texts are Isaiah 20:3–6; Jeremiah 43:11–13; 46:13–26; Ezekiel 29:1–16; 30–32; Daniel 11:42–43; and Joel 3:19. A primary motif in several of these passages is a call for the drying up of the Nile River. Ezekiel 30:12, for instance, proclaims: "[Thus says the Lord God,] 'I will make the Nile canals dry and sell the land into the hands of evil men. And I will make the land desolate, and all that is in it, by the hand of strangers; I, the Lord, have spoken.'" Zechariah 10:11 similarly announces God's judgment on Egypt: "And He will pass through the sea of distress, and strike the waves in the sea, so that all the depths of the Nile will dry up; and the pride of Assyria will be brought down, and the scepter of Egypt will depart."

Our intention in this chapter is to determine why the theme of a waterless Nile appears so frequently in Hebrew prophetic texts and to explain precisely what the motif means. Here again, the Egyptian setting and background information will help us in our quest. Our method of analysis will be to investigate the historical background of the most representative and important curse on the Nile. In that manner a good amount of information will be gleaned that can be applied to all the Old Testament curses on the Nile.

A Representative Curse and Its Background

The passage we will consider is Isaiah 19:5–10:

5. And water from the sea will be dried up;[1]
And a river[2] will be desolate and dried up.[3]
6. And rivers will stink;[4]
The Nile canals of Egypt[5] will be low[6] and desolate;
Stalk and papyrus reed[7] will be decayed.
7. Bare places[8] (will be) near the Nile,[9] near the delta;[10]
And every place of sowing of the Nile (basin) will dry up, will be driven out, and will be no more.
8. And the fishermen will mourn;[11]
And all who cast a fishhook into the Nile will lament;
And those who spread nets on the top of the waters will languish.
9. And the workers of combed linen and the weavers of white cotton will be ashamed.
10. And her appointed ones[12] will be crushed;

1. The translation is the author's. The Septuagint translates the first line: "And the Egyptians will drink water by the side of the sea." Apparently the Greek translators understood *mayim* to be *miṣrayim* ("Egypt"), and the verb *niššĕtû* to be related to the Hebrew verb *šātāh* ("to drink"). No such emendations are necessary. The passage makes perfect sense as referring to the Red Sea crossing in Exod. 14 as a paradigm of a future curse upon Egypt.
2. The singular here likely refers to the Nile River, mentioned later in the pericope.
3. The two Hebrew verbs are also used in Gen. 8 in regard to the dried earth after Noah's flood. *Yābēš*, in particular, reflects land that is intensely dry. The ground that Israel crossed in the midst of the Red Sea is also termed *yābēš*.
4. A hapax legomenon; see R. Yaron, "The Meaning of ZANAḤ," *VT* 13 (1963): 237–39.
5. An abbreviated form of Egypt used elsewhere in Hebrew poetic literature (2 Kings 19:24; Isa. 37:25). Some argue that *māṣôr* stands only for Lower Egypt, and one scholar believes it refers to the cataracts of the Nile. See P. J. Calderone, "The Rivers of 'Masor,'" *Biblica* 42 (1961): 423–32.
6. The verb *dālal* means "to be low, hang down." Here it probably refers to the Nile inundation that supplies Egyptian canals. The curse, then, is that the Nile will not rise, but stay low.
7. The Hebrew *sûph* may be etymologically related to Egyptian *twf(y)*, "marsh plant, papyrus."
8. The Septuagint interprets *ʿārôt* to mean "reeds, green herbage." That rendering may be correct because the Egyptian word for papyrus is *ʿrt* (*WAS* 1:213). Thus, this may be a loanword. On the other hand, the term may derive from the Hebrew verb *ʿrh*, which means "to be bare, naked." See J. Reider, "Etymological Studies in Biblical Hebrew," *VT* 2 (1952): 115–16.
9. This is probably an Egyptian loanword. See H. Eising and J. Bergman, יאר, in *TDOT* 5:359–63.
10. The Hebrew literally says "the mouth of the Nile."
11. Cf. Isa. 3:26, where the same word (*ʾānāh*) is used, also in conjunction with *ʾābĕlû* ("they will lament").
12. *BDB* believes *šātîtêah* derives from *šāt*, and therefore refers to working classes. Actually, it may be related to *šātat*, "to appoint," and it would then reflect the upper classes of Egyptian society in contrast to the hired workers of the second half of the verse. Consequently, all ranks of society will be troubled and dismayed by the curse on Egypt. I. Eitan's argument ("An Egyptian Loan Word in Isa 19," *JQR* 15 [1924–25]: 419–22) that this word is Egyptian is not very convincing.

A Relief from the Tomb of King Ra-hotep: Fishing in the Nile. *Courtesy of the Staatliche Museum, Berlin.*

All hired workers will be sad[13] of soul.

Before we can arrive at a proper interpretation of our text, it is necessary that we first determine its historical setting. The curse against the Nile is part of a broad, sweeping series of oracles that the prophet Isaiah pronounced against a host of foreign powers. Most of the oracles in Isaiah 10–23 are introduced with the term *maśśā'*, "a burdensome word."[14] The first verse of each oracle specifies the nation being maledicted by Isaiah: Assyria (10:5); Babylon (13:1); Philistia (14:29); Moab (15:1); Damascus (17:1); Cush (18:1); Egypt (19:1); Edom (21:11); Arabia (21:13); and Tyre (23:1). There is no consensus as to which imprecations the prophet Isaiah actually spoke or wrote, although there is no good reason to believe he did not compose them all.

---

13. *'agĕmê* is a hapax legomenon. The biblical writer employs it as a play on words with verse 15, which speaks of bulrushes (*'agĕmôn*) having no work.

14. The term *maśśā'* in Old Testament prophetic texts introduces a speech of minatory, threatening character. Some scholars argue that *maśśā'* merely means "utterance, oracle," but the across-the-board menacing nature of the term demands a translation that reflects hostility.

Few passages in the Old Testament have been chronologically and historically scrutinized as much as has Isaiah 19. Various suggestions have been presented regarding the historical milieu of Isaiah's curse upon Egypt; most of them have centered on the identification of the "mighty king" that will rule over Egypt (19:4). Candidates have included Assyrian monarchs (Sargon II, Sennacherib), Persian rulers (Cambyses), and the Seleucid kings of Syria (Antiochus Epiphanes).[15] Some have argued that this figure is more likely an Ethiopian or Cushite monarch from the late eighth century B.C., such as Piankhy or Shabaka.[16] Other scholars believe that no specific king or historical period was intended by the author.[17] James Coffman concludes that "it is probable that the prophet is not alluding to an individual king at all. The description would fit any of the Assyrian kings, including Esarhaddon and Assurbanipal who actually conquered Egypt."[18]

A majority of recent scholars seem to place Isaiah 19 in the 720–702 B.C. range, although there is disagreement regarding which specific events are in view.[19] Even Donald Redford, who is skeptical of almost everything in the Bible, regards Isaiah 19 as an accurate description of the political situation in Egypt at the end of the eighth century B.C.[20] But to say that Isaiah 19 refers to the period between 720 and 702 B.C. is not all that helpful. Several critical political and military events occurred during this eighteen-year period that would be proper settings for the Isaiah 19 prophecies. For example, Assyria under Sargon II invaded Philistia and came to the very borders of Egypt at least three times in that period.[21] Although some scholars hesitate to attempt it, determining the precise historical setting behind Isaiah 19 seems possible. In order to accomplish that task, we must provide a general brief overview

---

15. For an overview of options tendered by early biblical scholars, see G. B. Gray, *A Critical and Exegetical Commentary on the Book of Isaiah I–XXXIX* (New York: Scribner, 1912), 321.

16. J. Bright, *A History of Israel*, 3d ed. (Philadelphia: Westminster, 1981), 281; J. H. Hayes and S. A. Irvine, *Isaiah the Eighth-century Prophet* (Nashville: Abingdon, 1987), 253–58; and J. D. W. Watts, *Isaiah 1–33* (Waco: Word, 1982), 248–62.

17. H. Hailey, *A Commentary on Isaiah* (Grand Rapids: Baker, 1985), 162; E. J. Kissane, *The Book of Isaiah*, 2 vols. (Dublin: Browne and Nolan, 1941, 1943), 1:215; and E. J. Young, *The Book of Isaiah*, vol. 2 (Grand Rapids: Eerdmans, 1969), 16.

18. J. B. Coffman, *Commentary on Isaiah* (Abilene: Abilene Christian University Press, 1990), 174.

19. E.g., Hailey, *Commentary on Isaiah*, 156, comments that "the probable date of the events of this chapter is the period of the Assyrian threat to Judah (720–702 B.C.)."

20. D. B. Redford, "The Relations between Egypt and Israel from El-Amarna to the Babylonian Conquest," in *Biblical Archaeology Today* (Jerusalem: Israel Exploration Society, 1985), 192–205; and idem, *Egypt, Canaan, and Israel in Ancient Times* (Princeton, N.J.: Princeton University Press, 1992), 351.

21. See N. Na'aman, "The Brook of Egypt and Assyrian Policy on the Border of Egypt," *TA* 6 (1979): 68–90.

of the Egyptian political and economic scene during the latter half of the eighth century B.C.

The policies of the Libyan pharaohs (e.g., Shoshenk I) at the beginning of Dynasty 22 resulted in nearly a century of peace and prosperity for Egypt (ca. 945–860 B.C.). However, with the reign of Takelot II (ca. 860–835 B.C.), Egypt descended into a period of decline and conflict. By the mid-eighth century B.C., the centralized authority of Egypt had been divided into the hands of numerous local dynasts (this fragmentation of power had actually begun in the ninth century B.C., and thus dominated the political horizon of Egypt for nearly a century and a half).[22] Anyone traveling to Egypt in the last half of the eighth century would have encountered no fewer than seven fiefs, including those of the great chief of the Me(shwesh), two kings in Lower Egypt, two kings in Middle Egypt (at Herakleopolis and Hermopolis), and the temple estate of Amon in the Thebaid. The legitimate king of Dynasty 22 directly controlled only Tanis and its environs, Athribis, and Memphis; all other lords temporal, while they offered him lip service, ran their bailiwicks independently.[23]

In addition, Egypt had lost control of Nubia (Cush, Ethiopia), which had gradually become an independent state with the end of Dynasty 20.[24] The disintegration of centralized authority and power in Egypt left the country weak and open to outside aggression, which appeared in two forms in the second half of the eighth century B.C.—Nubia and Assyria.

After Nubia gained its freedom from Egypt, a power center started to develop at the capital of Napata. The Nubian state was characterized by a revivalist attitude, the desire to reinstate earlier Egyptian culture in place of the culture of the recent New Kingdom. The Nubians preferred as a model the glorious years of the Egyptian Old and Middle Kingdoms, "a species of Egyptian culture that was somewhat old-fashioned and fraught with a solemn, conservative piety."[25] In art and architecture, for example, the Nubians looked to early Egypt for inspiration. Royal tombs at Napata were modeled after Old Kingdom pyramids, and they included scenes of Old Kingdom funerary ritual. The Nubians also exploited traditional religious ideas regarding kingship, *ma'at*, and symbolic unity.[26] They had great zeal for the Egyptian god Amon, who had been worshiped at Napata since early in Dynasty 18.

22. J. H. Breasted, *A History of Egypt* (New York: Scribner, 1937), 547.
23. Redford, "Relations between Egypt and Israel," 195; and W. Holscher, *Libyer und Ägypter* (Glückstadt: J. J. Augustin, 1937).
24. C. Aldred, *The Egyptians* (London: Thames and Hudson, 1961), 153.
25. Redford, *Egypt, Canaan, and Israel*, 343.
26. B. G. Trigger et al., *Ancient Egypt: A Social History* (New York: Cambridge University Press, 1983), 243.

By the last third of the eighth century B.C., Egypt had grown so fragmented and impotent that the rulers of Napata sought to assert some control over it. In 728 B.C. Piankhy "began the absorption of Egypt."[27] At this time, Tefnakhte, a ruler of various nomes in the western delta, attempted to expand his holdings by advancing southward with a large army.[28] Piankhy responded by marching his troops northward and engaging Tefnakhte in a series of battles. According to the Piankhy Stele, the Nubians shattered the forces of Tefnakhte, penetrated as far as Memphis, and forced the delta dynasts to pay tribute.[29] How great the submission truly was is debatable, for "although Piankhy claims to have trounced Tefnakhte, it is significant that he did not proceed with his army beyond Memphis, and was satisfied with token submission of the Delta."[30] Apparently Sais, the capital of the western delta, was stronger than Piankhy indicates in his triumphal stele. After the invasion he loaded his ships with treasure and sailed back to Napata at the fourth cataract of the Nile.

Piankhy's return to Nubia did not mean that the Ethiopians held no sway over events in Egypt after their departure. Piankhy's sister, Amenirdis I, for example, continued to serve as coregent and the "Divine Consort of Amon" at Thebes, a position she had held since 735 B.C. Her rule there had neutralized the powerful *imperium in imperio* of Thebes and solidified Piankhy's control of that important Egyptian city.[31] Piankhy likely maintained garrisons in other strategic towns of Egypt.[32] His northern border at this time probably extended far into Egypt, possibly even as far as Asyut.[33]

Egypt itself, however, was not completely shackled by the Nubians. Brisk trade by land and sea between Egypt and foreign nations to the north is evident from archaeological remains of this time. The Egyp-

---

27. Breasted, *History of Egypt*, 539.
28. K. A. Kitchen, *The Third Intermediate Period in Egypt (1100–650 B.C.)* (Warminster: Aris and Phillips, 1973), 362–63.
29. Erected in the temple of Amon at Napata, this magnificent granite stele bore inscriptions on all four sides recording in detail Piankhy's military campaign to the north. See B. Porter and R. L. B. Moss, *Topographical Bibliography of Ancient Egyptian Hieroglyphic Texts, Reliefs, and Paintings*, 7 vols. (Oxford: Oxford University Press, 1927–64), 7:217; N.-C. Grimal, *La Stèle triomphale de Pi(ankh)y au Musée du Caire* (Cairo: IFAO, 1981); *AEL* 3:66–84; and *ARE* 4:406–44.
30. Redford, *Egypt, Canaan, and Israel*, 346.
31. Aldred, *Egyptians*, 153. In addition to a superb statue from Karnak and a tomb and funerary chapel at Medinet Habu, Amenirdis is named in a desert graffito at Wadi Hammamat; see Kitchen, *Third Intermediate Period*, 382.
32. *ARE* 4:421.
33. Redford, *Egypt, Canaan, and Israel*, 343.

tians traded with Lebanon for timber,[34] and commerce seems to have taken place even between Assyria and Egypt.[35]

Piankhy probably died in 716 B.C., and he was buried in his pyramid at Kurru, with a team of horses to serve him in the afterlife.[36] Piankhy's brother Shabaka, who had married one of Piankhy's daughters, succeeded him.[37] Political sectionalism continued to dominate Egypt at the time of Shabaka's accession to the throne of Nubia. Three rulers vied for leadership in Lower Egypt: Osorkon IV (ca. 730–712 B.C.), ruling in Tanis as the last king of Dynasty 22; Shoshenk VI(?) at Leontopolis, the final ruler of Dynasty 23; and Bakenranef (Bocchoris, ca. 720–712 B.C.) at Sais. Because of the factionalism, Shabaka attacked Egypt early in his reign, conquered it, and annexed it. According to Manetho (*Aegyptiaca*, fragment 65), Shabaka took Bocchoris captive, and then burned him alive. The Nubian assault appears to have taken place no earlier than 712 B.C.[38]

The archaeological record confirms Shabaka's reunification of the north and south (including Nubia). Artistic representations of Shabaka picture him wearing the double uraeus that symbolizes the two lands of Upper and Lower Egypt. He is called the "King of Egypt and Kush."[39] Shabaka's rule in the north is further proved by the appearance of his name in annual records of the Nile level at Karnak and on donation-steles at various sites throughout the delta.[40] He likely installed a Nubian governor in Sais, and he maintained rule over various oases of Egypt, such as the Bahria Oasis, where his building blocks were found.[41] Shabaka erected enclosure walls in temples of Upper and Lower Egypt. He apparently was a strong and energetic monarch.

Shabaka advanced the policy of the Nubian monarchs by looking to earlier periods of Egyptian history for inspiration. He assumed the prenomen Neferkare' ("He of beautiful countenance"), which was prin-

---

34. H. Tadmor, "Philistia under Assyrian Rule," *BA* 29.3 (1966): 86–102.

35. H. Tadmor, "The Campaigns of Sargon II of Assur: A Chronological-Historical Study," *JCS* 12.3 (1958): 77–100.

36. For the chronology of this period see K. Baer, "The Libyan and Nubian Kings of Egypt: Notes on the Chronology of Dynasties XXII–XXIV," *JNES* 32 (1973): 4–25; K. A. Kitchen, "Late Egyptian Chronology and the Hebrew Monarchy," *JANES* 5 (1973): 225–33; and D. B. Redford, "Some Observations on Egyptian Chronology of the Eighth and Seventh Centuries B.C.," *AJA* 8 (1977): 82–83. And, especially, see Kitchen, *Third Intermediate Period*, 2d ed.

37. *ANET*, 295.

38. Kitchen, "Late Egyptian Chronology," 228–29; D. B. Redford, "Sais and the Kushite Invasion of the Eighth Century B.C.," *JARCE* 22 (1985): 5–15; A. J. Spalinger, "The Year 712 B.C. and Its Implications for Egyptian History," *JARCE* 10 (1973): 95–101.

39. Redford, *Egypt, Canaan, and Israel*, 351.

40. Kitchen, *Third Intermediate Period*, 379.

41. Porter and Moss, *Topographical Bibliography*, 7:311.

cipally used of kings during the Old Kingdom in Dynasties 6–10.[42] Shabaka's building projects were reminiscent of earlier Egyptian history. He was the first pharaoh in centuries to build in western Thebes. For instance, the Nubian ruler partially decorated the central gateway that had originally been erected by Rameses II. He also built a colonnade in the forecourt of the temple area. In the temple of Amon (Djeser-iset) at Medinet Habu, which had first been built by Hatshepsut and Thutmosis III, Shabaka made some major alterations.[43] He constructed a chapel in the precinct of Amon at Karnak.[44] A building inscription on the north side of the fourth pylon attests to Shabaka's construction:

> [King Shabaka; he made (it) as his monument for his father], Amon-Re, lord of Thebes, presider over Karnak, restoring the great and august gate: "Amon-Re-is-Mighty-in-Strength," making for it a great overlay of fine gold, which the majesty of King Shabaka, living forever, brought from the victories, which his father, Amon, decreed to him; the great hall being overlaid with fine gold, the south column and the north column being wrought with gold, the two lower lips being of pure silver.[45]

And at Memphis he raised a chapel in the enclosure of the temple of Ptah (a structure primarily framed by Rameses II).[46]

Documentation for the reign of Shabaka is actually quite meager. Apart from the building programs we have mentioned there are few records and artifacts that witness to his kingship. He is mentioned in the record of the Nile levels at Karnak:

> Year 2, under the majesty of Horus: Sebektowe;[47] Favorite of the two goddesses:[48] Sebektowe; Golden Horus: Sebektowe; King of Upper and Lower Egypt: Neferkere; Son of Re: [Shabaka], living forever, beloved of Amon-Re, lord of Thebes, beloved of Montu-Re, lord of Thebes. The Nile, father of gods, was 20 cubits, 1 palm, 1 finger.[49]

A large scarab was also discovered from the time of Shabaka that commemorates his military prowess: "He has slain those who rebelled

---

42. Later pharaohs such as Rameses IX (ca. 1131–1112 B.C.) and Amenemnisu (ca. 1044–1040) also appropriated the prenomen Neferkare', but clearly the title was more characteristic of the Old Kingdom than any other period.
43. Porter and Moss, *Topographical Bibliography*, 7:165.
44. Ibid., 202.
45. *ARE* 4:454.
46. J. Baines and J. Malek, *Atlas of Ancient Egypt* (New York: Facts on File, 1980), 136.
47. Sebektowe, a name meaning "he who illumines the two lands," was assumed by Shabaka because of his reunification of Upper and Lower Egypt; see *WAS* 4:86–87; 9:219.
48. "The two goddesses" refers to Wadjet, the tutelary goddess of Lower Egypt, and to Nekhbet, the tutelary deity of Upper Egypt. Again, reunification is the point.
49. *ARE* 4:452.

against him in both South and North, and in every foreign land."[50] Shabaka ruled for thirteen full years until his death in about 703–701 B.C. Like Piankhy before him, Shabaka was entombed in Kurru.

The second major threat to Egypt at the end of the eighth century B.C. was Assyria. The Mesopotamian nation had begun to be a world power in the ninth century B.C. when it repelled the Arameans and then assumed the role of victorious overlord of southern Anatolia and northern Syria.[51] In the second half of that century, the Assyrians invaded Israel.[52] By the middle of the following century, Assyrian suzerainty was secure throughout Syria-Palestine. As early as 738 B.C., Azariah king of Judah recognized Assyrian authority and sovereignty—he had been recently defeated by the Assyrians as he headed a twelve-state coalition in rebellion.[53] Ahaz, the grandson of Azariah, paid vassal tribute to Tiglath-pileser III and declared, "I am your servant and your son" (2 Kings 16:7). One of the reasons for Ahaz's submission appears to have been the penetration of Assyrian forces into Philistia in 734 B.C.; they may have threatened the Judean kingdom from there. Judah's eastern neighbors Edom, Ammon, and Moab also paid tribute to Tiglath-pileser III at this time. Because of this major campaign in 734–732 B.C., the region from the Taurus Mountains in the north to the River of Egypt in the south paid homage to the Assyrian monarch, whether as provinces or vassal states.[54]

In the 730s a weakened Egypt sat between two power centers: Assyria to the northeast had been in a period of great expansion, and now it knocked at the very gates of Egypt; Nubia, to the south, was just beginning to strengthen, and it began to formulate an expansionist policy primarily directed to the north. Over the final quarter of the century, the local native rulers were caught in "the struggle between Kush and Assyria for the control of Egypt."[55]

---

50. Kitchen, *Third Intermediate Period*, 379; see also J. Yoyotte, "Plaidoyer pour l'authenticité du scarabée historique de Shabako," *Biblica* 37.4 (1956): 457–76.

51. H. Tadmor, "Assyria and the West: The Ninth Century and Its Aftermath," in *Unity and Diversity: Essays in the History, Literature, and Religion of the Ancient Near East*, ed. H. Goedicke and J. J. M. Roberts (Baltimore: Johns Hopkins University Press, 1975), 36–48.

52. M. C. Astour, "841 B.C.: The First Assyrian Invasion of Israel," *JAOS* 91 (1971): 383–89.

53. H. Tadmor, "Azriyau of Yaudi," *Scripta Hierosolymitana* 8 (1961): 270–71; and M. Cogan, *Imperialism and Religion: Assyria, Judah, and Israel in the Eighth and Seventh Centuries B.C.E.* (Missoula, Mont.: Scholars, 1974), 65.

54. W. W. Hallo, "From Qarqar to Carchemish: Assyria and Israel in the Light of New Discoveries," in *Biblical Archaeologist Reader*, vol. 2, ed. E. F. Campbell, Jr., and D. N. Freedman (Missoula, Mont.: Scholars, 1961), 174.

55. Trigger et al., *Ancient Egypt*, 245.

During the 720s Assyria's army was quite active in the west, and it ravaged certain countries in the region, most prominently the kingdom of Israel. According to some authors, the Assyrians invaded the capital Samaria no fewer than four times in that decade, the most devastating being an attack by Shalmaneser V in 725–24 and a final assault by Sargon II in 722–21.[56] Although the precise sequence of conflict is much debated, clearly the Assyrians brutally conquered Israel in a series of attacks and deported its population.[57] Egypt's role at the time of the destruction of Israel is not clear, although according to 2 Kings 17:4 the Egyptians, under the enigmatic King So, were in alliance with Israel against the Assyrians.[58]

After the fall of Samaria, Sargon II invaded southern Philistia in 720. During a conflict at Gaza, the Philistine king of Gaza fled to Egypt for protection. Egyptian troops came to his aid and met the Assyrians in battle at Raphia. The Assyrians were victorious. Sargon II chased the Egyptians back to their homeland, destroyed Raphia, and deported a large part of its population, some nine thousand people.[59] He returned in 716 for what appears to have been a minor campaign that is attested in a single prism fragment from Assyria.[60] In 712 Sargon II returned again with a more vengeful assault on Philistia, the main target being the city of Ashdod. The Annals of Sargon II relate what happened during the siege:

> Iamani from Ashdod, afraid of my armed force, left his wife and children and fled to the frontier of M[usru][61] which belongs to Meluhha[62] and hid there like a thief. . . . The terror(-inspiring) glamor of Ashur, my lord, overpowered the king of Meluhha and he threw him in fetters on hands and feet, and sent him to me, to Assyria.[63]

---

56. J. H. Hayes and J. K. Kuan, "The Final Years of Samaria (730–720 BC)," *Biblica* 72.2 (1991): 153–81.

57. See the discussion of N. Na'aman, "The Historical Background to the Conquest of Samaria (720 BC)," *Biblica* 71.2 (1990): 206–25; H. Tadmor, "The Campaigns of Sargon II of Assur," *JCS* 12.1 (1958): 22–40; and E. J. H. Becking, "De ondergang van Samaria" (Ph.D. diss., University of Utrecht, 1985).

58. For work on the identification of this king see A. R. W. Green, "The Identity of King So of Egypt—An Alternative Interpretation," *JNES* 52 (1993): 99–108; D. L. Christensen, "The Identity of 'King So' in Egypt (2 Kings XVII 4)," *VT* 39 (1989): 140–53; R. Borger, "Das Ende des ägyptischen Feldherrn Sib'e=So," *JNES* 19 (1960): 49–53; and H. Goedicke, "The End of 'So, King of Egypt,'" *BASOR* 171 (1963): 64–66.

59. Na'aman, "Brook of Egypt," 68–90.
60. Ibid., 71.
61. Egypt; see Tadmor, "Assyria and the West," 39.
62. Ethiopia.
63. *ANET*, 285.

Apparently, the Nubian king Shabaka, who probably began his rule of Egypt in 712 B.C., extradited Iamani to the Assyrians. Most likely he did so in order to maintain a semblance of friendly relations with the powerful Assyrians.

For the greater part of the last twenty years of the eighth century B.C., little hostility and conflict occurred between Egypt and Assyria. That Assyria attempted to foster commercial relations with Egypt is evident in an inscription of Sargon II: "I opened the sealed harbour of Egypt, mingled Assyrians and Egyptians together and made them trade with each other."[64] A clay seal-impression discovered at Nineveh and bearing the name of Shabaka and his figure in a victorious pose may reflect a political relationship (treaty?) between the Nubians and the Assyrians at this time.[65] When Shabaka died (ca. 703–701), he was replaced by Shebitku, who had served as coregent with Shabaka for some time.[66]

External peace soon ended in 701, however, when the Assyrian monarch Sennacherib led an invasion into Philistia as far as Ekron. Shebitku mounted an expedition against the Assyrians, and they met in the plains of Eltekeh. There the Assyrians appear to have suffered a reverse, which probably contributed to Sennacherib's withdrawal from Syria-Palestine.[67] Thus ended the period in which most scholars place the events of Isaiah 19.

A close inspection of Isaiah 18–20, which deals with Cush and Egypt, enables us to define the historical backdrop quite closely. Several considerations testify to a setting just prior to the Nubian Shabaka's invasion of Egypt in 712 B.C. and the Ashdod rebellion against Assyria in the same year:

1. In Isaiah 18 and 19 Cush and Egypt are treated by the prophet as separate lands. There is no indication in the text that Cush is in control of Egypt (or vice versa). This presents a terminus ad quem of 712 B.C., because after that date Egypt and Cush were unified under the rulership of Shabaka.

2. Isaiah 19:2 tells us that Egypt is in the midst of civil strife and war—"kingdom against kingdom." That appears to reflect Egypt just prior to Shabaka's conquest when at least three rulers were vying for power in Lower Egypt. The fragmentation of Egypt is apparent in verses 11–13, where two separate Egyptian power centers are mentioned: Zoan (Tanis) and Memphis.

---

64. Na'aman, "Brook of Egypt," 84; see also M. Elat, "The Economic Relations of the Neo-Assyrian Empire with Egypt," *JAOS* 98 (1978): 20–34.
65. Breasted, *History of Egypt*, 553; Kitchen, *Third Intermediate Period*, 380.
66. F. J. Yurco, "Sennacherib's Third Campaign and the Coregency of Shabaka and Shebitku," *Serapis* 6 (1980): 221–41.
67. Redford, *Egypt, Canaan, and Israel*, 353.

3. Isaiah 19:4 predicts that Egypt will be delivered "into the hand of a cruel master, and a mighty king will rule over them." Apparently at this point Egypt is independent, but will soon be taken over by a (foreign) king—that, of course, took place under the Nubian Shabaka.

4. Isaiah 18:2 implies that the political relationship between Assyria and Nubia is, if not good, at least workable. Such relations reflect the economic and political times between 720 and 701 under Piankhy and Shabaka.

5. Isaiah 20 treats Egypt and Cush together. In addition, "the Assyrian expedition of 712 to Ashdod is vouched for by the text, and is not disputed."[68] Thus Isaiah 20 represents a later time period than Isaiah 18–19 and gives us another terminus ad quem.

Although much of the material in these chapters is eschatological, the historical setting is evident. The backdrop is the fragmentation of Egypt and the imminent takeover of the land by the Nubian ruler Shabaka. The conquest of Egypt by Nubia is figuratively expressed in Isaiah 19:5–10 as the drying up of the Nile River.

The Nile Inundation

Why did the prophets use the motif of the drying up of the Nile when they pronounced doom on Egypt? The answer is suggested in the words of the Greek historian Herodotus (2.5): "For even though a man has not before been told it, he can at once see, if he have sense, that that Egypt to which Greeks sail is land acquired by the Egyptians, given them by the river."[69] The idea that Egypt is the gift of the Nile was hardly a new one when Herodotus wrote those words so many centuries ago.[70] The ancient Egyptians themselves looked upon the Nile as the primary source of their existence. In its inundation stage the Nile was considered to be "the giver of life to the two lands," "the lord of sustenance," "he who causes the whole land to live through his provisions," and the like. The celebrated "Hymn to the Inundation" proclaims:

> Hail to your countenance, Hapi,
> Who goes up from the land, who comes to deliver Kemet (Egypt). . . .
> Who brings food, who is abundant of provisions,

68. H. L. Ginsburg, "Reflexes of Sargon in Isaiah after 715 B.C.E.," in *Essays in Memory of E. A. Speiser*, ed. W. W. Hallo (New Haven: American Oriental Society, 1968), 47–53.

69. For a seminal study on the formation of the Nile Valley see W. C. Hayes, "Most Ancient Egypt. Chapter I. The Formation of the Land," *JNES* 23 (1964): 74–114.

70. J. G. Griffiths, "Hecataeus and Herodotus on 'A Gift of the River,'" *JNES* 25 (1966): 57–61.

Who creates every sort of his good things. . . .
Who is enduring of customs, who returns at his due season,
Who fills Upper Egypt and Lower Egypt. . . .
Everything that has come into being is (through) his power;
There is no district of living men without him.[71]

The proper name the Egyptians gave to the Nile was *itr(w)*,[72] but in its inundation stage they called it *ḥ'pi*.[73] The latter is also the name given to the Egyptian god of the inundation; in other words, the Egyptians believed that the rising of the Nile waters was the embodiment of a god. Hapi is regularly depicted as a hermaphrodite, a god with sexual traits of both male and female. He usually has pendent breasts and is pregnant, as on the relief of a sandstone pillar in the temple of Rameses II at Abydos.[74] He is frequently represented as bearing gifts of food for humans and gods. Obviously the Egyptians considered Hapi the god of fecundity and fertility. Their response on seeing the Nile in inundation is succinctly captured in the Pyramid Texts (581): "They tremble that behold the Nile in full flood. The fields laugh and river-banks are overflowed. The god's offerings descend, the visage of men is bright, and the heart of the gods rejoiceth."[75]

The physical benefits of a high Nile to the Egyptians are obvious, so we need not spend much time detailing them. At Wadi Halfa, near the southern border of Egypt, the Nile begins to rise in June and reaches its maximum height in September. Its flow at maximum height is about 800 million cubic meters per day, at its low point only 100 million. Such a massive amount of water provides irrigation for fields and brings fresh alluvial deposits to the riverbanks so that the use of fertilizers is unnecessary.[76] The ancient Egyptians rightly understood the inundation to be the source of their food supply:

---

71. The bulk of this translation is by J. L. Foster, "Thought Couplets in Khety's 'Hymn to the Inundation,'" *JNES* 34.1 (1975): 1–29. For a general discussion of various hymns to the Nile see R. T. R. Clark, "Some Hymns to the Nile," *University of Birmingham Historical Journal* 5 (1955): 1–30.
72. *WAS* 1:146–47. The Hebrew term for the Nile River is *yĕʾōr*, borrowed from the Egyptian *itr(w)*.
73. A. de Buck, "On the Meaning of the Name Ḥ'pi," in *Orientalia neerlandica (A Volume of Oriental Studies)* (Leiden, 1948), 1–22. See also A. H. Gardiner, *Egyptian Grammar* (London: Oxford University Press, 1957), 580.
74. For this depiction see V. Ions, *Egyptian Mythology* (New York: Bedrick, 1982), 107.
75. A. Erman, *The Literature of the Ancient Egyptians* (New York: Dutton, 1927), 10. The ancient Egyptians knew that the heliacal rising of Sothis, the Dog Star, coincided with the Nile's inundation; so when Sothis arose, the farmers prepared their fields for cultivation. See J. G. Read, "Early Eighteenth Dynasty Chronology," *JNES* 29 (1970): 1–11.
76. W. S. LaSor, "Egypt," in *ISBE* 2:31.

Ha'py gives life to the two lands; meat and food come into being when he rises.[77]

Ptah to Rameses II: "I give thee a great Nile, I endow for thee the Two Lands with wealth, produce, food."[78]

The Nile, whether inundated or not, also supplied fish as a food source of the people.[79]

Two very important plant crops, flax and papyrus, depended upon the Nile inundation. Flax is an annual plant cultivated for its fiber and seeds. Its fiber was manufactured by the ancient Egyptians into ropes and linen yarn for clothes and sails. Papyrus, of course, was the chief Egyptian writing material and an important export. The earliest boats on the Nile were constructed of papyrus reeds.

Because the Nile connected all the important parts of Egypt, the boat was the basic means of transport. It eased communication between all significant localities which were sited on the banks of the Nile itself. The running of cargo internally in Egypt was done primarily through shipping, and trade between Egypt and foreign countries was sometimes accomplished on the water. Other uses for boats on the Nile, such as movement of military forces, are well known and documented.[80]

Beyond the mere physical benefits bestowed on Egypt by the Nile inundation, the rising of the river was a great symbol of resurrection. It is sometimes compared in the ancient literature to the rising of the sun, which of course was the foremost physical emblem pointing to resurrection. Inundation was another sign of the cosmic circuit of life, death, and rebirth. A blessing upon the king reads: "I grant thee that thou mayest rise like the sun, rejuvenate thyself like the moon, repeat life like the flood of the Nile."[81] Because of the rebirth motif, the Egyptians often identified the Nile River with the god Osiris, who was not only the king of the dead and the underworld, but also lord of resurrection. Rameses IV thus extols the majesty of Osiris: "Thou art the Nile . . . gods and men live from thy outflow."[82]

---

77. For an excellent translation see K. A. Kitchen, *Ramesside Inscriptions I* (Oxford: Blackwell, 1993), 75.
78. *ARE* 3:404.
79. *ANEP*, 33–34.
80. Baines and Malek, *Atlas of Ancient Egypt*, 68–69.
81. See K. F. Piehl, *Inscriptions hiéroglyphiques recueilliés en Europe et en Egypte* (Leipzig: J. C. Hinrichs, 1886–95), vol. 2, plate 4.
82. J. Cerny, *Ancient Egyptian Religion* (New York: Hutchinson's University Library, 1952), 85, argues against the identification of Osiris with the Nile inundation. His argument is not very convincing.

The importance of the Nile to Egypt is further reflected in the emphasis placed upon the king's control of the Nile. Simply put, Pharaoh had power over the Nile River. According to a text from Dynasty 5, "It is Unas who flooded the land. . . . It is Unas who pulled up papyrus. It is Unas who reconciled the Two Lands."[83] Pharaoh was so identified with the Nile that he is referred to as "Ha'py, who overflows every day, who gives life to Egypt."[84] Pharaoh Akhenaten "calls himself a Nile for his people."[85] The idea is that Pharaoh is the true provider of sustenance for Egypt; it is he who floods the Nile, which in turn supplies the people with nourishing crops.

The connection between the king and the inundation was so strong that temple reliefs, especially during the New Kingdom, tied together the beginning of the rising of the river and the coronation of the Pharaoh. A typical inscription reads: "First month of the Inundation, New Year, the beginning of peaceful years, (Day) of the Coronation of the King of Upper and Lower Egypt. Union of the Two Lands. Circuit of the Walls. Festival of the Diadem."[86]

Correspondingly, a high Nile signified a prosperous reign. And thus Rameses II's desire for later kings: "May the full Nile come for you at his season."[87] Because the inundation symbolized a prosperous king and rule, the yearly levels of the Nile were commonly recorded for each Pharaoh's reign. At Semneh, for example, inscriptions on rocks above the Nile indicate the river's heights from the reign of Amenemhat III (ca. 1844–1797 B.C.) to Sebekhotpe II (ca. 1745 B.C.).[88] Similar records are found at the Great Temple of Karnak and elsewhere.[89] The inundation was a defining event of one's kingship.

While a high Nile was considered a great blessing for the land, sometimes the river rose too high. An inscription from the time of Smendes, the first king of Dynasty 21 (ca. 1070–1044 B.C.), records a catastrophic flood:

> Lo, his majesty sat in the hall [of his palace, when there came messengers, informing] his majesty that the canal-wall . . . which (Thutmosis III) had built, had begun [to fall to ruin]—forming a great flood, and a

---

83. H. Frankfort, *Kingship and the Gods* (Chicago: University of Chicago Press, 1948), 177.
84. N. Davies, *Rock-cut Tombs of El Amarna*, 6 vols. (London: Egypt Exploration Fund, 1903–8), 6:9–10.
85. *ARE* 1:181. An inscription of Tefibi, prince of the Lycopolite nome, claims that he "was a Nile . . . for his people."
86. Frankfort, *Kingship and the Gods*, 106.
87. *ARE* 3:208.
88. *ARE* 1:331.
89. *ARE* 4:339–453.

powerful [current] therein, on the great [pavement] of the house of the temple. It encircled [the front]. . . . [His majesty said] to them: As for this matter reported to me, there has been nothing in the time of my majesty from old, like it.[90]

In the third year of Osorkon III (ca. 785 B.C.), an inundation flooded two feet above the pavement of the temple at Thebes:

> The flood came on, in this whole land; it invaded the two shores as in the beginning. This land was in his power like the sea, there was no dyke of the people to withstand its fury. All the people were like birds upon its [ ], the tempest . . . his . . . , suspended . . . like the heavens. All the temples of Thebes were like marshes.[91]

Perhaps more devastating to Egypt were the years in which there was no inundation. Failure of the Nile to provide water was a nightmare and a curse. In the "Prophecy of Neferti" the prophet describes the land of Egypt under such conditions:

> The rivers of Egypt are empty, (so that) the water is crossed on foot. Men seek for water for the ships to sail on it. Its course is [become] a sandbank. The sandbank is against the flood; the place of water is against the [flood]—(both) the place of water and the sandbank. . . . Everything good is disappeared, and the land is prostrate because of woes.[92]

All the blessings of Egypt evaporate when the Nile fails to flood. Transportation is affected. For example, Uni, during Dynasty 6, sent men to get granite from quarries at Aswan, but it could not be transported because the water in the Nile was too low. Crops, of course, were adversely affected. A stele of Mentuhotep from Dynasty 11 describes such an event: "(When) a low inundation happened in the 25th year, I did not allow (my) nome to starve. I gave it barley and emmer from Upper Egypt and did not allow misery to overcome it before great inundations returned."[93]

Whereas a high inundation was connected with the coronation of a pharaoh, failure to flood was tied to the death of a king. When Thutmosis III died, the Nile was reportedly so low that "there was not enough

90. *ARE* 4:308.
91. *ARE* 4:369. Further examples of high floods that brought disaster to Egypt could easily be cited from the literature, such as an extreme inundation during the time of Pharaoh Amasis (ca. 570–526 B.C.).
92. *ANET,* 445.
93. Translation presented by J. R. Huddlestun at the annual meeting of the Society of Biblical Literature, Washington, D.C., Nov. 1993.

water to cover the secrets of the Netherworld."[94] To the ancient Egyptian, a low level of the Nile was a curse, a sign of disfavor from the gods. It paralleled the setting sun and the onset of darkness as symbols of infertility, loss, and death.

Isaiah 19:5–10 curses Egypt by calling for the Nile to be "desolate and dried up" (v. 5). Following that general prophecy is a remarkable description of the effects of an impotent Nile on the economic vitality of the land. Agriculture will be affected—the land will simply "dry up," and instead of lush, fertile croplands along the banks of the Nile, "bare places" will dominate (v. 7). The fishing industry will suffer severe hardship and "will languish" (v. 8). Finally, all those whose occupations depend on the crops produced by the flooding of the Nile will "be crushed" and "sad of soul" because there will be no plants to harvest and to work with. All the great blessings of the Nile, which are at the core of the Egyptian economy, will be destroyed when Isaiah's curse is fulfilled. Obviously the prophet was well informed about Egypt, and his prophecy of a failure of the Nile slammed hard at the heart of the land.

Isaiah could not have used a metaphor more powerful to declare the coming conquest of Egypt by Shabaka in 712 B.C. The death of the Nile represented to the ancient Egyptians the dissolution and downfall of civilization—no renewal, no revival, no regeneration. For all intents and purposes, Egypt would be destroyed.

The prophet knows that Yahweh is sovereign over all the events being foretold. "Thus saith the LORD" operates throughout the prophecy in Isaiah 18–20. The rise of Cush and Assyria, the fall of Egypt, the Ashdod rebellion all come to pass because Yahweh has so willed it. Even the rising and abating of the Nile River occur by Yahweh's authority and power. The Egyptians, we have seen, thought otherwise; to them Pharaoh governed the river, and as overseer he caused it to fall and rise. So a major theological antithesis dominates the biblical passages that curse the Nile: Who is lord of the earth? This antithesis is nowhere more richly expressed than in Ezekiel 29:3, 8–10:

> Thus says the Lord GOD:
> "Behold, I am against you, Pharaoh, king of Egypt,
> The great monster that lies in the midst of his rivers,
> That has said, 'My Nile is mine, and I myself have made it.'. . ."

Therefore, thus says the Lord GOD, "Behold, I shall bring upon you a sword, and I shall cut off from you man and beast. And the land of Egypt

---

94. C. Palanque, *Le Nil à l'époque pharaonique: Son rôle et son cite en Egypte* (Paris: E. Bouillon, 1903), 72–74.

will become a desolation and waste. Then they will know that I am the LORD.

"Because you said, 'The Nile is mine, and I have made it,' therefore, behold, I am against you and against your Nile, and I will make the land of Egypt an utter waste and desolation, from Migdol to Syene and even to the border of Cush."

Bibliography (1973–95)

Ahituv, S. *Canaanite Toponyms in Ancient Egyptian Documents.* Winona Lake, Ind.: Eisenbrauns, 1984.
Ahlström, G. W. *The History of Ancient Palestine.* Minneapolis: Fortress, 1993.
Aldred, C. *Akhenaten and Nefertiti.* New York: Viking, 1973.
———. *The Egyptians.* 3d ed. London: Thames and Hudson, 1987.
Aling, C. *Egypt and Bible History: From Earliest Times to 1000 B.C.* Grand Rapids: Baker, 1981.
Allen, J. P. *Genesis in Egypt: The Philosophy of Ancient Egyptian Creation Accounts.* New Haven: Yale Egyptological Seminar, 1988.
Allen, T. G. *The Book of the Dead; or, Going Forth by Day.* Chicago: Oriental Institute, 1974.
Arnold, D. *Building in Egypt: Pharaonic Stone Masonry.* New York: Oxford University Press, 1991.
Assmann, J. *Ägyptische Hymnen und Gebete.* Zurich: Artemis, 1975.
———. *Re und Amun.* Göttingen: Vandenhoeck and Ruprecht, 1983.
Baer, K. *Rank and Title in the Old Kingdom: The Structure of the Egyptian Administration in the Fifth and Sixth Dynasties.* Chicago: University of Chicago Press, 1974.
Baines, J. *Fecundity Figures: Egyptian Personification and the Iconology of a Genre.* Warminster: Aris and Phillips, 1985.
———, and J. Malek. *Atlas of Ancient Egypt.* New York: Facts on File, 1980.
Bartlett, S. C. *From Egypt to Palestine: Through Sinai, the Wilderness and the South Country.* New York: Arno, 1977.
Batto, B. F. *Slaying the Dragon: Mythmaking in the Biblical Tradition.* Louisville: Westminster/John Knox, 1992.
Bernstein, B. *Sinai.* New York: Viking, 1979.
Bierbrier, M. L. *The Late New Kingdom in Egypt: A Genealogical and Chronological Investigation.* Warminster: Aris and Phillips, 1975.
Bietak, M. *Avaris and Piramesse.* Oxford: British Academy, 1979.
———. *Tell el-Dabʿa.* Vol. 2. Vienna: Oesterreichische Akademie der Wissenschaften, 1975.
Bimson, J. J. *Redating the Exodus and Conquest.* Sheffield: JSOT, 1978.
Blacker, C., and M. Loewe, eds. *Ancient Cosmologies.* London: Allen and Unwin, 1975.

Bleeker, C. J. *Hathor and Thoth.* Leiden: Brill, 1973.
Borghouts, J. F. *Ancient Egyptian Magical Texts.* Leiden: Brill, 1978.
Brier, B. *Ancient Egyptian Magic.* New York: Morrow, 1980.
Brothwell, D., and B. Chiarelli. *Population Biology of the Ancient Egyptians.* London: Academic, 1973.
Brunner, H. *Grundzüge der altägyptischen Religion.* Darmstadt: Wissenschaftliche Buchgesellschaft, 1983.
Bryce, G. E. *A Legacy of Wisdom: The Egyptian Contribution to the Wisdom of Israel.* Lewisburg, Pa.: Bucknell University Press, 1979.
Butzer, K. W., and L. G. Freeman, eds. *Early Hydraulic Civilization in Egypt.* Chicago: University of Chicago Press, 1976.
Cerny, J., and S. Israelit-Groll. *A Late Egyptian Grammar.* 2d ed. Rome: Pontifical Biblical Institute, 1978.
Childs, B. S. *The Book of Exodus.* Philadelphia: Westminster, 1974.
Clifford, R. J., and J. J. Collins, eds. *Creation in the Biblical Traditions.* Washington, D.C.: Catholic Biblical Association of America, 1992.
Coote, R. B. *Early Israel: A New Horizon.* Minneapolis: Fortress, 1990.
Darby, W. J., P. Ghalioungui, and L. Grivetti. *Food, the Gift of Osiris.* London: Academic, 1977.
D'Auria, S., P. Lacovara, and C. Roehrig. *Mummies and Magic.* Boston: Northeastern University Press, 1988.
David, A. R. *The Ancient Egyptians: Religious Beliefs and Practices:* Boston: Routledge and Kegan Paul, 1982.
Davies, G. I. *The Way of the Wilderness: A Geographical Study of the Wilderness Itineraries in the Old Testament.* Cambridge: Cambridge University Press, 1979.
Dothan, T. *The Philistines and Their Material Culture.* New Haven: Yale University Press, 1982.
Dumbrell, W. J. *Covenant and Creation.* New York: Nelson, 1985.
Epsztein, L. *Social Justice in the Ancient Near East and the People of the Bible.* London: SCM, 1986.
Fairman, H. W. *The Triumph of Horus.* Berkeley: University of California Press, 1974.
Faulkner, R. O. *The Ancient Egyptian Coffin Texts.* 3 vols. Warminster: Aris and Phillips, 1973–77.
———, E. F. Wente, and W. T. Simpson. *The Literature of Ancient Egypt: An Anthology of Stories, Instructions, and Poetry.* New Haven: Yale University Press, 1973.
Finn, T. M. *Early Christian Baptism and the Catechumenate: Italy, North Africa, and Egypt.* Collegeville, Minn.: Liturgical, 1992.
Fox, M. V. *The Song of Songs and the Ancient Egyptian Love Songs.* Madison: University of Wisconsin Press, 1985.
Frankfort, H. *Kingship and the Gods: A Study of Ancient Near Eastern Religion as the Integration of Society and Nature.* Chicago: University of Chicago Press, 1978 reprint.
Frith, F. *Egypt and the Holy Land in Historic Photographs.* New York: Dover, 1981.

Garbini, G. *History and Ideology in Ancient Israel.* New York: Crossroad, 1988.
Gardiner, A. H. *Egypt of the Pharaohs: An Introduction.* London: Oxford University Press, 1974 reprint.
Germer, R. *Flora des pharaonischen Ägypten.* Mainz: Zabern, 1984.
Giveon, R. *Footsteps of the Pharaohs in Canaan.* Tel Aviv: Hamador Liydi'at Ha'aretz Batnuah Haqibutzit, 1974. (Hebrew)
———. *The Impact of Egypt on Canaan.* Göttingen: Vandenhoeck and Ruprecht, 1978.
Goedicke, H. *The Report of Wenamun.* Baltimore: Johns Hopkins University Press, 1975.
Goedicke, H., and J. J. M. Roberts, eds. *Unity and Diversity: Essays in the History, Literature, and Religion of the Ancient Near East.* Baltimore: Johns Hopkins University Press, 1975.
Gorg, M. *Aegyptica—Biblica: Notizen und Beiträge zu den Beziehungen zwischen Ägypten und Israel.* Wiesbaden: Harrassowitz, 1991.
Griggs, C. W. *Early Egyptian Christianity: From Its Origins to 451 C.E.* Leiden: Brill, 1991.
Har-El, M. *The Sinai Journeys.* San Diego: Ridgefield, 1983.
Hayes, J. H., and J. M. Miller, eds. *Israelite and Judaean History.* Philadelphia: Westminster, 1977.
Helck, W., and E. Otto. *Lexicon der Ägyptologie.* Wiesbaden: Harrassowitz, 1975.
Herrmann, S. *Israel in Egypt.* Naperville, Ill.: Allenson, 1973.
Holladay, J. S. *Cities of the Delta.* Part 3, *Tell el-Maskhutah.* American Research Center in Egypt Reports 6. Malibu, Calif.: Undena, 1982.
Hornung, E. *Conceptions of God in Ancient Egypt.* Ithaca, N.Y.: Cornell University Press, 1982.
Houlihan, P., and S. Goodman. *Birds of Ancient Egypt.* Chicago: Bolchazy-Carducci, 1985.
Ions, V. *Egyptian Mythology.* New York: Bedrick, 1982.
Irwin, J. T. *American Hieroglyphics: The Symbol of the Egyptian Hieroglyphics in the American Renaissance.* New Haven: Yale University Press, 1980.
Israelit-Groll, S., ed. *Pharaonic Egypt: The Bible and Christianity.* Jerusalem: Magnes, 1985.
———. *Studies in Egyptology Presented to Miriam Lichtheim.* Jerusalem: Magnes, 1990.
Jacq, C. *Egyptian Magic.* Chicago: Bolchazy-Carducci, 1985.
James, T. G. H. *The Archaeology of Ancient Egypt.* New York: Walck, 1973.
———, ed. *Excavating in Egypt.* Chicago: University of Chicago Press, 1984.
Joines, K. R. *Serpent Symbolism in the Old Testament.* Haddonfield, N.J.: Haddonfield House, 1974.
Kamil, J. *Coptic Egypt: History and Guide.* Cairo: American University in Cairo Press, 1987.
Kater-Sibbes, G. J. F. *Apis.* Leiden: Brill, 1975.
Keimer, L. *Die Gartenpflanzen im alten Ägypten.* Vol. 2. Mainz: Zabern, 1984.
Kemp, B. J. *Ancient Egypt: Anatomy of a Civilization.* New York: Routledge, 1989.

Kitchen, K. A. *The Bible in Its World.* Downers Grove, Ill.: InterVarsity, 1978.

———. *Pharaoh Triumphant: The Life and Times of Ramesses II.* Warminster: Aris and Phillips, 1982.

———. *The Third Intermediate Period in Egypt (1100–650 B.C.).* Warminster: Aris and Phillips, 1973.

Knapp, B. *The History and Culture of Ancient Western Asia and Egypt.* Belmont, Calif.: Wadsworth, 1988.

Kuntzmann, R. *Le Symbolisme des jumeaux au Proche-Orient ancien: Naissance, fonction et évolution d'un symbole.* Paris: Beauchesne, 1983.

La Farge, H. A., et al., eds. *Museums of Egypt.* New York: Newsweek, 1980.

Leahy, A. *Libya and Egypt in the First Millennium B.C.* New York: Routledge, 1988.

Levinson, J. D. *Creation and the Persistence of Evil.* San Francisco: Harper and Row, 1988.

Lichtheim, M. *Ancient Egyptian Literature.* 3 vols. Berkeley: University of California Press, 1975–80.

Lipinski, E. *State and Temple Economy in the Ancient Near East.* Leiden: Brill, 1979.

Lucas, A. *Ancient Egyptian Materials and Industries.* London: Histories and Mysteries of Man, 1989.

McCurley, F. R. *Ancient Myths and Biblical Faith.* Philadelphia: Fortress, 1983.

Manniche, L. *City of the Dead: Thebes in Egypt.* Chicago: University of Chicago Press, 1987.

Moran, W. L. *The Amarna Letters.* Baltimore: Johns Hopkins University Press, 1992.

Morenz, S. *Egyptian Religion.* Ithaca, N.Y.: Cornell University Press, 1973.

Murray, M. *Saqqara Mastabas.* London: Histories and Mysteries of Man, 1989.

Newby, P. H. *Warrior Pharaohs.* London: Faber and Faber, 1980.

Nibbi, A. *Ancient Egypt and Some Eastern Neighbors.* Park Ridge, N.J.: Noyes, 1981.

Nicholson, E. W. *Exodus and Sinai in History and Tradition.* Richmond: John Knox, 1973.

Niditch, S. *Chaos to Cosmos: Studies in the Biblical Patterns of Creation.* Decatur, Ga.: Scholars, 1985.

Nyrop, R. F. *Area Handbook for Egypt.* Washington, D.C.: U.S. Government Printing Office, 1976.

Perdue, L. G. *Wisdom and Cult: A Critical Analysis of the Views of Cult in the Wisdom Literature of Israel and the Ancient Near East.* Missoula, Mont.: Scholars, 1977.

Posener, G. *Cinq figurines d'envoûtement.* Cairo: Institut français d'archéologie orientale, 1987.

Prados, J. *L'Invasion de la Méditerranée par les peuples de l'océan.* Paris: Editions l'Harmattan, 1992.

Rainey, A. F., ed. *Egypt, Israel, Sinai: Archaeological and Historical Relationships in the Biblical Period.* Tel Aviv: Tel Aviv University Press, 1987.

Redford, D. B. *Akhenaten, the Heretic King.* Princeton: Princeton University Press, 1984.

———. *Egypt, Canaan, and Israel in Ancient Times.* Princeton: Princeton University Press, 1992.
Ritner, R. K. *The Mechanics of Ancient Egyptian Magical Practice.* Chicago: University of Chicago Press, 1993.
Romer, J. *Ancient Lives: The Story of the Pharaoh's Tombmakers.* London: Weidenfeld and Nicolson, 1984.
———. *People of the Nile.* New York: Crown, 1982.
Rothenberg, B., et al. *Sinai: Pharaohs, Miners, Pilgrims, and Soldiers.* Washington, D.C.: J. Binns, 1979.
Rousseau, P. *Pachomius: The Making of a Community in Fourth-Century Egypt.* Berkeley: University of California Press, 1985.
Ruffle, J. *The Egyptians: An Introduction to Egyptian Archaeology.* Ithaca, N.Y.: Cornell University Press, 1977.
———. *Heritage of the Pharaohs.* Oxford: Phaidon, 1977.
Russmann, E. *The Representation of the King in the XXVth Dynasty.* Brooklyn: Brooklyn Museum, 1974.
Sadek, A. *Popular Religion in Egypt during the New Kingdom.* Hildesheim: Gerstenberg, 1987.
Samuel, A. E. *From Athens to Alexandria: Hellenism and Social Goals in Ptolemaic Egypt.* Louvain, 1983.
Sandars, N. K. *The Sea Peoples.* London: Thames and Hudson, 1978.
Sarna, N. M. *Exploring Exodus: The Heritage of Biblical Israel.* New York: Schocken, 1986.
Sasson, J. M., ed. *Civilizations of the Ancient Near East.* 4 vols. New York: Scribner, 1995.
Schmandt-Besserat, D., ed. *Immortal Egypt.* Malibu, Calif.: Undena, 1979.
Shafer, B. E., et al., eds. *Religion in Ancient Egypt.* Ithaca, N.Y.: Cornell University Press, 1991.
Simpson, W. K., and W. M. Davis, eds. *Studies in Ancient Egypt, the Aegean, and the Sudan.* Boston: Museum of Fine Arts, 1981.
Spalinger, A. J. *Aspects of the Military Documents of the Ancient Egyptians.* New Haven: Yale University Press, 1982.
Spenser, A. *Brick Architecture in Ancient Egypt.* Warminster: Aris and Phillips, 1979.
———. *Death in Ancient Egypt.* Harmondsworth: Penguin, 1982.
Stiebing, W. H. *Out of the Desert? Archaeology and the Exodus/Conquest Narratives.* Buffalo: Prometheus, 1989.
Strobel, A. *Der Spätbronzezeitliche Seevölkersturm.* Berlin: W. de Gruyter, 1976.
Strouhal, E. *Life of the Ancient Egyptians.* Norman, Okla.: University of Oklahoma Press, 1992.
Trigger, B. G. *Nubia under the Pharaohs.* Boulder, Colo.: Westview, 1976.
———, B. J. Kemp, D. O'Connor, and A. B. Lloyd. *Ancient Egypt: A Social History.* Cambridge: Cambridge University Press, 1982.
Tufnell, O. *Scarab Seals and Their Contribution to History in the Early Second Millennium B.C.* Studies on Scarab Seals 2. Warminster: Aris and Phillips, 1984.
Uphill, E. P. *The Temples of Per Ramesses.* Warminster: Aris and Phillips, 1984.

Van Seters, J. *In Search of History: Historiography in the Ancient World and the Origins of Biblical History.* New Haven: Yale University Press, 1983.

Voss, M. H., et al., eds. *Studies in Ancient Egyptian Religion.* Leiden: Brill, 1982.

Walton, J. H. *Israelite Literature in Its Cultural Context: A Survey of Parallels between Biblical and Ancient Near Eastern Texts.* Grand Rapids: Zondervan, 1989.

West, J. A. *Serpent in the Sky.* San Francisco: Harper and Row, 1979.

Westendorf, W., ed. *Aspekte der spätägyptischen Religion.* Wiesbaden: Harrassowitz, 1979.

White, J. B. *A Study of the Language of Love in the Song of Songs and Ancient Egyptian Poetry.* Missoula, Mont.: Scholars, 1978.

Wildung, D. *Egyptian Saints.* New York: New York University Press, 1977.

Wiseman, P. J. *Ancient Records and the Structure of Genesis: A Case for Literary Unity.* Edited by D. J. Wiseman. Nashville: Nelson, 1985.

Scripture Index

Genesis

1 28, 118
1–2 73
1:1 44, 45, 64
1:1–5 115, 116
1:2 28, 66, 114, 115
1:3 44, 66
1:4 67
1:6 67
1:6–7 67
1:6–8 115
1:6–13 116
1:8–11 61
1:9 67, 68
1:9–13 115, 116
1:10 116
1:11 69, 116
1:14 61, 67, 69, 116
1:14–18 69
1:14–19 115
1:16 66
1:18 67, 116
1:20 61
1:20–21 70
1:20–23 115, 117
1:21 86
1:22 61
1:24 61
1:24–28 70
1:24–31 115, 117
1:26 61
1:26–28 117
1:27 71
1:28 46, 72, 114
2:7 70, 71
3 46
3:7–11 46
3:17–18 46
3:19 70
3:20 62
3:21 45n
3:24 46
4:2 62
5:29 46
6:14 114
8 230n
8:5 64
9:1 114
11 114
11:4 114n
12:10–20 162n
14:19 44, 65
25:26 62
25:27 127
37:35 43
37:36 74, 77, 78, 80, 81
39:1 74, 77, 78, 80, 81
40–41 227
40:8 228
40:11 227
40:16 227
41:1 227
41:8 227
41:13 227
41:45 75
41:50 75
42:38 43
44:29 43
46:20 75
46:26–27 114
47:11 126

Exodus

1–15 96, 113
1:1–5 114
1:7 114
1:10–11 114n
1:11 125, 128, 129
2:3 114, 134
3:19–20 83, 154
4 93
4:2–3 86
4:9 68
4:21 96
5:1 83
5:10 83, 119
5:19 113
5:21 145
6:1 83, 154
7 93, 117, 120
7–12 104, 115, 117, 118, 120
7:3 96
7:4 83, 154
7:5 120
7:8–13 49, 85, 86, 94, 103

253

7:9–10 86
7:11 94
7:12 85
7:13 96
7:15 87
7:15–25 109, 115, 116
7:15–8:15 115
7:17 120
7:19 116
8:1–6 110
8:3 117
8:16–24 110, 115
8:17–18 117
8:19 120
8:22 120
9:1–7 111, 115
9:8–17 115
9:9–10 117
9:12 96
9:18–10:20 115, 116
9:19 117
9:22 116, 117
9:25 116, 117
9:34 102
10:1 96
10:2 109
10:5 116
10:7 120
10:10 113
10:12 116
10:15 116, 127
10:20 96
10:21 116
10:21–29 112, 115
10:23 117
10:27 96
11–12 115
11:5 117
11:7 113
12–19 121
12:12 109, 117, 119
12:37 130
13–15 114
13:4 136n
13:17 137
13:17–18 132
13:18 144

13:21 114
14 230n
14:4 96, 120
14:8 96
14:11 145
14:11–12 145
14:16 68, 85
14:18 120
14:21 114
14:22 68
14:25 120
14:26 85
14:29 68, 114
15:4 134
15:12 85
15:16 83, 154
15:23–26 145
15:23–27 123n
16:1 136n
16:2–3 145
16:3 145
17:2–3 145
17:3 145
19:16–18 32
19:20 64
20:4 43
22:1 81, 82
22:30 127
31:17 44
32:12 113
32:22 113
38:1–3 45n

Leviticus

11:44 48
19:28 42

Numbers

11–12 121
11:1 113
11:4–6 145
11:5 145
11:5–6 145
11:31–35 123n
12:16 133

13:21–22 144
13:22 127
14:1–4 145
14:2–4 145
14:25 144
16:11–14 145
16:13 145, 146n
16:30–33 43
20:2–5 145
20:5 113, 145
20:14–21:4 139
21 139, 143, 147, 148, 149, 155
21:1 144
21:3 143
21:4–9 142, 143, 144, 146, 154
21:8–9 149, 151
21:12 133
21:18–19 201
21:18–20 133
25:1–3 42
33 122, 123, 125, 128, 133, 137, 140, 141, 143
33:1 122
33:1–49 121
33:2 122, 123
33:3 122, 125, 143n
33:3–4 122
33:3–8 123–36
33:4 108
33:5 125, 130, 143n
33:6–7 131
33:7 131, 133
33:9 123n
33:9–40 136–39
33:10 136
33:10–11 144
33:11 133
33:12–13 136
33:15 133
33:17 123n
33:34 138
33:35 137
33:36 138
33:37 139

Scripture Index

33:38–39 139
33:45b–50 140
33:50–56 122

Deuteronomy

4:3 42
8:15 146
9:18 113
10 121
11:4 134
18:9–11 42
18:10–11 49
21:1 127
32:2 69n
32:10 115
32:11 114
32:27 122
32:33 87

Joshua

2:10 134
4:22 68
4:23 134
11:20 96
15:33 198
15:43 198
15:59 201
19:15 192
19:29 193
19:38 201
24:6 134

Judges

1:19 195
1:33 201
5:15 195
8:24 74n

1 Samuel

8:15 77n
9:23–24 80, 82
27:10 198
30:14 198

2 Samuel

3:3 164
8:16–18 179
20:23–26 179
23:4 69n
23:8 198
23:13–39 169

1 Kings

1 168
3:1 161, 162
4 165, 166
4:2–6 179
4:21–22 166
7:8 162
9:15 161
9:16 162, 163, 179
9:24 162
9:26 135, 138, 144, 169
10:18–20 169
10:28–29a 161
11:1 164
11:1–2 162
11:40 179
14 188
14:21 164
14:23 42
14:24 42
14:25 162n, 180
14:25–26 173, 187n
15:12 42
18:28 42

2 Kings

3:22 106n
3:27 41
11:12 167, 168
16:7 237
17:4 238
18:4 142
18:13 173
19:16 173
19:20 173
19:24 230n
23:4–10 49

23:7 42
24:1–10 173
25:8–20 80, 82

1 Chronicles

2:9 201
2:26 201
2:27 201
2:33 200
2:48 202
2:55 198
4:11 198
4:16 196
4:20 198, 199
6:15 173

2 Chronicles

8:11 162
12:2–4 174
12:4 187n
32:1–22 173
32:30 123

Nehemiah

9:6 44

Esther

1:10 79n
1:12 79n
1:15 79n
2:3 79n
2:14 79n
2:15 79n
2:21 79n
4:4 79n
4:5 79n
6:2 79n
6:14 79n
7:9 79n

Job

1–2 44n
1:6–12 44

6:5 69n
9:6 43
26:11 43
26:13 87
28:1 123
38 55
38:4–6 43
38:6 43
38:17 43
38:27 69n, 123

Psalms

8:3–4 34
8:5 46
8:8 70
11:4 43
18:15 43
19:1 44, 67
19:6 125
24:1–2 46, 55
33:6 45, 61
74:13 86, 92
78 213
78:12 127
78:43 127
88 43
89:14 169
91:13 87
104 55
104:2 43
104:5 43
106:7 134
106:9 134
106:22 134
106:28 42
107:33–35 123
136:13 134
136:15 134
139:8 44n
148:5 45
148:7 86

Proverbs

8:30 43
9:2 81

15:16–17 208n
22:17–18 212–13
22:17–25 211–15
22:17–24:22 211, 213, 215
22:19 213
22:20 213
22:21 214
22:22 214
22:23 214
22:24 214
22:25 214
27:25 69n

Ecclesiastes

1:2 47

Isaiah

3:26 230n
6 146
10–23 231
10:5 231
10:18 149
11:6–9 47
13:1 231
14:29 146n, 231
15:1 231
17:1 231
18–19 239, 240
18–20 239, 245
18:1 231
18:1–2 114n
18:2 240
19 232
19:1 31, 231
19:2 239
19:4 240
19:5 245
19:5–10 229–30, 240, 245
19:7 245
19:8 245
19:11–13 239
19:15 231n
20 240

20:3–6 229
21:11 231
21:13 231
23:1 231
26:11 122n
27:1 86, 87
29:16 56, 64
30:6 146n
34:11 66
35:1–2a, 9–10 47
37:25 230n
38:10 43
40:22 43
45:9 56, 64
56:3–4 79n
56:3–5 77n
59:19 149
64:8 64
65:17–19 47
66:1 44

Jeremiah

4:23 66
24:7 47
31:31–34 47
32:40 47
33:14–16 47
43:11–13 229
46:13–26 229
46:25 113
49:21 135

Ezekiel

1:22–25 67
10:1 67
29:1–16 229
29:3 92, 117, 245
29:8–10 245
30–32 229
30:12 229
37:26–27 47
42:11 125
43:11 125
44:5 125

Daniel

1:3 79n
1:7 79n
1:8 79n
1:9 79n
1:10 79n
1:11 79n
1:18 79n
3 71
11:42–43 229
12:3 67

Hosea

6:3 125
9:10 42

Joel

2:31 106n
3:19 229

Amos

9:3 87

Micah

5:8 122

Zechariah

3 44n
3:1 44
9:16 149
10:11 229

Luke

4 44n

Romans

6:23 46n
8:20 47n
8:21 47n

Hebrews

11:3 45n

Revelation

4:11 46
12:9 44n

Subject Index

Abel-, 194, 200
Abydos, 175
Adamah, 195
Adam and Eve, 46
Adar, 200
'Adar, 199
Administrative structures of Solomon, 167–68, 178–79
"Admonitions of Ipu-wer," 223
Adoraim, 191
Afterlife, attaining the, 96–98, 102, 118
Aharoni, Yohanan, 139, 144, 170
Ahaz, 237
Aijalon, 187, 192
'Ain Qedais, 199
'Ain Qedeis, 138
'Ain Qudeirat, 138
Akhenaten, 243
Albright, William, 78, 79n, 181–82, 184n, 196
Aling, Charles, 76
Allegory in dreams, 226, 227
Almon(-diblathaim), 140
Amarna, 221
Amemit, 97–98
Amenemhat I, 119, 223
Amenemhat III, 93
Amenemnisu, 236n
Amenemope, 164, 209. *See also* "Instruction of Amenemope"
Amenerdis I, 234
Amenophis II, 122
Amenophis III, 140, 165, 184

Amon, 36, 58n, 69–70, 183, 233; temple of, at Karnak, 99n, 174, 180, 236
Amon-Re, 111, 112
Amulets, 88, 98, 149n. *See also* Scarabs
Anath, 40–41
Angels, 44
Ani, 96–98
Animals: creation of land, 70, 117; destruction of, 111
Animate nature of all creation, 37
Anointing, 168
Anthrax, 105, 106
Antiochus Epiphanes, 232
Anu, 37
Anubis, 97, 113
Apion, 100
'apiru, 25n–26n, 128
Apis, 111
Apocalyptic, 224
Apsu, 30, 38–39, 55n
Arad, 143–44; of the House of Jeroham, 200
Architectural imagery in the creation account, 43
Architectural parallels, 170
Arishot, 132
'ārōb, 110
Article, translation of Hebrew, 192, 198
'Aruna, 187, 193
Ashdod, 238, 239, 240, 245
Asherah, 42

259

Ashna, 198
Ashur-dan II, 188n
Assyria, 188, 232, 233, 237–39, 240, 245
Astrology, 221–22, 228
Atharim, 144
Atum, 57, 58–59, 60–61, 62n, 67, 69, 70
Axe, double, 163
Azariah, 237

Ba, 96, 97
Baal, 31–32, 40–41; Peor, 42
Baal-zephon, 131–33
Babel, 114
Babel and Bible (Delitzsch), 28n
Bādal, 67
Bahria Oasis, 235
Bakenranef, 235
Bāla', 85
Balance of truth, 97–98, 118
Ball, E., 168
Bārā', 45
Battlefield Palette, 151
Batto, Bernard, 135
Beale, Greg, 102
Beatty Papyrus, 225–27
Beersheba, 187
Beginning of creation, 64
Běhēmāh, 117
Beit-Arieh, Itzhaq, 137
Beitzel, Barry, 134
Ben-Hanan, 198
Běrē'šît, 64
Bergman, Jan, 68
Berlin Hymn, 65
Beth-Anath, 200–201
Beth-Horon, 187, 192
Beth-Olam, 193
Beth-Shean, 184, 186, 191; Stele, 190; Valley of, 195
Beth-Ṣoba, 194
Beth-tappuah, 187, 194
Bible and mythology, 27–32
Bietak, Manfred, 126, 127
Biran, Avraham, 160
Birds, creation of, 70, 117

Bitter Lakes, 132–33
Bleiberg, E. L., 130
Blood, water turned to, 105, 106–7, 109–10, 116
Boats, 242
Bocchoris, 235
"Bocchoris and the Lamb," 224
Boils, 105, 111, 117
Book of Am Duat, 148
Book of the Dead, 56n, 96, 97n, 98, 100n, 102
Book of the Gates, 88, 147–48
Boustrophedon, 186
Breath of life, 71–72, 110
Bronze serpent, 142–55; as symbol of destruction of Egypt, 149
Brunner, Hellmut, 169
Bubastis, 177, 180n
Bubastite Portal, 174, 180–87, 190–202
Budge, E. A. Wallis, 99, 208–9
Building motif for the structure of the universe, 43
Bull cults, 111
"Butcher," Potiphar as, 81–82
Byblos, 178, 189
Bytdwd, 160

Cambyses, 232
Canaanite view of reality, 40–42
Canal, defensive, 131, 134
Cassuto, Umberto, 86
Chaos: at creation, 66; to order, exodus as, 115. See also Order
Charms, 87, 97n. See also Amulets; Scarabs
Chester Beatty Papyrus III, 225–27
Child sacrifice, 41, 49
Clements, Ronald, 205
Coats, George, 145, 147
Cody, Aelred, 167
Coffman, James, 232
Coogan, Michael, 32
"Cook," Potiphar as, 76, 80–82
Coregency, 168
Coronation: of Pharaoh, 36, 243; ritual, Judean, 167–68

Cosmic wars, 28, 30, 36, 38–39, 63
Cosmogony: Egyptian, 36–37, 55; Genesis and Egyptian, 53–73; Mesopotamian, 38–40; Hebrew, 44–46
Cosmologies: ancient Near Eastern, 33–49; Egyptian, 34–37; Mesopotamian, 37–38; Canaanite, 40–41; Hebrew, 43–44, 48
Couroyer, B., 211
Craftsman, creator as, 64
Creation: Hebrew and Mesopotamian accounts of, 27–31, 53–54; Mesopotamian account of, 59n, 63; in Egyptian cosmology and Genesis, 64–72; manner of, in Genesis, 44–45; manner of, in Egyptian cosmology and Genesis, 56–64; pattern of, 45; out of nothing, 45, 62–63; comprehensive nature of, 65; days of, 66–70, 73, 114–17; narrative and the Book of Exodus, 113–17
Creator in Egyptian cosmology and Genesis, single, 55–56
Crocodile, 86–87, 110; wax, 93
Crown, Pharaoh's, 89–92, 93–94, 147, 151, 152, 235
Cryer, Frederick, 221
Cultural mandate, 114
Cumont, Franz, 221
Curses on the Nile, 229–46
Cush. *See* Nubia
Cyclical view, 35n, 41

Dakhla, 176
Darkness (plague), 105, 106, 112, 116
David, 159, 160, 168, 178; house of, 160; thirty men of, 169
Davies, G. I., 132
Days of creation, 66–70, 73, 114–17
Dead, communication with the, 42, 48, 222
Death: in Egypt, 36, 145; of Pharaoh, 244. *See also* Mummification
De-creation, plagues as, 113–17
Deir el-Bahari, 176
Deir el-Medinah, 220
Delitzsch, Friedrich, 28

Democracy, primitive, 37–40
"Demotic Chronicle," 224
Demythologizing of pagan legends, biblical, 28–29
Derek hā'ăthārîm, 144
deVaux, Roland, 167, 168
DeVries, Carl, 211
Dibon, 140
Divination, 42, 48, 219–28
Division: of cosmos, twofold, 65–66; of sky and earth at creation, 67
Djadjaemonkh, 84
Dog Star, 241n
Dophkah, 136
Double axe, 163
Dream, 222, 224–28; omens, 225–27
Drioton, E., 210–11
Driver, S. R., 28
Drought, 41. *See also* Nile, drying up of the
Dry ground, 68, 116, 230n
Dung beetle, 98–101

Ea, 30, 38, 39, 55n
Ebers Papyrus, 99
Edom, 26, 139, 144, 195, 199, 237
'ēdût, 167–68
Egypt as land of mystery, 219, 228
Egyptian view of reality, 34–37, 55; and Genesis, 53–73
Eighth plague, 105, 106, 112, 115, 116
Eisenlohr, August, 13
Eissfeldt, O., 133n
Ekron, 239
Elements of the universe, 34–35
Elliger, K., 169
El-mat(t)an, 201
Elohim as creator, 44, 61
'ĕlōhîm, 28
Encampment, 125, 133
Enlil, 37
Ennead, 90n, 97–98
Enuma Elish, 29–31, 38, 55n, 59n, 62n, 63
Erman, Adolf, 209–10, 213
'Eṣem, 196
Etham, 130–31

et-Taiyiba, 191
Eunuch, 77–80, 82
Eve, 46
Ex nihilo creation, 45, 62–63
Exodus, 121–41; historicity of, 24, 25, 141, 143n; account, Egyptian elements in the, 85n; as re-creation, 113–15
Extispicy, 220
Ezion-geber, 137–38, 169, 197

Fall, cosmic, 46–47
Feather of truth, 97, 118
Federn, Walter, 225
Fertility, Canaanite obsession with, 41–42
Fiery serpents, 146–49
Fifth day of creation, 70, 115, 117
Fifth plague, 105, 106, 111, 115
Finkelstein, Israel, 125
Firmament, 67
First-born, death of, 105, 106, 107, 113, 117
First day of creation, 66, 114, 115, 116
First plague, 105, 106–7, 109–10, 115, 116
Fish: creation of, 70, 117; death of, 110
Flax, 242
Flies, 105
Flood: Hebrew and Mesopotamian accounts of a great, 27–28, 29; Nile, 243–44
Fort of . . . , 196, 198; Abram, 196; Tilon, 199
Fourth day of creation, 69, 115, 116
Fourth plague, 105, 110–11, 115, 117
Free, Joseph, 76–77
Frogs, 105, 106, 110, 117
Funerary papyri, 98

Gage, Warren, 113
Gardiner, Alan, 135, 149, 225
Gath-padalla, 187, 193
Gaza, 190, 238
Geb, 60

Genesis: and Mesopotamian literature, 25, 27–31, 53–54; and Egyptian cosmogonies, 53–73; creation narrative and the Book of Exodus, 113–17
Gezer, 161, 162, 163, 170, 179, 190
Gibeon, 187, 192
Gilgamesh, 27, 28, 33
Giveon, Raphael, 163
Glueck, Nelson, 26, 137, 139
Gnats, 110
God: as designer of the universe, 43; sovereignty of, 46, 48, 95, 103, 110, 111, 120, 245
Gods, creation of, 36–37, 38, 48, 55n, 56, 58–61, 72. *See also* Theogony
Gods, immanence of, 47
Gods, wars between, 28. *See also* Cosmic wars
Gods of Egypt: plagues as polemics against the, 108–13; standards as embodiments of the, 151, 154
Gōme', 114
Grasshoppers. *See* Locusts
Grdseloff, Bernhard, 186, 192
"Great Hymn": to Khnum, 56, 70, 72, 93n; to Amon, 69–70; to Atum, 70; to Aton, 71
Green, Alberto, 166
Gressmann, Hugo, 210
Grintz, Y. M., 76, 81
Grumach, Irene, 210
Guard, Potiphar as captain of the, 80–82

Hail, 105, 106, 112, 116, 117
Hall, H. R., 142
Halpern, Baruch, 24–25
Hamilton, Victor P., 108n
Ḥānāh, 125
Hapharaim, 186, 191
Hapi, 109, 240–41, 243
Hardening of Pharaoh's heart, 96–103
Haremhab, 128
Haremsaf, 180
Ḥartōm, 94
Hathor, 111

Ḥāzaq, 96
Hazer-Gaddeh, 198
Hazor, 161, 170
Heart: hardening of Pharaoh's, 96–103; scarabs, 101–2
"Heavens and the earth," 44, 65–66
Hebrew view of reality, 43–47, 48–49
Hebron, 127
Hedjkheperre setepnere, 177
Heidel, Alexander, 53, 72
Hekhet, 110
Heliopolis, 60, 130
Hengstenberg, Ernst, 92, 94, 104
Herakleopolis, 166
Hermopolis, cosmogony of, 66
Herodotus, 35n, 146n, 219, 240
Herrmann, Siegfried, 187
Herzog, D., 210
Hezekiah, 142, 173n
Hieratic numerals, 170
High places, 42
Hillock, primeval, 36, 57, 59, 68–69
Historicity of the Old Testament. *See* Scholarship, present-day
Hoffmeier, James, 54, 84
Holladay, John, 129
"Holy," 48
Hor, Mount, 139
Horapollo, 100
Hormah, 143–44
Horses, Solomon's import of, 161
Hort, Greta, 105–6
Horus, 93, 98, 102, 119, 152; eye of, 91; Sons of, 226
htm, 130
Huddlestun, J. R., 24n
Hughes, George, 182
Humans: purpose of, 30, 39, 46, 48, 72; creation of, 37, 70–72, 110, 117
Humbert, P., 213
Hyksos, 128
Hymns: to Amon, 68; to Khnum, 69; to Aton, 70; to Re, 70; to the Nile, 109; to the Inundation, 240

Iamani, 238–39
ỉb, 96

Ibn Ezra, 94
Idols, Canaanite, 42
Image of God, 30, 71
Imhotep, 111
Immanence of the gods, 47
Inanimate objects charged with power, 89, 151
Incubation, 225
Insects, 105, 110, 117
"Instruction for King Meri-ka-Re," 71, 119, 206n, 225
"Instruction of Amenemope," 70, 205–16
"Instructions of King Amen-em-het," 206n
"Instructions of Ptah-hotep," 206n
Introductory formula in wisdom literature, 213
Ipu-wer, 223
Isis, 98, 111, 148
Israel: Stele, 26n; unfaithfulness of, 42, 146; and Judah as targets of Shishak, 187; Assyrian invasion of, 238
Itinerary, Hebrew, 121–41
Iye-abarim, 140

Jabel Madurah, 139
Jebel Nebi Harun, 139
Jeroboam, 166n, 179, 188n
Jerusalem, 187n, 188
Jezreel Valley, 186, 187, 189, 196
Jochebed, 114
Joines, Karen, 148
Jonckheere, F., 79–80
Joseph, 74; story of, 23, 73, 75, 79; and dream interpretation, 227–28
Jotbathah, 138
"Journey of Wenamon," 169, 178n
Judah and Israel as targets of Shishak, 187
Judgment, future, 96–98

Ka, 59, 90n, 93, 96, 97
Kābēd, 96
Kadesh-Barnea, 138–39
Kadish, Gerald, 80

Karnak, 26n, 90, 99n, 174, 177, 178, 180–87, 190–202, 236; levels of the Nile at, 235, 236, 243
Keil, C. F., 25
Kevin, R. O., 210
Kheprer, 57, 58, 69, 100, 111
Kheti, 88, 148
Khirbet Burin, 187, 193
Khirbet Futeis, 196
Khirbet Zubâlah, 197
Khnum, 56, 67, 70n, 93n, 110
Kibroth-hattaavah, 123n
Kinnim, 110
Kitchen, Kenneth, 75–76, 133, 164n, 166–67, 168, 174, 211
Krahmalkov, Charles, 140
Kuk, 36
Kurru, 235, 237

Laban, 187, 202
Lachish Letters, 173
Lambert, Wilfred, 25, 54
Lance, H. Darrell, 163
Lanczkowski, Gunter, 224
Land, creation of, 68
Lecanomancy, 222–23, 228
Lepsius, Karl, 184
Letters to the dead, 222, 224
Libanomancy, 220
Lice, 105, 106, 110
Light, creation of, 66, 116
Linguistic contacts between Israel and Egypt, 26
Lion Palette, 151
Literary creations, plagues as, 107–8
Locusts, 105, 106, 112, 116
Logos doctrine, 61
Lyons, H. G., 176

Maacah, 202
Ma'at, 35, 36, 118–20, 169, 205, 233
Maatkare, 177
McNeile, Alan, 94
Magic, 28, 30–31, 39–40, 41, 42, 48, 84, 91, 92, 94–95, 101, 148, 149n, 151, 219–28
Mahanaim, 187, 191

Malamat, Abraham, 164
Manetho, 180n, 181, 182, 235
Marah, 123n
Marduk, 28, 29, 31, 39–40, 55n
Marriage alliances, 164–65, 175, 177; of Solomon, 161, 162–65, 179
Maśśā', 231
Master craftsman, the creator as, 64
Masturbation (method of creation), 37, 59–60, 61, 100n
Mazar, Benjamin, 143, 186
Mazĕkîr, 167
Measurements, Egyptian, 170
Medinet Habu, 90, 152, 236
Megiddo, 161, 170, 184–86, 187, 189, 190, 192
Memphis, 125, 177, 234, 236, 239
Memphite theology, 55, 56, 60, 61, 62–63, 102
Mentuhotep I, 152, 244
Merneptah, 26n, 224; Victory Stele, 222n
Mesha Stele, 160
Mesopotamia, divination in, 220, 221, 223, 226–27, 228
Mesopotamian creation story, 55, 59n, 63. *See also* Enuma Elish
Mesopotamian literature, parallels in Genesis to, 25, 27–31, 53–54
Mesopotamian view of reality, 37–40
Metalworker, the creator as, 64, 67
Meyer, Eduard, 107
Migdol, 130–31; name, 195
Milgrom, Jacob, 121
Military itinerary, 122, 141
Milk and honey, land with, 146n
Miller, J. M., 173n
Mining expeditions, Egyptian, 136
Miqĕwēh, 116
Mitanni, 184
Moab, 26, 139, 237
Monotheism, 30, 48, 72
Montet, Pierre, 23, 95, 163
Moon, creation of the, 69, 116
Morenz, Siegfried, 55, 68
Morgenstern, J., 45
Môṣā'êhem, 123–25

Moses: birth of, 114; as chronicler of Numbers, 122–23
Mosquitoes, 105, 110
Mot, 40–41
Mummification, 36, 101, 102
Mummu, 30, 38–39
Murmuring motif, 144–46
Murrain, 105
Mystery, Egypt as land of, 219, 228
Mythology, Bible and, 27–32

Na'aman, Nadav, 144
Nāḥāš, 86–87
Name-rings, 183–84, 186
Names of objects as essential to their creation, 62
Namlot, 176
Napata, 233–34
Narmer Palette, 151
Natural disasters, plagues as, 104–7
Nature, gods as personifications of elements of, 35, 36, 37–38, 40, 47–48, 60
Naveh, Joseph, 160
Naville, Edouard, 129
Nebuchadnezzar, 173
Necromancy, 42, 48, 222
Neferkare', 235
Neferti, 223–24
Negev, 198
Něḥōšet, 147
Nehushtan, 142
Nekhbet, 89, 167–68, 236n
Nēs, 149–51
Nevin, Alfred, 94
New Year's Day, 36
Nile, 35, 70, 105, 109–10; curses on the, 229–46; drying up of the, 229, 230, 240, 244–45; level at Karnak, 235, 236, 243; inundation, 240–45
Ni-Maat-Re, 93
Nine Bows, 190
Ninhursaga, 38
Ninth plague, 105, 106, 112, 115, 116
Noah, 114
Northern route, 132, 133n, 137
Noth, Martin, 142, 188

Nubia (Cush), 178, 188, 189, 233–37, 239, 240, 245
Numerals, hieratic, 170
Nun, 35, 36, 57–58, 61, 62. *See also* Primordial waters
Nut, 35, 60, 112

Oboth, 140
Octead, 66
Oesterley, W. O. E., 210
Omens, dream, 225–27
Onam, 201
Oppenheim, Leo, 226
Oracles, 220–21, 228; dreams as, 226, 227
Order: and chaos, 30, 36, 38–39; to chaos, plagues as, 115–17, 119; Egyptian concept of order, 118. *See also* Ma'at
Osiris, 91, 98, 242
Osorkon I, 177, 182n, 183
Osorkon III, 244
Osorkon IV, 235

Palestine List, 140
Papyrus, 242; Sea of, 134–36
Papyrus Anastasi III, 135, 145
Papyrus Anastasi V, 130
Papyrus Leiden 348, 25n, 128
Papyrus of Ani, 96
Peet, T. Eric, 24, 76
Peleth, 200
Pelusium, 125, 131
Penuel, 194
Pepy, 99
Per-Atum, 129
Per-Wadjit, 89
Petrie, W. M. Flinders, 23, 105
Pharaoh: and the serpent-crest, 89–92, 93–94, 147, 151; hardening of the heart of, 96–103; plagues as attacks against, 113, 119–20; and *ma'at*, 119; failure to identify, 162n; as the dominant subject of oracles, 221; and the Nile, 243, 245
Philistia, 163, 187, 238, 239
Phoenicia, 178

Piankhy, 232, 234–35, 240; Stele, 234
Pi-hahiroth, 131, 133–34
Pithom, 128–30
Plagues, 85, 104–20; as natural disasters, 104–7; as literary creations, 107–8; as polemic, 108–13; as de-creation, 113–17
Plant life, 69
Pliny the Elder, 100
Plutarch, 100
Polemic, biblical, 31–32, 83–85, 92–94, 102–3, 108–13, 118, 154–55
Polytheism, 28, 29, 47
Posener, Georges, 118, 210
Potiphar, 74–82; the name, 75–77, 82; as title, 76
Potiphera, 75
Potter, the creator as, 56, 64–65, 70, 93n, 110
"Potter's Oracle," 224
Pratico, Gary, 137
Prenomen, 177
Priesthood and oracles, 221
Primeval hillock, 36, 57, 59, 68–69
Primitive democracy, 37–40
Primordial waters, 38, 61, 62. *See also* Nun
Prism of Sennacherib, 173
Properties, doctrine of, 149n
Prophecy, 223–24; against Egypt, 229–46
"Prophecy of Neferti," 119, 223–24, 244
Prostitution, temple, 42, 49
"Protests of the Eloquent Peasant," 224
Proverbs and the "Instruction of Amenemope," 205–16
Pr-Rameses, 126
Psusennes II, 164, 175, 177, 179
Psylli, 95
Ptah, 56, 60–61, 62–63, 67, 70, 111, 224
Ptah-hetep, 119
Punon, 140
Pyramid Texts, 57

Qantir, 126–28, 129
Qāšāh, 96
Qĕdēšîm, 42

Rabbah, 190
Rabbith, 190
Rad, Gerhard von, 167–68
Rāḥap, 114
Rameses (city), 125–28, 129, 133
Rameses I, 152
Rameses II, 25n, 126, 128, 140, 178n, 184, 236, 243
Rameses III, 90, 152
Rameses IV, 242
Rameses IX, 236n
Rameses XI, 169
Ranke, Hermann, 75
Raphia, 187, 202, 238
Rāqîa', 67
Ray, J. D., 227
Re, 35, 36, 56n–57n, 58n, 69, 70, 88, 90n, 102, 111, 112, 148
Rebirth motif, 35, 242
Re-creation, the exodus as, 113–15
Redemption, cosmological, 47
Redford, Donald, 23–24, 73, 75, 76, 85n, 126, 127, 159, 161, 166, 167, 174, 182, 232
Red Sea, 134–36, 169, 189; dividing of the, 68, 84, 154, 230n
Reeds, Sea of, 134–36
Rehob, 184, 186, 191
Rehoboam, 173–74, 180, 187n, 188
Reliefs on the Bubastite Portal, 182–87
Resurrection, symbols of, 88, 112, 242
"Rider of the clouds," 31
Rituals, Canaanite, 41–42
Robinson, T. H., 188n
Rod. *See* Staff
Rome, 90n
Rowley, H. H., 142
Rubuti, 190
Ruffle, John, 214, 215
Rylaarsdam, J. Coert, 107

Sabbath rest, 73

Sacrifice, child, 41, 49
Sais, 234, 235
Samaria, 238
Sapek, 197
Saqqara, 57n, 111
Śārāph, 146–47
Sargon II, 232, 238–39
Śar haṭṭabbāhîm, 74, 78, 80–82
Sārîs, 77–79, 82
Sarna, Nahum, 23, 123
Sa-ta, 88
Satan, 44
Sayce, Archibald H., 23, 66
Scarabs, 95, 98–102, 236
Scholarship, present-day: on Egypt and the Bible, 13, 23–27; on the ten plagues, 104–8; on the exodus, 121, 141, 143n; on the bronze serpent, 142; on the united monarchy, 159–61; on Old Testament history, 172–74; on wisdom literature, 205–7
School tradition, 207
Schulman, Alan, 164, 165
Scott, R. B. Y., 170
Scribe, 167
Seasons, 35, 41
Sebektowe, 236
Second day of creation, 67, 114, 115, 116
Second plague, 105, 106, 110, 115, 117
Sed Festivals, 154
Seebass, Horst, 78
Sekhmet, 111
Ṣelem, 71
Self-generation: of gods, 36, 48, 57–58, 100; of dung beetles, 99, 100n
Semneh, 243
Senehem, 112
Sennacherib, 173, 232, 239
Separation motif in cosmogonies, 67, 68, 69
Serabit el-Khadem, 136
Sĕrîs parĕ'ōh, 74, 77–80
Serpent: worship, 88, 89; charming, 95; bronze, 142–55

Serpent confrontation, 85–103, 117, 120, 154; as a paradigm of the plagues, 85–86; as combat between deities, 86; irony in the, 92–94
Serpent-crest, 89–92, 93–94, 147, 149n, 151
Serpents: in ancient Egypt, 87–92; as protectors, 88; fiery, 146–49; winged, 146
Seth, 91; Sons of, 226
Sethos I, 122, 128, 148, 154, 184, 190
Seventh plague, 105, 106, 112, 115, 116, 117
Sex, Canaanite obsession with, 41–42
Shabaka, 232, 235–37, 239, 240, 245; Stone, 55, 60, 62, 102
Shalmaneser V, 238
Sharuhen, 201
Shebitku, 239
Shedsunefertem, 175
Sheol, 43
Shipping enterprises of Solomon, 169
"Shipwrecked Sailor," 88n, 148
Shishak (Shoskenk I), 90, 122, 162n, 164n, 165, 166, 172–202, 233; reign of, 174–80; figure of, on the Bubastite Portal, 182; Stele, 184–86, 192
Shoshenk VI, 235
Shu, 35, 37, 58–59, 60, 112
Shuhathites, 198
Shunem, 186, 191
Shupak, Nili, 207
Siamun, 162–63, 164, 179
Ṣibĕ'ōt, 122
Silsileh Inscription, 180–81
Similars, principle of, 226, 227
Simons, J., 134
Simpson, D. C., 210
Sinai: Mount, 32, 137; Peninsula, 123, 136–37
Sixth day of creation, 70, 115, 117
Sixth plague, 105, 106, 111, 115, 117
Smendes, 177, 243
Snake. See Serpent
Snofru, 84, 119, 223
So, 238
Socoh, 187, 193

Solomon, 159, 161–70, 174n, 178–79, 189; marriage of, 161, 162–65, 179; taxation system of, 165–67, 179; administrative structures of, 167–68, 178–79
Sôpēr, 167
Sothis, 241n
Sovereignty of God, 46, 48, 95, 103, 110, 111, 120, 245
Speaking as method of creation, 45, 61–62, 63
Speiser, E. A., 25
Speos Artemidos, 152
Sphinx, 225
Spies, way of the, 144
Spitting (method of creation), 37, 58–59, 100n
Staff, 85, 151; of Aaron, 86–87, 92–94
Standards, 149–54, 155
Starting point, 125
Static view of history, 35–36
"Strong arm," 83, 84, 154–55
Sucathites, 198
Succoth, 130–31, 133
Sun, 35, 99, 112, 242; creation of the, 69, 116; god, 100, 148. See also Re
"Sun-Hymn of Haremhab," 58n
Suppiluliumas, 164
Sympathetic magic, 148

Ta'anak, 186, 191
Ṭabbāḥ, 80–82
Tabeh, 138
Taharqa, 90
Tahpanhes, 132
Takelot II, 233
Tanis, 126–27, 163, 175, 177, 233, 235, 239; Stele, 90, 112
Tannîn, 86–87, 117
Tanutamon, 89, 224
Tany, 164
Tatenen, 56
Taxation system of Solomon, 165–67, 179
Tēbāh, 114
Tefnakhte, 234
Tefnut, 37, 58–59, 60, 112

Těhôm, 28, 29n
Tell 'Arâd, 199
Tell Dan, 160
Tell Daphneh, 132
Tell el-Kheleifeh, 137–38
Tell el-Maskhuta, 129, 130, 177
Tell es-Seba', 197
Tell Jemmeh, 201
Tell Malhata, 144, 200
Tell Masos, 144
Tell Ratabah, 130
Tenth plague, 105, 106, 107, 113, 115, 117
Teti, 99
Thebes, 175–76, 180, 234, 236, 244
Theogony, 28, 30, 48, 72. See also Gods, creation of
Thiele, Edwin, 163n
Third day of creation, 67–69, 114, 115, 116
Third plague, 105, 106, 110–11, 115, 117
Thirty chapters of "Amenemope" and sayings of Proverbs, 213
Thompson, Thomas L., 159, 172n, 173
Thoth, 69, 97
Throne design, 169
Thunder at Sinai, 31–32
"Thus says . . . ," 83–84
Thutmosis I, 151, 180
Thutmosis III, 122, 140, 152, 184, 193, 244
Thutmosis IV, 65, 225
Tiamat, 28–29, 38–39, 55n
Tiglath-pileser III, 237
Timsah, Lake, 135
Tirzah, 195
Tjeku, 130
Tōhû, 115; wābōhû, 66, 116
Topographical lists, Egyptian, 140
Trade: Solomon's, 169; Egyptian, 234–35; Shishak's, 178; routes as reason for Shishak's invasion, 188–89
Transjordan, 139–41, 187, 191
Trap, metaphor of the, 214
Tulul edh-Dhahab, 191

Tutankhamun, 99, 101
Ṯwf(y), 134–35
Twofold division of the cosmos, 65–66
Tyre, 169

Ugaritic myths, 27, 32, 40–41, 54n
Unas, 90, 243
Unfaithfulness of Israel, 42, 146
Uni, 244
United monarchy, 159–71, 178
Universe: elements of the, 34–35; as God's abode, 43; creation and structure of the. *See* Cosmogony; Cosmologies
Uphill, E. P., 130
Uraeus, 89–92, 93–94, 147, 151, 152, 235
Userkaf, 119
Utnapishtim, 27

Van Seters, John, 107–8, 173n
Vegetation, 69, 116
Via Maris, 187, 189

Wadi Halfa, 241
Wadi Tumilat, 129, 130, 131
Wadjet, 89, 91n, 149n, 236n
Ward, W. A., 100n
Wast, 183
Waters: above and below, 67; separation and gathering of, 116; primordial, 38, 61, 62. *See also* Nun

Water turned to blood, 105, 106–7, 109–10, 116
Wayeheset, 176
Webaoner, 93
Wenamon, 169, 178n
Wente, Edward, 126, 182
Westcar Papyrus, 84, 92
Williams, Ronald, 170, 211
Wilson, John A., 55
Wilson, J. V. K., 29
Wisdom literatures, Egyptian and Hebrew, 205–7
"Wisdom of Ani," 206n, 209

Yabāšāh, 67–68
Yābēš, 230n
Yadin, Yigael, 161
Yād rāmāh, 122
Yaham, 184, 187, 193
Yahuda, Abraham S., 23, 26n, 64, 71
Yam sûph, 134–36, 144
Yehallel-el, 196
Yeraza', 195
Yeroham, 201
Yewepet, 176
Yorda, 202
Yurza, 201

Zalmonah, 140
Zemaraim, 195
Zevit, Z., 108n
Zoan, 127, 239

John D. Currid is associate professor of Old Testament and chair of the biblical studies division at Reformed Theological Seminary in Jackson, Mississippi. He earned his Ph.D. degree in archaeology from the Oriental Institute at the University of Chicago.